F

Inscribing the Time

The New Historicism: Studies in Cultural Poetics
Stephen Greenblatt, General Editor

Inscribing the Time

Shakespeare and the End
of Elizabethan England

Eric S. Mallin

UNIVERSITY OF CALIFORNIA PRESS
Berkeley · Los Angeles · London

University of California Press
Berkeley and Los Angeles, California

University of California Press, Ltd.
London, England

© 1995 by
The Regents of the University of California

Chapter 1 appeared in a slightly shorter form in
Representations (vol. 29, winter 1990).

Library of Congress Cataloging-in-Publication Data

Mallin, Eric Scott.
    Inscribing the time : Shakespeare and the end of
Elizabethan England / Eric S. Mallin.
        p.   cm.   (The New historicism ; 33)
    Includes bibliographical references (p.) and
index.
    ISBN 0–520-08623-6 (alk. paper)
    1. Shakespeare, William, 1564–1616—
Contemporary England.   2. Literature and
history—England—History—16th century.
3. Great Britain—History—Elizabeth, 1558–
1603.   4. Historicism in literature.   I. Title.
II. Series.
PR2910.M32   1995
822.3′3—dc20
                                        94-28943
                                                CIP

Printed in the United States of America
9 8 7 6 5 4 3 2 1

The paper used in this publication meets the
minimum requirements of American National
Standard for Information Sciences—Permanence of
Paper for Printed Library Materials, ANSI
Z39.48-1984.

For my mother,
and the memory
of her mother

Contents

Acknowledgments

I am delighted to acknowledge those who have helped, directly or indirectly, with this book.

Thanks go to the University of California Press for permission to reprint chapter 1, which appeared in a slightly shorter form in *Representations* (vol. 29, winter 1990). I would also like to acknowledge the English Department of the University of Texas at Austin for giving me two important things: ample time to write and a fine place to work.

Leah S. Marcus and Frank Whigham have been guiding lights in my time at Texas, and their generosity has been sustaining. Dolora Wojciehowski read much of the manuscript and made several brilliant suggestions, sometimes causing me to wish that she had written it. John P. Rumrich worked through the book heroically, staying enthusiastic about it even when I could not. I thank them all for their remarkable collegiality. I would also like to express deep appreciation to Bill Sutherland, Joseph Kruppa, and Wayne Lesser for finding ways to make my life easier throughout the arduous process of completing the manuscript.

Doris Kretschmer of the University of California Press has been extremely helpful and attentive, shepherding this work in a timely manner (despite my delays) through various stages of production. The Press's three anonymous reviewers offered excellent suggestions on matters both essential and ornamental. At a critical stage in the preparation of the book, Melissa Gilbert cheerfully provided superb research assistance.

Inscribing the Time had its origins as a Stanford University dissertation written under the auspices of David Riggs, John Bender, and Ronald Rebholz. They helped me, as someone once said, to acquire form and to avoid pitfalls; they also prepared me for some of the pleasures of Shakespeare studies. Michael T. Gilmore, Alan Levitan, and Allen Grossman first introduced me to literary analysis before I could fully understand what they were teaching, but some of what they taught and how they taught it has stayed with me. I am grateful for that, and my readers should be too.

I have also learned from my friends. Hilary M. Schor and Christopher Ames have been smart, steady, and extraordinarily supportive long-distance companions for many years now. Others who have helped with this work or with more important matters: James Bookless, Peggy Bradley, Seth Brody, Paul Howe, Ronald H. Iscoff, and Leonard Lipitz.

My best influences have taught me to read, to reason, and not to give up too soon. Elissa Mallin-Dawe first showed me the power of art to express strange joy. Rebecca W. LaBrum teaches me daily about love and labor; she remains my most important colleague. And my mother, Sonia R. Lipitz, gave me everything I needed to complete this book. The project and its author could not have made sense without her.

Introduction

I

History never repeats itself, but it offers analogies.

    J. E. Neale, Essays in Elizabethan History

This book is a study of three Shakespeare plays—*Troilus and Cressida,* *Hamlet,* and *Twelfth Night*—in their contemporary historical contexts. These plays disclose three very different accumulations of English political and social anxiety during the tense transitional years between the Elizabethan and Jacobean regimes.[1] I argue that the dramas imagine their stories as versions of contemporary history: they contain formations and deformations of plots, ideologies, events, and psychological accommodations at the end of the Elizabethan era. Throughout I shall claim that "history"—by which I narrowly mean the specific past of Renaissance sociopolitical and literary conditions—proves in Shakespeare's theater to be a constant force with variable coefficients. Sometimes history is the direct referent of the dramatic business; more often it is the deferred, submerged conspirator in the plot; at still other times it proves to be an alienated, hostile presence dislodging the work from secure moorings or meanings.

    Shakespeare's Troy, Denmark, and Illyria are not repetitions of England; they are, as the epigraph from J. E. Neale is meant to suggest, analogies.[2] As analogies of history the plays constantly approximate and appropriate forms of the real—governmental organizations, physiologi-

cal processes, spiritual struggles—in their fictions. My arguments depart from some new-historical studies by taking the texts' topicalities
not only as referent but as literary *structure*; the contemporary history
materially shapes and misshapes the drama. I examine in the first chapter the way divisive Elizabethan court politics and self-delusional ideologies are mapped into the chiastic relationships of violence in *Troilus and
Cressida*. In chapter 2 I consider another cultural fact with structural
implications for the plays: epidemic disease. In *Hamlet* (as to a lesser
extent in *Troilus and Cressida*), the idea of contagion afflicts the root
relations of language, mind, and rule, and these relations have clear historical correlates—not necessarily determinants but, again, definite
analogies.

The study of plague in *Hamlet* continues figurally in the third chapter
with a reading of selected contaminating histories in James's royal succession. By a "contaminating" history I mean an episode or memory
that problematizes the tidy order and meaning of the new reign—specifically, a set of events that interacts with and undermines Shakespearean
theatrical architecture. In *Hamlet*, contagion and succession are complementary topical anxieties, but to come to terms with these we must confront an even more sharply focused issue of locality: the status of the text
itself. In chapters 2 and 3, I examine the second or "good" quarto of
Hamlet because that text registers most suggestively, and recoverably,
the material interactions of imagination and history. Of course, just because a text interacts with its environment does not mean that it necessarily becomes culture's glassy essence. *Hamlet's* formal and textual perturbations are anything but passively reflective of the turmoil at the end
of Elizabeth's reign. Aesthetic products typically rewrite their surrounding circumstances. To do so, however, they often submerge or displace
the historical referent to ease the stress of the moment—thus speaking
volubly about that moment and subliminally reintroducing stress. In the
final chapter, on *Twelfth Night*, I attempt to dislocate my own premises,
that is, to read referentiality that has moved away from the moment of
theatrical production. In Illyria, Shakespeare shifts the contextual frame
away from 1601. With its memorial treatment of "a kind of Puritan"
threat, its mediated courtships, and its unalloyed feminine triumphs,
Twelfth Night tries to evade the present and sets itself back in the historical middle distance.

These texts sometimes ruthlessly display, sometimes avoid or inter
history's most upsetting implications. They convey multilevel anxiety,
concentrations of cultural trauma that they do not, indeed cannot, fully

organize or analyze. And 1600 to 1603 are especially good years—keeping in mind the Renaissance double edge of the phrase "good years"—to examine.[3] The late Elizabethan era had a preternatural sense of its own ending; the close of the period was self-consciously likened to the end of Troy, a great civilization in its death throes. At the same time, the hope of a new king compensated for the debility, as many male courtiers saw it, of an aged queen. This was, in other words, a period bristling with half-revealed personal, ideological, and political activity. My original idea for this study was to seek in historical information some wattage to brighten these plays' dimmer passageways. But as the inquiry progressed, it became apparent that "information" itself offered only elusive simulacra of historical meaning; and the semantic slipperiness, the limited capacity of histories to fix their own (let alone Shakespeare's) significances, led me to the present set of readings, which seek to analyze how language and local knowledge codetermine Shakespearean evasiveness.

This book, then, attempts to illuminate three temporally contiguous plays by excavating their possible relations to historical origins and contexts. To some extent, however, the idea of origins is a fiction, a magic bullet that shatters interpretive obstructions to the past; an origin, like a reference, is really only an infinite regress of references. Like origin and reference, context too represents a construct shaped from a desire to know, to stabilize what is always in motion. The notion of context in postmodernity must seem a quaint and factitious convention. Nonetheless, it is an indispensable one. Understanding that the historical context is to some extent an arbitrary construct does not alter the fact that such constructs are epistemological necessities which orient cognition in crucial ways. If we connect verbal texts to social ones, we cannot but admit that people live, know, converge, fail, fight, create, and adapt in contexts, experienced not as arbitrary but as the bounded real. This reality is factored through a wide array of social possibilities: gender and sexuality, class and status, race and creed. What makes the idea of contexts epistemologically thorny is that persons in different subject positions move through a broad range of experience or Althusserian "lived relation to the real"; "the real" changes, depending upon one's aesthetic or historical contextualization of the particular subject position. Context inevitably alters the understood nature of persons and their histories.

This interdependence of text (historical subject, aesthetic object) and context (historical moment, ideological condition or structure), however lacking in explicit social reference, is neatly figured in Wallace Ste-

vens's well-known poem "Anecdote of the Jar." This work smartly reverses polarities of text and context, properly erasing each as a separate
entity. The poem's speaker sets or has set an object, a text of sorts, in a
notoriously general region or context:

> I placed a jar in Tennessee,
> And round it was, upon a hill.
> It made the slovenly wilderness
> Surround that hill.[4]

Even though uncontained, the context is "made" to do the bidding of
the text; the jar enforces compliance from the wilderness. But the text,
the jar, is itself literally a container: it is a figure for context, ajar to the
possibility of (semantic) openings and closings; and the slovenly wilderness, seemingly the frame for the jar, itself stands for a very traditional
artistic *text*—unruly nature, tamed by art. So Stevens's opening stanza
engulfs in one landscape of understanding the interpenetration of text
and context, both of which inhabit and disrupt the frame that describes
them. Some of the theoretical difficulty of contexts can be alleviated in a
Stevensian way, by seeing them as continuous with or transparent to the
text—or better still, as having been created or made to surround the text
by the text, even as the jar eventually "took dominion everywhere" inside the poem and inside the landscape it controls.

Shakespearean contexts always recreate this border indeterminacy:
the plays extend from the formations that are their subtextual subject.
Far from being the preserve of disinterested cultural information, this
theater is always a version of what it contains, implicated in the world it
describes. As Fredric Jameson has said:

> The literary or aesthetic act . . . always entertains some active relationship
> with the Real; yet in order to do so, it cannot simply allow "reality" to perse-
> vere inertly in its own being, outside the text and at a distance. It must rather
> draw the Real into its own texture. . . . The symbolic act therefore begins by
> generating and producing its own context in the same moment of emergence
> in which it steps back from it, taking its measure with a view toward its own
> projects of transformation.[5]

A flexible category in and of itself, "context" varies dramatically as well
among recent Renaissance literary theorists. For some new historicists, a
relevant frame for interpretation may be far displaced from the text's
temporal or spatial vicinity. The margins of context can stretch out over
oceans, years, and artistic forms. For example, to Stephen Greenblatt,
an Albrecht Dürer print shows something critical about the representa-

tional status of rebellion which is reconfigured in Shakespeare's 2 *Henry VI*; a story about French hermaphroditism furnishes a way of understanding sexual homologies and erotic exchanges in *Twelfth Night*.[6] Walter Cohen calls this interpretive technique "arbitrary connectedness": "The strategy is governed methodologically by the assumption that any one aspect of society is related to any other. No organizing principle determines these relationships: any social practice has at least a potential connection to any theatrical practice. . . . The commitment to arbitrary connectedness inevitably limits the persuasiveness of much new historicist work."[7] Cohen proceeds to expose some of the contradictions in Greenblatt's work, but he admits that because "theater itself is a contradictory institution," the desultory evidentiary procedures of new historicism are somewhat mitigated "at a higher level of abstraction." Cohen is right to perceive virtues and flaws in the technique. This mode of reading tends not to be *specifically* explanatory because it so often strays far from the text at hand; but it does often work "at a higher level of abstraction" to dissolve the notion of context in a productive rather than reductive way. This hermeneutic reminds us that an element of arbitrary connectedness inheres in every interpretive act. What, after all, counts as a "relevant" piece of information? The "arbitrary" or perhaps nonlocal form of new historicism reconstructs ideological or discursive formations and practices and relates them to semantic flashpoints in a given text. But for all its sophistication, the method frequently depends on the presumption of a stable set of historical meanings which, however unpredictably connected, tend to cast an even light over the ragged surfaces of the text. "Power," "authority," even "gender" have often worked similarly in new-historicist readings over severely differing contexts, and history in this discipline can come to seem too disciplined, a surprisingly confined signifier.

For better or worse, I have sought to limit arbitrariness by focusing on a specific temporal region of disruption: the transition from the Elizabethan to the Jacobean regimes. I have also tried to convey the sense of flux and destabilization inherent in this historical moment. As much as possible, I confine my inquiries here to local pressures that operate, often unpredictably, within a space of change.[8] Because I am not describing a general "poetics of culture" so much as a particular poetics of the theater's use of culture, I am pledged to pertinent contexts insofar as these can be determined and curtailed. Locality, employed as a main interpretive template, allows the critic to read the literary text through its *most probable* stresses and histories and to delimit the profusion of narratives that cause both arbitrary and likely influences to blend. Local reading can narrow the bewildering semantic range of the plays by pinning them to a nearby context; it can also, however, enlarge a drama's signifying potential should the text (like *Hamlet*, for instance) fail to specify limitations to contextual meanings. Because contexts, like "historical moments," *are* theoretically infinite, construing them always involves an act of containment, a resistance to the alluring fact or alternative story.

Here, then, are some of my self-imposed interpretive guidelines in this book. Although it is difficult to mark the termini of historical moments, I have generally confined my analyses to the period defined in the book's subtitle, or—as in the case of Scottish succession history and the early Puritan movement, discussed in chapters 3 and 4 respectively—to those histories which have clear and ongoing implications for this period and these texts. Likewise, I have attempted to limit context spatially. This book assumes that these are English histories that Shakespeare is on the verge of writing; their foreign settings distantiate reference only to secure, not frustrate, local interest. Given the fact that fashion, religion, and even genre circulate among nations, it may seem unnecessary to restrict topicality to English concerns, which could never—as some of the breathless reports of foreign ambassadors attest—remain strictly English. But in this particular historical niche, Shakespeare's plays concern themselves with the cultural peril of specifically English politics and ideology. These dramas are hardly cogent vehicles for jingoistic sentiment; but their central concerns are local, however broadly representative (i.e., "universal") that locality manages to be. Finally, I proceed on the assumption that historical contexts must demonstrably *play into* plot, theme, genre, image, or staging; the drama's central literary features must be apposite to or cognate with some significant cultural fact or presence and so create a representational resonance with history. Selective narrowing of contexts offers the best chance to recover the intercourse between text and time. I have tried, then, to slow down the frames of historical reference that blur past in Shakespeare's plays; or to put it another way, I have placed the jar of the text within and about its known historical conditions.

The trick word in that last sentence is "known." This book attempts to deploy but also to extend and reconfigure the historically known. No small presumption for a nonhistorian, this effort can nonetheless be justified by the nature of historical knowledge, which I take to be largely documentary—that is, textual, and thus always legitimately subject to rereading. An interpretive instability must be acknowledged at once: the past that I read through Shakespeare's texts has already been read by those texts and finessed, over time, by generations of historians and critics; and the idea of the theater that I attempt to nourish through cooked (i.e., selected and processed) data cannot provide any certain access to the lived past of the plays. This dilemma of mediated histories can be eased if we see the text itself as an historical repository, with a direct, participatory relation to its time. In this regard, we may follow Foucault's early work in attempting to establish "archaeologies" of knowledge resident in cultural productions.

Perhaps an analogy in more traditional archaeological terms is in order. One interesting formation common in the Middle East is the tell, a hill-shaped site on which several generations or even civilizations have successively built. An artificial construct—"the accumulated remains of one or more ancient settlements"[9]—the tell stands to a modern age as comprehension's rough draft, a version of historical fact anticipating the refinements of taxonomists, curators, and theoreticians. Compressing the past, the site presents a convenient if deformed epitome of cultural activity. Because the tell displays without making definitive disclosures, it is, befitting its homonym, a kind of narrative. Like any story, the tell is an occasion for analysis, the groundwork for topical understanding.

To read literature by way of the past, one may usefully regard the text as a tell-like structure: a repository of tiered and culled histories compressed into shapes that forerun meaning. The archaeological site resembles the literary artifact in that both comprise superposed layers of significance.[10] The more deeply submerged the level, the more difficult it is to retrieve and reconstruct without altering it—but the better preserved that level may be because of its chthonic embeddedness. In texts as in tells, crucial referentiality tends not to be disposed too close to the surface. The archaeological model offers the hope that some trace essence of the real can be reclaimed—certainly not without losing some data, but perhaps without scattering entirely the forms of the distant past. The literary artifact differs in important ways, of course, from the tell, particularly in its constitutive materials: the verbal work assembles subliminal, cognitive, and tonal elements from its culture, the "prior historical or ideological *subtext*," in Jameson's words, of the society (*Political Unconscious*, 81). But the analogy of text to tell *can* illuminate the theoretical pitfalls of interpretive excavations. In hoping to find the thing in itself, the past-as-it-was, archaeological work may accidentally erase periodic or epochal divisions; later historical intrusion often disturbs the stratifications that can, in the best case, act as a diachronic key to the local(e). What is more, because of its spatial limits, the tell, like the text, is bound to skew the sample of cultural activity; it cannot be fully representative. Finally, the structure can silently, unintelligibly absorb encounters with other civilizations by which the culture under study has become enriched or infected. The uncertainties of reading such a dig suggest some of the hazards of historical inquiry. But the site, like the text, remains opaque to every understanding that is *not* historical.

So in arguing that Shakespeare's theatrical plots tell versions of historical events or meanings, I depend on this flexible, archaeological sense of "tell": a provisional ordering of artifacts; a narrating of uncertain histories that have been assembled but not wholly interpreted. The plays write across regimes, conjoin the real and the fictive, without always marking the boundaries. This uncertainty leads us to the notion of inscription.

In exercising the conceit of the tell—the articulate culture or artifact—I have begun to define inscription through an antithetical term. For inscribing, or writing-in, is the opposite of telling, or speaking out. Yet they are complementary opposites. Whereas the tell speaks a collective voice, synecdochically sampling or disinterestedly compressing a whole cultural structuration, inscription posits selective, individual agency and intentionality: a person who inscribes is up to something. When Shakespeare writes the culture that shapes his texts, he becomes more than merely an indifferent producer of cultural objects or a medium through which events are told; he is also reader, redactor, and rhapsode. Meanings lodged in scriptive acts are rarely governed completely by a unified authorial intention. But the "author function" that belongs to the name of Shakespeare is hermeneutically useful and not necessarily simplistic. What's in that name is the presupposition of a set of conscious designs that the plays and their staged histories sometimes obey, sometimes subvert. To understand the idea of inscription—the idea that history is, and is susceptible of, representation in texts—we must accept that there are points at which text, history, and authorial intention work in concert, points where they clash, and yet other points where they conspire to create ambiguous impressions. The theater writes and records *diffuse* cultural intentions, transcending any single historical subject's or author's business or desire. But this characterization of the stage should not obliterate the notion of the author, the inscriber. True to my own poststructural academic contexts, I understand the text as multiple: the intersection of a range of discourses. Thus the early modern culture as a whole can be said to have helped write Shakespeare's plays, even as late-twentieth-century American culture helps write the way I interpret them. If the dramatist cannot avoid inscribing the time into his texts—whether or not he intends the ramifications of the inscriptions[11]—he also has the ability to reconstitute, through "the fierce endeavor of [his] art," specific histories in particular ways.

One locus for theater's inscriptive intertwining of cultural and authorial intention, and one that bears heavily on my readings of each of these plays, is the repeatedly staged historical figure of Queen Elizabeth. There was little doubt that playwrights and poets placed her in their work in various guises. She spoke of her own position as theatrical ("We princes, I tell you, are set on stages, in the sight and view of all the world duly observed," she is famously supposed to have said),[12] and the theater borrowed a royal prestige by openly and subtly performing her. What emerges from the practice is the multiplicity of her perceived selves, an impression of polymorphism partly created and partly perceived that did not always accomplish its stated goal of honoring her. In the well-known letter of 1589 "annexed" to the first edition of *The Faerie Queene*, Spenser wrote to Walter Ralegh of his allegorical method in the poem, a representational strategy of the sort that I have tried to retrieve and analyze in this book:

> In that Faery Queene I meane glory in my generall intention, but in my particular I conceiue the most excellent and glorious person of our soueraine the Queene, and her kingdome in Faery land. And yet in some places els, I doe otherwise shadow her. For considering she beareth two persons, the one of a most royall Queene or Empresse, the other of a most vertuous and beautifull Lady, this latter part in some places I doe expresse in Belphoebe, fashioning her name according to your owne excellent conceipt of Cynthia, (Phoebe and Cynthia being both names of Diana.)[13]

This somewhat coy description of the poem smooths over the political dissonance inherent in these allegorical divisions, separations, and multiple namings. By confessing that "in some places els, I doe otherwise shadow her," Spenser is edging toward a statement about the darker, more shadowy representations of Elizabethan policy and character in the poem, made justifiable by the *human* imperfections in the "most vertuous and beautifull Lady." This "letter of the authors expounding his whole intention in the course of this work" cannot possibly live up to its billing, because the author's understanding of his own intention is at once veiled and extraordinarily conflicted. There are designed *and* accidental leakages of meaning in the allegorical technique—Spenser's multiple personifications of Elizabethan qualities and strategies—that no account of intentions can caulk. It would be wrong to suggest that the fragmentary inscription has a life *all* its own; but the life it receives from the poet certainly outlives attempts (even the poet's attempts) to confine it semantically. The point is that, as Spenser admits but understates, inscription is multiple in practice and result, and it is not completely answerable to intentionality. Any text that attempts to collate multiple historical realities will find itself, or those realities, fragmented, like a cubist work that tries to represent three dimensions on a single surface. Thus the meanings of history suffer, in literary inscriptions, emergencies of disjunction, contradiction, and discord. These crises may have been part of an original perception about the particular subject, but they may also arise as a result of that subject's incarnation in representational flesh of many figures. Such an aesthetic procedure opens the text to oppositional, unflattering, or uncontrolled lineations.

We can stay with the example of the queen. John Lyly's *Endymion: The Man in the Moon* (c. 1591) stages the metaphorics of frustrated courtiership in Elizabeth's sphere. Endymion, the lover who fails of favor (indirectly, Lyly himself) has wasted his youth in worship of the unattainable monarch, here mythologized as Cynthia. In love with the moon, Endymion is cast into a forty-year sleep by Cynthia's jealous rival, Tellus, who has failed to secure his affections and seeks to prevent those affections from aiming elsewhere. Homage to the queen brings (at first, it seems) no rewards, only a horribly premature senescence; but finally the ruler restores Endymion to youth with a kiss. By the end of the play, Cynthia, still romantically unattainable, becomes somewhat less emotionally distant as she manages and sanctions several romantic couplings which secure the comedy. But more interesting than the main plot of deflected romance is a mirroring subplot featuring an amusing braggart warrior named Sir Tophas. Like Endymion, whom he resembles in his narcissism and his appetites, the *miles gloriosus* finds himself in love with a powerful woman, one just as unattainable in her way as is the queen. Sir Tophas's choice is none other than an old witch, Dipsas, the enchantress who was employed by Tellus to cast the spell on Endymion. The inscriptive mechanism here could scarcely be more conflicted. Endymion's predicament can be traced to three women, a trinity that is subliminally a unity: an unattainable queen, a jealous lover, and a haggard, ugly witch. "Without a doubt Endymion is bewitched," his friend Eumenides comments long *before* the spell is cast (1.1.116).[14] The clear parallel of Dipsas and Cynthia, and the rivalry (converging on indistinguishability) of the queen and Tellus, conspire to undermine what the play seems to announce: the supposed incomparability of Cynthia. The multiplicity of the queen's images and roles—goddess on earth, mystical provider of bounty, controller of erotic relationships at court—activates an artistic process that admits unfavorable aspects of Elizabeth's (human and monarchical) personality into the representational field. And these aspects, of course, will bear differential weight depending on the temporal and social context of the work.

I think that Lyly attempts a genuine if misguided contribution to the queen's mythology in this play, fending off—with mixed success—some of the more unbecoming associations of inconstancy, distance, and tyranny with which the moon could be associated, so as to claim for Elizabeth an image (as did Ralegh in "The Book of the Ocean to Cynthia") of eternally regenerating youth and gravitational power. But this is, as the figure of Dipsas suggests, an image with some local, temporal pressure on it. For in 1591, the queen was fifty-seven years old. Around the last decade of her reign, inscriptions of Elizabeth could no longer evade the force of time; the years gathered on the monarch's mortal body and on her image in texts. By the end of the decade the problem had grown plangent. Thomas Dekker, for example, begins *The Pleasant Comedie of Old Fortunatus* with this sugary exchange:

> 1. Are you then travelling to the temple of *Eliza?*
> 2. Even to her temple are my feeble limmes travelling. Some cal her *Pandora*, some *Gloriana*, some *Cynthia*: some *Belphoebe*, some *Astraea*: all by severall names to expresse severall loves: Yet all those names make but one celestiall body, as all those loves meete to create but one soule.
>
> (Prologue, 1–6)[15]

All these names, however, have their own mythologies, which can collide to form impacted ideological contradictions that undercut the supposed obeisant intent. One wonders, for instance, how the troubling sexual image of Pandora and the implications of the unstable Cynthia ("still inconstant, yet never wavering," as Lyly ambivalently calls her [3.4.223]) rhyme with the juridical seriousness of the Astraea name. Writers under the queen's impress—"Elizabethan" writers—frequently played these images off one another, some to an effect of bland homage, but others to the discord sounding here. The problem is not simply that the profusion of royal images becomes unmanageable; as I discuss in my treatment of *Troilus and Cressida*, the more serious point is that the profusion sometimes betrayed an inability to remain unambiguously enthusiastic about the queen. Dekker's play appeared in 1599, in Elizabeth's sixty-sixth year, and the topic of Eliza (whose age goes unmentioned in the passage) is introduced by two old men. The younger generation, of which Dekker was part, had conspicuously greater difficulty than do these characters in sustaining such praise. It is hard to imagine that the darker subtext of the queen's age *purposively* lurks beneath the lavish praise of Elizabeth at the beginning of Dekker's play; it is harder still to suppose that the taboo subject of her years does not figure into the meanings of this passage. A reading of inscription cannot resolve intention, but it can suggest the conditions that enable and strain it.

As a study of inscriptive processes, this book is a close reading of history's functional complexity in Shakespeare's plays. Alan Liu's insight that new historicism's formalist biases and vocabulary generate many of its characteristic interpretive maneuvers will apply here.[16] The technologies of close reading can profitably describe—and of course, produce—qualified destabilizations of historical meaning. New-critical principles can also tease surprises from the intercourse between texts and events that seem by now exhausted or overread. (Surely there is no justification for two more chapters on *Hamlet* unless a new play or a play readable in new ways emerges from the attention.) Close reading works well in explicating the appearance of history in texts because that appearance is precisely the aggregate of details. Inscribing is a miniaturist operation. These plays deform and re-form significant events and issues, but they also register a plenum of minute historical impulses. Consequently, recovering the historical signified depends on dilation, on magnifying textual and temporal quiddities. History in these plays tends not to be painted in broad allegorical strokes or to gesticulate wildly as in *roman à clef* farce. Rather, it figures a deflection and reduction of the real.

One consequence of the theater's sensitivity to subliminal environmental conditions is a loss of continuity *between* signals from the culture. Theatrical representations of history tend toward the broken, the intermittent, and thus tend not to sponsor perfectly cogent schemas or worldviews—as would, for instance, certain types of allegory. The failure of texts to inscribe their cultures with perfect coherence is not necessarily an aesthetic failure; indeed, it may show the playwright's genuine attempt at mimesis—a "true" perception about the fragmentary nature of the historical world. Alternatively, the sheared-off sense of history in texts may highlight the author's ability to forge staggered, fractal, or composite images and understandings of material reality. The aleatory nature of topical reference in the theater deprives us of one benefit that new criticism bestowed: the luxury of neat, readable patterns. It is often difficult (again, as the chapters on *Hamlet* testify) to resolve analyses of conflicting and sometimes unintelligible data, no matter how narrowly the historical contexts are construed.

I do not mean to claim that these Shakespeare plays are entirely unhinged from pattern or (especially) from one another. Indeed, even with their different genres, their divergent tonalities and referential structures, these three plays have some striking similarities. In fact, a prominent trope of similarity occupies each work: emulation in *Troilus and Cressida*, contagion in *Hamlet*, and echo in *Twelfth Night*. These features are not purely rhetorical tropes such as Quintilian or Scaliger described. Instead, each of these figures has a structural or thematic implication. Experienced readers of Shakespeare will already be familiar with the symbolic extensions of these tropes: they include the plays' common obsessions with twinning, surrogacy, imitation, exchange, disguise, influence, and repetition. Each of the tropes functions in the plots of the plays as a decentering device, splitting off privilege, identity, or force from its sanctioned possessor and redistributing it among other claimants for power or sympathy. Echo, which I read as pertinent to *Twelfth Night*'s subtext, is perhaps the most common and benign of these figures. As a trope with its own mythography, it carries a history of passivity, even potentially a kind of generosity; echo seizes but returns, in the act of seizure, the voice of the other. By contrast, emulation (*Troilus and Cressida*) and contagion (*Hamlet*) are more explicitly violent, appropriative forms of similitude, befitting their plays' thematic and generic indications. These three rhetorical structures organize plot and the limits of dramatic subjectivity; they also suggest important aspects of the theater's inscriptive procedures. I take these figures (themselves quite similar and intertwined) to be metonymic of each text's relationship to its histories. That is, tropes of similarity are rhetorical models for the dramas' intercourse with the culture they recreate. Internally, the tropes offer a version of order and organization. Yet, as René Girard has argued, a structure based on recursion or (especially) imitative doubling promises not order but dissolution, endless reciprocal agon.[17] The same contradiction obtains for the texts' similitudes of culture. The act of reproducing the historical field would seem to promise some sort of categorical or mimetic order; in fact, the inscription of the time yields endless perturbations in meaning. The trope of resemblance within a work, like the theater's intussusception of literary features and parallel historical forms, implodes neat distinctions between text and history and coerces the breakdown of representational categories.

The texts' rhetorical recursions of their contexts, complicated as they are, call to mind an area of scientific inquiry known popularly as chaos theory. Recent investigations have labeled as "chaotic" certain physical phenomena which resist classification or description by Newtonian paradigms. Chaos systems include weather patterns, heart fibrillation cycles, the motion of objects immersed in liquids, and the formation of coastlines. What fascinates researchers of chaos is the presence of order within the apparently ungoverned arena of activity. Patterns arise from these systems' tendency to proliferate self-similarity. That is, a chaotic event makes recombinant, symmetrical patterns out of a portion of the system as a whole.[18] The general notion involves not just symmetry but *replication* across scale. The representationality of chaos systems is the issue here: the systems' smallest niche tends to iterate, in general shape with further formal disruptions, the larger complex. And the presence of form embedded in turbulent structures—let us think of them as texts— holds out the possibility that some stability could exist in even thoroughly nonlinear structures or aesthetic products.[19] The infinite contexts of history are a chaos system of which the works of Shakespeare, and of every writer, are a self-similar part. So it should not surprise us that these works imperfectly replicate the folds, whorls, and dynamisms of the larger surround.

The appeal (and of course, the problem) of chaos theory is its accessibility to so many intuitions; many metaphoric connections to the chaos paradigm can be made without strain. One such connection, central to this book's concerns with contagion as a cultural habit, is through the idea of the virus, the unpredictably replicating mechanisms of which are only now coming to be understood. Without original DNA of its own, a virus is involved in the hostile production of a self-similarity derived from a host organism. Texts are, of course, more and other than chaotic propagations of history, more than viral reproductions of an unresisting cell of the real. The disease metaphor, however, conveys the parasitic intimacy of texts and contexts, as well as the dangers of dissolving the boundaries between them. Susan Sontag has mentioned that "immunologists class the body's cancer cells as 'non-self,' " as distinguished from the "self" of original biological material.[20] But that nonself is eerily produced by some combination of environmental factors, systemic debility, and genetic substance, a set of causes which problematizes the virus's destruction, linked as the germ is to the self that houses it. Conditions that trigger the growth of a virus, the outbreak of a war,[21] or the creation of a Shakespeare play are deeply unpredictable: the avatars of coincidence, of causes mysterious or always insufficiently explanatory. As an account of cultural or artistic formation, a chaos or contagion model makes more sense than deterministic theories because the innumerable influences of culture are, at their core, random events with only satellite predictabilities. The mathematician Benoit Mandelbrot, writing about the calculations needed to generate a statistical model of a coastline, could well be discoursing about art and its relation to history when he notes that a deterministic approach "would be . . . doomed to failure because each coastline is molded through the ages by multiple influences that are not recorded and cannot be reconstituted in any detail. The goal of achieving a full description is hopeless, and should not even be entertained" (quoted in Hayles, *Chaos Bound*, 167). This statement, ideologically deficient if applied to cultural formations, nonetheless carries a useful reminder for historicists: the text's conditions of production simply cannot be specified in full. Effects in the world are not necessarily linear or proportionate to their causes; an effect such as a text is especially, thankfully unpredictable, and always at some distance from its "cause."

If the work of art were merely a recursion of chaotic historical patterns, or a "tell" whose layers comprise cross-sections of its own founding culture, it would then seem to lack all autonomy. Once we posit that cultural influences produce, however unpredictably, textual effects, the idea of the text's utter contingency is inevitable. Inscription initially offers hope here, insofar as it signifies artistic control and agency: if the culture can be inscribed in the text, then the latter automatically contains, neutralizes, or otherwise manages the former. But this account of the process is incomplete. The act of inscribing history in texts may *begin* authorially as an attempt to contain or reify chaotic meanings (which is how my readings of literary historiography began). But it more often becomes, in spite of itself, the practice of *protracting* and replicating a chaos of histories through the artistic medium. In the case of the three plays studied here, their thematic tropes of similarity evoke principles of apparent internal and referential order—only, as I have said, to break down formal categories and perspectives. Just as the resemblances of Hector and Achilles, Hamlet and Claudius, or Viola and Sebastian are the occasion for large-scale confusions, so the texts' self-similarity to the environing histories of which they are part dissolves the ontological boundaries between the theater and its influences, analogues, and intertexts. History, latent in the plots of the dramas, dissolves the self/nonself or external/internal dialectic that feeds the formalist hunger. Shakespeare's plays, which have until fairly recently been regarded as antiseptically literary, are in fact thoroughly touched (the Renaissance term for "contaminated" as well as "maddened") by the elements of the time. One assumption underwriting this book is that textual ambiguity or aporia complexly embodies historical undecidability. More than an adjuvant factor in textual paradoxes and cruxes, history is a causal one. In this respect inscription is *both* an intentional and an inevitable act: the result of authorial choice and cultural compulsion. Even in cases of Shakespeare's deliberate deployment of referentiality, unexpected complications inherent in the facts break forth, rattling the author's grasp of the operations. Inscription-as-control can be alarmed by inscription-as-infiltration. The culture inscribes, lodges itself in texts; the texts, in turn, with *and* without authorial sanction, write out the meanings of this occupancy.

II

One ought to resist the temptation, even in introductions, to make axioms out of uncertainties. Still, such formulas are useful as positional markers. So I shall claim, first, that the significance of an historical moment is always unknowable at that moment, just as the *originary* relation of texts to their contexts is indeterminate. Some historical episodes, which from our current vantage point appear to have only a single meaning, doubtless had, at the time, numerous semantic registers. In the second quarto of *Hamlet*, I argue, Shakespeare inscribes among other things the physical and psychic danger of the bubonic plague. This inscription accords nicely with a career genre transition; after *Hamlet*, the happy ending becomes nearly impossible for Shakespeare, or at least extremely expensive. But even though the historical fact of contagion keeps company with Shakespeare's canonical shift to tragedy or tragicomedy, different responses to the disease—literary and otherwise—were certainly possible. The event, that is, was coded across a wide range of generic possibilities, and these possibilities complicate easy assumptions about the valence of the historical fact. There is, for example, the Jonsonian take on plague, staged in *The Alchemist* (1609), where persons of wit, opportunity, and weird fortitude can triumph hilariously; or Thomas Nashe's *The Unfortunate Traveller* (1593), a major plague text, where disease launches a plot that sprawls toward the grotesque and away from pathos or tradition. Thomas Dekker's plague pamphlets (1603–36) conduct, like Nashe's work, brilliantly inventive genre experiments in which sickness brings on a kind of civic psychomachia. From another angle, Christopher Marlowe fashions in *Tamburlaine* (c. 1587) an heroic (or antiheroic) version of the world-conquering pestilence that challenges both simple Aristotelian responses such as pity or terror and simple moral reactions which usually prevail in cultural crises. And Shakespeare was quite prepared in other works— *Love's Labor's Lost, A Midsummer Night's Dream, Twelfth Night*—to deploy the idea of plague or contagion as a comic device, a trick of desire and group psychology. Thus, what ought to be the most legible events— the most appalling tragedies or, conversely, the happiest occurrences— are not necessarily inscribed or interpreted in a uniform way. Even more threatening to a single view of the meaning of a particular historical phenomenon is the possibility of contemporary indifference: the chance that, as Auden comments on Brueghel's *Icarus*, some persons will simply sail calmly on, unimpressed with marvelous disaster.[22] Indeed, these are responses encoded in Jonson's and Dekker's works about the plague. So I am led to a second axiom: the semantic impact of a particular history will always be a projection backwards by an invested reader or culture.

As an example of the ways in which works of art produce relativity about the history they inscribe, I would like to consider briefly another plague of current vintage and its inscription in a work of popular culture. The usefulness of this example will be in its reminder that the thick physiological obsessions of tragedy are certainly not peculiar to the Renaissance and that these obsessions are always factored by historical forces.[23] To anticipate some of my readings of Shakespearean interactions with history, then, and to bring some diffuse interpretive issues in this book into focus, I offer a brief topical reading of a recent work of American cinema.

In David Cronenberg's remake of *The Fly* (Twentieth-Century Fox, 1986), the tragic hero, brilliant scientist Seth Brundle, suffers from motion sickness. Because he cannot get quickly from place to place without feeling queasy, he invents an elaborate teleportation machine, a multi-chambered construction organized through a computer that codes and recodes the material to be transported. The astounding device vaporizes objects in one chamber and reassembles them, supposedly unchanged, in another. However, there are some glitches in the process: at the beginning of the movie, Brundle can teleport only inanimate objects, because, as he explains it, there is something about flesh that the central processing unit of the computer does not understand. The hero explains the problem to Veronica, a journalist who has been documenting the experiment and has also recently become his sweetheart. After their lovemaking, Brundle has the insight which enables his triumph and disaster: computers are stupid, he says, and know only what you tell them; "I must not know enough about the flesh myself; I'm going to have to learn." He acquires the requisite knowledge—the movie is silent about how—to enable teleportation of living things.

One evening, slightly drunk and worried about Veronica's fidelity (actually, she has left for the evening to end a relationship with a former partner), Brundle rashly decides to teleport himself. But in the course of the experiment, a common housefly fortuitously enters the transportation chambers, and Brundle's genetic components are somehow fused and encoded with the fly's on his reassembly; the computer interpolates the conflicting genetic data to create what eventually becomes a monstrous hybrid, a man-insect. (Later, when he understands what has occurred, Brundle notes with wonder that his teleporter has become a gene splicer.) In Cronenberg's version, the transformation is not immediately apparent, and the audience does not at first know what effect the entry of the fly into the "telepod" will have on the subject. As it happens, the maiden voyage turns out to be the one that kills him.

Veronica soon notices Seth undergoing some alarming metamorphoses. The formerly calm, rational man becomes psychotically energetic and grossly appetitive, both gastronomically and sexually. But as the first signs of his mutation become evident, another strange thing happens on screen, this time concerning the movie's conversation with contemporary culture and history. Even after he understands how the experiment has miscarried, how he has been genetically fused with the fly, Seth tells Veronica that he has contracted an illness, *not* suffered a hideous accident: "You were right; I'm diseased, and it might be contagious somehow. . . . I think [the sickness] is showing itself as a bizarre form of cancer. . . . I'm just going to disintegrate in a novel way, and then I'll die." These lines are given their gloss by Brundle's increasingly scary appearance. His skin becomes mottled, lesioned; not yet teratoid, in the early stages of his metamorphosis he merely looks disturbingly ill. He looks, in fact, like he has contracted Kaposi's sarcoma, a rare and disfiguring ("a bizarre . . . a novel") form of skin cancer that is one of the best-known signs of patients with Acquired Immune Deficiency Syndrome (AIDS).[24]

Seth Brundle's dilemma diverges palpably from that of the "typical"

Introduction   19

American AIDS victim, the HIV-positive homosexual male. Still, certain points of contact are figured and deflected. Brundle's transformation is marked by heightened sexual desire and promiscuity, characteristics frequently assigned early in the epidemic, even by sympathetic authors, to members of the gay community, who were constantly pilloried for failing to control their "unnatural" urges and thus for spreading the sickness.[25] Furthermore, Brundle's enabling knowledge, the understanding that facilitates his teleportation experiment (and the acquisition of the symbolic disease) is definitively erotic, a learning about the flesh, as he puts it; AIDS, of course, is most commonly contracted through sex. The eroticism of the disastrous experiment is further featured when Brundle conducts his self-teleportation in the nude; the film offers no explanation why he cannot pass through the chamber fully clothed. His unfaithful deed (a betrayal of the woman who is, he thinks, betraying him) is a private engagement of the naked flesh. It is also an act that has been infiltrated by a sort of virus. If Brundle comes to resemble in some measure a victim of disease, the fly is the pathogen, a natural, random, invasive element—an unnoticeable detail of daily life that can become deadly. Just as the flea was for so many centuries virtually unthinkable as the culprit in bubonic plague outbreaks, so the movie insect wreaks havoc out of all predictable proportion to its apparent power. But the fly may be an appropriate symbolic vessel for fears about AIDS in ways the movie never fully intends or understands. And in this *unconscious* communication with its context, the film can be interpreted as an inscriptive document, read in ways similar to the readings of Shakespeare in this book. The insect's more unsavory characteristics and appetites appeal, in a way, to expectations and prejudices that lie deep beneath the film's nervousness about (homo)eroticism. Promiscuous breeder, revolting gourmand—a point we are not cinematically spared—and diseased coprophage (a feature we never have to confront), the fly subliminally focuses the deepest antihomoerotic impulses of heterosexual culture. It is associated not only with sickness in general but more specifically with a conflation of food, sex, and excrement. The most toxically antihomosexual persons in our society fixated early in the AIDS crisis on these associations and charged gay men with sexual habits indistinguishable from the natural behavior of the insect. In 1983, Dr. Paul Cameron of Nebraska referred to the male homosexual community as "a living, breathing cesspool of pathogens. . . . Here is a subclass of people who, as a function of their sexuality, are consuming prodigious amounts . . . of fecal material."[26]

The Cronenberg fly not only produces a symbolic virus in the main character. It also induces unrealized associations with a progressive and fatal ailment that plays upon a particular late-twentieth-century fear—the fear that knowledge of the flesh can lead to disease and death. To interpret the film and its pivotal creature in an historical context, the viewer must understand the fly's dual function as *origin* of sickness (i.e., as metaphoric virus) and as victim of the sickness, a convergence the plot makes plain: after his internalization of the insect's genetic code and his transformation, the scientist becomes, as he calls himself, "Brundlefly." Figuring at once the undetectable germ, the carrier and victim of illness, and, more obliquely, a set of prejudices about the HIV-infected male, the insect and the scientist absorb and disperse historical indicators in a nonlogical way. Yet the "fly," like the movie itself, filters, contains, but does not exactly highlight its cultural referent. The movie's most bitter and pointed allusion to the AIDS crisis is quite indirect: it comes in an ironic aside that comments on what brutally stupid moralists have said about the disease—that it is, in effect, God's (or Nature's) revenge against homosexuals. In attempting to explain to Veronica the significance of his transformation, Seth notes in passing, "I seem to be stricken by a disease with a purpose, wouldn't you say?" Other than this comment, however, the hero's demise has little or nothing to do explicitly with AIDS, and homosexuality does not have a voice in the story.

Brundle's brief resemblance in *The Fly* to an AIDS patient did not mark a watershed moment for Hollywood's treatment of the disease, nor did it change the ways in which it was possible to think about sickness; indeed, the presence of AIDS or new-disease discourse in the movie has gone largely unnoticed.[27] So why is the truncated, slanted reference there at all? Even though the movie cannot be said to be "about" the ailment in any extensive way, Brundle's lesions are signs, modern versions of the plaguy death tokens which cried "No recovery" (*Troilus and Cressida*, 2.3.179) about victims of pestilence. History insinuates itself in *The Fly* like a disease. Neither a perfect nor perfectly conscious metaphor for the hero's suffering, AIDS still functions subliminally to warn us of the despair and the terror of bodily deterioration which await many a victim of the illness; this is the precise fate awaiting Seth Brundle. The analogy between Brundle and that of an AIDS patient tells—in the archaeological sense—the encroaching tragedy of the hero: this utterly unbelievable fiction alludes askance to a morbidly prevalent, too-common horror story in our midst. Brundle's idiosyncratic fate, his complete singularity, would seem to quarantine the AIDS references within the barrier of the bizarre plot; the character seems to defeat similitudes. This, however, is exactly the lesson that we have had to learn, that the demography of pandemics has taught: diseases cross population boundaries and distribute risk; and, as I shall suggest through reading Shakespearean tropes of similarity, epidemics enforce likeness within and beyond the margins of texts.

The veiled allusion, the undeveloped undertone are objects of legitimate critical study now that texts can be turned inside out to show how they have swallowed history. There are more obviously significant motifs in *The Fly* than the one I have been discussing;[28] the work "means" much the same thing, has the same effect on an audience, without the filmic language of disease penetrating it. Cronenberg's horror fiction cannot and does not pretend to make people think responsibly (or at all) about the consequences of the AIDS epidemic; indeed, the film's generic classification as popular horror fiction would seem to absent it from the burden of *serious* historical referentiality, although I think it is a mistake not to take its allusions seriously, however indirectly they are presented. The historical presence of AIDS contributes to *The Fly* a discourse of disaster, a tone of mortality; but the nuances of such a discourse are sheathed and dormant in the text, and they can (and usually do) pass without notice.

As these speculations about cinema are meant to imply, the meaning of history in texts is at once substantial and fleeting, the product of control and accident. What may begin as a half-conscious authorial strategy to manipulate historical reference can become the interpreter's prophylactic effort to constrain infectious meanings that have escaped artistic constraint. In Shakespeare's middle or transitional plays, the real—figured in this book as Queen Elizabeth and the earl of Essex, the first Jacobean plague, the Puritan movement—has an impact that must always be interpolated, projected backwards, because we cannot know the extent to which cultural turmoil affects individual mental landscapes. If matters of public record such as momentous changes in politics or demographics can become inseparable from the nerve and fiber of a literary text, so too can a general unease or a private array of complex pleasures and inconveniences. Many of the specific and local conditions of imaginative production will never be recovered: the weather, the mood of friends, the gate receipts for the month. Shakespeare's work remains walled off, by reason of its temporal and cultural distance, from the kind of intimate historical comprehension that would entirely confirm the readings I undertake. Indeed, even my personal anxieties—

which doubtless helped me select the histories I interpret as undeniable textual presences—control these readings haphazardly, not deterministically.

Historical referentiality in Shakespeare's work must always evoke dire doubt. The proportions and arrangement of this book derive from this doubt, from my advancing conviction about the simultaneous vitality and elusiveness of topical meanings in Shakespeare's theater. Indeed, even as these readings make strong claims for Shakespearean inscriptions of his time, they move steadily away from the assumption of the plays' *direct* topical correspondences with their culture. The way I have arranged them here, the three dramas demonstrate an increasing resistance to history, describing an arc from a fairly neat if problematic deployment of historical character and event (*Troilus and Cressida*) through an extremely murky contagion of referentiality (*Hamlet*) to the virtual absence of significant local reference (*Twelfth Night*). *Hamlet*, Shakespeare's most epistemologically unstable play and the most unstable text in its relation to histories, gets the bulk of my critical attention here; it is framed by one-chapter studies of the topically cogent historical satire and the allusively disjunctive comedy. The two bracketing texts occupy less space in my reading of Shakespeare's contextuality because they are in some sense less bothered about the presence of history within their borders.

To move from Troy to Illyria, with Denmark between, is to travel from mixed genre to fixed genre. My artificial scheme tentatively suggests that when Shakespeare's middle plays stray from generic regularity, they cleave to referentiality, as if history's anchor actually freed form from convention. The gender coordinates of the texts also shift as this study moves from Troy's compromised tragic world to Illyria's melancholy comic one. Specifically, in this arrangement, the potential for an undiminished female power gradually increases, and misogyny decreases accordingly. Perhaps this, too, is the upshot of genre—Linda Bamber's *Comic Women, Tragic Men* paradigm comes to mind[29]—but whereas in other comedies a latent misogyny can be sensed beneath female trials and triumphs, in *Twelfth Night* women are, for once in Shakespeare, portrayed not as trivial, enervated, or emasculating figures but as pleasurably forceful practitioners of their complicated wills. I hope that the movement to Illyria in this book works as something of a corrective to the much decried and denied new-historicist tendency to undervalue feminist theory and consciousness. Perhaps the marginalization of the topic to the penultimate paragraph of this introduction seems only to confirm the tendency. But the transformations of gender hierarchies and erotic potencies in these plays are central concerns of this book. These transformations inscribe history; they figure the social structures and possibilities of female power in the Renaissance. Such issues, it should be noted, are so often subordinated to masculinist concerns in the plays themselves—*Twelfth Night* excepted—that it is sometimes difficult to restore referentiality to the feminist project. This difficulty, however, should itself become the subject of historicist readings.

Michel de Certeau reminds us that the "project of historiography is the inverse of the poetic one":

> [Historiography] consists of furnishing discourse with referentiality, to make it function as "expressive," to legitimize it by means of the "real," in short, to initiate discourse as that which is supposed to have knowledge. The law of historiography functions to obscure nothingness, to suppress the void, to fill the gap. The discourse must not appear separate from its referents. The absence or loss at the origin of its construct must not be unveiled. . . . Literary history's function is to tirelessly restore referentiality; it produces such referentiality and forces its recognition from the text. Literary history thus . . . transforms the text into an institution, if we define the institution as the instrument which renders credible the adequation of discourse and reality by imposing its discourse as the law governing the real.[30]

This bracing cynicism about the historiographical project can stand as a sentry at the gates of my readings, warning passersby that referentiality is about to be restored—but "the absence or loss at the origin" of history or discourse will *not* be veiled. In fact, I am interested in contributing to Shakespearean reinstitutionalization in de Certeau's terms, even though theatrical discourse *cannot* be fully adequated to the real. How, then, is the restoration of referentiality to the text to be justified if this referentiality lacks truth value or ontological necessity? For my purposes, the saving notion lies in the pluralization of contexts, the *multiplicity* of reference in which discourse circulates, whether that discourse is historiographical, poetical, or the speaking practice of everyday life. Just as de Certeau argues that "one can regard historiography as something of a mix of science and fiction" (203), so shall I regard Shakespeare now as a mix of historical facts and theatrical fictions, both of which draw (on) a similitude of the real.

ONE

Emulous Factions and the Collapse of Chivalry

Troilus and Cressida

In *The State of England Anno Dom. 1600*, Thomas Wilson describes a country besieged. Despite its renowned military force and well-fortified capital city, England suffered a pervasive fear of attack. Frequent skirmishes with Ireland and rumors of imminent Spanish invasion fostered a national preoccupation with war. Indeed, Wilson's description of private arsenals portrays an entire country armed and at the ready for battle:

> For the provisions of armour every howseholder is charged to have in his howse, in a readiness, such armes as is appointed by the Commisioners, and there is no howseholder so poore that is not charged with some thing, at least a bill, sword, or dagger, who soever he is, unless he be a beggar.[1]

This late Elizabethan obsession was born of vigilance against a foreign menace, but it also had an ideological component. It manifested the monarch's personal symbology: invasion was a metaphoric threat to the inviolate Virgin Queen and her realm. Policy and ideology converged in England's national energies, which were directed largely to defensive as opposed to aggressive or interventionist ends.[2] Wilson notes, for instance, that the "comon souldiers that are sent out of the realme be of the basest and most unexperienced, the best being reserved to defend from invasion" (*State of England*, 34). Rarely conciliatory, the country neither escalated hostilities (profiteering missions excepted) nor sought peace.

England's concomitant state of siege was, oddly, a marker of success.

As long as the country (like its queen) could repel attack, it would maintain power. In her famed speech to the troops at Tilbury in 1588, anticipating an incursion by the Spanish Armada, Elizabeth provocatively declaimed her credo:

> I am come amongst you . . . to lay down for my God and for my Kingdom and for my people my honor and my blood even in the dust.
>   I know I have the body but of a weak and feeble woman, but I have the heart and stomach of a king, and of a king of England too, and think foul scorn that Parma or Spain, or any prince of Europe should dare to invade the borders of my realm; to which, rather than any dishonour shall grow by me, I myself will take up arms.[3]

The first sentence syntactically implies and withdraws eroticism ("I am come . . . to lay down . . . my honor and my blood") in its expression of Elizabeth's military intentions. Taking up arms here is a wholly self-protective measure. The queen means to defend against an invasion that could, like a sexual violation, engender ignominy. Elizabeth at Tilbury disclosed the psychological effect of her policy: the edgy passivity of waiting for an attack. Invasion anxiety produced a military strategy and a national condition of nervousness, inspiring such elaborate preparations as were seen at Tilbury and other points of entry.[4] Like Cressida in *Troilus and Cressida*, the country lay on its back to defend its belly, "at all these wards," "at a thousand watches" (*Troilus and Cressida*, 1.2.250).[5]

Cressida's words to Pandarus describe both a sexual and a martial strategy, one that befits a play about a war that began as a rape. Her paradoxical description of defense—she will lie upon her back to defend her belly, "upon my secrecy, to defend mine honesty; my mask, to defend my beauty" (1.2.248–49)—can also be taken as a peculiarly Elizabethan mode of behavior. The queen maintained her symbolic and literal inviolability through vigilant wards and watches, but she admitted feminine vulnerability as a defense of her (masculine) authority. With the heart and stomach of a king but the body of a weak and feeble woman, Elizabeth made substantial ideological gains from a seemingly susceptible posture. Cressida's policy (unsuccessful though it is) articulates, on a minute scale, a version of Elizabeth's; the play world of *Troilus and Cressida* (c. 1602) comprises far more comprehensive and complicated stagings of late Elizabethan ideology, policy, and events. The neurosis of invasion made England something of a Troy, a nation ten years at war without strong hope of either victory or truce. Troy, be-

sieged and paralyzed, imaginatively refigures the troubled last years of
Tudor rule.

                              I

England's disengaged, perpetual militancy in the 1590s was replicated in
a hostile atmosphere at court. Protracted struggles with Spain and Ireland magnified tensions within the upper levels of government. The nobles divided along anti- and pro-war lines. The Cecil family—William
Cecil, Lord Burleigh (treasurer of the realm) and his son Robert (secretary to the queen)—led the faction that promoted peace with Spain and
Ireland. The opposing, militant faction followed Robert Devereux, the
second earl of Essex.

The conflict between Essex and the Cecils was no mere set-to between
common political opponents; it was in fact a central social drama in the
last years of the reign. Even though, as Thomas Wilson suggestively
notes, there were "some good Lawes made to avoid emulacion amongst
noblemen and gentlemen and also factions,"[6] those laws must have
functioned to entice by seeming to prohibit. For as is generally recognized, the proliferation of emulation and factions was a crucial characteristic of Elizabeth's method of rule. From the beginning of her reign
the queen had employed factionalism as a kind of ecosystem.[7] To prevent challenges to the monarchy, the nobles were encouraged to conceive of one another as the sole obstacles to positions of greater and
greater strength. Factionalism, like the national military posture and
Cressida's misunderstood sexuality, was essentially defensive, a strategy
to control and redirect hostility. The French ambassador extraordinaire
to England in 1597, André Hurault, sieur de Maisse, noticed that

> The court is ordinarily full of discontent and factions, and the Queen is well
> pleased to maintain it so, and then the Lord Treasurer, old as he is, is exceed-
> ingly ambitious and finds nothing but amusement in these court broils, and
> his son is altogether immersed in them.[8]

In their brisk campaign for force and place, Elizabeth's nobles did much
of her work for her.

Robert Naunton later wrote of the queen that "the principall note of
her raigne will be that she ruled much by faction and parties, which she
herself both made, upheld, and weakened as her own great judgement
advised."[9] Certainly, early in her rule, Elizabeth circumscribed most of
the factional conflict she created. But if aristocratic hostility was the

product of an imposed plan, there were indications at the end of the sixteenth century that the design could not contain its materials. The courtiers who came to the fore in the 1590s had an ambitious slyness about them that Burleigh and Leicester dared not display when Elizabeth was in her prime.[10] The usually perspicacious queen was late to acknowledge the new climate; in 1601 she lamented, "Now the wit of the fox is everywhere on foot, so as hardly a faithful or virtuous man may be found."[11] The overreaching peers produced more intense struggles than Elizabeth had anticipated, and these struggles disrupted the delicate balance she had sustained for so long. When Essex finally led an armed contingent against Whitehall in 1601, the coup was directed against the earl's rivals, not against the queen. The faction system was curiously effective in deflecting hostility from Elizabeth; nevertheless, the struggle for prominence at court precipitated the abortive rebellion.[12] "A good quarrel to draw emulous factions, and bleed to death upon" (2.3.75) overwhelmed the structure of rule that Elizabeth had used for some forty years. Designed to restrain disorder, factionalism actually fueled it. The system, as Essex's career ultimately suggests, backfired violently.[13]

It was apparent even before the rebellion that factions extended far beyond Elizabeth's intentional influence. Administrative divisiveness became the widespread norm. Even Wilson, who was only a tangent to the circle of the court, could observe:

> In all great offices and places of charge they doe allwayse place 2 persons of contrary factions and that are bredd of such causes, or growne to such greatness, as they are ever irreconcilable, to the end, each having his enemyes eye to overlooke him, it may make him looke the warilier to the charge, and that if any body should incline to any unfaithfulnesse in such charges of importance as concern the publicque safety, it might be spied before it be brought to any dangerous head. ... This is seene allwayse in ye Towre, the place of most trust, where the Lieftenant and Stuard, master of the Ordnance and Lieftenant of the same, have been ever in my remembrance vowed enemyes, and this is too apparent in the Deputyes of Ireland & Govnor of Munster att this time and heretofore. (*State of England*, 42–43)

The drift of Wilson's political science is clear. The faction system was necessarily unstable, for it deployed mighty opposites in critical and adjacent posts; the nation balanced uneasily in conflict. From the court to the Tower to the proxy government in Ireland, hostility prevailed as internal policy grew precarious and public. Court battles at the end of the reign had their stormy center in the Essex and Cecil conflict, yet they surpassed policy or even personality and entered a different category, that of inescapable governmental rift. Proliferating factions seemed to manifest a pathological disunity of political structure and spirit, a contagious emulation of disorder. The most prominent feature of the reign in its last years was this spreading agon inside it; internal strife prolonged external problems and diseased the realm.

In *Troilus and Cressida*, Shakespeare transforms a de facto Elizabethan policy and its unforeseen consequences into a central plot complication of the Trojan War story. Or we might say that he inscribes and augments the resemblance between a major crisis of that story and a crucial political problem of his time. The *Iliad* begins with a civil war for supremacy between Achilles and Agamemnon. Achilles soon withdraws from the fighting to protest Agamemnon's appropriation of his "prize," Briseis; his absence hamstrings the Grecian forces, which remain ineffective until his return. But rather than portray the Greek dilemma in Homeric terms as an offended hero's protest against rapacious authority, Shakespeare frames the crisis as a plague of personal interest groups. Vexing factionalism underlies the failure of the Greek army and compels Ulysses to expound on the loss of "degree." He attributes the prolongation of the Trojan War to administrative neglect and a consequent divisiveness in the camp:

ULYSSES: Troy yet upon his bases had been down
             And the great Hector's sword had lack'd a master
             But for these instances.
             The specialty of rule hath been neglected;
             And look, how many Grecian tents do stand
             Hollow upon this plain, so many hollow factions.
                                            (1.3.75–80)

Ulysses' speech inaugurates a topical representation of internecine political strife and its effects. Just as irreconcilable enemies seemed to infect every limb of English government, so hollow factions spread among the Greeks and fragment the militia.

Inattentive, ineffectual authority and an entirely self-centered nobility generate this turmoil. Agamemnon, allegedly the leader of Greece, is incapable of diagnosing or even noticing the problem besetting his command. Indeed, Ulysses' declamation on degree undercuts (and thus comments sharply on) the general's clumsy attempts to rationalize the army's protracted failure (1.3.1–30). The aristocracy, indifferent to disorder, constantly engages in purposeless (nonteleological) acts of subversion, and these acts prove irresistible. Explicating the Greeks' woes, Ulysses cannot help but perform the disruptive thing he decries: first by taking center stage from Agamemnon and indicting "the specialty of rule"; next by openly confessing his scorn for his superior ("The general's disdained / By him one step beneath" [1.3.129–30]); and finally by enviously locating the blame for the army's failures in a fellow warrior, thus reflexively proving his point and perpetuating the problem of divisiveness. According to Ulysses, the Grecian problem is nearly featureless, emptied out, unreadable—hollow factions in hollow tents upon a plain—yet there is one clear signifier: "The great Achilles, whom opinion crowns / The sinew and the forehand of our host" (1.3.142–43), disturbs the order of things.

Achilles derives his muscular sovereignty from "opinion," an essential feature of any court dynamic. He becomes the only consensus agent of force in the world of Troy; the entire war, it seems, is his prerogative. Power is situated, negotiated, burlesqued in his tent in a great parody of Elizabethan peer affairs. The Achilles faction engages in councils, political intrigue, satire, the gossip of the pampered, and even court entertainments: Thersites "is a privileged man" (2.3.60) such as monarchs had. When Ulysses admits that "opinion crowns" his colleague-out-of-arms the "sinew and the forehand" of Greece, he inadvertently grants to Achilles the figurative body of governance. Significantly however, such ad hoc, unsolicited power makes him an engine of disruption. His tent-keeping is all the rage—a fashion trend that sparks contagious anger. Achilles's withdrawal generates furious, single-wing factions such as Ajax, a poor emulator of *casual* autonomy. Ajax, "grown self-will'd," mimics Achilles, "keeps his tent like him; / Makes factious feasts" (1.3.190–91). This unconscientious objector has begun to damage the Grecian cause through imitative inaction and editorialization; he rails "on our state of war / Bold as an oracle" (1.3.191–92). Thus Achilles's preference for his private "faction of fools" (2.1.121) amounts to an insurrection; his absence from the wars is a power that mimeographic emulation makes perilous. No army, no administration, can afford such a trend of departures. Achilles's power in subversive *absence* ironically figures the decentering of force relations in Troy. The most potent warrior, the former glorious image of heroism, undoes hierarchy simply through his seclusion.

In 1598, some three or four years prior to *Troilus and Cressida*, George Chapman published an unfinished translation of the *Iliad* with a dedication to the earl of Essex. To Chapman, Robert Devereux had

a nearly mythic stature; he represented demidivinity, an even more heroic "type" than that of the courtier-soldier-scholar. The work is
therefore inscribed "To the Most Honored now living Instance of the
Achilleian vertues eternized by divine Homere, the Earl of Essex."[14]
This address enacts the requisite fawning over a potential patron, but
it also represents a personal and a cultural perception. For Essex *was*
an exemplar of Achillean attributes in England (whether these were
virtues or not is at question). The Venetian ambassador Francisco
Contarini, writing in 1599, unequivocally calls him "the greatest personage in England, the man who has enjoyed more of the Queen's
favor than anyone else."[15] Essex's dashing demeanor and restless self-
promotion contributed to his aura of glory, but his most visible attribute was his aggressive militarism. De Maisse reports that "Among the
courtiers the Earl of Essex is the chief person in the Realm. . . . He is
entirely given over to arms and the war, and is the only man in England who has won any renown thereby" (*Journal*, 33). Devereux
took enthusiastic part in the most conspicuous state military operations; his heroism at Rouen (1591) and Cadiz (1596) was already the
stuff of national legend. But when he fell from favor at court, when
the factional turmoil there grew oppressive, or when his proposed war
policies met with royal indecision or disapproval, the earl also frequently indulged in a disruptive, Achillean reclusiveness. De Maisse repeatedly describes Devereux as an absence more than a presence: "The
Earl of Essex, for his part, is very independent; on the least pre-text
given him he withdraws and would go to his own house" (18). The
friendly and sympathetic ambassador arrived in England after Essex's
return from the failed campaign to the Azores; although de Maisse
often sought an audience with the sequestered earl, he met again and
again with only rumors: "According to report [Essex] was feigning illness, and had been in disgrace with the Queen since returning from his
voyage" (33).

Essex's surly withdrawals were well known to Chapman; as a result,
"the 1598 *Iliads* discloses Chapman's studied, eccentric attempt to apol-
ogize for Achilles's isolation."[16] Chapman's promotion of the earl as
Achilles is a sustained justification of an individualist whose separation
from society is intended to indict corrupt social practice. The dedication
to Essex continues:

Most true Achilles (whom by sacred prophecie Homere did but prefigure in
his admirable object and in whose unmatched vertues shyne the dignities of

the soule and the whole excellence of royall humanitie), let not the Pessant-common polities of the world . . . stirre your divine temper from perseverance in godlike pursute of Eternitie. (*Chapman's Homer*, 504)

The Homeric Achilles is the perfect figure for an Essex apologia because, as Cedric Whitman has said, "integrity in Achilles achieves the form and authority of immanent divinity, with its inviolable, lonely singleness, half repellent because of its almost inhuman austerity, but irresistible in its passion and perfected selfhood."[17] Like his Homeric archetype, Chapman's Achilles is a sensitive, wronged warrior who righteously withdraws from the battle to confound Agamemnon's overweening authority. But any extensive pursuit of the parallel produces a more complicated reading. Essex's withdrawals, unquestionably a challenge to power, were neither so simply virtuous nor so clearly motivated as Chapman implies: indeed, they were transparently a form of insubordination. What was more troubling, particularly regarding the implications of factionalism for the order of the reign, was that the earl attracted in his absences a following of "desperate and disreputable professional soldiers" who, according to de Maisse, had been "ill-recompensed" by court rivals (*Journal*, 49). This entourage formed a countercourt to which Essex retreated in times of extreme stress. As his fortunes waned, the earl became progressively difficult to appease, and his independence was seen as a palpable threat.[18] The "greatest personage in England" was a constant locus of political instability.

In referring to Essex as Achilles, George Chapman accidentally creates an obtrusive irony. For Achilles, the greatest of the Greeks, is also, like Essex, a terrific nuisance. In the late 1590s, Devereux had indeed become the "now living instance" of Achillean attributes: an honored fighter who sulked, surrounded by his thuggish Myrmidons (his malcontent soldiers and courtiers) when honor was out of reach. He came to embody the dark side of martial individualism. After the earl's unsanctioned, rash return from the Irish wars and immediate confinement for disobedience in 1599, Chapman's ideal of a nearly unblemished heroism no longer seemed plausible. Interestingly, it was an ideal in which Shakespeare had participated, though with characteristic caution. The following passage from *Henry V*, while rejoicing in Essex's anticipated triumph, seems aware of him as a rival force and nervously subordinates praise for the general to plaudits for the monarch. After imagining Henry being swept into London like some conquering Caesar, the chorus compares the reception Essex will probably receive, if all goes well:

As by a lower but by loving likelihood,
Were now the general of our gracious Empress,
As in good time he may, from Ireland coming,
Bringing rebellion broached on his sword,
How many would the peaceful city quit,
To welcome him! Much more, and much more cause,
Did they this Harry.
                                        (Act 5, Chorus, 29–35)[19]

But following the earl's rebellion and fall in 1601, the epic, heroic ideal no longer even seemed *possible*. With the subversively sequestered Achilles, Shakespeare erases and rewrites Chapman's portrait of independent heroism. Of course, the parameters of the heroic had already been erased and redefined. For Essex inscribes as much as he is inscribed; he is part of the cultural pen and ink, the material conditions of conceptual possibility for *Troilus and Cressida*.[20]

Shakespeare's Achilles, in turn, figures the motivational complexity and problematic centrality that were, in another context, Essex's own. As Chapman would prefer to forget, context is inescapable. No matter how far Achilles removes himself from the wars, he inevitably affects and is implicated in "the Pessant-common polities of the world." He is pulled back to the battle, even as Devereux was inexorably drawn to court and is drawn by the play world: a subject pressured by representational politics in which he participates fully and in which character and selfhood are always being read and written.[21] In his period of disgrace Essex complained that "they print me and make me speak to the world, and shortly they will play me upon the stage."[22] He was correct. The revisionist portrait of fugitive power in *Troilus and Cressida* evokes an historical moment in which "Pessant-common polities" and their representation are not only unavoidable, but contagious.

Thus does the rhetoric of contagion, essentially a language of *context*, cling suggestively to Achilles in the play. Ulysses describes him as suffering from a terminal disease: "He is so plaguy proud that the death-tokens of it / Cry 'No recovery' " (2.3.178–79). But plagues spread. Achilles is the premier victim *and* carrier of epidemics, for while his arrogance quarantines him, his eager imitators disseminate the politics of avoidance. His withdrawal makes him ever more the focus of war and the plague of factions.

The contagious centrality of Achilles has a dramaturgic element about it. Determined to prove insubordination, Ulysses hilariously recites the send-up of Nestor and Agamemnon that Patroclus performs for the Achilles faction (1.3.151–84). What Ulysses actually demonstrates, however, is the subversive communicability of Achilles' local theater. The indignity to which Patroclus and Achilles subject the Greek council in their coterie playhouse becomes an irresistible script for Ulysses' outrageous performance; rebelliousness infectiously, dramatically reproduces itself. *Troilus and Cressida* encrypts the theater's assault on authority, and in the process introduces another Devereux-Achilles overlay. For the most probable historical context of an encounter between Essex and Shakespeare involves just this issue of contestatory theater. By commissioning Shakespeare's company, the Lord Chamberlain's Men, to play *Richard II* on the eve of his uprising in 1601, the earl meant to incite some form of revolt through the mimetic enactment of a deposition.[23] He hoped, that is, to use the theater as a contagiously subversive force. Achilles, irresistibly imitable, analogously spreads subversion both factional and theatrical. Both Essex and Achilles suffer and transmit a plague which, as the hegemony sees it, weakens the bones of state: "And in the imitation of these twain . . . / . . . many are infect" (1.3.185–87). The pathogenic figures spread "an envious fever" that makes everyone "sick / Of his superior" (1.3.132–33), corrupted by the contagious desire for a degree of autonomy denied by the very notion of "degree."[24]

The play defines with precision the social and historical mechanism of this illness: "pale and bloodless emulation" (1.3.134). In trying to goad Achilles back into the wars, Ulysses flatters him with a tableau of his former greatness. He says even the gods suffer from jealousy of the hero: Achilles' "glorious deeds but in these fields of late / Made emulous missions 'mongst the gods themselves, / And drave great Mars to faction" (3.3.188–90). Emulation and its product, factionalism, always flourish together through the collapsing of difference, even presumably the ontological difference between men and gods. Because court factionalism was an equilibrating structure, it spurred the nobles to augment the distinctions that it dissolved. Their circular solution was emulation, which Joel Fineman (drawing on René Girard's work) defines as "that paradoxical labor of envy that seeks to find difference in imitation"; it is "the emotional modality appropriate to the scheme of differentiating violence between equals."[25] Emulation at Elizabeth's court was a method of advancement: imitate your fellow courtier so completely as to make him obsolete.[26] In a system that promoted nullifying balance, that calibrated power relations to the disadvantage of those most actively engaged in it, every self-creative gesture produced only imitation. The "hollow factions" to which Ulysses refers exactly configure this business of copying what one seeks to destroy. Fineman pertinently notices that emulation is "a desire divided against itself . . . best illuminated by Freud's ambiguous account of an ego whose identifications are simultaneously subjective and objective, narcissistic and anaclitic" ("Fratricide and Cuckoldry," 107). Such desirous hostility, "the noblest hateful love" (4.1.34), is always an impulse in those who seek to demolish rivals they depend upon, rivals who are the very impetus for self-formation.[27] Despite its psychological complexity, the emulative impulse is not an individual or personal but rather a viral, systemic phenomenon. Those who occupy a grid of social roles on the same level in a given organizational structure (courtiers, assistant professors, executives) tend to be rendered competitively indistinct.

In *Troilus and Cressida*, the problem of emulation is particularly keen for the Greeks, whose statesmen and soldiers are of nearly identical lofty rank. The Grecian forces include "sixty and nine that wore / Their crownets regal" (Prologue, 5–6)—independent princes, interchangeable members of an aggregate, disunified aristocracy that lacks a compelling account of intrinsic value or difference. When Ulysses says "emulation hath a thousand sons / That one by one pursue" (3.3.156–57), he conjures the assembly-line nightmare of patriarchal violence that produces indistinguishable persons.[28] Society fosters contagious imitations that frustrate the distinctions it pretends to treasure.

What is mesmerizing about the idea of emulation in the drama is its metacultural conflation of *two* historical coordinates: the obsessive competition between the aptly named "peers" of the realm; and the conditions of Shakespearean representation.[29] For as a mimetic act, emulation is always to some extent an aesthetic one as well. It is a poetics of success through imitative conduct. Political behavior and aesthetic form appropriate and infiltrate one another; as the nobility enacts an increasingly hostile drama of imitative gesture and stratagem, the Shakespearean theater implicates itself in this historical context by emulating it— simultaneously articulating and debasing the cultural referent. Portrayed within but also enacted by the play, emulation escapes containment; it is always an ailment, an infection coursing within and without. Just as violent emulation in the Elizabethan court wrought havoc on cultural templates such as honor, nobility, and distinction, *Troilus and*

Cressida, too, contaminates what it copies. The emulous drama treats the overtold tale of Troy but displaces its predecessor and competitor texts through its escalating, sarcastic violence and its radical obliteration of the ideologies that no longer validate that tale. This drama is an enterprise sick with its own knowledge of contemporary dramatic, political, and erotic practice. The Shakespearean emulation of the Troy story is a profoundly deforming project of literature reading history.

II

"Dame," fait il, "j'ai bien oï parler
de vostre pris, mais che n'est ore mie;
et de Troie rai jou oï conter
k'ele fu ja de mout grant seignorie;
or n'i puet on fors les plaches trover . . . "

"Lady," says he, "I have indeed heard talk
of your greatness, but there is nothing left of it.
I have also heard talk of Troy,
how it was once a great power;
nowadays they can just barely find the site."
                                                    Conon de Béthune[30]

The Trojan War is a battle between two sets of courtiers for possession of a queen. The story thus frames the essential social and political dynamic of the Elizabethan court, where the Cecil and Essex factions sought, in Lawrence Stone's words, "control of the Queen's purse and person."[31] But if Shakespeare replicates some parallels between English court affairs and the tale of Troy, he also skews others, setting the picture of contemporary politics curiously awry. The most obvious and important breach between the play and its cultural context is that neither the Trojan nor the Greek side has a figure much like Elizabeth. Political force in Ilion resides solely in the doddering patriarch Priam and his boisterous boys; the Greek camp, too, is as far from a gynocracy as imaginable. The Trojans and Greeks, as combatants for a totemic sexual and material site—the body of Helen—emulate the crises of the Elizabethan aristocracy through fragmented outline and indirection.

The relationship of a literary work to a culture that sponsored, coerced, or prohibited it has been nicely defined by Edward Said as "the *eccentric*, dialectical intermingling of history with form in texts."[32] But if Shakespeare's interminglings are eccentric, they are also for the most part symbolic, purposeful, motivated. The example of court parties suggests just such a production of meaning. Factionalism for many years bore Elizabeth's imprimatur and signature, yet the author of strife in the Grecian camp is not a ruler but a courtier. (Or two courtiers, inasmuch as Ulysses diagnoses and so recreates the problem that Achilles has caused.) However, this canted parallel, far from signifying the text's distance from its historical moment, actually reproduces the major topical problem. Courtier control over the factions in Greece configures an impotence in royal or monarchical authority *with respect to* such structures. Agamemnon's estrangement from his own authority and from his fellow kings enables factious insubordination. Likewise, the presentation of factional rivalry as first a plague and then an ex post facto policy—"Their fraction is more our wish than their faction" (2.3.101), Nestor says of a potential Achilles-Ajax alliance—underscores a current governmental failure. Elizabeth's regulatory mechanism takes dramatic form as a hierarchical and organizational nemesis. Dissimilar arrangements in the play and culture highlight analogical similarities: they are differences encoded to show sameness and ultimately to insinuate deficiencies of contemporary rule. But some disjunctions are less easily decoded than others.

In associating the Grecian camp with Elizabeth's court, the play deflects the single *expected* correspondence between text and world. For Geoffrey of Monmouth's mythographic account of Britain's origins had long since established an identity between England and Troy. Aeneas's great grandson Brute or Brutus was said to have founded Britain after the fall of the ancient city. In Spenser's formulation, "noble Britons sprong from Trojans bold, / And Troynovant was built of old Troy's ashes cold" (*Faerie Queene*, 3.9.38). If London (Troynovant) is regarded as a phoenix sprung from the ashes of a great civilization, then the recognizable English problem of factionalism in *Troilus and Cressida* symbolically afflicts the wrong side.

What can we make of this alteration? It seems at first to confute the cherished Tudor myth of Trojan origins, a myth that was becoming increasingly unconvincing toward the end of the queen's reign. As Frances Yates explains, Elizabeth's ancestors "were of Welsh or ancient British descent. When the Tudors ascended the throne of England, so runs the myth, the ancient Trojan-British race of monarchs once more resumed the imperial power and brought in a golden age of peace and plenty."[33] Or so it might have appeared for much of the queen's rule. But by the end of her monarchy, this story was assailed convincingly; the historicity of "Brutus" was in considerable doubt. The figure was skeptically dismantled by no less an authority than Elizabeth's historian, William Camden:

> Geffrey Ap Arthur Monmouth, foure hundred yeares ago, was the first . . .
> that to gratifie our Britains produced unto them this Brutus, descended from
> the gods, by birth also a Trojane, to bee the author of the British Nation. . . .
>   Furthermore . . . very many out of the grave Senate of great Clerks, by
> name, Boccace, Vives, Hadr. Junius, Polydore . . . and other men of deepe
> judgement, agree joyntly in one verdict, and denie, that ever there was any
> such in the world as this Brutus: also, that learned men of our owne country,
> as many, acknowledge him not, but reject him as a meere counterfet. . . . [34]

The unreliability of mythification is variously portrayed in *Troilus and Cressida*, most memorably in Achilles' assertion that he has killed Hector after the Myrmidons have in fact done the deed. Yet the debunking of myth cannot by itself explain specific transmogrifications such as the assignment of a characteristic English problem to the Greeks instead of the Trojans.

What can better account for the Shakespearean alteration is the text's formal "dialectical intermingling" with its historical contexts. The play's plot formation schematizes its proximate relation to late Tudor conditions. For history is *not* reproduced eccentrically in *Troilus and Cressida*; it is disposed bilaterally. Both Greek and Trojan camps recollect contemporary political acts and structures; both sides, and their transactions, establish compelling circuits of text and world. The Trojans in the play are coextensive with the Greeks in their referentiality; they simply evoke other aspects of a specifically Elizabethan dissolution. Troy differs in the heavier *ideological* freight of its representations.

Throughout the drama, the sons of Priam identify themselves with the forms and conventions of chivalry. They cleave to a traditional ideal of knighthood and "honor": courage, loyalty, dedication to cause and ruler and lady. (The Trojans suffer occasional lapses when it occurs to them that cause, ruler, and lady are irremediably separate; for much of Elizabeth's reign, these were three in one.) The Trojan chivalric ideal derives its literary impetus from the romance epics of the Middle Ages; in *Troilus and Cressida* the medieval heritage of the story seems to belong almost exclusively to the Trojans.[35] The Greek lords are situated stylistically in the late Renaissance, surprisingly contemporary in the weary cynicism of their political maneuvers. The Trojan men, by contrast, emerge through attitude and language as vaguely antiquated. But only vaguely: their courtly behavior in love and battle, musty-seeming enough by 1600, nonetheless recreates a crucial facet of the Elizabethan cult.

The chivalric premise lay behind virtually every late Tudor court formality: progresses, pageant entertainments, anniversary celebrations, diplomatic embassies, conferrals of dignities. The enactment of the ideal in the period was, on its surface, an expression of monarchical glory and the nobles' undying fealty. But chivalry, enthusiastically resuscitated for Elizabeth's reign, survived (like the story of England) with something of a false genealogy. Chivalry barely managed to contain its hereditary discord and contradictions. In its medieval form, chivalry masked savage and unregenerate self-interest; deadly sins were meliorated only by their veneer of martial glory. In some cases the line between chivalry and criminality was frighteningly thin. The European Middle Ages suffered a scourge of *condottieri*, mercenaries who sought the honor of wars "by birth and vocation" but whose greedy ravages were comparable to the effect of an epidemic.[36] Knighthood glorified bravery and martial prowess, but in so doing, it legitimated and rewarded rapacity. Yet this ambivalence was, it could be argued, always part of the courtly appeal. To William Caxton (in the preface to Malory's *Morte D'Arthur*), the Arthurian tales contain

> many joyous and playsaunt hystoryes and noble and renomed actes of humanyte, gentylnesse, and chyvalryes. For herein may be seen noble chyvalrye, curtosye, humanyte, frendlynesse, hardynesse, love, frendshyp, cowardyse, murdre, hate, vertue, and synne. Doo after the good and leve the evyl.[37]

The apposition of "humanyte, gentylnesse, and chyvalryes" with "cowardyse, murdre, hate, vertue, and synne" suggests that exemplars of good and evil intertwine in the literary courtesy tradition. Moral ambivalence lends it force as an expression of human history and motivations. The chivalric sanctioning of greed, violence, and adultery (service to a woman was typically service and love of an already married woman) led Tudor humanists such as Roger Ascham to decry the "bold bawdry and open manslaughter" of the knightly ethos.[38]

So chivalry came to the Elizabethans as a problematic, even tainted form. In the later Middle Ages, a strategic manipulation had helped salvage it as a code of honor. Malcolm Vale has written that in order to "secure the allegiance of the nobility and the knightly classes, princes and monarchs found it expedient to graft the powerful concept of personal honour on to that of loyalty to the sovereign."[39] That is, the knights and nobles negotiated a new relationship to monarchy in which they sacrificed some of their autonomous power. What did they gain? The theatrical pleasures of distinction, recognition, even safety—a life, as Francis Bacon once recommended to Essex, in the light, not in the heat. Elizabethan chivalry at its apex successfully replayed this contractual relation. The chivalric mode was an agreement and commodity as much as a style of service; it had incalculable exchange value as a means to favor, priority, and place. In turn, bestowing honor and honors for opulent, ostentatious service, the queen deployed chivalric conventions to maintain the order of the court. Chivalry became a tough container of vastly different contents and discontents: it managed the gelid, bookish formalities of aristocratic homage as well as the boiling rivalries of the most ambitious nobles. It provided a stage upon which factionalism was performed. The queen's Accession Day tilts and progress entertainments used the chivalric mode to help enclose potentially disruptive bids for glory in a stabilizing theater of service.[40]

This ambition/containment dialectic was pressured late in the reign by the problems, as Louis Montrose notes, of "gender and generation."[41] In the Elizabethan version of chivalry, "the essence of knighthood was service to a lady";[42] faithfulness to an unattainable erotic object became a condition of courtier success. The neochivalric cult combined medieval, military thematics of honor and loyalty with amorous overtones to ensure the queen's utter centrality. But these thematic threads could not be woven without entanglements. The Elizabethan redaction of courtly practice was jeopardized in the 1590s by the ruler's increasing generational distance from her courtiers. The problem operated on the literal and figurative levels: neither Elizabeth's age nor her long-employed maternal symbology could comfortably accommodate erotic aspects of her image. The erotic-maternal juxtaposition can never be, past a certain point, entirely comfortable.[43]

The queen's image was "comprehensive, diffuse, and ambiguous," but her self-fashionings became contradictory; in their contradictions, unbelievable.[44] The object of erotic obeisance who took no lovers was somehow the mother of her country who had no children. Despite such disjunctions, the aging queen remained a potentially bounteous maternal figure in economic terms, dispensing the milk of patents and monopolies to her youthful, needy nobility. Elizabeth's motherly persona was by far the most psychologically and chronologically forceful of her self-constructions in the last decade of her reign. The young courtiers, unruly sons more than lovers (and never spouses), found and placed themselves in a conflictual relationship with this female po-wer.[45] The symbolic and physical signs of Elizabeth's advanced age sorted ill with her Tilbury persona—defensive, inviolable, but entic-ing—and with the chivalric premise of her eternal desirability. I do not mean to say that advanced years and sexuality are incompatible, nor that attractiveness vanishes at any particular point in life; simply that the image of eternal freshness and youth, upon which the chivalric fic-tion to some extent depends, is impossible to sustain once bodily cor-ruption becomes unarguable. And in Elizabeth's case, the disintegra-tion of the courtly mode, or at least of its efficacy, coincides with that corruption. Late Tudor chivalric performances and the poetry that recreates them tried mightily to circumvent the harsh fact of decline, but the effort fell short and sometimes backfired. For instance, George Peele's *Anglorum Feriae* records the Accession Day tilt of 1595 and celebrates Elizabeth's recent escape from the Lopez assassination plot. The work describes the queen in glowing, reverential language, but the poet's account concludes with a curious prayer: "May she shine in beautie fresh and sheene / Hundreds of yeares our thrice renowned queen."[46] Surely Peele means that the mental image of Elizabeth's pre-sent beauty should endure forever? But his words summon instead the specter of the anile monarch, in the thirty-seventh year of her reign, counternaturally living on and on, enthroned, embalmed, for centu-ries. The chivalric gesture toward her physical beauty, in denying the fact of mortality, turns back on itself.

Other disruptions of the chivalric were more clearly intentional. In 1598, while deliberating about whom to appoint to the lord deputyship in Ireland, Elizabeth fell into a bitter dispute with the earl of Essex. During one particularly heated argument, the earl—erstwhile flower of latter-day Tudor chivalry—was reported to have turned his back scorn-fully on his sovereign as he added a vicious insult: he said "her condi-tions were as crooked as her carcase."[47] To comment on the queen's aged and deformed body constituted an attack upon it, and Elizabeth promptly struck her former favorite. Not one to back down, Essex laid his hand on his sword hilt. The death knell of chivalry sounded by this episode reverberates until the end of the reign. Essex repeated his disobe-dience on a larger scale in Ireland and yet again in his rebellion. Eliza-beth's inevitable physical deterioration was not just the subject but the enabling fact of Essex's effrontery; her physical vulnerability liberated transgressive impulses and removed a fulcrum on which the nobility once safely balanced its powers and desires. For all the strength of Elizabethan chivalry, it ran a great risk in locating ideology in the queen's body natural.

Underlying the problem of the declining chivalric image was the basic issue of gender difference: Elizabeth's political potency was a thorough cultural anomaly. Montrose reflects with admirable understatement that "the political nation—which was wholly a nation of men—sometimes found it annoying or perturbing to serve a prince who was also a woman, a woman who was unsubjected to a man."[48] This chafing was worsened by abiding resentment of Elizabeth's manipulative intrusions in courtiers' personal lives. It was not enough to plight political troth: the queen's men were expected to maintain the appearance of sexual fidelity to her, or ever so cautiously to submit their alternate desires for her approval.[49] The Virgin Queen, insistent cynosure of male attention, directed the court complex of romance and sexuality—an arrangement that defines delayed gratification. Many of Elizabeth's sharp political maneuvers were conducted within this complex but were frequently misread as solely gender-related phenomena. When Ambassador de Maisse sought to learn from Elizabeth whether England would actively pursue the Spanish wars, he could obtain only equivocal answers: "They labored under two things at this Court," he concluded, "delay and inconstancy, which proceeded chiefly from the sex of the Queen" (de Maisse, *Journal*, 115).[50] The ambassador meant, in his exasperated, androcentric way, that delay and inconstancy are female traits, but they also characterized the monarch's politic sexuality. Delay and inconstancy were precision tools for social maintenance, as integral to maintaining stability in a male-pressured court as were the emulous rivals themselves. Through "delay" the queen wisely employed the erotic understanding that avails Cressida—until the Trojan woman is trapped in the Grecian world of men, and "inconstancy" becomes the only option:

> Yet hold I off. Women are angels, wooing:
> Things won are done; joy's soul lies in the doing.
> That she belov'd knows naught that knows not this:
> Men prize the thing ungain'd more than it is.
>
>   (1.2.291–94)

The fact that men prize the thing ungained, or desire what they do not have, was the motivational and regulatory foundation of Elizabethan factionalism *and* chivalry.

Yet constant striving for inadequate emolument (political, fiscal, or psychosexual) may eventually have undermined loyalties. About Elizabeth, de Maisse believed that "if by chance she should die, it is certain that the English would never again submit to the rule of a woman" (*Journal*, 11–12). Frustrated by the queen's cagey responses to his overtures for information, he can hardly be taken for a disinterested reporter of prevailing opinion. But the ambassador's irritable comment activates the possibility that deferred gratification fueled some men's hostility for female rule.

The problem with maintaining the chivalric ideal was thus not solely in upholding the fiction of Elizabeth's infinite desirability but more generally in sublimating the multiple, intensely strenuous conditions of that desirability. The court was dissilient, generationally fractured, manned (as it were) by an increasingly impatient and acquisitive nobility. The unworkability of the courtly mode in the late 1590s was in some sense its deep, gender-related *insincerity*: dedicated masculine self-interest took precedence over obligatory chivalric service to a woman. However, the precarious genius of Elizabethan chivalry was that it offered the courtier pleasures and rewards precisely compensatory for tensions in gender relations. Late Tudor chivalry was a forum for the visibility of masculine courtier power.

Elizabeth's Accession Day tilts provided the most public site of this power. Styled after medieval chivalric antecedents, the tilts were annual celebrations of the queen's ascendance to the throne.[51] They featured displays of martial prowess in which gentlemen and nobles jousted across a barrier; the man who splintered the most lances won a prize from the queen. Like *Troilus and Cressida*, bear baiting, and public executions, the tilts translated violence into theater. Tonally at deep odds with the persistent, encroaching reality of war, such chivalric exhibitions achieved a golden world of amusing and sanitized discord. But while the tournament served as an ideological state apparatus, cementing the symbolic association between the defense of the country and the chivalric defense of the monarch, it also publicized a critical difference between the queen and her men. The act of war—Elizabeth's Amazonian symbology notwithstanding—was the indisputable area of male superiority, of male *control*, in this reign. Both warfare and the artificial chivalric theater of the tilts offered the courtier an outlet for aggression that was not controlled by the queen. The tournaments' kinetic dispersal of masculine energy may have alleviated some tensions, but it generated others. For public mock-warfare afforded irresistible and inspiring self-exposure. The courtier's physical strength, horsemanship, and glory became the subjects of the tournaments; Elizabeth became an honored object, a motionless spectator and recipient of sincere or disingenuous attentions. The young nobility, glory-seeking and militant, flushed with its own greatness, upstaged the monarch. In reanimating the dormant, genetic dangers of medieval chivalry, the tilts delimited a male arena that necessarily excluded the female except as observer. Such an exclusion achieved, if only momentarily, the dream of masculine power at court, but this dream was not easily shaken.[52]

The functions and dysfunctions of Elizabethan chivalry take us back to *Troilus and Cressida*, where the Trojans manifest in single-combat challenges and tournament activity a comparable employment and diminution of the courtly enterprise. In Troy, the failure of the chivalric mode is related to profound resentment of the woman for whom the nobles fight; yet that resentment is implicated not in the age or dominance of the erotic object but in its redefinition. For in Shakespeare's Troy, emulous, furious male desire is its own and only object. The realignment of the erotic impulse underlies the vexed state of Elizabethan and Trojan courtliness.

III

The first staged meeting of the Greeks and Trojans sets the divisive, conflicting tones of chivalry in *Troilus and Cressida* at a high pitch. Aeneas visits the Greek camp in act 1, scene 3, to deliver Hector's single-combat challenge, thus initiating the Trojans' mock-heroic discourse. But Aeneas's failure to recognize his interlocutor, coupled with the parodic, stylistic excesses of his attempts to do so, threaten to cause all conversational middle ground to cave in:

> AENEAS: Fair leave and large security. How may
> A stranger to those most imperial looks
> Know them from eyes of other mortals?
>
> AGAMEMNON: How?
>
> AENEAS: Ay.
> I ask, that I may waken reverence,
> And bid the cheek be ready with a blush
> Modest as morning when she coldly eyes
> The youthful Phoebus.
> Which is that god in office guiding men?
> Which is the high and mighty Agamemnon?
> (1.3.222–31)

An actor might deliver Aeneas's speech with either foppish sincerity or snooty contempt. It contains both these elements as well as a seemingly gratuitous homoerotic overtone of a blushing bride in an aubade. Agamemnon responds to the speech with a marvelous aporia: "This Trojan scorns us, or the men of Troy / Are ceremonious courtiers." He knows that either he is being insulted or that the peculiar Trojans always speak this way. Agamemnon's perplexed gloss exposes the two poles of Elizabethan chivalric meaning: ceremony as courtesy, ceremony as subversion. Once Aeneas delivers Hector's challenge, the sincerity of the courtly mode becomes no less suspect.

The challenge itself is a protest against prevailing conditions. Although it is peacetime in Troy (a truce is on), Hector is "resty grown" (1.3.262) and seeks disruption. Out of the boredom and anxiety that settle on soldiers prevented from creating their performative fame, the greatest Trojan tries, through Aeneas, to pick a chivalric fight with the Greeks. He does so in terms of a defense of his lady's excellence and honor:

> If there be one among the fair'st of Greece
> That holds his honour higher than his ease,
> That feeds his praise more than he fears his peril,
> That knows his valour and knows not his fear,
> That loves his mistress more than in confession
> With truant vows to her own lips he loves,
> And dare avow her beauty and her worth
> In other arms than hers—to him this challenge:
> Hector, in view of Trojans and of Greeks,
> Shall make it good, or do his best to do it,
> He hath a lady wiser, fairer, truer,
> Than ever Greek did couple in his arms;
> And will tomorrow with his trumpet call
> Midway between your tents and walls of Troy
> To rouse a Grecian that is true in love.
> If any come, Hector shall honour him:
> If none, he'll say in Troy, when he retires,
> The Grecian dames are sunburnt and not worth
> The splinter of a lance. Even so much.
>   (1.3.264–82)

Hector's invitation to the "sportful" combat is not motivated by either a need or desire to defend his wife, Andromache, who remains unnamed in the speech. Indeed, the woman in the challenge functions as a deeply ambivalent rhetorical construct. This pandering, mediated invitation

reads Elizabethan courtly behavior and draws its substance from the
fount of contemporary cultural practice.[53] Hector's challenge employs a
language of courtly love as a pretext for military activity, but the primary impulses of the speech are antifeminist and, correlatively, homoerotic.

The Trojan challenge is a calling-out—the colloquialism neatly implies the open, theatrical nature of such invitations—with no named
adversary. Hector plays the role of champion against all comers that Sir
Henry Lee, and later the earls of Cumberland and Essex, performed at
the tilts.[54] Queen's champion was a coveted role in the tournaments; it
publicly denoted a serious honor, establishing a link between romantic
and military elements at the ideological core of the Elizabethan cult.[55]
There is a critical difference in the case of the proposed Trojan tournament, however. The fact that conferred order and sense on the mock-
jousts in Elizabeth's time, their raison d'être, was the presence of the
queen. But at Hector's challenge, and more significantly at the chivalric
duel itself in act 4, no woman can validate the terms of the fight because
no woman is there. The duel both excludes women and removes authority figures as well, for neither Agamemnon nor Priam sets the battle
conditions: at the duel of Hector and Ajax, Aeneas and Diomedes play
the marshals of the lists to determine the extremity of the combat. The
chivalric challenge and the following tousle produce a male arena *of
courtier rule*, an Accession Day tilt for nobles only, with no queen invited. Hector's tournament-style love challenge, phrased in honor of his
mistress, is like a game for schoolboys only—no girls allowed.

In the absence of women, real and representational, Hector generates
a homoerotic discourse. He calls on "the fair'st of Greece," but he
means the men. After an insinuation that vows between warriors and
women are always "truant," he appeals to any Greek who can avow his
lady's "beauty and her worth / In other arms than hers." The wordplay
depends of course on the two meanings of *arms*, but the "other arms"
are not merely weaponry: they are, pointedly, Hector's limbs as well.
His invitation is designed to make the Greek lovers unfaithful to their
women. The Trojan hero in this speech becomes a surrogate object of
desire.

Aeneas plainly announces that the enterprise is homoerotic: Hector
will call "to rouse a Grecian that is true in love." If any should "come"
after Hector arouses him, the Trojan will do him honor.[56] Now erotic
bonding between warriors is common enough in literature, although it is
generally directed toward a beloved companion, not an enemy.[57] What

makes this speech particularly interesting is that it does not posit an enemy. Instead, the language deflects the expected hostility from the chivalric rival to the traditional putative chivalric love objects. The speech denigrates women in the guise of their defense; it exculpates the men from and implicates the women in any negative outcome of the duel.[58] Should the Greek warriors fail to meet Hector, he will not blame them; rather, he'll slander the Grecian dames, who, he will say, are "sunburnt and not worth / The splinter of a lance." "Sunburnt" connotes "infected with venereal disease"; the splintered lance suggests an impaired penis: the Grecian dames, Hector will say, are not worth the risk of syphilis.[59] Chivalric style cloaks the most uncourtly, hostile sentiments in gleaming armor. At the same time, such meanings are probably not in the range of Hector's intentions. The fissures in the Trojan monument to chivalry are plastered over by habit of force.

Hector's challenge pricks dramatic tension because the Greeks conspicuously lack any women in their camp at this point. What they *do* have, however, is the only openly conducted homosexual relationship in the Shakespearean canon. Achilles and Patroclus are lovers, and their private bond is substantial: it is the only loyalty that manages to survive the depredations of the war.[60] Granted, their relationship is seen as an unholy alliance by the Greek council, but *not* for sexual reasons; the politicos are angry only that Achilles, and "with him Patroclus / Upon a lazy bed the livelong day / Breaks scurril jests" (1.3.146–48), mocking what is left of Grecian authority. (Thersites views the lovers as "preposterous," but he is scarcely a touchstone for acceptable social activity.) The male-enfolded desire of the Greeks is especially compelling contextually because, as Ulysses notes, Hector's love call *does* have an intended object: "This challenge that the gallant Hector sends . . . / Relates in purpose only to Achilles" (1.3.321–23). The arms that Hector finally uses to rouse Achilles from his drowsy tent are battle arms that destroy Patroclus, his obstacle for Achilles' attentions. Achilles seeks horrible gratification for the loss, catching Hector "unarm'd": "this is the man I seek" (5.8.10).

Given the noncourtly, masculine-oriented, disgruntled Grecian soldiers, it is odd how quickly, albeit awkwardly, Agamemnon and Nestor respond to Hector's challenge, as if chivalry were a transcultural value. Although the chivalric style is more appropriate to the Trojans' situation, it speaks to the concerns of both camps by performing a slick, ceremonious devaluation of women and by claiming the worth of a lousy fight. Sure enough, the Greek response to Hector implicitly continues chivalric misogyny in—and beyond—the play world. Responding to Aeneas, Nestor boasts that if no young champion can be found, he will meet Hector to defend the honor of his own lady—a very old lady, who, as Nestor says, "Was fairer than his grandam, and as chaste / As may be in the world" (1.3.298–99). Along with the doubts about female chastity that infiltrate the subjunctive last line, Nestor's words conjure a dicey contemporary tableau: the uncomfortable, possibly ridiculous defense of an ancient woman's virtue. Aeneas, courtier extraordinaire, snidely answers, "Now heavens forfend such scarcity of youth" (301). Like Nestor's lady, and like the image of the aged Elizabeth buried beneath his language, chivalry itself is creaky, out of date. Nearly all the Trojans speak the language of chivalric romance as an ideological safety hatch for their criminal wife-stealing and their latent misogyny. But of the Greeks, only the faintly daffy Nestor can respond in the courtly way to Hector's challenge. The idiom of knightly sincerity is nearly obsolescent slang to the Greeks, because only their older generation can apprehend what has clearly become unintelligible to the rest of them: the concept of defending a woman's honor.

The repressive misogyny in the ranks may be ascribed in part to fears of inadequacy and doubts about female constancy, both arising from the circumstances of this particular war. In Troy, when the heterosexual premise holds, the knight fights for a lady on whom "thousands of rival desires converge";[61] the female chivalric beloved therefore becomes not (like Elizabeth) a source of joy and sustenance but (like Elizabeth) the fount of doubt and paranoia. After the woman's inevitable rejection of most of those desires, she is transformed by the rejected suitors into something hateful, while the men are strangely exonerated for any hint of misconduct in the courtship game. Diomedes illuminates this process in the most violent verbal attack on a woman in the drama. In an interview with Paris (4.1.69–75), he aims such vitriol at Helen ("For every false drop in her bawdy veins / A Grecian's life hath sunk") that an audience may briefly forget that the war is a product of Paris's, not Helen's lusts; and, more tellingly, that Diomedes had earlier expressed his consensual desire for the Grecian queen:

AENEAS: Had I so good occasion to lie long
            As you, Prince Paris, nothing but heavenly business
            Should rob my bed-mate of my company.
DIOMEDES: That's my mind, too.

                                              (4.1.4–7)

But Paris remembers the exchange and ironically undercuts Diomedes' vituperation with his own brand of misogyny: "Fair Diomed, you do as chapmen do, / Dispraise the thing that they desire to buy" (4.1.76–77). Denigration of the female erotic object spreads through the armies—a subtextual twin of emulous factionalism. Following the transfer of Cressida to the Greeks, Ulysses proposes the "general kissing" reception ceremony, a mock-chivalric ritual strongly evocative of a group rape. When it is Ulysses' turn to claim a kiss, Cressida cleverly denies him. He then savagely denounces her as one of the "sluttish spoils of opportunity / And daughters of the game" (4.5.62–63). This outburst is patently retributive for her neat humiliation of him before his fellows; but Hector's sennet sounds immediately after Ulysses' angry speech, and the entire Greek presence on stage cries: "The Trojan's trumpet." So despite evidence to the contrary, Cressida's wantonness is made to seem contagiously irrefutable through unanimous aural contamination—"The Trojan (s)trumpet."[62] Cressida's trumpeted transformation by group accord reveals the armies' conspiracy to honor their own unlovely psychic arrangements.

If the courtiers' misogyny arises from rejected or frustrated heterosexual desire, as it seems to do in the case of Diomedes and Ulysses, that desire is nonetheless *always* ratified in the company of men. The general kissing scene has a powerfully homoerotic, locker-room edge; Cressida becomes a means by which the men measure their masculinity against one another. Worth noting is that both Achilles and Patroclus participate in the kissing of Cressida; it is not so much that the lines of homo- and hetero-eroticism blur in Troy as that one sexual form is the frame or container for the other. Just as Hector's jaunty genital challenge eliminates women as serious contenders for male attention, the kissing of Cressida replays on a small scale the larger occasion of the war: the use of a woman as pretext and pretense for the enthusiastic display of male desires to and before other men: "Hector, in view of Trojans and of Greeks, / Shall make it good, or do his best to do it." Helen is not the goal of the war: she is its local excuse. Women bring armies of men together. And like the adjective *chivalrous* itself, warfare definitively excludes women.

Even Troilus's one-shot affair with Cressida is a plot device to perpetuate and intensify the masculine engagement. Troilus raises no objection to her exchange for Antenor because he is conditioned to think of the trade of a woman for a man as a good swap. Certainly, the transaction energizes both sides. At the moment of her exchange, Troilus and

Diomedes indulge in a mutually arousing display of chivalric chest thumps and antichivalric taunts, all the while ignoring the silenced woman. The warriors now have an excuse to excite one another as Cressida vanishes against the backdrop of their reflective interests. The mechanism of the courtiers' conflict may seem to be, as René Girard would have it, mimetic desire, both men having been inspired by the other's interest in the woman; but that triangulation distorts the *obvious* vector of desire in this scene.[63] Everything here, and in the play as a whole, moves along the patent or submerged axis of homoeroticism, the dedication to male intercourse. The imaginative disappearance of women is a necessary consequence—possibly a goal—of the emulous, self-obsessed conflict.

Eve Kosofsky Sedgwick has offered salutary warnings against seeing in male homosexuality a simple "epitome, a personification, an effect, or perhaps a primary cause of woman-hating."[64] She demonstrates with respect to Shakespeare's sonnets that textual misogyny "plays off against the range of male bonds" (33)—"homosocial," not necessarily sexual bonds—which can foster a heterosexuality that eclipses women and is "relatively unthreatened by the feminization of one man in relation to another" (36). But in *Troilus and Cressida,* male homosocial relations so thoroughly exclude and debase women that the unconscious misogynistic project is made to seem necessary and reasonable. In fact, the bond between men in both Troy and Elizabeth's court "plays off against" (causality being unrecoverable here) the need to achieve or dislocate, retrieve or dominate, the source of female power. Hector's challenge is an invitation to eliminate by homosocially replacing the woman's social value as an object of sexual activity. Men feminize themselves in other ways to appropriate other female prerogatives: Achilles and Essex both play Cressida's and Elizabeth's game of keep-away to secure their own desirability, positioning themselves homosocially to decenter the woman. The two genres of homosocial behavior in the text can be seen as chivalric or antichivalric, Hectoresque or Achillean: the first is active, specular, militant, conservative, apparently (not really) heterosexually inflected; the other is listless, covert, pacifistic, and passively subversive, clearly (not entirely) homosexually inclined. But no matter what the sexual direction of homophilia may be, *all* male relations in Troy work to the detriment of the females. This fact can be dramatically startling. For instance, Troilus and Pandarus enjoy their traffic in woman, the Cressida business, as a way of honing and fulfilling their mutual desires.[65] Cressida's tryst with her lover ends abruptly in act 4, scene 2, when her uncle arrives to mock her. Bothered at his intrusion, she utters a half-knowing, haunting understatement: "I shall have such a life" (4.2.22). Troilus and Pandarus soon share a dirty joke at her expense; some thirty lines later, word comes of her exchange for Antenor.

The certain failure, the disaster of heterosexual relations that is the Trojan War story enforces a presumptive preference for homosocial configurations in this text. After Ulysses reveals a shameful (heterosexual) reason for Achilles' withdrawal from the fighting—"'Tis known, Achilles, that you are in love / With one of Priam's daughters" (3.3.193–94)—he tries to reenlist the hero with this rich apothegm: "And better would it fit Achilles much / To throw down Hector than Polyxena" (3.3.206–7). Ulysses' homoerotic goad to manly action, a replay of Hector's to the Greeks, is quickly seconded by Patroclus:

> A woman impudent and mannish grown
> Is not more loath'd than an effeminate man
> In time of action. . . .
> Sweet, rouse yourself.
>   (3.3.216–21)

Sedgwick's point about a male heterosexuality that eclipses women is especially relevant to Achilles, who conducts a secret affair with Priam's invisible daughter Polyxena but a fairly public dalliance with Patroclus "upon a lazy bed the livelong day" (1.3.147). Achilles' ambivalent sexuality (addressed with the required antifeminist injunction) completes and complements Hector's chivalric evacuation of heterosexuality in the love challenge. What is defined as "effeminate" here is passivity, but that is the very thing that marks Achilles' heterosexuality: for his female beloved, Polyxena, has made him pledge his withdrawal from the wars. Love for women prevents fighting; love for men demands it, as Patroclus here (and later, by his death) calls Achilles back to the battle. Whereas both Hector's and Achilles' heterosexual relationships end in separation, the two greatest warriors end with one another, in a kind of homosocial consummation.

The desire for communion with men in a military or sexual context may have an inward-turning, self-directed valence to it. As a result of his colleagues' entreaties, Achilles expresses a physical need to see his counterplayer, but the terms of his desire suggest something disturbing about its nature and perhaps its historical formation:

I have a woman's longing,
An appetite that I am sick withal,
To see great Hector in his weeds of peace,
To talk with him, and to behold his visage,
Even to my full of view.

(3.3.236–40)

Achilles conceives of his desire as feminine (and thus, of course, debilitating) but describes it suggestively in narcissistic terms. He hungers to
see Hector in his own condition, unarmed, entented; it is an essentialist
and emulous desire, bent to fit a narcissistic frame. Emulation, that conflictual loss of difference, is itself narcissistic—a social model of relations that turns outward only to feed inward, a self-obsessing, self-pro-
moting, and self-destroying infinite regression or motivational loop. The
emulous desire is for the self to resemble another which it already resembles by virtue of the very desire. And while both terms, emulation and
narcissism, signify a destructive imitation, they also allude to a problematic structure of love. If there is a psychological point in this play on
the continuum between homosocial and heterosexual desire, an inter-
stice where Achilles resides, it is the vortex of emulous narcissism, in
which the male can conceive of himself as female (via the male other) in
order to respond completely to a self-directed need. Male narcissism in
the text is a cognate of homophilia that parodically depends on a heterosexual view of relations.[66]

The exigencies of imitative narcissism also describe the chivalric project, which provides male participants with the kind of reflective self-
gratification that females, by definition, cannot supply. When Hector
and Ajax finally meet for their knightly duel, Aeneas explains to Achilles
that "This Ajax is half made of Hector's blood; / In love whereof, half
Hector stays at home" (4.5.83–84). Achilles instantly understands the
fight in erotic terms: "A maiden battle, then? O, I perceive you" (4.5.-
87). These warriors will draw no blood from one another, and so will
remain unpenetrated, maidenly. Narcissism too is maidenly, foreclosing
consumption. Hector's reluctance to fight Ajax à l'outrance suggests
not an incest taboo so much as a way of preserving and enclosing the
image of the self in the enemy:

Let me embrace thee, Ajax.
By him that thunders, thou hast lusty arms;
Hector would have them fall upon him thus.

(4.5.134–36)

Hector's chivalric acts are fully emulous and homophilic; his meetings with Achilles, then, have the symbolic density of self-encounter about them. In *Troilus and Cressida*, the chivalric and the narcissistic merge when the armies come passionately together, pitched in their extremity toward a mutually glorifying violence. The warriors are mirror lovers in arms—rivals in love.

IV

To what extent do these conflicting sexual registers reproduce an Elizabethan court complex? In what ways can we recover the historical reality of such potentially undifferentiated terms as narcissism and homosocial bonding for a reading of *Troilus and Cressida*? Certainly, the social fact of these categories is exceedingly hard to specify. Narcissism is a hugely inclusive, inchoate designation; male bonds have been ever present in patriarchal social and literary texts since (at least) the *Iliad*. To apply "narcissism" as a periodizing concept, I appeal only to the (non-clinical) notion of an ultimately self-destructive self-interest; for "homosocial bonds," those relations between men that exclude, degrade, or imaginatively obliterate women. That the conjunction of these terms can signify in any delimited, historical fashion is a hope I pin on the earl of Essex, the axial figure in *Troilus and Cressida*'s cultural referentiality. Essex again evokes relevant coordinates—in his unavailing obsession with his own image and influence and in his masculinist strategies for circumventing and subduing the queen's centrality.

The presence and absence of Queen Elizabeth within systems of male self-regard is crucial here. I have described factionalism and chivalry as specific productions and dispositions of her court's sexual politics. Only through the absent presence of Elizabeth, refracted in the dim light from Shakespeare's Troy, can "narcissism" and "homosocial relations" be seen as correlative descriptions of compensatory historical structures. The queen grants meaning to these taxonomies of selves at war.

War: it is a hypnotic object of male attention; for Essex, it was also a homosocial escape route from the power of his monarch. In the sphere of Mars, far more than in that of Venus, Essex could achieve unsubjected and purposely irritating freedom from female rule. His martial attitude was forged at the beginning of his court career in sympathy with a group of poor younger sons of the gentry who chose military instead of aristocratic service; the post-Armada skirmishes offered an outlet for their blocked social energies. In spite (or because) of the strong royal suspicion of courtier entourages, Essex became spiritual and martial leader of several of these men: he wrote, "I love them for mine own sake, for I find sweetness in their conversation, strong assistance in their employment, and happiness in their friendship. I love them for their virtues' sake and for their greatness of mind. . . . If we may have peace, they have purchased it; if we must have war, they must manage it."[67] This male esprit de corps seems to have fueled, at a later point, the earl's radical misconduct. After he was installed as commander of the English forces in Ireland, repeated conflicts with Elizabeth about financing and strategy arose. The Irish campaign was a fiasco of disobedient self-determination and monarchical disapproval.[68] Essex went so far as to forge a symbolic alliance with men of war against the queen; but this bond was, significantly enough, with the enemy. After a particularly harsh disagreement with Elizabeth, Essex symbolically aligned himself with the rebel Tyrone by negotiating a truce with him in direct violation of the queen's orders. He found in the Irish adversaries a compelling image of his own impulses; he wrote pointedly to Elizabeth that "the people in general have able bodies by nature, and gotten by custom ready use of arms. . . . In their pride they value no man but themselves . . . ; in their rebellion they have no other end but to shake off the yoke of obedience to your majesty."[69] This alarming report obviously functions as a self-description, uncovering the courtier's will to power; the Irish, like Essex, "value no man but themselves," and seek to shake off their obedience to a woman. When Essex returned to England unbidden, Elizabeth was all too aware of his trespass upon her power: "By God's son I am no Queen; that *man* is above me;—Who gave him command to come here so soon?"[70] Her fury seems as bound to the issue of sexuality as hierarchy: no man was above her, nor would ever be.

It was not only in international war games that Essex formed alliances with men as antidotes for servitude to a woman. He responded to the stormy faction fights of the late 1590s by repeatedly retreating to "his bed" at home, accompanied by his band of disaffected warriors and soldiers (de Maisse, *Journal*, 49). Thus, Devereux extended a homosocial sphere of male rule from the public and active to the private, passive life. But even when he seemed to be serving his monarch, Essex managed Hector's chivalric trick of undercutting and defying what he allegedly defended. Gestures of apparent homage to Elizabeth were in fact often transgressions against her commandments.[71] In 1589, Essex undertook a voyage with Sir Francis Drake to Portugal to escape perceived restraints at court. Letters he left behind infuriated the queen by asserting that he "would return alive at no one's bidding" (*DNB*, 877). On arrival in Lisbon, the earl assumed a ceremonious demeanor in the exaggerated Trojan style; he boldly challenged any of the soldiers in the Spanish garrison to break a lance in the name of their mistresses and his queen.[72] Two years later, in the midst of the siege of Rouen, Essex wrote to the Marquis of Villars, asserting "that I am better than you, and that my Mistress is fairer than yours."[73] Predictably, his conduct again offended Elizabeth, whose fairness he was supposedly advertising; but the contemporary French chronicler was most impressed by "the knight-errantry of Englishmen" (*DNB*, 877).

Knight-errantry, subversive chivalry, was an enduring masculine appliance of self-promotion; it sometimes even literally wrote narcissism into its user's manual. In Francis Bacon's tilt device for Essex in 1595, the earl played Erophilus, love's lover; the goddess of self-love, Philautia, attempted to sway him from Love (Elizabeth) to narcissistic self-indulgence. The bad joke of the tilt is that Essex's elaborate conceit and flamboyant appearance shouted his narcissism louder than it could possibly proclaim his service. But the tilt speeches and some of Bacon's accompanying marginalia suggest that the provenance of the performance was anti-Elizabeth sentiment, narcissistic *and* homosocial. For two years prior to the tilt, Essex had sought the position of solicitor general for Bacon, his protégé and secretary. The fervent attempt was an act of deep friendship and also a bid for political leverage; the earl wanted to install his man in a lofty perch. But shortly before the Accession Day ceremonies, Elizabeth finally rejected the suit, and both friends were crushed. Essex's tilt device, supposedly all about the virtues of self-sacrifice, is tinged with bitterness. In one of the speeches, Philautia says that she has been told "the time makes for you"; in the margin beside these words Bacon wrote in Essex's private copy: "That your lordship knoweth, and I in part, in regard of the Queen's unkind dealing, which may persuade you to self-love."[74] The performance is so thoroughly narcissistic, so aggressively self-glorifying that Elizabeth felt no compulsion to suffer all of it: "The Queen said, that if she had thought there had bene so moch said of her, she would not have bene there that night; and soe went to bed."[75] On this evidence both Roy Strong and Richard McCoy suppose that the tilt failed spectacularly, but that notion assumes the queen was supposed to like it. On the contrary: the tilt angrily repaid her for her "unkind dealing." Essex and Bacon put their private bond to the service of an oppositional narcissism, with Essex at the center of his gaudy proclamation of homage. The departure of Elizabeth

from her own Accession Day party merely achieved in fact what had
already been performed in chivalric discourse.

But this warped chivalry dislocates more than the monarch; it displaces the earlier, old-historicist, reflective identification of Essex with
Achilles.[76] For there is no obvious sense in which the Greek partakes of
the culture of chivalry as the earl so relentlessly did. Once we lose the
certitude of the Essex-Achilles identification in Shakespeare's play,
mustn't the historical reading be abandoned or severely qualified? Not
really. Several years ago, James E. Savage suggested that Hector evokes
the earl of Essex more consistently and convincingly than does Achilles.
Savage argued that the Trojan Hector bears a fame for gentleness and
courtly conduct that alludes to the renowned knightly side of Devereux.[77] It is Hector who has, in Troilus's words, a "vice of mercy," and
Hector to whom Aeneas refers when he announces that "the glory of our
Troy doth this day lie / On his fair worth and single chivalry" (4.4.145–
46). And it is Hector, not Achilles, who suffers Essex's fate: death at the
hands of a rival group. The Cecil contingent had long amplified through
innuendo Essex's ambitions and desire for self-rule.[78] Apprised in Ireland of the Cecil faction's barbed insinuations, the earl felt like a man
exposed to a mortal assault:

> I am armed on the breast, but not on the back. . . . I am wounded in the back,
> not slightly, but to the heart. . . . I lay open to the malice and the practice of
> mine enemies in England, who first procured a cloud of disgrace to over-
> shadow me, and now in the dark give me wound upon wound.[79]

His prophetic words fantastically shadow Hector's unarmed demise at
the Myrmidons' hands in Troilus and Cressida: Essex and the Trojan
both meet their ends as failed heroes against strategic conspiracy, the
victims of a gang killing. Although Savage underestimates Hector's capacity for antiheroism, as does Hector himself, substantial parallels do
recommend an Essex inscription in Hector.

We cannot easily purchase this identification without exchanging
George Chapman's for it; but in disavowing the Achillean, faction-lead-
ing Essex to obtain the Trojan, chivalric version, the reader merely sacrifices one prescriptive referentiality for another. Robert Devereux's contradictory responses to his own heroic stature discourage a reading that
nominates a single candidate as his theatrical representative. He personi-
fies Jean Howard's apt comment about history: "not objective, transparent, unified, or easily knowable and consequently . . . extremely

problematic as a concept for grounding the meaning of a literary text."[80] It is therefore appropriate that neither Achilles nor Hector is a monochrome block of separable signification. In the two warriors' reflective, homosocial, and emulous relationship, the historical coordinates of Shakespeare's text may be recovered. To excavate the complex unity of the Essex inscription, let us look at the crisis point of Hector's courtly "character"—his heartless slaughter of the speechless Greek soldier.

In five lines near the end of the play, the entire chivalric premise with which Hector has been identified collapses:

Enter one in [sumptuous] armor.

HECTOR: Stand, stand, thou Greek; thou art a goodly mark.
            No? wilt thou not? I like thy armour well:
            I'll frush it and unlock the rivets all
            But I'll be master of it. Wilt thou not, beast, abide?

Exit Greek.

            Why then, fly on; I'll hunt thee for thy hide.
                                                    (5.6.27–31)

The Renaissance audience must have had a weird, hallucinatory sense of déjà vu at this moment. A beautifully attired anonymous knight enters the field of battle; mute, he encounters a chivalric opponent. This scene uncannily resembles one particular tournament and Accession Day conceit. The figure of the Unknown Knight, who entered the lists anonymously, was an integral part of the tilts from medieval times.[81] In Elizabeth's tournaments, Essex himself likely appeared disguised as the melancholy Unknown in 1600, which might have represented a last-ditch effort to return to royal favor.[82] Appearance in the lists as an Unknown Knight, speechless and gorgeously clad, betokened a special status. Not just anyone could be the Unknown. The role signified a courtier's distinctive position at a given tilt: he would enter in exquisite disguise to plead a specific grievance or to announce extraordinary chivalric service to the queen.

But Hector kills him. The *inconnu* hunted down and butchered represents a once glorious chivalry, now encumbered and made vulnerable by its own dazzling image. The play's climactic commentary on chivalry remembers the fate of Narcissus and figures a symbolic suicide. Hector, central chivalric force in Troy, kills the most recognizable Elizabethan image of chivalric privilege, reducing it to a beast for slaughter. In so doing, he destroys the courtly ideal as it almost existed in the play. He diminishes it to a coveted exterior, contaminating through his greed its life spirit. And in fact, on closer inspection, Hector discovers that the ideal has become entirely flesh, a corrupted thing. Beneath the armor he finds a "most putrefied core, so fair without," whose "goodly armor thus hath cost thy life" (5.8.1–2). The gaining of the armor, however, costs Hector his life as well. For he disarms, satisfied with the kill, and gives Achilles an opportunity to murder him most unchivalrously. Hector's appeal to fair play ("I am unarm'd: forego this vantage, Greek") resounds hollowly, for in viciously seeking and obtaining the merely external, he suicidally destroyed the image of what he was—an image that served, however deceptively, to protect him. Achilles is effective and brutal force in rhyming complement to Hector's own, absent the ideological trappings. His Myrmidons, speechless unchivalric Unknowns all, exact the necessary death of the rival, adjunct self.

A well-documented theatrical custom extends the interpretive borders of this scene. In a contemporary production of *Troilus and Cressida* the actor playing the Unknown Knight might have worn armor that once belonged to a member of the nobility. Elizabethan acting companies customarily purchased entire wardrobes from the estates of noblemen who wore such finery on formal occasions—such as the Accession Day tilts.[83] If Hector did murder an Unknown clad in a queen's man's armor, the audience would have witnessed an unmistakable tableau of the death of Elizabethan chivalry. But in the last years of the reign this death was visible enough, even without the Shakespearean scene.

In the conversation between decadent Trojan and English knighthood, in the suicidal encounter with the Unknown, the "pervasive cultural presence" of Essex is again palpable.[84] As the central actor on the buckling stage of late Elizabethan chivalry, and as the fractious noble who repeatedly sabotaged his own stature as heroic cultural representative, Essex dictates a necessary complication of literary inscriptions. A simple substitution of vehicles for the Essex tenor is inadequate practice because the earl's career at and away from court was always marked by the narrow oscillations of service and self-aggrandizement. It is thus not only possible but *necessary* to see the configuration of Hector-Essex in simultaneous, both/and relation to that of Achilles-Essex. The image of Robert Devereux, that is, bifurcates in the two central adversaries of *Troilus and Cressida*.

V

The characterological division of Essex's image responds to a clearly perceived duality in Devereux himself. He lived two interanimated but antagonistic lives, logical contradictions of power. The dark, sulking court player and homosocial warrior was also periodically the queen's loving favorite, serviceable and dutifully adept; but such contradictions were increasingly difficult to manage. The earl's aptitude for chivalry, itself a conflictual mode, brought him into the bright circle of fame, thrillingly close—but always subject—to the female power he sought to control. Essex, a product of the court relations which he so discomfited, reified the fissures in Elizabethan policy and ideology. His representational filiation into Achilles and Hector similarly anatomizes the endless divisiveness, the proliferating internecine violence, arising from social and ideological discord. The late Tudor overreliance on factionalism institutionalized an emulous chaos that chivalry (because of its own debilitations) could ultimately neither mask nor control.[85] The peculiarly Elizabethan dislocation defined by *Troilus and Cressida* is that gap between England's martial, chivalric glory, of which Essex was the final, desperately flawed representative, and the darker realities of the political present, circa 1600, to which he contributed in no small measure and which finally overwhelmed him. Through and around the Devereux crux, *Troilus and Cressida* dramatizes a world riven by its own implacable conflicts: "those wounds heal ill that men do give themselves" (3.3.-228). And they *are* men's wounds.

Unlike English wars fought under the aegis and for the glory of the queen (against the Spanish Armada, for example), Shakespeare's Trojan War—like the interminable Irish guerrilla conflict—progressively loses the ideological, erotic focus it once had and thus its protective mantle of "cause." This Troy finally discards the inspirational fiction of a central female figure, an Elizabeth, a Helen, or a Cressida. The latter two caricatural antitypes of the queen are portrayed as deeply flawed and wholly contingent upon external (strictly male) valuation and control. If this portrait sketches a courtier wish, it also expresses an orientational shift in fin de siècle politics. Just as the Trojan men of chivalry are disinclined to protect or preserve Cressida, Elizabeth's best men—Essex *and* Cecil—were in the late 1590s already making secret overtures to the male monarch in Scotland. The queen was vanishing. Male bonds were forming that covertly circumvented the female monarch at the end of her reign.[86] The overcoming of feminine presence, will, and influence is a prominent movement of the last act of *Troilus and Cressida*, and it is played on both sides. Cressida is abandoned by Troilus, who never once voices a desire to regain her; instead, he wants Diomedes to "pay the life thou ow'st me for my horse" (5.6.7).[87] Her strategy of delayed gratification fails miserably with brutish Diomedes, the new antichivalric courtier.[88] Polyxena, the absent feminine principle (the woman as cipher), cannot block Achilles from battle once Patroclus dies. The Greek hero plunges back into the fray and cancels the last vestige of female influence in Troy, thus articulating Essex's deepest desires in the Irish campaign: to be engaged in warfare without being subject to the dominion of a woman. Instead, every woman in the play is herself subjected—to the whims, lusts, negligence, or fury of courtiers. The retrieval of Menelaus's queen, the alleged goal of the war, enrages virtually every Greek who troubles to think about it. Helen, reduced by Troilus to a "theme of honour and renown, / A spur to valiant and magnanimous deeds" (2.2.200–201), disappears from the play entirely in the third act. She emerges only as a reference after that, and a hated one: "Name her not now, sir," Menelaus warns Hector, "she's a deadly theme" (4.5.180).

The play registers the absence of female power, mediating between the fact and the fantasy of a profound, ongoing diminution of Elizabeth's potency; but *Troilus and Cressida* always blames the male aristocracy for the world's disasters. Courtiers' narcissism becomes endless, shared self-immolation: "No space of earth shall sunder our two hates," Troilus spits (5.10.27). The factionalized Greeks encode a critique of Elizabeth's failed political manipulations, but they more directly evoke the paralyzing self-interest of the Essex and Cecil groups. The Trojans manifest the self-deceptive vogue of revivified knighthood in the queen's reign, but the woman, the supposed object of their destructive exercises, cannot be faulted for the attention (such as it is). The text's insistence on the determining force of homosocial relations dismantles the potentially subversive contraption of its own historical referentiality.

But *Troilus and Cressida* always undoes its subversions. Its exiguous relation to contestation stems from the thorough redundancy of that act in a political landscape lacking a clear authority; there is nothing, or not enough, to subvert. If the play deforms and dismantles the myth of the Trojan War in the process of emulating its own historicity, it also implies that deformation is the only possible construction of a reality between history and fiction, one in which the failed present is overtaken by a darkling future; in which meaning is thoroughly engulfed by the endless procession of dissolving historical moments:

Time hath, my lord, a wallet at his back,
Wherein he puts alms for oblivion,
A great-sized monster of ingratitudes.
                    (3.3.145–47)

This grim reading of human significance is enabled by the widespread neutralization of ideology in Troy and England. Both worlds lie paralyzed in a chasm between ideologies, without effective symbolic organizations of political value.[89] If ideology has a perceptual, even heuristic function, it bestows but also requires a focal point, a way of assimilating (possibly mystifying or subsuming) the relevant data of cultural upheaval and social disorientation.[90] Not only is such a point of focus absent from the Trojan War, but it was also rapidly dematerializing in the last years of Queen Elizabeth's reign.

The fall of Ilion and the scattering of the Grecian lords occur sometime beyond Pandarus's infectious epilogue; those events are not far off, but neither are they staged. *Troilus and Cressida* holds the conclusion of this tale in abeyance because a substitute version of authority—the only hope against the epidemic of disintegration—was yet to arrive. When it did, in 1603, the worst outbreak of the bubonic plague in forty years came with it.

TWO

Word and Plague
in the Second Quarto *Hamlet*

On the day of James Stuart's unhurried descent from Scotland to claim his kingship—April 5, 1603—London's Court of Aldermen was busy. The magistrates ordered poor relief, more watches, and a vagabond round-up for St. George's Parish, an impoverished, unlucky neighborhood in Southwark.[1] These orders had little to do with James's imminent arrival. They were instead the first official response to news of the bubonic plague, which was reported in the suburbs on March 3. The ailment triggered the clicks and whirs of civic rule and the intrusive vigilance that signals governmental anxiety. But there was good reason for the nervousness: the most recent major outbreak, in 1593, had killed about 13 percent of the city's inhabitants.[2]

Warning signs of the disease coincided roughly with rumors and machinations of the Scottish succession. Plague was spied in the well-traveled corridors of commerce, war, and diplomacy: 1599 in Portugal, 1601 in Spain, 1602 in the Low Countries. In the summer of 1602, the Privy Council prohibited both imports and immigration from Amsterdam, where the epidemic was in full, awful bloom. September of that year saw the port of Yarmouth suffer eighty plague deaths in one week, after which domestic trade with the town was suspended for over a month. And slowly, during the winter thaw, sickness began to take hold in the poor pockets and edges of London. It emerged in curious contemporaneity with the change of rulers.

The new king thus met a formidable obstacle to his kingship. During

the week of May 5, 1603, plague killed eleven in London and the outly-
ing wards. Apprised of the danger, James skirted the city, taking a royal
barge under London Bridge to visit the Tower on May 11; he then
promptly departed for Greenwich. By May 26, the weekly plague total
had reached thirty-two. After the bills of mortality were reported, James
ordered everyone who was not already at court to leave London before
the end of the term (June 6) and not to return until the coronation. As
late as June 28, when the force of the outbreak was indisputable, Dudley
Carleton wrote that although "the Sickness doth spread very much, and
it is feared it will prove a great plague . . . the Coronation holds at the
appointed time, which shall be performed with much solemnity and all
the old ceremonies observed."[3] James dearly wanted the ceremonial acknowledgment of his status, but he was caught between the need for
public legitimation and self-preservation. On July 6 the coronation was
reluctantly postponed, "owing to the growth of Plague and the fear that
those coming to see our Coronation may spread it in the country," and
thus the king deferred "all state and pomp accustomed by our progeni-
tors . . . [and] our solemn entry and passage through our City of London
for this time" (Nichols, *Progresses*, 1:198–99). Monarchical progress
and ceremony were literally botched, disrupted by those purplish, swollen nodes and lesions called plague botches, which marked the disease
and its victims. Throughout the summer of 1603, the weekly mortality
count increased geometrically—from more than 30 on June 2 to 263 on
July 7; and then, shockingly, to 1,396 by July 28. Before the sickness ran
its course, "there died in London 38,244; of which number there were
30,578 of the Plague."[4]

The epidemic of 1603—which kept theaters closed for the better part
of a year, prevented royal residence in London, and, strangely, brought
Shakespeare's acting company under the king's protection—did not of
itself signify an unimaginable alteration.[5] As Thomas Dekker's pamphlet *The Wonderfull Yeare 1603* demonstrates, it was the concatenation
of Elizabeth's death, James's seemingly redemptive accession, and the
unusually bad outbreak that had such a devastating impact on England
that year. In this chapter and the next, I shall consider some of the literary implications of this historical sequence. The Shakespeare play that
figures this history most intensely—the history, that is, of monarchical
death, succession, and widespread disease—is *Hamlet*.

But which *Hamlet*? As recent textual criticism has emphasized, there
are three major versions of this play: the first quarto (Q1, 1603), the
second quarto (Q2, 1604), and the first folio (F, 1623). Textual studies

have also stressed that the compositional dates and the relative authority of these texts—their essential relation to each other—cannot be determined with certainty.[6] The practical effect of this conundrum is to foreclose confidence about the historical situation, and situatedness, of all the *Hamlets*.[7] Indeed, most of the material in the play is impervious to precise dating. This fact helps pave the way for an argument that, to some critics, will smack of historical implausibility: specifically, that the 1604 quarto (whose composition is generally thought to date from 1600–1601) has some relation to the three watershed events of 1603. Theoretically, Q1, Q2, *or* F could inscribe the historical episodes in question, because Elizabeth's death, James's accession, and the plague's arrival occurred just before the publication of the first quarto (the title page says the play "hath been diuerse times acted by his Highnesse seruants," which dates the text after May 19, 1603, when Shakespeare's company became the King's Men). Practically, however, it would have taken a prodigiously speedy rewrite for the events of 1603 to have found their way intelligibly into Q1. And while the Folio text could easily incorporate these events, we cannot stabilize an historical reading from the Folio *Hamlet*, since that text could have been revised well after the years 1603–4 (the quartos, obviously, could not). Thus, if the events of James's succession year do have any trace or resonance in the play, the second quarto text should provide the richest historical indicators.[8]

Even if the second quarto was written well prior to 1603, the appearance of the text *after* that wonderful year is an index (or perhaps an obscure prologue) to a history of the play's meanings—which reverberate uncannily with the events that barely preceded Q2's publication. Q1 was printed when the memory of Elizabeth was still fresh and the presence of a king was a novelty. Q2 appeared after James had been on the throne for less than a year; the plague still raged ferociously in London and was in some sense interfering with his reign. At the very least, then, the two quartos stand in radically different relationship to the crucial transitional events of the time. In considering the environment in which the texts *appeared*, I can make modest claims about the ways in which they inscribe their local contexts, and I can make these claims without unwarranted speculation about the provenance of temporally indeterminate underlying manuscripts. An historically factored reading of the *Hamlet*s of 1603 and 1604 can begin to rationalize some of the striking differences between the two dramas.

This chapter is about the symbolic and structural operation of plague in the second quarto of *Hamlet*.[9] In 1604, a resonant context existed for

the text's thematic of disturbed kingship and national disease, two topics that become intensified in the transit from Q1 to Q2. My reading
here will serve as the first half of a larger argument, which I shall complete in the next chapter, about the second quarto's intensely complicated topicality. For now let me say that the traces of epidemiological
history that punctuate the 1604 *Hamlet* work in concert with anxieties
about succession in the text, and I shall construct my reading around
these two axes. To make the point about topical intervention more effective, I shall examine some of the "good" quarto's (admittedly immense)
differences from Q1, in hopes of showing some ways in which references
to and dramatic structures of contagion multiply textually in the later
work—after sickness had achieved local dominance.[10] From this point
on, unless otherwise noted, any reference to *"Hamlet"* will be to the text
of the second quarto (1604).[11]

Shakespeare's most endlessly perplexing drama figurally reanimates
the force that plagued the early moments of James's reign—that radically destabilizing, brutal fact of bodily and cognitive danger. To a remarkable degree, the play internalizes the epidemic crisis as a crisis of
form: disease offers a structural template that produces unstructuring.
In staging contagion, *Hamlet* suggests that a single influence, effectively
transmitted, can permeate and radically discompose the consciousness
of an entire culture. One corruptive force can ruin the world.

I

Derek Traversi has noted that "the action of *Hamlet* is, in its inner logic,
the progressive revelation of a state of disease."[12] The point could be
taken further: *Hamlet*'s plot is a virtual schematic of plague. The play's
sickly images are neither inert nor ornamental; its language of bodily
corruption metastasizes. What results is a subliminal thematic of contagion: a progressive dispersal of weakness, delusion, passion, and violent
physical decomposition among a growing number of susceptible bodies.

Contagion in *Hamlet* is figured primarily as poisoning, a somatic and
linguistic act which is always, sooner or later, deadly. The metaphoric
relationship of plague and poison in the Renaissance stemmed from a
contemporary perception about their material connectedness: the belief
that one literally contained and dispersed the other, that the essential
stuff of infection was toxin. Indeed, in plague pamphlets and other medical tracts the most common synonym for "infection" was "poison" or
"venom."[13] For instance, Stephen Bradwell, a Caroline physician, de-

fines plague as "a Popular Feavor venemous and infectious, striking chiefly at the Heart."[14] Bradwell provides an especially interesting taxonomy of the poison resident in pestilence:

> This Putrid Plague, is ... venemous, which is granted of all both Physitians and Philosophers. Now by *Venom* or *Poyson*, we commonly understand some thing that has in it some dangerous subtle quality that is able to corrupt the substance of a living body to the destruction or hazard of the life thereof. This working is apparent in this *Sicknesse*, by his secret and insensible insinuation of himself into the *Vitall spirits*, to which as soone as hee is gotten, he shewes himselfe a mortall enemy. . . . His subtle entrance, his slye crueltie, his swift destroying; the unfaithfulnesse of his *Crisis*, and the other *Prognostick Signes*; and the vehemencie, grievousnesse and ill behaviour of his *Symptomes*, all being manifest proofes of his *venemous quality*. (Bradwell, *Physick*, 6; italics in original)

We should spend a moment with this description, for its claims and contradictions epitomize the cultural discourse about the plague. To Bradwell, this disease is not merely fatal, but immoral: it conducts surreptitious assaults on the wholesome or innocent body, employing poison as its agent. The writer's tendency to allegorize the physical damage done by plague arises from a hermeneutic impulse as much as a medical one. Discussing the "venom or poison" inherent in the disease offers authoritative diagnostic stability—both physicians and philosophers agree on the taxonomy—and the everyday reader can also "commonly understand" it. But for all his confidence in having associated plague with the substance, Bradwell cannot provide a respectably precise technical definition of venom: he describes it, rather limply, as "some thing that has in it some dangerous, subtle quality" that endangers or destroys life. What is this thing? The physician's certitude expands and contracts throughout the description. "This working is apparent," he avers, recovering temporarily, but in the next phrase the disease gets the better of him; it is "secret and insensible," and its symptomatology baffles him: "The unfaithfulnesse of his Crisis, and the other Prognostick Signes" frustrate the diagnostician. Bradwell's loaded clinical attributes for the plague (subtle, sly, swift, unfaithful, vehement, grievous) substitute moral fury for comprehension. Finally the interpretive difficulty of the sickness—the "ill behaviour of his *Symptomes*"—surprisingly becomes the occasion for diagnostic confidence about it, and a circle of hermeneutic redundancy forms. The plague must be the product of venom because its elusiveness is venomous. We know what it is because we don't know what it is.

The function of "poison" in plague tracts is to control anxiety about the unknowable—to explain plague by assigning it a physical cause and thus to delimit that which escapes understanding. But poison is an analogy, a deferral, rather than an explanation. Physical venom does resemble plague in the manner (if not the scope) of its destructiveness. But poison's particular relevance to *Hamlet* lies in the epistemological problem it claims and fails to explain. When the Ghost tells Hamlet that "thy Vncle stole / With iuyce of cursed Hebona in a viall, / And in the porches of my eares did poure / The leaprous distilment" (D3), it pretends to solve a crime the sources, motives, and ramifications of which have not begun to be rooted out. Fatal, undetectable, finally uncontrollable, toxin in the play functions as it did in plague tracts: an all-encompassing explanation that cannot account for much. Even though the Ghost depicts King Hamlet's demise in allegorical terms as the simple upshot of poisonous Evil's infectious, treacherous invasion and destruction of Good, this explanation (like Bradwell's) leaves copious gaps. Claudius's poison may be the original vial of disorder, the revealed, *physical* cause of King Hamlet's death; but what matters in the play, what animates and infects it, is poison's psychic residue: that which is borne from the Ghost to young Hamlet. The historical transformation of the king into the Ghost produces a crucial change in the *idea* of poison: toxin alters from a physical to a cognitive fact, a change that is marked by the Ghost's astounding transformation from victim to transmitter of destruction. And so the specter materializes as the drama's prime figurative poisoner—an agent provocateur who, as several critics have noted, pours another venom, the virulent narrative of his death, into Hamlet's ears.[15] This narrative envenoming proliferates and proves contagious. For once having absorbed this rhetorical toxin, the son disseminates it in various forms throughout the Danish court, where it enters *all* ears. This plague constitutes Hamlet's characteristic business at Elsinore, his *normal* mode of relationship.[16]

The venom Hamlet ingests, the imaginative poison, has a time-release quality: it is let out, little by little, whenever Hamlet speaks to the quarantined population at Elsinore. His own plaguy speech becomes the drama's plot piston—not merely a lubricant but the vital moving part, animating the desultory sequence of events. For if murder "will speak / With most miraculous organ" (G1), so will Hamlet; after the interview with the Ghost, he seeks to disrupt the court through notions, not potions. Remarkably, the literal and figurative poisons have the same effect: Every character to whom Hamlet speaks with venom, with bitterness and anger, is doomed to die. The catalogue is striking: Polonius, Ophelia, Laertes, Claudius, Gertrude, Rosencrantz and Guildenstern— all feel the sting of the central carrier's verbal barbs. We cannot exclude Hamlet himself from this list, as his self-lacerating language incites the danger that consumes him; he is autoinfected at the last. Perhaps most remarkable, the *only* characters who die in the play are the ones Hamlet has verbally assaulted. In his essay "Of the Power of the Imagination," Michel de Montaigne prepares the theatrical scene played out in Denmark:

> But all this may be attributed to the narrow seam between the soul and body, through which the experience of the one is communicated to the other. Sometimes, however, one's imagination acts not only against one's own body, but against someone else's. And just as a body passes on its sickness to its neighbor, as is seen in the plague, . . . likewise the imagination, when vehemently stirred, launches darts that can injure an external object.[17]

As with the plague, clear causal evidence is elusive, but considerable circumstantial clues point to the fatal virulence of Hamlet's imagination as reified in his language; his words endanger the body as much as they imperil the mind. His discourse, and the knowledge that fires it, have an *uncanny* power to derange and destroy.

In his magnificent work on the nature of contagion (1546), Girolamo Fracastoro (Fracastor) takes care to distinguish the poisonous from the contagious.[18] He bases his contagion theory on similitude, the idea that "the infection is precisely similar in both the carrier and the receiver of contagion; we say that contagion has occurred when a certain similar taint has affected them both" (Fracastor, *Contagion*, 3). But he flatly denies that poisons can produce likeness: "poisons cannot, strictly speaking, cause putrefaction or engender in a second individual a principle and germ of exactly the same sort as was in the original individual. The proof of this is that persons who have been poisoned are not contagious to others" (49); thus, "when persons die of drinking poison, we say perhaps that they were infected, but not that they suffered contagion" (3). Fracastor categorizes poisons as primarily material or spiritual, depending on which parts of the person they afflict, and his description of the spiritual type harmonizes with the opening crises of *Hamlet*: "Those [poisons] that operate by spiritual images can destroy by . . . producing an intolerable sadness. But they can generate nothing similar to themselves" (49).

Because Fracastor's theory pivots on the idea of similitude, it lends itself to a rhetorical and psychological as well as a purely medical reading of contagion. His discussion rigs a useful theoretical framework for the application of contagion theory to *Hamlet*. The play does not, of course, hammer out a structure built solely from the treatise's terms and propositions; but it does engage the essential metaphor of Fracastor's work. For in *Hamlet*, similitude *is* the fertile, poisonous ground of plot and character; the impulse for likeness engenders rampant similarity, parallelism, repetition, and doubling. Shakespeare employs the Fracastorian idea mainly by distributing the physical fact of infectious likeness to the moral, affective, and imaginative spheres. The symbolic ramifications of biological contagion theory receive a compelling gloss from René Girard, who enlarges (with anthropological intent) the microscopic features of Fracastor's original observations; here is Girard's characteristic statement on the literary function of plague imagery and theme: "The plague is universally presented as a process of undifferentiation, a destruction of specificities."[19] This reading of the disease can be mapped back into Fracastor's understanding that contagion produces deadly likeness. The destructive similarity that befalls bodies in epidemics afflicts minds and motives in Denmark.

Claudius obtained his brother's place, wife, and privilege through emulous fratricide, and so began the cycle of imitation and the production of likeness—read "contagion"—that ensnares his nephew. The Ghost in turn imitates Claudius by trying to engineer a murder; he calls for filial loyalty, an enforced similarity that will produce a like-minded revenger and replicate regicide.[20] Hamlet becomes, in several ways, a similitude of both fathers. The rhetorical strategy employed yet disavowed in the revenge overture to Hamlet also has Fracastorian overtones: the spirit produces *sympathy* ("Alas poore Ghost" [D2]). Although the Ghost expressly denies this as its goal ("Pitty me not, but lend thy serious hearing / To what I shall vnfold" [D2v]), its tale cannot but be a pathos machine, concocting and refining the myth of the father's victimage. Sympathy, the emotional correlative to contagion, manipulates identification on behalf of a sufferer to reproduce and propagate—perhaps alleviate—suffering. Fracastor's great treatise *De Contagione* begins with a long excursus called *De Sympathia*, in which he outlines the sympathy or natural attraction necessary to produce an effective contagion between objects in the world. He asserts throughout that bubonic plague is a vast pathology of sympathy, a heightened relationship between disparate, converging entities—identity run wild (Fracastor, xxxiv). *Hamlet* portrays a poison that, *pace* Fracastor, does indeed engender contagions of similarity, in material and metaphoric ways. This venom has mercurial, variable form and function. It is an elusive, unstable substance, with one exclusive channel of entry, one avenue of force: the ear. The play's toxin is language.

The historical force of plague, so metaphorically suggestive, can become translated into textual or dramatic structure. Some evocative differences in the quartos imply that the later text internalizes something of its pathological environment. Hamlet rails wildly at Ophelia following the "To be or not to be" soliloquy in pestilential terms—"Ile giue thee this plague for thy dowrie"—and this line occurs in both early texts. But in the 1604 quarto, his poisonous language generates a rhetorical and psychic similarity. Ophelia's commentary suggests that she catches the very disorder that she hears in the prince: "O what a noble mind is heere orethrowne! / The Courtiers, souldiers, schollers, eye, tongue, sword . . . / quite quite downe" (G3). Her earlier reference to *herself* as possessing a "noble minde" (G2v), and the unintelligible implied sequence "Courtiers . . . eye, souldiers . . . tongue, schollers . . . sword" suggest that Ophelia has been damaged, instantaneously, by Hamlet's ferocious rant. Her reaction in the first quarto is altogether more controlled or, as it were, less infected: "Great God of heauen, what a quicke change is this? / The Courtier, Scholler, Souldier, all in him, / All dasht and splinterd thence, O woe is me" (E2). In Q2, we can sense a contracted disturbance.[21]

A more fantastic example of the depth and scope of verbally caught similarity occurs in Laertes' subjection by Claudius near the end of the play. Plotting Hamlet's death by duel, the king suggests that Laertes could easily "choose / A sword vnbated, and in a pace of practice / Requite him for your Father" (M1). Laertes assents, and his response is surprising:

> I will doo't,
> And for purpose, Ile annoynt my sword.
> I bought an vnction of a Mountibanck
> So mortall, that but dippe a knife in it,
> Where it drawes blood, no Cataplasme so rare . . .
> . . . can saue the thing from death
> That is but scratcht withall.
>
> (M1)

What makes this addition to the plan so interesting is that Claudius did not think of it first. Laertes devises the poisoned sword trick, which depends on the notion of an unbated point but is more clever; when the king then proposes the hamfisted expedient of the poisoned chalice as a fail-safe maneuver, we can see that something has gone awry with the notion of character. To bring Laertes to this pass, Claudius has had to poison him slowly against Hamlet, using crafty insinuations that epitomize the play's movement of verbal corruption. No mental giant, Laertes has descended into the Charybdis of a superior intelligence; but he has emerged with something of that intelligence. He seems to have caught the very *idea* of poison from the primal poisoner, the king. In the first quarto the whole scheme—duel, sharp sword, and poison tip—is Claudius's idea, and Laertes follows stupidly along: "*King.* Nay but Leartes, marke the plot I haue layde. . . . / *Laer.* T'is excellent, O would the time were come!" (H3–H3v). But in the second quarto, after the onset of plague, character and interiority prove unstable, and subterfuge is a communicable attribute as it becomes possible to catch the habit of dissembling—an ailment of soul, of self.[22] This moment epitomizes a radical, inevitable invasion of history into *Hamlet*: pestilence infiltrates theater as a characterological device of communicated similarity. Shakespeare highlights the plaguy nature of this contraction by the unusual designation for the unction Laertes will daub on his sword: "Ile tutch my point / With this contagion, that if I gall him slightly, it may be death" (M1). As Falstaff notes in another context, "It is certain that either wise bearing or ignorant carriage is caught, as men take diseases, one of another; therefore let men take heed of their company."[23]

   Hamlet's contagion of identities begins with the verbal corruption first imposed by the Ghost. And the plague of this word poison is dispersed dementia and semantic instability: trouble in mind.

II

The Ghost's tale to Hamlet provides the seed—the *seminarum*, or the germ—of an imaginative disease that has grimly literal consequences.[24] The story enfolds horrors and toxic contradictions, and it generates in Hamlet a deep-seated paranoia about sexuality, about the body's fragility, and about the possibility of basic moral distinctions; the narrative proves deeply, perhaps entirely influential. Laertes prepares the audience for the Ghost's appearance and effect on Hamlet—as well as for Hamlet's later effect on Ophelia—when, in lines with no first-quarto antecedent, he adjures his sister, "In the morn and liquid dew of youth / Contagious blastments are most imminent" (C3v).[25] Laertes simply means that the innocent are susceptible to the corruptions of the world, to sexual assault, yet his warning presently assumes a dramaturgic reality he could not have dreamed: the Ghost's imminent words are contagious blastments that threaten Hamlet's innocence. This threat is configured sexually and psychically, for the seed of the Ghost's tale impregnates the son's imagination. When the Ghost earlier appeared to Horatio, it occupied a temporal space analogous to a barren sexual one—in "the dead wast and middle of the night" (C2)—and it was mute. But the aural assault on the prince helps the spirit achieve compensatory potency and recover a measure of power lost in the cuckolded king's slack, unconfessed demise.[26] Figuratively impotent until it speaks, King Hamlet's image embodies the multivalent force of the word "spirit"—a vital power, a mysterious transcendent breath, an absconding demon, a seminal substance. The father revivifies himself by poisoning the heir. The Ghost's narrative resembles a perverse incarnation; it is a rape ("so am I bound to hear," Hamlet says) or seizure of body and mind that also recollects the Annunciation, insofar as Mary's fertilization with Christ was in some early patristic traditions accomplished aurally.[27] And to set the time right, to redeem it when men least think he will, Hamlet, like Mary an unsuspecting receptacle, must carry the father's desire to term—even if he feels "vnpregnant of my cause" (F4v). Whether configured as disease, rape, or something more spiritual, spectral language has a physical impact on him; prematurely burdened, profoundly aged by the dreadful words, Hamlet's body inherits the Ghost's psychological torment: "o fie, hold, hold my hart, / And you my sinnowes, growe not instant old, / But beare me swiftly vp" (D3v). This most ruminative of dramas repeatedly devolves into focus on physicality—the body's primacy over politics or ideology; its magnetic resonances with other bodies; its supreme contours of need.[28]

The Ghost's narrative provides grisly clinical details of King Hamlet's murder and describes not merely a death but a pathology. The spirit is the end-product of Claudius's "leaprous distilment" (D3); it pictures itself as having caught a decanted disease. After the poison was poured in King Hamlet's ear, "a most instant tetter barckt about / Most Lazerlike with vile and lothsome crust / All my smooth body" (D3). The symbolic transformation entailed in King Hamlet's unsavory end as a self-described Lazar or leper must explode Hamlet's preconceptions about his father; at the least, those ideas cannot survive the account wholly intact.[29] For, even more than plague or syphilis, leprosy signified an abiding *moral* condition. The sickness was the "disease of the soul"; not a public or general ailment, the affliction was a private marking, God's personalized judgment upon the individual's state of grace.[30] In spite of itself, then, the Ghost betrays the poisoning as King Hamlet's own imaginative and spiritual corruption; the disfiguration encases heavenly judgment. What is more, lepers (like plague victims) suffered extreme social quarantine in hygienic exile, such that the transition from king to leper would represent the most profound downward mobility (although examples of leprous kings were not uncommon in biblical and medieval iconography).[31] Corporeal evidence to the contrary, however, the Ghost instead plays several lofty roles in its recitation—the jealous and angry God, the virtuous victim, the terrible seeker of vengeance—none of them humble or self-blaming. In short, the account of the king's noble blamelessness strains belief; the loathsome crust over the elder Hamlet's postmortem image expresses an internal disease manifested, as well as an external contagion absorbed.

The dead king's malady inspires a thematic plague partly because of the diagnostically convergent character of diseases in the Renaissance. Leprosy and plague were symptomatically and etiologically similar, both entailing topical disfiguration and moral condemnation.[32] What is more important, leprosy, like bubonic plague, was known and feared as a hideously efficient contagion. The Ghost's account, eidetically marking the father as leprous, seeds the very idea of King Hamlet as dangerous, a figure not to be worshiped but shunned like the plague.[33]

In spite of this text's obsessions with the body, pestilence in *Hamlet* is epistemological. On one level, the Ghost's disease is gossip, or information: it is the bad news you get when you grow up and discover nasty things about your relatives. But on a deeper level, the plague is *knowledge*: not necessarily a field of empirical truths, but rather, those disarticulated perceptions, suspicions, and anxieties which pressure the phenomenology of the self so as to secure, subvert, or marvelously direct it. Because this knowledge is plainly (but complexly) intolerable, it can make mad—especially in reagent and recombinant forms with already present doubts and vulnerabilities. The Ghost's revelations push Hamlet to perceive a depravity in the world that surpasses even his most dismal presuppositions. The prince's worst suspicions about Claudius ("O my propheticke soule! my Vncle?") have been more than confirmed and his fears about his mother intensified. But a distortion that Hamlet can at first barely detect contaminates the otherworldly signals he receives: currents of explosive anger, physical revulsion, and psychic violence cascade from the voice of the beloved father, the sickening ghost-king. And

it is not only the content but the style of the speech that must infect
Hamlet's already shaky cognitive and emotional condition. At the point
of its most furious denunciation of Claudius, the Ghost begins to hiss
like the snake in Denmark's unweeded garden: "I that incestuous, that
adulterate beast, / With witchcraft of his wits, with trayterous gifts, / O
wicked wit, and giftes that haue the power / So to seduce" (D3). If the
ambiguous pronominal referent here is not itself a sort of disclosure—"I
that . . . beast"—the tone of the speech is sufficiently ugly to throw
Hamlet off the track of father worship.[34] Along with his other radical
revisions, Hamlet must begin to confront incipient doubts about the
source of the message—evidently a tainted source, full of dark dubiety
and rage. The prince's "knowledge," then, fails as reliable, disinterested
fact; it is potent but morbidly scrambled. When he seeks to pass it on, it
carries only the clarity of hunch or, at best, desire. The play as a whole
comes to revolve around and resemble the static in Hamlet's mental
field. Both Hamlet and the audience must somehow translate into sense
a knowledge that can never cohere, even *on reflection*, because it
emerges from a corrupt origin.[35] The Ghost's risible injunction for disinterested revenge—"But howsomeuer thou pursues this act / Tain't not
thy minde"—comes too late, because it comes after his own account:
after, that is, Hamlet has *already* been tainted.

Impure data rarely offer clear directions or yield fully intelligible solutions—garbage in, garbage out. The father's disintegrative voice crip-
ples Hamlet's capacity to determine what he knows as well as an audience's ability to construe what can be known. Surely the Ghost possesses
painful facts we can pity it for having.[36] But we cannot recover those
facts precisely. Celebrated as this feature of *Hamlet* is, it defrauds plot
and makes character unintelligible. For instance, in calling Claudius
"that incestuous, that adulterate beast" in the second quarto (D3), the
specter subtly adds a charge to Q1's "he, that incestuous wretch" (C4),
a charge that unfortunately implicates Gertrude—though unclearly—in
the original crime. The second quarto version of the Ghost's speech is
largely similar to that of the 1603 text, but it contains some unique tonal
confusions that contribute to Hamlet's troubles. Q2's Ghost oscillates
between rage at Claudius, egocentrism, and blame of Gertrude, sometimes emphasizing the second and third features at the expense of the
first: "O Hamlet, what a falling off was there / From me . . . / . . . and to
decline / Vppon a wretch whose naturall gifts were poore / To those of
mine." The sexual jealousy of these lines continues in the puzzling injunction, absent in Q1, to "let not the royall bed of Denmarke be / A

couch for luxury and damned incest" (D3v). Hamlet has been conscripted here to prevent Claudius's continued sexual, not political reign;
revenge for the murder has all but dissolved as a motivating factor. As if
to blur the message further, the Ghost amends the first quarto's relatively benign instructions about Gertrude—"Leaue her to heauen, / And
to the burthen that her conscience beares" (Q1, C4v)—with this erotically sadistic wish: "leaue her to heauen, / And to those thornes that in
her bosome lodge / To prick and sting her" (D3v).

As we might expect, the Ghost's account in the two texts produces
distinctly different reactions from Hamlet. Since the spirit concentrated
on Claudius's perfidy in Q1, Hamlet, left alone on stage, exclaims in
that text: "a damnd pernitious villaine, / Murderous, bawdy, smiling
damned villaine" (C4v). But in Q2 the prince's animus takes two directions at once:

> O most pernicious woman.
> O villaine, villaine, smiling damned villaine.
>   (D3v)

In the second quarto, Hamlet has been contaminated by the Ghost's
sex nausea and its peculiarly muted antifeminist rage at the queen. We
can say that the entire quarto is so contaminated, for in that text Gertrude's culpability in the original crime remains unresolved, as I shall
discuss in the next chapter. This is not only an issue of textual gender
politics; it is a question of epistemological possibility. The second quarto
lacks several interpretive amenities which Q1 provides, such as Gertrude's direct denial of Hamlet's accusations in the earlier text: "But as I
haue a soule, I sweare by heauen, / I neuer knew of this most horride
murder" (G3). And Q2 deletes such useful unfoldings as the first
quarto's private interview between Horatio and the queen, where Hamlet's friend reveals that Claudius did in fact plan the prince's murder
(Q1, H2v). The Ghost's story in Q2 is part of that text's project to obscure the play's prehistory, to bury a precious and enticing cache of
facts. Notoriously, this is information that Hamlet and the critics both
desperately need.[37] Indeed, the broad effect of the Ghost's seminal
speech in the second quarto is the transmission of a textual, global disease of poisonous doubt and factual deficit. The narrow effect of the
speech is to guarantee Hamlet's paralysis through contradictory, muddled signals: murder your uncle, taint not your mind, purge the throne of
lust and incest, leave your mother to heaven but leave her bosom to be
pricked and stung; remember me.

Since knowledge in Denmark is plaguy corruption and language the poisonous vehicle of its transmission, it follows that Hamlet's education through ghostly utterance will be monstrously difficult to assess. To be sure, the lesson was a bad one, full of false starts, misdirection, obscure language, and other perplexity. It is not surprising, then, that Hamlet's initial response to the lecture is shortsighted: he declares "it is an honest Ghost" (D4), contrary to all appearances.[38] He has repressed some of the specter's most glaring, mortifying disclosures: that the beloved king's soul suffers mightily in "sulphrus and tormenting flames" for the "foule crimes done in my dayes of nature"; that the tale of its secret prison house could harrow, freeze, start, part, the body of the listener; that the king was "sent to my account / Withall my imperfections on my head" (D3). What are these flames, crimes, punishable and unabsolved imperfections? Hamlet's jarring, partial knowledge that the father was not all that either Hamlet had supposed does not crystallize in an epiphany, but rather emerges in a striking and entirely appropriate *theatrical* proliferation of doubt and duality. Hamlet's newly destabilized epistemology is the caught sense of shifting moral categories—the dissolving difference between Hyperion and a satyr, between luminous Good and toxic Evil.

The first sustained manifestation of this troubled knowledge comes in the speech that Hamlet requests from the player, Aeneas's tale to Dido about Troy's destruction. In this splendid passage, Shakespeare invests the avenger Pyrrhus with several of Hamlet's imagined roles in the revenge drama—the impulsive warrior and the loyal avenging son he wishes to be but also, prominently, the terrifying regicide that he rightly fears he will become if he fulfills his revenge obligations. In Hamlet's opening prompt to the speech ("the rugged *Pirrhus*, he whose sable Armes" [F3v]), however, the avenger's appearance mainly represents Hamlet's newly "disowned" knowledge of his *father's* fearsome debilities.[39] Pyrrhus is scarcely human; he has an unnatural skin encrustation, the cooked blood of families smeared over him and hardening in the flaming city. He has been "bak'd and empasted with the parching streets / . . . rosted in wrath and fire, / And thus ore-cised with coagulate gore, / With eyes like Carbunkles" (F3v). The ghost of King Hamlet, itself swathed in "sulphrous and tormenting flames," and the leprous freak king that the Ghost has described, "barckt about . . . with vile and lothsome crust," are conflated in the description of the terrible burning, encrusted revenger. We cannot know why Hamlet loves this story so much except, as we would suppose in this context, as some form of motivation to revenge. But the Troy speech is countermotivating, and desperately unclear. It summons a hideous image in which the perpetrator of retributive violence is literally disfigured by the remains of his victims.

The figure of Pyrrhus is a murky hallucination of convergence, a contaminated set of references. In remembering this figure, Hamlet has subliminally processed the Ghost's narrative of the king's death and condition in the afterlife as his father's *similarity* to a profane and vicious father-killer who, like the Ghost, is "hellish": "the hellish *Phirrhus* / Old grandsire *Priam* seeks." The Ghost has been imaginatively transformed from a victim of violence into a vengeance-seeking berserker. In creating an image of King Hamlet as a demonic horror, the Ghost forms an image that, like plague, destroys through similitude. For by blasting the image of the beloved parent, by replacing the peerless father with a figure of intense moral and physical deformity, the Ghost both corrupts Hamlet and impossibly complicates his task. Spectral narrative has infected Hamlet with the shadow of a doubt, one that slides beneath the stage of mind and whispers: cure the disease you worshiped.

Verbal contagion is actually a spreading *cognitive* disorder that allows other contagions such as evil, insurrection, and ambiguity to proliferate erratically, to make something rotten out of what was once, as Ophelia calls Hamlet, "the mould of forme" (G3). Epistemological plague in the second quarto *Hamlet* finally excresces in what might be called a *contamination of category*. There is in the state a general seepage, a miscegenation of positive and negative attributes; the categorical indistinguishability of good and evil, a Girardian undifferentiation, is a threat to perception and psychic organization that occurs at all levels. For instance, we have seen that in his rage, the hellish Pyrrhus seeks Priam "with eyes like Carbunkles" (F3v)—that is, with burning, blistering eyes. This description, absent from Q1, collates with the Player's account of how Hecuba's grief would affect the gods: it "would haue made milch the burning eyes of heauen" (F4). Both hellish and heavenly occupants have eyes that burn, a peculiar resonance that figuratively equates two ordinarily well-separated categories. Sustaining this same important confusion, Hamlet describes himself in the next soliloquy as "prompted to my reuenge by heauen and hell" (G1). This line, also missing from the first quarto, is as useful a key to the hero's confusions as we are likely to find. And in a world where hell and heaven are indistinguishable, it should not surprise us that (again in Q2 alone) Claudius describes his love for Gertrude as "my vertue or my plague, be it eyther which" (L3).

If the Ghost engenders deep category corruptions that threaten lines of knowledge and clarity, it also produces a more concrete theatrical disturbance. When Ophelia brings back her credulous report of the prince in his probable antic disposition, her description provides another discomfiting vista of similitude: Hamlet looks "pale as his shirt"; he acts in pantomime, raising a sigh "pittious and profound," and gives her a look "so pittious in purport / As if he had been loosed out of hell / To speake of horrors" (E2). He looks, in other words, Ghostly.[40] If Hamlet's disposition *is* purely antic here (as he had warned it would be), a clownish, controlled madness to flummox the court, what can we make of his resemblance to the Ghost? He may think he is being antic, but Hamlet cannot deflect a single disturbance that he feels; he both lives and confers every one. Ophelia's report registers Hamlet's too-accurate imitation of "pittious" disorder; he fails to control what he resembles, as the contagion of similarity overtakes him.

Hamlet's subliminal acknowledgment of the militant spirit's vast deprivation of soul, and its possible representation of his father's intense internal deformity, has no positive outcome. Significantly, when Hamlet does manage directly to confront his father's debasement—that is, when he can clearly state the bleakest implications of the Ghost's story—his own steepest characterological decline begins. It is as if the raw knowledge, finally processed, becomes piercingly contaminating. I refer to the moment when Hamlet chances on Claudius at prayer, and uses the Ghost's information to rationalize postponing revenge:

> A tooke my father grossly full of bread,
> Withall his crimes braod [*sic*] blowne, as flush as May,
> And how his audit stands who knowes saue heauen,
> But in our circumstance and course of thought,
> Tis heauy with him: and am I then reuendged
> To take him in the purging of his soule,
> When he is fit and seasond for his passage:
> No.
> Vp-sword, and knowe thou a more horrid hent.
>
> (J1v)

Hamlet acknowledges the uncertain status of his father's soul, maybe even with a subliminal recognition (in the imprecise pronominal referents) of the victim's similarity to the murderer.[41] Assuming that "his crimes" and "his audit" are King Hamlet's, we can perceive the son accepting the appetitive, sinful, human reality of the man that was his father. But this newly confronted knowledge, which would ordinarily be an important adaptive stage in the mourning process, has a surprisingly ill effect. As a direct consequence of this understanding, Hamlet now prepares to perform an act far worse than anything Claudius has done—worse even than anything the Ghost has requested. Hamlet now sets about the task of soul-damning. Determined to catch—to kill—the king amidst "some act / That has no relish of saluation in't / . . . that his soule may be as damnd and black / As hell whereto it goes," Hamlet precipitously enters the realm of the stock revenger, the hero contaminated and diminished by desires more awful than those that animated the original crime. Critics who argue that the prince simply tries here to postpone what he finds repugnant must ignore Hamlet's underscored resemblance, during Claudius's prayer, to the villainous Pyrrhus at the murder of Priam: just as the prince hesitates with his sword aloft, so for a moment does Pyrrhus, whose weapon, "declining on the milkie head / Of reuerent Priam, seem'd i'th ayre to stick" (F3v)—a statuary resemblance particular to Q2. No longer the good Christian son bearing the logos of a new dispensation, Hamlet has temporarily put on the mask of classical avenger whose sense of justice at once transcends and degrades human prerogative. He now embraces the moral vacancy of the revenge code, not merely daring damnation but indulging infection.

If we translate Fracastorian plague theory to metaphorical terms, the Ghost imposes contagion's similitude, an equivalation of carrier and receiver. The spirit forces a reproduction, a self-duplication already extant nominally between Hamlets.[42] It must recreate the desires and energies of the king, so it orders the son to venture into an area of expertise—the single combat, the struggle with the enemy—which was peculiarly the elder Hamlet's own. This project fails. But the injunction produces an ancillary effect in the designated avenger: in Fracastor's terms, an upheaval "precisely similar" to the Ghost's, a rough decomposition of internal order and stability. Hamlet, that is, inherits the father's moral and psychic inflammations. The plot parodies christological doctrine here, twisting the issue of *homoiousion*: Is the son of like substance to the father? Now that the paternal figure has become an unholy Ghost, what is the status of the son's relation to it? Even if Hamlet owns a measure of integrity, a piece of dissimilarity, it *is* his father's awful business that he goes about—and that he speaks about.

III

The bubonic plague always activated fears and metaphors of communicability. Even when Thomas Lodge describes the moral and tactile etiology of the disease, he frames the sickness in linguistic terms: "For very properly is he reputed infectious, that hath in himselfe an euil, malignant, venemous, or vitious disposition, which may be imparted and bestowed on an other by touch, producing the same and as daungerous effect in him to whom it is communicated, as in him that first communicateth and spreddeth the infection."[43] The specter of verbal peril—the danger in conversation, in respiration, in the atmosphere that carries smells, sounds, words—frequently hovers on the margins of Renaissance plague tracts and, we may assume, in the consciousness of both the sound and the sick in epidemics.

The most commonly ascribed material cause of the disease was the atmosphere, and a huge anxiety attends this cause. Plagues were thought to arise from corrupt air; the uncivic stench that rose from piles of decaying bodies did little to alleviate the worry.[44] In emphasizing the poisonous and versatile action of contagion, Stephen Bradwell points out how difficult it was to avoid the disease: "Such sicke bodies infect the outward Aire, and that Aire again infects other Bodies. For there is a *Seminaire Tincture* . . . that . . . mixeth it selfe with the Aire, and piercing the pores of the *Body*, entreth with the same *Aire*" (*Physick*, 6–7; italics in original). The popular etiology finds its way into Shakespeare's work in Hamlet's evaluation of Denmark's air-quality index: the corrupted world becomes, in his imagination, "a foul and pestilent congregation of vapours"—code for a plague world. Similar atmospheric descriptions recur in the canon, sometimes even in comic contexts; for instance, Orsino recalls that when he first saw Olivia, "Methought she purg'd the air of pestilence" (1.1.19). Hamlet's query about the Ghost's provenance and baggage ("Bring with thee ayres from heauen, or blasts from hell") is therefore environmental as much as eschatological: he voices a specific concern that the spirit represents a familiar physical threat.

The danger of the air has a diagnostic appeal like that of poison: it seems to offer a firm cause for the unknowable ailment. But the plague pamphleteers who located the disease "in the air" did not of course locate it at all: they merely expressed its mysterious ubiquity, which is the real point of the atmospheric etiology. Plague envelops, but it also penetrates. As air, especially as breath, it configures an outside which cannot be kept out; Bradwell emphasizes this point with his language of intru-

sion ("piercing the pores of the *Body*, entreth with the same *Aire*").[45]
Many measures were taken to secure purity against the danger. The infected were, when indoors, to be surrounded by a sweetened, perfumy haze, and visitors were to breathe through pomanders: "Let him hold in his mouth a peece of Mastic, Cinamon, Zedoarie, or Citron pill, or a Clove." Obviously this arrangement made communicating with the patient quite difficult, and other suggestions made it harder still: "Let him desire his sicke friend to speake with his face turned from him."[46] Most writers explicitly warned the uninfected not to speak with the ill, and here we detect one of the primary social disruptions of the disease.

In a pestilent culture, all conversation carries risk; intimate spaces of encounter hold the greater dangers. Epidemics interrupted social intercourse in prohibitive ways—death first among these; the disturbance of speech, another. Here is Lodge on the vulnerability of those who lived with the afflicted:

> They that dwell continually with those that are infected with the plague, are in great danger to receiue the same infection . . . by reason that they . . . receiue their breaths, and smell their corruptions, and sucke in the infected ayre of the infected houses wherein they converse; which is a thing very dangerous.[47]

Lodge's tract concludes with antisocial precautions for the healthy: "We ought to flie from the conuersation of those that are infected" (L3). But the close or personal encounter was not the only source of worry. All intercourse, public or private, spiritual or secular, meant danger; no utterance was safe. Since the plague floated about on vapors, it could be carried on any raft of words. Curses uttered by King Lear ("Now all the plagues that in the pendulous air / Hang fated o'er men's faults light on thy daughters!" [3.4.67–68]) and Timon of Athens (who wishes "a planetary plague, when Jove / Will o'er some high-vic'd City hang his poison / In the sick air" [4.3.109–11]) conflate the aery pestilence with the metalinguistic possibility of producing plagues through speech. Some writers imagined the inevitability of infection as a result of any verbal (suspirative) act. In "The Triumph of Death," John Davies pictures a pastor who imperils himself with his own sermons: "oft whilst he breathes out these bitter words, / He, drawing breath, draws in more bitter bane: For now the air, no air but death affords."[48]

Plague putrefied the air necessary for both biological and communal, communicative existence. At the same time, the pestilence, like most national crises, ignited a desperate discourse: remedies and prayers, quarantine and burial rules, bleak and inspirational anecdotes, bills of mortality, lamentations public and private. Plague fostered conditions of stressful contrariety—making communication necessary, making it terrifying. Even the urge to converse, to engage with others, becomes a killing urge in plague time; several writers noted with dismay the perverse pleasure some persons took in scattering their infections.[49] Epidemics demonize the social impulse and so dismantle a culture's most basic operation: the ability to form a whole without dissolving or destroying the parts. The connections and disjunctions created by plaguy speech are especially compelling symbolically—that is, useful to the literary imagination—because in many respects, plague is *flawless* communicability. Contagion does not impede intercourse in any simple way; indeed, it perfects it, like a language that has become too horribly efficient.

There is a linguisticity to contagious disease. Plague mimics discourse in several respects: in its sociability, its mimetic productions, and its structural properties. First, the sickness depends on an interlocutor, and like dialogic language, it constructs and occupies interstices between sender and receiver: plague establishes societies, parodic though they are. Second, germs create similar attributes among a wide range of sufferers; they form or compel a single identity, and in this respect they mimic the infectious actions of words, which—to function intelligibly—must clear the social terrain of boundaries between persons. Shared speech and shared symptoms create landscapes of likeness. Finally, pestilence, like language, has an intrinsic architecture, a syntax. It pronounces sentence on the body, making it a vessel of sequentially signifying marks (spots, fever, swelling, buboes and death tokens, dementia, death) that evoke a deep structure, an underlying form or principle.[50] For virtually all Renaissance commentators, the deep structure of contagion is sin; some shape of depravity (indeterminate though that may be) underlies every bubonic plague outbreak. The ailment articulates death and agony from the materials of human turpitude. Infectious ailments and effective discourses both dissolve the protective membrane that keeps selves separable.

A dense paradox lies at the heart of the discourse/disease juncture: that which enables and secures safety can also pose an insidious threat. The potential comfort of social interaction inevitably entails a risk of contamination. By forming and defining relations, "ordinary" conversational language simultaneously smudges clear, protective boundaries. (We do not need to consider here those extreme verbal instances, such as the confession and the accusation, which foreground personal vulnerability and danger.) Long before it can be an efficient vehicle of desire, discourse marks desire's port, a primal signpost for the place and need of connection. But too often, sometimes imperceptibly, diction becomes dictation, and verbal gestures of intimacy shift into effacement, into domineering acts of discursive narcissism. Speech exposes or binds a speaker to others in the giddy pleasure of making oneself known, but in dyadic relations, a disequilibrium of this pleasure produces a less rosy result: the absorption or obviation of the other's voice. And if the will to discourse proves strong, persuasive, infective, and if that discourse is (as all human language must be) flawed by the ordinary deformations of want, rage, humility, embarrassment—in other words, by affect—then the contaminatory force of the language can prove virulent and even destructive. Truly, the establishment of a shared semantic premise, what might be called the contagion of meaning, is inherent to *all* language; contagion is a basic operational fact of communication. But if language exceeds its *normative* infectious function, it can become an instrument of social death—the virtual obliteration of the interlocutor.

Hamlet stages the transgression of linguistic norms many times over as it shows discursive dominations of subjected listeners. At Elsinore, language transmits a speaker's psychic disruptions to alleviate his or her own mental pressure. The plaguy transmission of subjectivity takes several forms in the play: obsessive narrative (from the Ghost); lewd trope (Hamlet to Ophelia; then, once she has fully internalized a version of madness, Ophelia to the court); anxious choral commentary (Hamlet to Claudius in the *Gonzago* scene); or loveless familial imperative (Polonius to Ophelia, Hamlet to Gertrude, Claudius to Laertes—substitute father to surrogate son—and the loquacious Ghost again). In each case, the words flood the vulnerable interiority of the auditor with the speaker's perceptual or ethical derangements. Pestilential speech thus differs from biosocial contagion in its nature as a practice, its conditional production of human (not necessarily conscious) will.

At least one Renaissance account of the plague regards it explicitly as a species of dangerous language, if not human language. During the dreadful outbreak of 1603, Roger Fenton wrote *A perfume against the Noysome Pestilence*, a sermon that supplies an evocative causal linkage between pestilence and the spoken word:

> The word which commonly is used in Scripture for the pestilence is deriued from a verbe that signifieth to speake, as some thinke, because, where it is,

euery one speaketh of it, enquireth after it, how it encreaseth, what remedies
there be for it . . . what be the symptomes, & qualities of it: wherefore since
it is a thing so well knowne, as every one is able to discourse of it; I shall need
speak the lesse. Onely this much in a word: since we haue so long hardened
our harts against the voice of God, speaking vnto vs; it seemeth now that hee
will indeede speake with vs, in a iudgement so quick, that vnless some speedie
atonement be made with all expedition; hee is but a worde and a blow: that
since we would not heare him, we shall now feel him, for the word which
Moses here vseth (properly translated Plague) signifieth Smiting: and such a
smiting as is fearefull and terrible for impenitent sinners to thinke vpon.[51]

The claim that scriptural plague declines etymologically from a word
that means "to speak" is, so far as I know, unique, and Fenton seems
uncertain about it too ("as some think").[52] The association of plague
with eschatological punishment he then cites is more traditional. But
other divines testified to the sickness's auditory impact. Henoch Clapham, for instance, gives anecdotal evidence of those plague-stricken patients who "felt and heard the noise of a blow; and some of them have
upon such a blow found the plain print of a blue hand left behind upon
the flesh."[53] For these churchmen, plague is a communiqué from God,
aurally or somatically received, requiring attention in exchange for redemption: "since we would not heare Him, we shall now feel him." The
epidemic is the last chance to hear a message that the populace has willfully failed to heed ("we have so long hardened our hearts against the
voice of God").

Fenton identifies one phenomenological crux of epidemics in the lan-
guage-knowledge-disease cluster: the pestilence infiltrates and disrupts
both comprehension and speech, and so secular language about pestilence is *discourse* in the absence of *understanding*. These were, as Hamlet himself reminds us, nearly synonymous terms in the Renaissance:
"Sure he that made vs with such large discourse / Looking before and
after, gaue vs not / That capabilitie and god-like reason / To fust in vs
vnvsd" (K3v). But to the preacher, there is an immense chasm between
speaking and knowing where the plague is concerned; although he says
"since it is a thing so well knowne . . . I shall need speak the lesse," his
sarcasm on this point is palpable: plague is of course not at all well
"known" in the sense of "understood." The point of the dubious
"plague equals speech" etymology is that the sickness, a subject of colloquy, *cannot* be rationalized through language. God speaks plague
using a grammar of physical disintegration, a grammar that sinful humanity can never understand. Epidemics trammel the rational parts.

Like any natural disaster, plague was indeed customarily interpreted as a divine message: an index to the endless text of meanings that we cannot read; a warning of incandescent agonies that promise no recovery and surpass all description.[54] What distinguishes epidemic sickness from other catastrophes, however, is that it intensifies fears not only about the rationality of the universe—the knowability of divine design—but, more concretely, about discourse and its risks. The bubonic plague always activated terrors of communicability, and this anxiety produced a serious *cultural* threat. For where pestilence reigns, conversation is feared as a disease vector, and fear of communicative existence is paranoia about society.[55] If Fenton suggests that divine language produces plagues on earth ("hee will indeede speake with vs"), he is doing no more than replicating an intuition about the destructive potential of *human* discourse. And human language amidst cultural upheavals can mimic such disorder, at once describing and scattering discord.[56]

In pestilential environments, disease infiltrates and occupies discourse as one of its fatal matrices. *Hamlet* inscribes this process as the signal event of the play: the Ghost penetrates and ventriloquizes the hero, speaking its deadly desires first to and then (imperfectly) through him. To an extent difficult to gauge, Hamlet is a channel or conductor for the fractious words of the dead, for death, to enter the world. The Ghost, a mere verbal construct and projection deprived of material praxis as such, spews polluted language which Hamlet absorbs, deploys, and redistributes as his primary tool for revenge. The prince keenly feels this discourse's violence, this seizure that the language-Ghost has made, but he willfully misrecognizes it as the oppressions of *others'* language: he fiercely demands of the transparent Guildenstern, "Why looke you now how vnworthy a thing you make of me, you would play vpon mee . . . and there is much musique excellent voyce in this little organ, yet cannot you make it speak" (H4). To control the speech of others, then, becomes Hamlet's dearest project and best chance at success, as with the *Gonzago* playlet:

> Speake the speech I pray you as I pronoun'd [*sic*] it to you, trippingly on the tongue. . . . Be not too tame neither, but let your owne discretion be your tutor. (G3v–G4)

And he asks Gertrude not "to rouell all this matter out / That I essentially am not in madnesse, / But mad in craft," to which she responds with dire truth, "if words be made of breath / And breath of life, I haue no life to breath / What thou hast sayd to me" (J4v). The impulse to control other speakers, to speak through them, repeats the treatment he has received from the Ghost; Hamlet behaves as he has been practiced on, an abused child repeating abuse. (This recursiveness is a normative sociological form of contagion.) Even granted his directorial impulses, however, Hamlet finds it difficult to control the language wherein he is *self*-constituted. His logorrhea neither expresses nor coordinates any stability—psychological, semantic, or political. Elsinore seems to him at first a world of transparent types: the good father, the bad stepfather, the faithless schoolboy chums, the betraying sweetheart, the fatuous counselor, the ditzy courtier. But the transparencies grow opaque, and Hamlet fashions an arcade of verbal curtains and distractions which occlude his own access to clarity. Unable to perceive clearly, he conducts his business at court in a dangerous linguistic whirlwind; his speech demolishes where it touches down.

Michel Foucault once began a lecture by expressing his desire to "have slipped surreptitiously into this discourse . . . I should have preferred to become aware that a nameless voice was already speaking long before me, so that I should only have needed to join in."[57] His wish "to be on the other side of discourse from the outset, without having to consider what might be strange, frightening, and perhaps maleficent about it" (51), betrays a thoughtful logophobia, an anxiety not dissimilar from what Hamlet feels and produces:

> . . . anxiety about what discourse is in its material reality as a thing pronounced or written; anxiety about this transitory existence which admittedly is destined to be effaced, but according to a time-scale which is not ours; anxiety at feeling beneath this activity (despite its greyness and ordinariness) powers and dangers that are hard to imagine; anxiety at suspecting the struggles, victories, injuries, dominations and enslavements, through so many words even though long usage has worn away their roughness.
>
> What, then, is so perilous in the fact that people speak, and that their discourse proliferates to infinity? Where is the danger in that? ("Order of Discourse," 52)

These questions bear significantly on *Hamlet* and Shakespearean language in general. For Foucault, as for Shakespeare, power relations (destined to conclude with that terrible sequence, "injuries, dominations and enslavements") are factored almost entirely through words. His tragic soliloquy suggests that "what discourse is in its material reality" is something altogether alien, if not hostile, to "this transitory existence," largely because the "existence which admittedly is destined to be effaced" seems incommensurate with a life made up of so many, such long-lived words. What frightens Foucault about discourse, about its powers and dangers, may be the fatal vision it ultimately summons and his own absolute, nearly unconscious absorption into that vision; language is a poststructuralist memento mori. To "slip surreptitiously" into discourse, as Foucault wished, would be to attain a coveted invisibility from language, an undetectable use of but not subjection to it, an invisibility which amounts to immortality. Individual human life, fragile and inconsiderable, is strangely out of scale with and curiously irrelevant to the field of verbiage which enables and survives it.

Foucault's understanding of discourse as "a violence that we do to things, or in any case a practice that we impose on them" ("Order of Discourse," 67), converges with language's broad function in *Hamlet* as a peril to the (discursively formed) selves at its mercy. What is the danger in the fact that people speak? It is the entomologist's danger: pinning, classifying, paralyzing a reality that is always more fragile and complicated than the instruments of evaluation. It is the actor's danger: the threat that spoken, scripted words obviate a subjectivity that always recedes *as a result* of the words, alien and unowned. And finally it is the subject's danger, the worry that injuries, dominations, and enslavements limn the entire horizon of the verbal surmise.[58] Perhaps, then, Foucault anxiously imagines that language (which, logically, has no agency, no existence unformed by a human intelligence) carries a dream of its own perfection: to function seamlessly across the difference of persons and exist finally irrespective of them. This is the discourse of plague. It produces the paranoid impression of the user becoming the used—yet who has not felt this, felt bracketed and vaporized by the words that choose us? Thus conceived, language exploits human intercourse and form merely as vehicular ciphers to convey its own infectious potency. Foucault finally feared the nightmare of a discourse whose utility effaces its covert power and danger. Hamlet subscribes to an obliterative discourse whose (marginal) utility *is* its danger.

IV

Success for Hamlet balances on the wobbly hope that language can service epistemology—specifically, that he can, counterintuitively, learn by speaking. But by the time he is ready to administer the theatrical test of Claudius's guilt through the doctored *Gonzago* performance, the investigative instrument of his language has become grossly miscalibrated by earlier accidents and trials. A hermeneutic uncertainty principle emerges: the observation or explanation of an object changes that object. Its position alters as it is being explained; or the light cast varies the outlines, the shape, the apparent substance of the thing. Thus the presumed evidence and the knowledge that claims authority from that evidence get dislodged. Interpretation always changes the understood parameters and contents, the perceptual reality of a text; certainly a soiled or misaligned measuring device will more radically alter notions about that which is under study and may even alter the object itself.[59] In *Hamlet*, the object under study *does* change. Hamlet cannot read (observe, engage, attack, interpret: infect) Claudius and Polonius, Ophelia and Gertrude, Rosencrantz and Guildenstern, without wreaking ontological havoc on them—without transmitting destructive contagion.[60]

Hamlet tries to deploy language as a periscope, a surveillance instrument that keeps him hidden, but the investigative act itself, and particularly the disturbances he has inherited from the Ghost's own discourse, confound his best attempts, both revealing and betraying him. His language typically proves perversely ineffectual, an exploratory scalpel that operates against his self-interest; it alienates the prince from the court he has disordered, incurring quarantine, expulsion, and attempted execution. His words always have a profound density and oracular charge; they gesture cleverly, like the witches' ambiguities in *Macbeth*, to recondite knowledge and inside information. But his language also betrays a relentless incompetence, a failure to achieve its own ends or secure its desired meanings.

Hamlet's words routinely trouble understanding. Always about to mean *something*, they usually trail off into insoluble ambiguity; like the apparently random malice of epidemics, Hamlet's speech aims at multiple targets, diverges noticeably from its apparent intention, and characteristically demolishes category distinctions as it undermines its own illusion of purpose at every turn. Subtly and all unknowingly, Hamlet in language becomes a disease even as he tries to become its cure. For instance, after the player delivers the Hecuba speech, Hamlet decides that theater itself can be used as a diagnostic measure:

> For murther, though it have no tongue will speake
> With most miraculous organ: Ile have these Players
> Play something like the murther of my father
> Before mine Uncle, Ile observe his lookes,
> Ile tent him to the quicke, if a doe blench
> I know my course.
>
> (G1)

The apparent meaning of the prince's plan is undermined by a kind of septicemia of ambiguity. By saying he will tent his uncle to the quick, Hamlet means he will both attend to or watch him carefully, *and* that he will become or employ a "tent," a medical instrument that probed and cleaned a wound. But a tent was also used to "keep open or distend a wound, sore, or natural orifice" (*OED* sb3, def. 2): metaphorically, that is, to prolong or exacerbate it. In an age ignorant of antiseptics, such a device would actually foster infection. Interestingly, the *OED* gives the following alternate spellings for "tent" in the sixteenth and seventeenth centuries: "teynte, taint, taynt." Thomas Nashe exploited the implicit connection:

> Debt and deadly sinne, who is not subiect to? with any notorious crime I neuer knew him tainted; (& yet tainting is no infamous surgerie for him that hath been in so many hote skirmishes).[61]

"Tent" for "taint" was an operative Renaissance pun. Hamlet's first act as a doctor or diagnostician, then, strongly suggests an act of contamination: the probe of Claudius, the potentially prophylactic examination, will simultaneously taint him to the quick. So when the prince says (in lines absent from Q1), "If a doe blench / I know my course," he seems already imaginatively to have killed the king: if Claudius responds properly he'll be as good as dead, a "corse" Hamlet knows, a corpse his tainting has infected. For Hamlet, the desire to know and the wish to kill are not sharply differentiated. The eerie pun also suggests that the intended victim will be Hamlet, too—"I know *my* course"—and thus his self-knowledge doubles here as the knowledge of his mortality. (In fact, all of Hamlet's knowledge henceforth seems to depend on the outcome of the *Gonzago* playlet.) A final ambiguity of the speech undoes any possibility that the prince can remain detached from the disease he studies. Having decided that the play is his best empirical tool, the thing "wherein I'll catch the conscience of the King," Hamlet unknowingly becomes as good as his word: to catch the king's conscience means not only to ensnare it but to contract it.

Hamlet catches and prolongs an ailment remarkably like the disease he seeks to purge; he both bestows and contracts ghastly cognitive illness. His discourse amplifies his noetic crisis. It propagates contagious similitudes that bind self and other, that undermine category distinctions between suspicion and proof. His language thus seeds collective neuroses and discord, but it cannot make reliable differentiations or draw reasonable conclusions.

The prince thinks that the best way to root out an infection is to spread it linguistically. A moment at the *Gonzago* scene will help show just how complicated this assumption is, how deeply language is implicated in the structure of plague, and most important, how contagion structures the body of Hamlet's discourse.

When Claudius has begun to grow uncomfortable with the play-within-the-play and challenges the prince about the plot, Hamlet seizes his chance to tent his uncle. He does so by yoking the themes of poison and audition:

KING: Haue you heard the argument? is there no offence in't?
HAM: No, no, they do but iest, poyson in iest, no offence i'th world.

                                                                            (H2v)

Hamlet's response seems peculiar on several counts: there has been no discernible jest from the players, and likewise no literal poisoning has yet occurred or been mentioned in the playlet. We should read Hamlet's answer instead as another trim pun that comments reflexively on the action of toxic language in Denmark. Hamlet twice implies in his answer to the king that there is no threat or offense on stage: first, because the players are only joking; and second, because to "poyson in iest" is, here, to "poison ingest." In one respect, the players are the ones who absorb the prop of the stage poison, confining the offense to their stage and leaving "no offence i'th world." But there are no unserious jokes in Denmark: the ingestion pun implies that expressing and consuming are the same act. Logically, the wordplay has no point. The players should not ingest what they speak; only the audience should—especially Claudius, concerned as he is with what there is to hear, with how toxin operates aurally. Yet the pun has a subliminal logic: speakers are constantly corrupted with their own language. They are susceptible to the venom of their own oratory; at some point, no poisoner remains safe from his corruption, an axiom *Hamlet* takes as a story guide. Because a word spoken must first be harbored and nourished in the womb of the imagination, heard first internally by the speaker, a constant bidirectional danger accompanies the speech act, even, presumably, the soliloquy. Hamlet's fondest dream is that he can remain untouched by the depravity he has heard and spoken about his uncle; but as soon as he articulates a position, diagnoses an ailment, it becomes his own, his tainted mental property.

Because word-poison constitutes the play's theme and structure, it compels a metadramatic consideration of what is heard or ingested in a performance, *as opposed to* what is merely seen. While the stage murderer pours his venom into the ear of the sleeping king, he metalinguistically addresses his brew, which is akin to describing one's own words as one speaks them:

LUC: . . . Thou mixture ranck, of midnight weedes collected,
         VVith *Hecats* ban thrice blasted, thrice inuected,
         Thy naturall magicke, and dire property,
         On wholsome life vsurps immediatly.
HAM: A poysons him i'th Garden for his estate . . .

(H3)

An exquisite ambiguity attends "inuected," a word automatically changed by all modern editors to Q1's (and F's) "infected"—a change which severs the semantic ligature between a hostile linguistic act (the thrice-blasted invective of Hecat's "ban") and the corruption or infection inherent in that act (already implied by the word "blasted"; recall Laertes' warning, "contagious blastments are most imminent"). Also operative at the phonetic margins is "inflected": cursed (invected) alterations of meaning, unwholesome (infected) usurpations of life, take linguistic form in poison, inflected in several toxic curses.

As if to underscore the critical function of the spoken thing, when the stage murderer Lucianus pours venom into the ear of the sleeping Player King, Claudius fails to respond immediately, even as he had notoriously failed to respond during the preceding dumbshow which reenacts the historical crime. It might be more accurate, however, to say that Claudius is not *permitted* to respond to Lucianus's perfidy—not, at least, until Hamlet peppers him with a comment on the scene:

HAM: A poysons him i'th Garden for his estate, his names *Gonzago*, the
         story is extant, and written in very choice Italian, you shall see anon
         how the murtherer gets the loue of *Gonzagoes* wife.
OPH: The King rises.

(H3)

The scene could be staged many ways, of course, but the text seems to indicate that it takes Hamlet's pushy gloss to get a rise out of Claudius. The king, that is, responds to Hamlet's narrative rather than his dramaturgy; he is affected not by what he sees—a usurper pouring poison into the ear of a sleeping king—but by what he hears: a commentary about that action. Thus, Claudius's earlier nonresponse to the dumbshow makes perfect sense. Yes, the king saw the prefatory mime, but he could not respond to what he could not hear.[62] His subsequent vigorous reaction to Hamlet's eager narrative secures a simple point: for knowledge to have power, for information to take hold, it must enter *through the ear*. In a theatrical world where language holds hegemonic force, the dumbshow can by definition have no effect.

Hamlet's gadfly pestering of the king during the players' speeches thus helps cement a point that could not have been neatly, definitively made *without* the prefatory mime. However, once Claudius does react to the narrativized murder, we cannot be sure which aural facts have registered most potently; we cannot at this moment know what, exactly, bothers him.[63] *The Murder of Gonzago* could have had ratiocinative value, but Hamlet dashes that possibility by making open threats against Claudius throughout—by speaking. For in identifying Gonzago's murderer as "one *Lucianus*, Nephew to the King" (H2v), rather than, as Denmark's history would have it, brother to the king, the play-within-the-play becomes a murder threat, broadcast clearly from nephew to uncle. And in being so aggressively confrontational about the primal event, Hamlet entices a reaction *not* to the mise-en-scène but rather to his own narrative about it. He speaks daggers to Claudius while the players play, the poison pours. In a mirrored repetition and reversal of plot history, Hamlet aurally poisons Claudius—infects him—in these central scenes. As Nigel Alexander notes, one vital aspect of *The Murder of Gonzago* is that its presentation "convinces Claudius that he is diseased. He diagnoses this disease as Hamlet and attempts to cure himself by sending the Prince to execution in England."[64] The thing to catch the king's conscience becomes instead a telegraphed homicide warning (as well as an oedipal promise of replacement: "you shall see anon how the murtherer gets the loue of *Gonzagoes* wife"). *The Murder of Gonzago* is a surefire bet to terrify Hamlet's adversary, but not necessarily to reveal him. Yet neither Hamlet nor the drama openly acknowledges this problem.

Lucianus propounds an ambiguity which escapes the prince's rhetorical control; the figure self-deactivates as an instrument of discovery. I do not think it has been generally noticed that the name "Lucianus" has an exemplary rhetorical ancestry. In Puttenham's *Arte of English Poesie*, the Greek rhetorician and satirist Lucian is invoked in connection with the figure of radical verbal doubt: *amphibology*, or what

Puttenham calls (with apt resonance for *Hamlet*) the "vicious speach":

> When we speake or write doubtfully and that the sence may be taken two
> wayes, such ambiguous terms they call *Amphibologia*, we call it the ambigu-
> ous or figure of sence incertaine. . . . [T]hese doubtfull speaches were used
> much in the old times by . . . false Prophets . . . to abuse the superstitious
> people, and to encomber their busie braynes with vaine hope or vaine feare.
>   *Lucianus* the merry Greeke reciteth a great number of them, deuised by a
> coosening companion one Alexander, to get himselfe the name and reputa-
> tion of the God *AEsculapius*, and in effect all our old Brittish and Saxon
> prophesies be of the same sort, that turne them on which side ye will, the
> matter of them may be verified.[65]

Puttenham's syntax prevents us from knowing whether Lucianus merely
recounted someone else's deceptive ambiguities or actually profited
from fraudulent self-representations constructed on his behalf; and thus
the example perfectly embodies its subject. The ambiguous word "re-
citeth" and the unclear referent "himselfe" both create an amphibology
that anticipates Hamlet's intense binary deployment of "Lucianus"—a
figure who may represent either Hamlet or Claudius, "turne them on
which side ye will." Shakespeare may not have known Puttenham's brief
excursus on rhetorical duplicity, but its intricate anticipation of *Hamlet*'s thematic obsessions is suggestive. Puttenham's Lucianus (or Alexander) used the devious, outrageous fabrications to deceive people into
thinking he was a god. But not just any god: Aesculapius is the Roman
god of medicine and healing. Just as verbal ambidexterity was exploited
amphibologically to achieve a false identity as a healer—and Puttenham
is suggestively silent on how this exploitation was managed—so Hamlet
uses Lucianus, a figure of *theatrical* duality and "sence incertaine," "to
encomber" Claudius "with vaine hope or vaine feare": specifically, to
tent him to the quick.

   Although the stage poisoner perfectly represents the division and convergence of Hamlet and Claudius, thus serving a *symbolic* function, the
figure also undoes its *dramaturgic* function by crippling the evidentiary
value of the *Gonzago* playlet. For all his clever plotting, writing, direct-
ing, Hamlet has stupidly tipped his hand: Claudius now knows the harm
his nephew means him (that much has been communicated unequivocally), and immediately after storming out of the performance, the king
seals a letter ordering Hamlet's death: "I like him not, nor stands it safe
with vs / To let his madnes range, therefore prepare you / I your com-

mission will forth-with dispatch, / And he to *England* shall along with you" (H4v).

Without fully grasping the ambiguities that contaminate his results, Hamlet has nonetheless become intensely aware of his own infectious potential. Directly after the playlet, Guildenstern informs Hamlet that the king is "meruilous distempred . . . with choller" (H3v), and Hamlet now disavows the physician's role that he said he would assume when tenting Claudius to the quick: "Your wisedome should shewe it selfe more richer to signifie this to the Doctor, for, for mee to put him to his purgation, would perhaps plunge him into more choller." The pun on "collar" is less important than the comminatory surface sense. Abrogating the doctor's role with this threat, Hamlet seems finally to have discarded the equivocation that summoned Lucianus. But even if the prince has successfully tented (opened, probed, and worsened) the wound of Claudius's febrile conscience, infective doubt should remain: audience doubt.

We confront a contaminating menace to rationality here. A moment of profound unintelligibility is treated by the play *as if it made sense*; a passage that ought to plant doubt in the minds of everyone (speaker, interlocutor, audience) slides into an apparent resolution that actually contains the germs of further dissolution.[66] Despite Claudius's guilt, it is theatrically illogical at this point to credit Hamlet's apparent triumph at having found him out; Hamlet ought not to be triumphing at all, only laying ground for further inquiry. For the king's response to the playlet is far from a lucid confession, especially given Hamlet's threatening contribution to that response. To the redactor/director of *Gonzago*, the play has had its desired effect; not so to Horatio, however, whose less sanguine interpretation of the event remains shrouded in his usual laconic, noncommittal idiom:

HAM: O good Horatio, Ile take the Ghosts word for a thousand pound. Did'st perceiue?
HOR: Very well my Lord.
HAM: Vpon the talke of the poysoning.
HOR: I did very well note him.

(H3)

Again, talk of the poisoning, rather than its spectacle, most concerns Hamlet. But it is the *prince's* toxic talk of the poisoning, not Lucianus's, that has made the issue of confirmation—the informational value of "the Ghosts word"—moot. And Horatio's response clarifies the problem: what Hamlet takes to be concentrated truth has been diluted in the matrix of the experiment. The friend's minimalist intercourse here hardly constitutes a ringing endorsement. Asked if this performance piece would not earn Hamlet a fellowship in "a cry of players," Horatio responds with chin-stroking caution: "Half a share." Half shares and partial evidence are all the play allows. An illuminating contrast to Horatio's rejoinder occurs in the first quarto, where the friend plays the eager informant and volunteers this intelligence after the show: "The king is mooued my Lord" (Q1, F4v). The certitude of the first quarto evaporates time and again into the airy, poisonous ambiguity of the second. Rules of evidence and conclusion dissolve in Q2, with a consequent peril to rationality.

  Gonzago is supposed to be a crucial test of Claudius's guilt, a test to be graded by Horatio's response. But then the play abandons the response as insignificant: Hamlet hears what he wishes to hear, and ignores his friend's halfhearted replies. The text constantly arranges such situations: dramatic avenues that hold out the promise of proof, knowledge, or orientation, but prove to be merely dead-end corridors lacking legible markings. The clog in verbal logic that corrupts the *Gonzago* performance and its aftermath characterizes *Hamlet*'s meanings, which pivot on irrational conclusions, confused assertions, and faulty word choices. The tainted mixedness of what Hamlet accepts (on the surface, at least) as unequivocal data corrupts what he accepts (on the surface) to be his knowledge. The reason for his ready acceptance of poor information is clear enough. In response to Guildenstern's aggrieved requests for greater conversational clarity after the *Gonzago* playlet, Hamlet confesses what we may already have gathered:

HAM: Sir I cannot.
ROS: What my Lord.
HAM: Make you a wholsome answer, my wits diseasd.
                              (H3v)

He is not only a diseased wit himself but the cause of diseases in others. The aftermath of the *Gonzago* performance shows Hamlet at his nervous worst: linguistically disturbed, spoiling for a fight, marginally incoherent. In a giddy spin the prince recklessly uses others for rhetorical target practice, sometimes purposefully, more often gratuitously; he disregards the obvious danger to himself and becomes an exceptionally mobile and potent vector of disruption, broadcasting his strain of sickness around the court.

From this point in the play, Hamlet's role as the spreader of cognitive illness crystallizes. In a famous exchange, the prince manipulates Polonius infectiously:

POL: My Lord, the Queene would speake with you, & presently.
HAM: Do you see yonder clowd that's almost in shape of a Camel?
POL: By th'masse and tis, like a Camell indeed.
HAM: Mee thinks it is like a Wezell.
POL: It is backt like a Wezell.
HAM: Or like a Whale.
POL: Very like a Whale.
HAM: Then I will come to my mother by and by.

(H4–H4v)

Hamlet enforces obedience to his unstable, fictive vision in exchange for a concession to visit Gertrude. But something more sinister is happening as well. This apparently trivial power game enacts on a small scale Hamlet's characteristic havoc: to break down the resistance of other subjectivities until they absorb his scattered perceptions and preoccupations. It is a wonderful feature of this exercise in imposed likeness that it depends on the perception of *similitude* ("it is like . . . It is backt like . . . Very like . . ."). This is contagion, the infective leveling of another consciousness. If it seems unusual to describe this scene in terms of plague, we should consider that the obliteration of individuality is the first social consequence of any epidemic, in which a vast number of persons contract the identical ailment. It will not be long before Ophelia, too, begins to act and speak as Hamlet did: mad, but not in craft. We should also consider that the interview with Polonius, although present in both quartos, is followed in Q2 alone by a passage that highlights Hamlet's Ghost-like, pestilential affinities: "'Tis now the very witching time of night, / When Churchyards yawne, and hell it selfe breakes out / Contagion to the world" (H4v). In the process of catching the king's conscience and the king's sickness, Hamlet becomes, in G. Wilson Knight's words, an "element of evil" whose poison causes the other characters to fall "like victims of an infectious disease."[67]

In overwhelming and dissolving identities through verbally imposed contagion, Hamlet breaks a plague to the world that speaks doom for the state. The implications of this power are most meaningful politically in the relationship of the so-called mighty opposites, Hamlet and Claudius. Their growing similarity—the plague that encircles them—is first fully visible after the *Gonzago* playlet. Following the performance, the king, as a result of Hamlet's words, has been in Guildenstern's phrase "meruilous distempred"; Rosencrantz then highlights the mutuality of infection by asking Hamlet: "Good my Lord, what is your cause of distemper . . . ?" (H4). Rosencrantz fails to realize that Hamlet's sickness is not unique property, not the prince's own, particular self; it is rather an appropriated force, a motile, communicable set of perturbations and compulsions. These *are* overwhelmingly persuasive.

Even before the *Gonzago* sequence, Claudius has felt the pressure of Hamlet's infectiousness. We can observe in what has been thought to be a textual error some compelling evidence of the range of Hamlet's influence. After eavesdropping on the prince, who has been excoriating Ophelia, Claudius determines that Hamlet should go to England for Denmark's neglected tribute; Polonius ill-fatedly asks for one last chance to discover Hamlet's real problem. The second quarto text records a variant so perfect that it seems a shame to emend it, worse still to ignore it. The king responds to Polonius's request with a line not present in Q1:

> It shall be so,
> Madnes in great ones must not vnmatcht goe.
>
> (G3v)

Most people think that "unmatcht" should read "unwatcht"; but because one of Hamlet's keenest talents is coercion, forcing others to act and think the way he does, what the king says here seems proper. The typesetter of Q2 has (perhaps accidentally) registered Hamlet's influential ability; with letter-perfect aptness, the text suggests that Claudius will intentionally, as Hamlet himself claims to have done, take on madness. Interestingly enough, and whether we read "unwatcht" or "unmatcht," the king had *just* determined, moments before, that Hamlet is in fact *not* mad. In the odd multiple negations this play so often employs, Claudius asked, "Love? His affections do not that way tend, / Nor what he spake, though it lackt forme a little, / Was not like madnes" (G3v). Perhaps in the king's quick self-contradiction, his assertion that Hamlet's sanity is madness after all, we can see that Claudius has indeed begun to match Hamlet's lunacy, to internalize it. Anyone who observes the play in performance will certainly be struck by the *intuitive* intelligence of Q2's reading: Hamlet drives everyone crazy. The only possible response to his illness is contagiously to adopt it, to not let it go unmatched.

V

An epidemic is a vast, dominating anxiety machine. Because of its enormous scale and the randomness with which it spread death, bubonic plague differed fundamentally from even the most disfiguring and agonizing illnesses such as syphilis and leprosy, which were generally regarded as unfortunate but individual afflictions. With its gigantic demographic impact, plague literally turned ailments of the self into ailments of the state. Such a transformation nicely describes the arc of *Hamlet*'s plot: the ravaged individual bears a disturbance from which the political sphere cannot remain shielded and from which it will not soon recover. The plague so radically disrupts the individual subject, so many individual subjects, that the entire culture comes to grief. We should not be amazed to find that the *notion* of epidemic sickness, once admitted into the kingdom of the text, behaves like the plague itself, escaping positional confines, moving centrifugally across difference among characters, meaning centripetally toward a core of impacted indeterminacy.

The plague's extensive presence in the text cannot be decoded in any formulaic way, and this difficulty has implications for a political reading. In the symbolic convergence of Hamlet and Claudius, the play complexly reproduces the historical encroachment, circa 1603, of the plague upon monarchy. But the posited allegorical identifications are contradictory and counter to topical expectation, revealing the trouble that Shakespearean theater has with its contemporary gestures. Certainly Claudius, the founding poisoner, must be read as the pestilent usurper, who introduces toxicity into the realm and displaces the man who could be the rightful heir. But his is also a notably orderly succession, a tidy statecraft, no matter how it was maneuvered. The deep disorders of the nation arise more from Hamlet's (and the Ghost's) frustrations than from Claudius's usurpation. It is the prince's actions that provide occasion for what historically was the plague's business: wreaking monarch-dislodging havoc and spreading "superfluous death" through the land. To the extent that pestilence configured both tyranny and insurrection, it is Hamlet who embodies the drama's primary plaguy force. We ought not to regard Claudius's *original* guilt as more severe than Hamlet's *originary*—that is, generative—criminality. Indeed, Claudius's rule would likely have been admirably coherent if left to its course. It is true that there would not have been much of a play if Hamlet had failed to oppose the suspected usurper. But the prince's remedies, his political actions, exacerbate the national illness.[68]

Claudius's own allusions to sickness, particularly to Hamlet as *his*
sickness, multiply after the prince gives disease free play by opening the
Pandora's box of theatrical indeterminacy with *Gonzago*. The king admits, while equating the prince with infirmity, that his own epistemological lack caused Polonius's death: "We would not vnderstand what was
most fit, / But like the owner of a foule disease / To keepe it from divulg-
ing, let it feede / Euen on the pith of life: where is he gone?" (K1). The
answer should by this point be obvious: Hamlet has been absorbed like
a virus into the very body of the monarch; he's begun to turn Claudius
into a Ghost ("the King is not with the body," Hamlet reminds Guildenstern), begun to efface him: "The King is a thing . . . Of nothing."
Certainly, the monarch feels his mortal body invaded; Claudius says
Hamlet rages "like the Hectique in my blood." But the sickness is not
easily purged, and Claudius realizes that a cure will come hard: "This
suddaine sending him away must seeme / Deliberate pause[;] diseases
desperat growne, / By desperat applyance are relieu'd / Or not at all"
(K2). Hamlet's de facto role as a vector or carrier of infection undergoes
a marvelous transformation: the hero (as in Roger Fenton's idea of the
divine word) *becomes* infection, tainting the already tainted world, further corrupting the monarchy. It is only through luck, through special
providence, that this disease is diverted from England; the shipborne
infection (a common cause of plague dispersal) finds its way back to
Denmark.

Some intertextual evidence supports this view of Hamlet's diseased
and kinglike disruptiveness. It has been shown that a probable source
for several of the play's political concerns is Philippe du Plessis-
Mornay's *Vindiciae Contra Tyrannos* (1579), a Huguenot meditation
on the responsibilities of the citizen to resist monarchical tyranny. This
text lays some of the groundwork for Shakespeare's representation of
Denmark through its unusual imagery of the tyrant's physical corruption of the body politic. However, if du Plessis-Mornay's descriptions of
tyranny have influenced Shakespeare's portrayals in *Hamlet*, they have
done so in surprising, inverted ways. Du Plessis-Mornay asserts: "Tyranny is like a raging fever. At the beginning it is easy to cure but difficult
to detect; afterwards, it is easy to recognize but very difficult to cure."[69]
But it is Hamlet who enacts this fever, "raging like the Hectique" in
Claudius's blood. Shakespeare offers a reversal of the expected roles of
tyrant and tyrannized, where the man customarily regarded as des-
potic—the usurper, the regicide—feels instead harried and harmed.
Claudius's other comment about diseases that must be relieved by des-

perate appliance may also have its precursor in du Plessis-Mornay: Hamlet has clearly become a difficult germ to cure. True, the king has committed "a brothers murther," which has "the primall eldest curse vppont" (J1); yet in clear and compelling terms—and not just to Claudius—the prince is the nation's contamination, the imbalancing virus. Once we regard Hamlet as the infecting agent in the Danish political body, it will not seem odd that in du Plessis-Mornay's terms, Hamlet, not Claudius, best fits the definition of the tyrant:

> But if a prince persistently subverts the commonwealth, if he brazenly perverts the law, if he shows that pledges, covenants, justice, and religion mean nothing to him . . . he is properly a tyrant. And by this name . . . he is branded an enemy of God and man.
>
> (*Vindiciae Contra Tyrannos*, 190)

Although Claudius perverted the law, Hamlet subverts the commonwealth in both a more widespread and a more spectacular fashion. The prince's steep moral descent reveals just how little "covenants, justice, and religion" mean to him. His willful damning of Rosencrantz and Guildenstern completes his earlier pleasure at the thought of ensnaring the king in some act that would foreclose his—Claudius's, that is—salvation.

The multiple contaminations introduced during *Gonzago* dissolve any illusion that Hamlet merely uncovers the sickness that he in fact so maniacally produces.[70] Shakespeare's affinity for balance and complementarity generates a hero who becomes morally comparable, through his own infectiousness, to the villain of the piece; although patently victimized, Hamlet develops into a brazen subverter of religious principle and human place.[71] The prince's transgressions are often underscored by spurious self-justifications, the most conspicuous of which comes after his callous butchering of Polonius: he piously intones, "Heauen hath pleasd it so / To punish me with this, and this with me, / That I must be their scourge and minister" (J4–J4v). This back-construction is a soulless apology for his own misdirected (but not unintended) violence. However, a scourge always resists intelligibility as a minister, and vice versa. In the Renaissance, bubonic plague was universally described as just such a divine scourge against human sinfulness. Yet these descriptions, which labored desperately for redemptive meaning, could not rationalize the epidemic.[72] The supposed divine provenance of the disease insufficiently explains the ruthless ruin of the blameless, the neutral, and the reprobate.

Hamlet, for all his linguistic scourging, cannot convincingly posit

moral causes for his actions. He has no interest in ministering to those he
will punish or in leading them to repentance; the closest he comes is
when he resolves to speak daggers to his mother, a resolution which
results in one accidental murder, a second ghostly visitation—and no
commitment whatsoever from Gertrude to keep away from Claudius's
bed. Like the bubonic plague, Hamlet becomes a tyrant whose destructive efficacy overtakes his ethical rationale. He claims divine sanction
for his cruelest acts: describing how he has delivered Rosencrantz and
Guildenstern to their unshriven deaths, he says, "Why euen in that was
heauen ordinant" (Niv). Compared to the prince, Claudius should earn
our respect: he never claims to act in anyone's interest but his own.

   Hamlet's affliction of Claudius effects a plaguy convergence of king
and adversary on the level of grammatical as well as theatrical referent.[73]
One familiar example comes in a soliloquy missing from Q1, "How all
occasions doe informe against me. . . . " Hamlet here questions his own
apparently flaccid response to powerful stimuli: "How stand I then /
That haue a father kild, a mother staind" (K3v). Hamlet seems to con-
fess, in grammatically ambiguous terms, the precise crimes Claudius has
committed. The words as they stand in the second quarto do bear some
figurative truth: Hamlet must have imaginatively killed off his father
(i.e., at least come to regard him as dead) in order to undertake the
necessary reality of revenge; and he must mentally stain his mother to
sully his intended victim, Claudius, and to sustain his own resolve. But
the lines are chiefly significant because they bespeak the play's now fully
articulated convergence of the hero and the villain.

   That convergence began in Hamlet's consciousness well before this
moment—perhaps as early as his request from the player for a speech
about Pyrrhus:

> One speech in't I chiefely loued, t'was *Aeneas* talke to Dido, & there about of
> it especially when he speakes of *Priams* slaughter, if it liue in your memory
> begin at this line, let me see, let me see, the rugged *Pirhus* like Th'ircanian
> beast, tis not so, it beginnes with *Pirrhus*, the rugged *Pirrhus*, he whose sable
> Armes . . .
>
> (F3–F3v)

What is Hamlet correcting from his false start to the tale Aeneas tells,
and what does he misremember? Somehow "Th'ircanian beast" slips
into Hamlet's consciousness as a modifier for "Pirrhus," and he realizes
he has gotten something wrong—but not entirely wrong. In the *Aeneid*,
Dido accuses Aeneas of treacherously abandoning her; significantly, she
uses the language Hamlet misapplied to Pyrrhus: "Traitor, no goddess

was ever your mother . . . No, your parent was Mount Caucasus . . . and tigers of Hyrcania nursed you."[74] A congeries of subterranean pressures alters Hamlet's memory of the passage, and these pressures figure his unspoken, troubled identification with the Trojan hero and with heroism in general.[75] For Dido's original reproof bubbles to the surface of Hamlet's lexical memory. It may recall to him, first, the already intense cognizance of Gertrude's nondivinity (especially in comparison to the "Hyperion" king): "no goddess was ever your mother." This awareness emerges again well into the player's speech when Hamlet impatiently asks the actor to "say on, come to Hecuba," as if requesting a proper, corrective model of spousal mourning.[76] In making the error, Hamlet may also be recording his subconscious preparation to perform Aeneas's signature infidelity—the rejection of a loving woman (Dido/Ophelia) for the sake of a heroic duty to which the whole cosmos has seemingly conscripted him. Finally, and most important, Hamlet's comparison of Pyrrhus to "th'ircanian beast" subtly restates one of the drama's basic assumptions: in a protagonist's least attractive or rational moments, he may be indistinguishable from a villain. Because not Pyrrhus but Aeneas is (allusively speaking) the original Hyrcanian beast, Hamlet's conspicuous misremembering actually remembers a classical precedent for confusing the heroic and the criminal, the new law and the outlaw. His identifications are delicate gyroscopes pulled by the contradictions of the revenge plot.

During *Gonzago*, Hamlet comes to understand, however ironically, his increasing similarity to Claudius: "Tis a knauish peece of worke, but what of that? your Maiestie, and wee that haue free soules, it touches vs not . . . This is one *Lucianus*, nephew to the King" (H2v). Later, as he prepares to accept the swordfight challenge, the prince reasserts his royal similitude: "I am constant to my purposes, they followe the Kings pleasure, if his fitnes speakes, mine is ready" (N3). In soul, in pleasure and fitness, Hamlet can equate himself to his uncle; but the specifically political ironies of the equation escape him. He finds himself in the familiar emulous bind of *Troilus and Cressida*: to destroy the rival always involves becoming the rival, assuming the other's place and identity. For Hamlet, similitude implies replacement. Hurled toward a likeness he must demolish—the analogy of kingship—the prince must sooner or later confront the responsibility of monarchy, a responsibility that would certainly fall upon him should he survive and be able to justify his revenge agenda (which would likely become suspect in the event of his survival). Hamlet's push toward revenge may well obscure other desires;

try as it might, the play cannot easily separate the substance of ambition from the farrago of motives for retribution.

The drama goes out of its way to avoid addressing this latent entanglement: for the heir apparent to murder the king signifies a succession. Does Hamlet come to resemble Claudius in order to destroy and replace him? Or must he destroy the king *as a consequence of* this resemblance, because the stage world is no longer big enough for both of them? The death of Claudius, we are meant to think, looms as the telos of all Hamlet's actions, but a key unspoken event inevitably awaits the king's death: the ascension of the *next* king. Most readers tend not to regard the prince as interested in politics per se. But Hamlet's darker purpose may be unknown to him, boring and familiar as it has been through history—a motivational cliché. Hamlet's revenge marks the final stage of an insurrection: his job is to dislodge the power he imitates.

Claudius, for one, is always vigilant about Hamlet's growing encroachment on his prerogative. In the midst of his self-absolving conversation with Laertes, the king receives the letter announcing Hamlet's return to Denmark—Claudius's first news that Hamlet is alive: "High and mighty, you shall know I am set naked on your kingdom[;] to morrow shall I begge leaue to see your kingly eyes, when I shal first asking you pardon, there-vnto recount the occasion of my suddaine returne" (L3v). The note seems to disavow political ambition; its mock-obsequiousness underscores the apparent differences in rank between the man within power and the one without. Claudius sharply reads through the phony formalities to dissect Hamlet's intentions:

KING: . . . if he be now returned
As the King at his voyage, and that he meanes
No more to vndertake it, I will worke him
To an exployt, now ripe in my deuise,
Vnder the which he shall not choose but fall.
(L3v)

Neither the letter to the king nor Claudius's response appears in the first quarto. The Folio reading is the choice of almost all modern editors, and it alters this passage considerably with a single word; but the reading is redundant and evacuates the considerable political implications of the speech: "if he be now returned / As checking at his voyage." Harold Jenkins in the Arden edition glosses "checking" as "shying, stopping suddenly in mid-course." The Folio reading oddly erases Claudius's suspicions about Hamlet's return, *and* it removes the identification between the two characters which Claudius in Q2 goes out of his way to notice. It is in the second quarto of 1604, the text adjacent to and replete with anxiety about disease and the succession, that the grappling over political place becomes clearest. Claudius says that if Hamlet means to give up the kingly role, then the prince will be vulnerable and must fall (die, descend in status). In other words, Hamlet's heralded return smacks of royal presumptions—and suggests to Claudius the frightening possibility, unmitigated (or even exacerbated) by Hamlet's rhetoric of obeisance, that the prince probably means to claim his royal rights. There is good reason for Claudius to imagine so; since Hamlet is alive, he has obviously defeated and likely discovered the plot against him. His return represents the most fraught convergence yet between the adversaries: a convergence not in soul or character, but in political position. However, Claudius says, if Hamlet does *not* prosecute his own kingship, if he means what he says in the letter and will not undertake the monarchy, then he can be victimized.

Claudius proves prescient, and Hamlet does not undertake to claim the monarchy he approaches. In the course of his eccentric insurrection, of his strange boldness mixed with stoic, pre-swordfight passivity, Hamlet abdicates the heroic: he deposes himself, not from the possibility of successful and glorious private revenge (already a heavily problematized notion in the Renaissance), but from the monarchy that would likely befall him pursuant to the act. Hamlet's abdication of heroism occurs in a gradual and roundabout way through the drama: he edges around, pesters, weakens, and finally kills the king, but he also carefully forestalls his own access to power. He o'errules kingship to a peace, to his own peace, but *only* once his exclusion from it proves irreversible. It cannot be coincidence that Hamlet's single attempt at regicide comes after he learns he has been poisoned and has "not halfe an houres life" left in him. Hamlet's imminent doom opens a decorous sliver of subversion in which the long-awaited revenge can occur, because the immense *political* consequences of the crime against the state can be evaded: his revenge, like the Ghost's, is virtually posthumous. Even so, as the prince breathes his last, he feels it necessary to ask Horatio to "report me and my cause aright / To the vnsatisfied."[77] The belatedness of the regicide, its very-last-minute character, should not be read as a failure of Hamlet's will. Rather, it must be seen *as* his will, an ingrained ideological sympathy with and obedience to historical conditions.

No matter how villainous the king or sympathetic the avenger, a staged regicide always had a certain electricity about it. The second quarto of *Hamlet*, contemporaneous with a deadly epidemic which ravaged the succession process, would have been supercharged in this regard. Elsinore's poisonous contagion upends kingship and reanimates the image of a regime pestered by disease. The surprise, of course, is that the disease is the hero. In Q2, a profound nervousness about the absence of monarchy competes with a parallel worry about an abscess in monarchy; these tensile anxieties pressure Hamlet's every act, his every deliberation. Well-founded fears about an ungoverned nation frame the text; "Long liue the King" is the play's (ironic) third line. And at the end, even after Claudius's villainy has been revealed and Laertes cries "the King, the Kings to blame" (O1), the play cannot quite loose its grip on the idea of a stable regime. For Hamlet's unthinking assault on the ruler causes the whole court to cry out in horrified voice, full with the memory of a gap in kingship: "Treason, treason."[78]

THREE

Succession, Revenge, and History

The Political Hamlet

I

Vpon Thurseday it was treason to cry God saue king Iames
king of England, and vpon Friday hye treason not to cry
so. In the morning no voice heard but murmures and
lamentation, at noone nothing but shoutes of gladnes &
triumph . . .

Behold, that miracle-worker, who in one minute turnd our
generall mourning to a generall mirth, does now againe in a
moment alter that gladnes to shrikes & lamentation.

Thomas Dekker, The Wonderfull Yeare 1603

Succession stories are about treason and the aversion of treason; the
definition of the word rides on the agenda of the victors.[1] In Thomas
Dekker's account of the lamentation, joy, then sustained plaguy misery
attendant upon James's accession, the arbitrariness of the designation
"treason" anticipates a more severe, less intelligible caprice.[2] Dekker
suggests that something has gone painfully, even supernally wrong with
the process of dynastic sequence—as if treason were itself being conducted outside the sphere of human influence, wreaking its disturbances
uncontrollably, absent of point or purpose.

By mid-May 1603, it was evident that James's glorious entry into the
city had become an evasive maneuver, a cowed, skulking dash from his
now dangerous subjects and from his princely role. For the presence of

bubonic plague forced the new monarch to dodge his own admirers. The crowds of gapers, gadabouts, and waterflies had already proven troublesome enough even before the disease was at its height. William McElwee writes that by the time James and his entourage had reached the northern city of York, two strains of preference seekers, the "north-bound English place hunters, and the impoverished Scots hurrying south for fear of missing the pickings, had swollen the train to a disorderly rabble of over a thousand which gave the King no peace and placed an intolerable burden on hosts."[3] On May 7, in the fields at the outskirts of London, the mob became "so greedy . . . to behold the countenance of the King, that with much unruliness they injured and hurt one another, some even hazarded to the daunger of death."[4] But with the epidemic in rising tide, the besieging admirers presented a still greater threat to one another and to the monarch. In plague time, service and homage looked like treason or insurrection: the pressure of the crowds, their thronging love, impinged too heavily on the royal body.

Plagues are harbingers and porous containers of disaster; the chaos that accompanied James to the throne augured ill for the reign. The sickness perfected anarchy, civic and national, because when an epidemic hit, the central authority figures were the first to surrender their physical place. Their absence facilitated the spread of the disease because laws designed to restrain it could not be enforced. Plague thus configured a treason abetted by the ruling politicians; the problem of fatal contagion, in other words, was inextricable from the problem of rule. With the epidemic in full swing, a Privy Council clerk, William Waad, wrote to Robert Cecil about the failure of local governance:

> Notwithstanding the Orders set down, there come Londoners from infected places into cottages in all the villages about London, and . . . presume no man or officer will lay hands on them, because it is known the sickness is in their houses. . . . The absence of the Aldermen from the City, and the Justices in the shire . . . hath bred liberty, and scope, in their lamentable cases and disorders.[5]

The disease caused a power outage and a displaced power surge; as the wealthy and influential fled the heavily infected areas, the disenfranchised and tainted became feared—because, for once, the consequences of disregarding them could be disastrous. In 1604, for instance, with the plague still raging, the mayor of York implored his fellow officials to remain in town: "The infection doth so greatly increase in this city that unless we the magistrates have great care and do take pains in the reliev-

ing of them, the poorer sort will not be ruled."⁶ Some of the moribund
populace rioted, actively seeking to spread their diseases. There were
stories of the sick endeavoring to infect the sound by thrusting themselves into their company and by dispersing linen and other personal
belongings on the streets of the city.⁷ The general disorder, in many
respects, was comparable to insurrection.⁸

Not only a threat to power, however, the epidemic behaved metaphorically as power's surrogate, its negative image. In the Renaissance,
and particularly at the inception of James's regime, plague was an ersatz
sovereign, an antithetical authority; it thus seemed a monarchical insur-
gence. The disease metaphorized a subversive strain *within power itself.*
Impervious and globally destructive, the sickness took on rhetorical
rule, perhaps as a result of its removal of kings and governors.⁹ When it
occupied a given place, it was said to "reign" there; spreading from
town to town, it was commonly described as being on progress.¹⁰ From
the human ruler's point of view, the only effective remedy for the sickness was to escape it, to keep in constant motion. However, flight compounded the problem of rule. Abandonment of place openly exposed the
impotence of the king to maintain centrality, to govern. And in James's
case, the plague vexingly accompanied the court. Throughout the summer of 1603, the Jacobean entourage carried contagion with them: from
London to Oatlands, Richmond to Woodstock, where two members of
Queen Anne's household died of the disease.¹¹ On September 17, at the
height of the mortality, Thomas Crewe wrote to the Countess of Shrewsbury, "The Queen removes hence today, the King upon Tuesday, towards Winchester, where will be a standing Court, unless the sickness
drive them thence, which hitherto hath followed them." A letter on the
same day from Thomas Edmonds to the earl of Shrewsbury confirms the
court's pessimism about the possibility of health: "We are now remov-
ing shortly to Winchester, where we shall stay till we have also infected
that place, as we have done all others where we have come."¹² Sure
enough, Winchester was contaminated just two weeks after the court's
arrival there; tireless with their lives at stake, they then escaped to Wil-
ton (Wilson, *Plague*, 107).

The court's self-consciousness about its own taint is compelling. Even
more significant is the nation's perception of the new regime's vulnerability. Suddenly, James was on an antiprogress, a royal egress. Forced to
flee, the new ruler appeared embarrassingly ordinary and mortal. The
body was too much with the king, his mortality in open view, but the
king was not with the political body, his people—and this separation,

necessary for survival, did extensive damage to James's image *as* a king. Looking back from the perspective of the revivified plague in 1609, John Davies of Hereford recalls the inauguration of the Jacobean regime:

> The King himself (O wretched Times the while!)
> From place to place, to save himself did fly,
> Which from himself himself did seek t'exile,
> Who (as amaz'd) knew not where safe to lie.
> It's hard with Subjects when the Sovereign
> Hath no place free from plagues, his head to hide;
> And hardly can we say the King doth reign,
> That no where, for just fear, can well abide.[13]

"Hardly can we say the King doth reign": although the king's fear is "just," the abject spectacle of the fleeing, self-exiled monarch was debilitating. While it is mean-spirited in the extreme to blame him for wanting to save his life, even James had to admit that his flight was politically undesirable. In a proclamation issued from Hampton Court on July 29, the king undermined the desired demeanor of mastery by confessing the scandal of his own disappearance: "The Coronation being happily over," the proclamation notes, "considering the evils the country suffers from the absence of its natural leaders . . . the King hereby commands all persons not detained at Court to depart at once."[14] Audibly relieved at the completion of his maimed rites, James evacuated the kingdom and, for a time, his own kingship. The epidemic dashed the ideological façade of monarchy's limitless ability to confer order and peace upon the kingdom, or to protect the bodies of the corporate whole. In the presence of plague, the human sovereign did *not* reign.

What should have been a joyous celebration of the Jacobean succession turned instead into cultural tragedy, a calamity of spectacular sorrow and terror. This alteration was the more painful in that it both mimicked and threatened a disaster which England had just narrowly escaped: political chaos. Although James's inheritance was in the works for several years prior to Elizabeth's death, and although most court insiders and many outsiders knew of the likely candidate, nothing was certain, and indeed, all comment about the question was severely interdicted.[15] So when the queen finally proclaimed James from her deathbed in March, the problem, in the words of one historian, "was settled before any other candidate had time to raise a disturbance, and, to the astonishment and relief of those who had been stockpiling arms against the queen's death, the succession crisis passed off in complete peace."[16] But by visiting confusion on a country that had just evaded it, by transfiguring the glorious into the miserable, plague thoroughly undid the preternatural pleasure of the succession.[17] Disease reanimated a national anxiety that had just been buried with the queen—the fear of having no monarch. Plague effected a surprise interregnum, replacing the ruler with nothing. As it happened, the pestilence continued to rage throughout the winter, and James had to wait nearly a year for his public coronation pageant. Between the death of Elizabeth (March 24) and the Stuart coronation (July 25)—in the enforced absence of visibly legitimate monarchy—the bubonic plague took hold of the nation.[18]

A new regime, frustrated, endangered, and forestalled; the king pestered from place to place by an inexorable, usurper-tyrant of a disease; the impeded succession causing the abdication of royal privilege immediately upon assumption of that privilege; the nation aghast at its own savage misfortune, at the impotence of the royal office—into this orbit of images I would like to project the next phase of *Hamlet*'s historical inscriptions and operations of meaning. The topic of the Jacobean succession, as many critics have noted, is intimate with the subject of *Hamlet* in history, especially as the story of the hero touches so tantalizingly closely at so many points on the story of King James's life. Before I rehearse some of these well-documented connections, however, I would like to explore the textual indicators of Hamlet's belated kingship. Until now I have stressed the play's intertwining of prince and villain-king as a primary effect of dramatic contagion; Hamlet's gradual assumption of tyranny registers his eccentric approach to the throne. This convergence makes an ethical point by intensifying the contradictions of Hamlet's task—that is, by sketching his approximation and configuration of that which he must kill—but it makes a political point as well: it seeds the notion of Hamlet *as* a king, blocked from the place which was his due. In 1603, plague spilled James from power. Barred from his own succession by nothing, by death, James lived the extended exclusion from place that Denmark's prince only rarely protests in the second quarto. *Hamlet* artistically renders obstacles not only to revenge but also to rule. These barriers may arise from within—as limitations of the susceptible, hesitant mind or vulnerable body. More often, they occur from without: from the massive ideological bulwark against regicide; the choking anxieties of court intrigue and family pressure; the immense weight of the past.

Interpretively disturbing possibilities are embedded deep within the history of national health that is inscribed in the second quarto of *Hamlet*. The great general treason of the bubonic plague of 1603 is that it seemed to be England's bodily reaction against the presence of a new king. In the wake of Elizabeth's death, the sickness seriously impaired the prestige or the charisma of the Scots monarch.[19] Whatever the eventual ramifications, the closer James got to London, to the seat of power and to his own visibility *as* a power, the more disorder accrued, and the closer he drew to infection.[20] Disease in *Hamlet* bears ironic historical lineaments. For the play bitterly imagines an accession tableau in which deadly treason takes over authority's place—at least until the true prince, the proper heir, can bring unmitigated disaster to the state.

II

The Ghost of King Hamlet tells the heir apparent many things in their first interview, but the political status of the youth goes conspicuously unmentioned; both royal Hamlets seem concerned about things other than the legalities of the succession. The Ghost never protests young Hamlet's loss of position, only his own. Nor does Hamlet himself, for most of the play, lament his preemption from rule. In spite of his disenfranchisement, however, other characters defer to him as being at or near the top of the political hierarchy. Yet he represses or deflects this position, and the obeisance due to it, as in this parting exchange with the guards on watch:

ALL: Our dutie to your honor.
HAM: Your loues, as mine to you, farewell.
                    (C3)

In valuing love over duty, reciprocity over rank, Hamlet here denies his social place and tries to establish a priority of affective authenticity over external form and service, a priority which will ultimately enable the antihierarchical act of regicide.[21] As much as he denies his stature, however, it remains obvious to other characters. Laertes, for one, seems quite convinced early in the play that Hamlet is the future king, and he employs that notion, alongside its allied bromide of the body politic, to discourage Ophelia from a romance with the prince:

LAER: His greatness wayd, his will is not his owne . . .
        . . . for on his choice depends
        The safty and health of this whole state,
        And therefore must his choice be circumscribd

Vnto the voyce and yeelding of that body
Whereof he is the head.
(C3v)

Laertes speaks as if the prince is already burdened with royal choices, as
if a new King Hamlet has been proclaimed and is considering a wife.[22]
Ophelia takes up a similar refrain when she calls Hamlet "Th'expectation and Rose of the faire state" (G3). It could be that Polonius's children keenly feel their own political marginality and so exaggerate Hamlet's proximity to the throne. But these lines seem prologue to some
promise that the play makes about Hamlet's aptness and destiny for
kingship, a promise that Fortinbras eventually apologizes for in Hamlet's absent presence: "he was likely, had he beene put on, / To haue
prooued most royall" (O2).

The extreme indirection with which the play broaches the hero's pri-
vation from rule lets us know that something weird has happened to the
procedure, not just the outcome, of the succession.[23] Hamlet's political
station is one of the play's legion mysteries. Although the king proclaims
him "the most imediate to our throne" and then invites him to "be as
our selfe in Denmarke" (C1), there ought to be some question—especially in the first scenes of the play—why the able-bodied, scholarly
youth is not *already* king. Yet no one utters a peep of protest against
Claudius. Because generations of critics have reminded us of Denmark's
elective monarchy, Hamlet's exclusion from the throne has been nor-
malized over time. But then it should seem just as odd that the only son
has failed to win election as it does that he has failed to inherit.[24] As a
"fact" of Danish culture, the elective monarchical process goes unmentioned, unexplicated, and wholly unquestioned until the last scene of the
play. Is the issue of succession in Denmark really clear, or simply unprotested? Has Claudius been unanimously elected, and by whom? By "the
people," or by a complicitous body of counselors and elders? By mystifying the procedure through which Claudius came to power, the drama
gives multiple impressions about mechanisms of state: they malfunction
while no one notices or cares; they are inherently corruptible; they are
mysterious, and not to be questioned or trusted. The drama plays a
game of royal bait and switch with the expected male inheritor and the
audience, throwing a cloak over the succession process. In late Elizabethan England, the image of a clearly legitimate heir who is stealthily
denied his place would be particularly appalling.

We need to know what the play resolutely refuses or is unable to tell:

the influence, if any, of the royal marriage upon the nation's choice; the political influence, that is, of the queen. But because we cannot determine whether Claudius's marriage to Gertrude preceded or followed his election, the succession mystery remains intact. The king himself seems to suggest that the marriage, shady at best in the light of his brother's funeral, followed his ascension to the throne: "Though . . . it vs befitted . . . our whole Kingdome, To be contracted in one browe of woe . . . Yet . . . we . . . thinke on him Together with remembrance of our selues. . . . Therefore . . . our Queene Th'imperial ioyntresse to this warlike state Haue we . . . Taken to wife" (B3v). Despite Claudius's sovereign and proprietary manner, his epithet "th'imperial ioyntress" for Gertrude implies an equivalence in their control of the kingdom and suggests at least the possibility that the king's rights go hand in hand with the queen's graces, her political indulgence. He is probably not just being courtly to his new bride; more probably, the phrase represents a prenuptial agreement, a legal consensus. But even if "Therefore . . . Haue we . . . taken to wife" implies a temporal sequence and thus the king's unlimited prerogatives, a deliberately elusive account of power emerges here; even Claudius's official version of cause and effect implies that Gertrude has been "taken" as an act of homage and remembrance (of "ourselves," no less), and for no other reason. The royal rhetoric constantly evades (but nervously alludes to) the king's contingent relationship to his own kingship: his dependence on high-level complicity ("Your better wisdomes, which haue freely gone / With this affaire along" [B3v]); his extrapolitical—that is, sexual—motivations; and his consolidation of power through legitimizing marriage. Claudius's indeterminately figured access to rule might then have derived primarily from the fraternal relationship of inheritance or from the marital one of coercive force.

For reasons that will become clear, I prefer the latter explanation. Hamlet's birthright (which admittedly may be no more of a "right" than that of the child of a United States president to inherit the office) may then have been effectively blocked by his mother's "o'erhasty marriage," which has *secured* the position to which Claudius may or may not have won election. I do not wish to land too heavily on this shaky interpretive plank. But the play sustains the possibility that whereas Hamlet's nobility descends patrilineally, it is impeded matrilineally— that is, matrimonially. "I say we will haue no mo marriage, those that are married alreadie, all but one shall liue" (G3), Hamlet bellows in a fit of unfeigned distemper. His rage against marriage may articulate a specifically political frustration that contains both psychological and historical ingredients. If he *has* been blocked or discouraged from kingship by his mother's wedlock, Hamlet's situation exactly reverses that of King James, whose mother, Mary Queen of Scots, provided him with the claim to Scotland's and eventually England's throne; additionally, Mary's bad marital choices actually *hastened* the Scottish prince's inheritance, as I discuss below. If Hamlet's exasperation at marriage *is* political, it remains the prince's only serious grievance that he does not expound upon at length—that the text does not wish to speak out loud. Hamlet's specifically marital, sexual hostility toward the mother who has not helped him secure a monarchy shields a more immediate historical antagonism: James's frustration with his political mother, Elizabeth, for her prolonged deferral of his English kingship.

The first quarto of *Hamlet* allows its protagonist to express political desire; when pondering the range of the Player's verbal potential, for example, Hamlet asks: "What would he do an if he hadde my losse? / His father murdred, and a Crowne bereft him?" (F1). The second quarto, however, postpones overt signs of Hamlet's aspirations just as carefully as it evades the political implications and intricacies of Claudius's election. Evidence of Hamlet's interest in kingship per se is spotty, and scarcely appears at all until the middle of the drama. In a rare moment of unguarded self-revelation susceptible of political interpretation, he does mention to Ophelia that he is "very proude, reuengefull, ambitious, with more offences at my beck, then I haue thoughts to put them in," and then he affirms and retreats from the confession: "wee are arrant knaues, beleeue none of vs" (G3). But after *The Murder of Gonzago*, Hamlet responds to Rosencrantz's question about the cause of his "distemper" by saying: "Sir, I lacke aduauncement" (H4). Perhaps he thinks he is being calculating—the response should look to the audience (and to Hamlet himself) like a lie—but let us assume for a moment that he has let something slip, that his heart's desire and mind's detachments can be traced to this missing commodity "advancement." After Hamlet expresses his "lacke," Rosencrantz helpfully replies that the prince should not worry about his hierarchical position, "when you haue the voyce of the King himselfe for your succession in Denmarke" (H4). This reply dovetails with Laertes' certainty about Hamlet's royal future, but it also enhances the impression of thematic contagion: Hamlet has the king's voice as a promise, as a possession. Voice is the text's symbolic vial of plague. A sinister and lovely polysemy, this double sense of voice resurfaces at the end of the play when Hamlet ambivalently endorses a more successful avenger than he has been: "I doe prophecie

th'ellection lights / On *Fortinbrasse*, he has my dying voyce, / So tell
him" (O1v). In Hamlet's last moments, the transfer of vocality and
power goes beyond a vote of confidence: it is a curse, a guarantee of life
caught in the vise of office and the fatal pressure of royal responsibility.
At the point of death, Hamlet, finally fully invested with a king's voice,
has for just a moment completely taken over the king's identity and
position, in precisely the same sense of his earlier self-recrimination,
"how stand I then / That haue a father kild, a mother staind"; the dying
voice he gives to Fortinbras figures an ironic bequest, a gift of death. In
a potentate's proclaimed or juridical will lies coiled fact: "I sentence" or
"I decree" signifies a performative linguistic act. During the play's last
moments, plot becomes plaguy Jacobean history: transitional monarchy
waits upon but also seemingly bequeaths mortality. Hamlet's political
apotheosis comes when his language attains, through the prerogative of
choosing a successor, monarchical tones; but his royal prerogative is
only and entirely coextensive with death—the end of the Hamlet family
line, if not the whole culture.

Since monarchical identity and demolition are interdependent in the
play, it makes good sense that Hamlet first openly confesses his political
interests when telling Horatio about his ruination of Rosencrantz and
Guildenstern. Hamlet has managed to trope (to turn verbally)
Claudius's scheme by killing the messengers, effectively erasing and rewriting the king's intentions. His expropriation of Claudius's plot crucially involves an imprinting of *kingly* identity: "I had my fathers signet
in my purse / Which was the modill of that Danish seale, / Folded the
writ vp in the forme of th'other, / Subcribe [*sic*] it, gau't th'impression,
plac'd it safely, / The changling neuer knowne" (N1v–N2).[25] Hamlet's
expert forgery and complex, murderous enfoldings (reversing the play's
opening command, "Stand and vnfolde your selfe") do him regal, not
yeoman service: he moves from resembling Claudius to overtaking him;
he assumes the king's monarch-function, a murderer's business. If identity is the vanishing point of resemblance, Hamlet begins to vanish into
identity with kingship once he fully surrogates both Claudius and King
Hamlet. The forged and folded letter resurrects the homicidal force of
the father, who is remembered in the signet; but that force is deployed by
fraud—that is, as Claudius would wield it. Hamlet's royal acts reunite
the deadly, sundered brothers of Denmark.

What gulls us into denial about Hamlet's darker deeds, his murders
and plots, is that they so entirely *are* the acts of a king, and we have been
hoodwinked into believing the prince's denials about his ambition. But

his practices are precisely those of a ruthless monarch, of one who will lustily devour enemies to nourish himself with power, and spit out the bones with no remorse. This realization takes Horatio aback:

HORA: So *Guyldenstern* and *Rosencrans* goe too't.
HAM: They are not neere my conscience, their defeat
        Dooes by their owne insinnuation growe,
        Tis dangerous when the baser nature comes
        Betweene the passe and fell incenced points
        Of mighty opposits.
HORA: Why what a King is this!

                                                        (N2)

Indeed—but which king? Horatio's customary taciturnity applies equally to Claudius, engineer of the first letter plot, and to Hamlet, its second engineer: "Why what a King you are!"

Hamlet's identity with royalty, his plaguy sameness with villainy, exposes his implication in specifically political desire. But he soon grasps one complication impeding this desire: tactical political success in Denmark follows on the heels of *erotic* success, and erotics are every bit as problematic for Hamlet as politics; the two are always interlaced. For instance, he perceives Claudius's achievement as a coherent mosaic of sex and statecraft, as he suggests to Horatio:

HAM: Dooes it not thinke thee stand me now vppon?
        He that hath kild my King, and whor'd my mother,
        Pop't in betweene th'election and my hopes,
        Throwne out his Angle for my proper life,
        And with such cusnage, is't not perfect conscience?

                                                        (N2)

These lines contain the play's (and Hamlet's) first specific complaints about a succession process which suddenly seems wholly suspect. Claudius's triumph now looks less electoral than erectional, as Hamlet assigns his own monarchical exclusion to his uncle's phallic deftness. In juxtaposition with "whor'd my mother," Hamlet describes the entrance of Claudius into monarchy as a specifically sexual breach, a popping in, reminiscent of Paris's costly intervention in Menelaus's love life: "For thus popped Paris in his hardiment / And parted thus you and your argument" (*Troilus and Cressida*, 4.5.27–28). Claudius's popping in, like Paris's, figures cuckoldry, but Hamlet (not his father) is the cuckold here; in the lines "whor'd my mother, / Pop't in betweene th'election and my hopes," Hamlet blames the king for sequentially impeding access to *two* oedipal prizes: the mother's sexuality and the father's authority.

As a description of Claudius's misdeeds, the phrase "pop't in" muddies the referent of Hamlet's desire, equating the maternal with the political space: each is erotically charged, sexually receptive, attainable. Again, the question of the succession remains unclear, the actual order of events *still* unresolved, but it is at last apparent at least to Hamlet that Claudius's adult heterosexuality has secured the election—the succession—at Hamlet's (unconsummated) expense. It is possible that he understood this mechanism earlier in the play. Significantly, in the politically potent sphere of his mother's bedroom, Hamlet records his *first* protest about the succession process when he calls Claudius "a cut-purse of the Empire and the rule, / That from a shelfe the precious Diadem stole / And put it in his pocket" (J3v). Having already been blocked by the Polonius family on the sexual path, the prince looks for a different erotics of advancement.

The Claudius model suggests that heterosexuality consummates political triumph, but it still takes an act of homoerotic violence to clear the way for that victory; and thus the bodies of Rosencrantz and Guildenstern become crucial props in Hamlet's rehearsal for the autocrat's part. Like Claudius, who destroyed his brother by pouring a dangerous juice into his unguarded orifice, Hamlet emulates the craft of kingship with a sexually coded assault of his two former friends:

HAM: Vp from my Cabin,
   My sea-gowne scarft about me in the darke
   Gropt I to find out them, had my desire,
   Fingard their packet, and in fine with-drew
   To mine owne roome againe.
         (N1)

His condition of being "vp" (erect), his groping to find them, the fulfillment of his desire, his fingering of their packet (letters, but also slang for genitalia), and his satisfied withdrawal all suggest homoerotic dalliance, intercourse, or in this case rape, stealthily mounted.[26] Syntactically, he has his desire *before* he fingers their packets, after he's groped them— the lines hint that the exchange of letters is *not* the prince's primary desire. Hamlet justifies his homoerotic destruction of Rosencrantz and Guildenstern by asserting that "their defeat / Dooes by their owne insinnuation growe" (N2); to unpack this comment, we may look to Thomas

Wilson's early description of rhetorical "insinuation": "a priuie twin-ing, or close creeping in, to win fauor with much circumstance."²⁷ The court spies are typically allied in Hamlet's mind with privy twining, a purely genital sexuality, as we see when he first greets them:

HAM: Then you live about her wast, or in the middle of her fauors.
GUYL: Faith her priuates we.
HAM: In the secret parts of Fortune, oh most true, she is a strumpet.
                                                                          (FIv)

Rosencrantz and Guildenstern's basely sexual nature metaphorizes their basely political nature, and teases out Hamlet's thinly disguised fury with them. Just after *Gonzago*, when the two companions have been sent to discover the cause of his "distemper," Hamlet accuses them of trying to manipulate him, to play on him like a pipe. He expresses a paranoia that appropriately mixes erotics and politics, a fear of being blown on, into, or away; he doesn't want to be fingered or handled as a mere instrument. He is so agitated that his metaphors begin to go off key: "you would plucke out the hart of my mistery . . . and there is much musique excellent voyce in this little organ." Then, collecting himself: "call mee what instrument you wil, though you fret me not, you cannot play vpon me" (H4).²⁸ Plucking out the heart of his mystery and fretting him are more apposite figures for stringed instruments, which Shake-speare could have furnished theatrically, were he so inclined. But instead he chooses the phallic pipe, another kind of little organ, as the stage vehicle: "wil you play vpon this pipe?" "My lord I cannot." The pipe, like the men and their surveillance mission, configures a sexual threat. Not wishing to be penetrated or plucked at, Hamlet will instead prove intrusive, protruding, and he takes his own digital, sexually charged re-venge on them.

In a line the second quarto lacks, Hamlet restates to Horatio his justi-fication for killing the king's instruments: "Why man, they did make love to this employment." The folio line helps clarify the prince's rage: he detests their servicing of the state at least as much as their disloyalty to him; he is repelled by their metonymic character as entirely sexual/ political beings. But his revulsion, I believe, is contaminated by fear of discovery, an anger at their relentless exposure of *his* political needs, unknown as he would like those to remain. The folio again is more explicit than the second quarto can be on this point, and fully illustrates Hamlet's resentment of the court spies. In another passage absent from Q2, Hamlet and the men engage in dark banter about Denmark: "To me it is a prison," Hamlet says in the folio. "Why," Rosencrantz replies, "then your ambition makes it one." Hamlet haughtily deflects the accusation ("O God I could be bounded in a nutshell and count myself a king of infinite space"), but the topic of Hamlet's cramped kingship and unfulfilled, shadowy ambition (as Guildenstern warns, "The very substance of the ambitious is but the shadow of a dream") infiltrates and pollutes the prince's lofty discursive space. Although he regards the subject as beneath him, as indeed he regards most desires as emanating from beneath, Hamlet in the folio lets slip a fixation on kingship in the act of denying it. Q2 manages to camouflage the fixation somewhat, but not completely. On learning from Rosencrantz and Guildenstern that the players are about to arrive, Hamlet's first words are: "He that playes the King shal be welcome" (F2).

Despite (or because of) the intrusions of the two functionaries, Hamlet defers, for as long as he can, his own involvement in the nexus of political and sexual desire. He defends against a world in which sexuality operates extensively within, on behalf of, as a substitute for, political strength. One important sign of Hamlet's deferral comes in his early, almost defiant use of the word "election" specifically to help articulate his *distance* from intrigue and influence: the word enunciates a pure love, untainted by politics. We know that the royal election, whatever form it took, did not go Hamlet's way. So it may be in part a form of psychological compensation that causes the prince, in tones of carefully emasculated passion, to speak love to Horatio, and to tell him that the most important election is affective.

HAM: Nay, doe not thinke I flatter,
        For what aduancement may I hope from thee . . . ?
        No, let the candied tongue licke absurd pompe,
        And crooke the pregnant hindges of the knee
        Where thrift may follow fauning; doost thou heare,
        Since my deare soule was mistris of her choice,
        And could of men distinguish her election,
        S'hath seald thee for herselfe.

                                                    (G4v)

By describing his soul's faculty of rational choice in feminine terms, Hamlet dissolves a masculinist Renaissance distinction between *anima* (fem., principle of life) and *animus* (masc., principle of intellection and rationality). As we saw in *Troilus and Cressida*, self-feminization has many functions for the male Shakespearean speaker; but here, self-denigration is not among them. Instead, Hamlet presents his mistress-soul as female but not as weak or vulnerable, a pledge to Horatio in an act of homosocial free will.[29] This expression of love complicates gender identity for two purposes: it allows Hamlet to deny sexuality, and it notarizes his repudiation of ambition. A feminine identity—adorned with rational, free will but unpolluted by sexual "will"—relieves Hamlet from the burdens of a male, court-constructed subjectivity in which intense sexual and social ambition are normative. He contrasts his love for Horatio with the beloved's inability to provide "advancement," but that inability is the very source of Hamlet's love: political engagement is precisely what Hamlet is avoiding by plighting troth to his friend. The word "election" here, even in the context of a discussion of Hamlet's soul, carries the harmonics of state more than religious doctrine. He contrasts the soul's elevated marriage seal with the crude sexual synecdoche of the candied tongue licking pomp, the pregnant knee of the flatterer—the slaveringly ambitious and bodily opportunistic. At this point in the play, prior to the *Gonzago* scene, Hamlet can still freely rush into Horatio's chaste and depoliticized affections: "giue me that man / That is not passions slaue, and I will weare him / In my harts core, / I in my hart of hart / As I do thee." Horatio is explicitly *not* "a pype for Fortunes finger / To sound what stop she please." To be phallically sexual is to be vulnerable; Hamlet professes a grateful, feminized chastity to his friend, for Horatio offers release from the power-soaked world, the world where "election" once and always represents a succession manipulated in bed. But Hamlet's attitudes change in the context of *Gonzago*, with his increased proximity to monarchy. Presently, the brutality of his interview with Ophelia ("Doe you thinke I meant country matters? . . . That's a fayre thought to lye betweene maydes legs" [H1]) and the putrid invective he afterward hurls at his mother ("Nay but to liue in the rank sweat of an enseamed bed . . . ") underline his sullied descent from matters of the soul to those of the groin—where he and the play locate vortices of political force.

Terror of the erotic accompanies and also encodes a fear of the political and, as such, conjures succession anxiety—Hamlet's and the play's. Queen Elizabeth's chastity cult, despite its ideological dissonances at the end of her reign, provided one kind of comfort, the little boy's safety of not having to imagine his mother (or grandmother) as a sexual being. But the fact of chastity also proved disturbing in that it meant the lack of an heir, which no ideological or iconographical manipulation could make good. Hamlet never enjoys psychic ease about *either* his queen mother's sexuality or succession politics in Denmark; Gertrude's erotic life not only fails to produce an unequivocal succession but actively mucks things up. The play is in this way a worst-case historical scenario, a tragic psychosis of the political unconscious in which anxieties about sex and politics constantly chafe one another. What if there *were* a rightful successor and he could not, so to speak, get in? Hamlet comes to embrace this imaginative despair. Just after his declaration of love to Horatio, the king and his train enter, and Claudius asks the prince how he fares. Apparently punning on the meaning of "fares" as "eats," Hamlet answers: "Excellent yfaith, / Of the Camelions dish, I eate the ayre, / Promiscram'd, you cannot feede Capons so" (H4). The more important pun, however, turns on statecraft, not gastronomy. The paranomasia of the politically discouraged resounds here: "I eat the heir" means that Hamlet is forced to consume his own ambitions and survive on only an airy promise of being the most immediate to the throne. It also means that we will have no more Hamlets, insofar as his dictum against wedlock ("I say we will haue no mo marriage") is self-consuming, and the succession will not pass lineally through him. At this point, he sees himself shut out of, and complicitous in, the predigested succession.

Yet the prince's revenge task would, if effective, presumably make the monarchy available to him—but Hamlet and the second quarto are exceedingly reluctant to consider this as a supporting motive. Hamlet as revenger apparent would compromise the purity (if any exists) of the desire for vengeance, because it would openly admit political craving. In pointed contrast, Laertes returns from France to avenge his father's death and directly challenges Claudius by leading a popular uprising. As if to underscore the process from which Hamlet has been excluded, Laertes' royal encroachment is framed as an election, albeit an unruly one:

MESSENGER: . . . the rabble call him Lord . . .
               The cry choose we, *Laertes* shall be King,
               Caps, hands, and tongues applau'd it to the clouds,
               Laertes shall be King, *Laertes* King.

                                                            (L1)

This extraordinary report glosses Hamlet's disappointments and political failures. It shows that Denmark's political forms are stable in all situations, if even the rabble and their rousers insist on their own election of a favored candidate ("choose we, *Laertes*").[30] It is significant that Hamlet, though "loued of the distracted multitude," never marshals a revolt of this sort—yet presumably he could, especially as his cause is even more reasonable, just, with more extensive ramifications than Laertes'. Why *doesn't* the prince stage an overt insurrection to convert revenge from the private to the public arena? The play as a whole suggests, as perhaps a vestigial recollection of Essex, that direct challenges to power will fail, which Claudius demonstrates by defusing Laertes' popular revolt without breaking a sweat. In any case, open challenge is for Hamlet inconceivable, for it would place him before the mirror of his repressed desires. These desires are not necessarily something he consciously wants and cannot, because of external restrictions, obtain; they are what, because of these restrictions, he cannot stand to believe he may want. He has long shied from political life, reluctantly remaining at Elsinore after his father's funeral, never fully pressing or protesting for his royal rights. He engages the court only in oblique, passive-aggressive disruptions, not in outright revolt; and he noticeably fails for most of the play even to mention his considerable political disappointments, which could serve quite nicely as "excytements of my reason and my blood" (K3v)—that is, as further motivations to revenge, if he wanted them.

But Hamlet's death-infected commitment to retributive murder becomes increasingly difficult to square with any civic impulse or will to office. The unacknowledged plot to secure political place—the succession plot—proves inimical to the urgent desire to do "bitter business" and obliterate monarchy, consequences and souls be damned—the revenge plot. Paradoxically, of course, Hamlet's revenge is prerequisite to his own succession. But the wild impulse and capacity for revenge and the orderly wish and capability to rule confute one another. Like negative and positive integers, they define mutually exclusive grounds. Further complicating this practical and ideological conflict is the para-dramatic level of discourse—that is, the historical context of the work. The play as a whole and Hamlet in particular skittishly engage a complicated desire that they can neither fully confront nor comfortably resolve: the desire, perhaps again translated from the Essex revolt, to contest and control monarchy, to master the space where authority resides—but not to occupy that space. Instead, contestation and control lead Hamlet to mimic the historical effects of that antimonarch, the bubonic plague: he will prevent the new king's peace and pleasure. He is like Lear's Fool in this sense: a reverse clown. His urge to interrupt authority's revels is a defective oedipal impulse. He seeks mainly to stymie the reigning force, not to seize it.

Hamlet's conflictual urges toward and away from kingship constitute one of the play's many insoluble contradictions. The text sustains an impressively steady inconsistency in its attitude toward Hamlet's possible succession. This waffling may have to do with dramatic necessity as much as ideological or historical conflict: if Claudius's election were portrayed as overtly illegal, or Hamlet's desire for rule showed too strong, the prince would have markedly less reason *not* to commit expeditious revenge. Still, after Hamlet's return from his perilous sea voyage, after his ghastly fight in Ophelia's grave and exciting narrative to Horatio about the plots he has overcome, the play seems ready to endorse the hitherto impossible dual ideal of Hamlet's readiness to take revenge *and* to reign. But remarkably, the text trumps the succession question one final time. Hamlet's "readiness" becomes a synonym for the anticipation of death, *not* for the belated ability to achieve revenge and royalty all at once: "there is speciall prouidence in the fall of a Sparrowe . . . if it be not now, yet it well come, the readines is all" (N3v).

How did the revenge and succession questions get diverted? Let me quote again Hamlet's tally of Claudius's crimes:

HAM: Dooes it not thinke thee stand me now vppon?
        He that hath kild my King, and whor'd my mother,
        Pop't in betweene th'election and my hopes,
        Throwne out his Angle for my proper life,
        And with such cusnage, i'st not perfect conscience?
                                                    (N2)

Hamlet asks Horatio two questions that the text of the second quarto only half-completes. The rhetorical immediacy of the queries obscures the fact that they are both missing the crucial referent, and that both are therefore grammatically incoherent. Does Horatio not think *what* "stand[s] mee now vppon"? Is *what* not perfect conscience? The referent of both questions—"To quit him with this arm"—is missing in Q2, and must (again) be supplied by the folio. Hamlet asks Horatio: don't you think I am justified, indeed, is it not perfect conscience, to requite Claudius for the harms he has done—to kill him? The folio does what the quarto cannot: it directly confronts the possibility of Hamlet as a justified regicide, a *political* revenger. The quarto seems racked by anxiety about the prospect of Hamlet's ambition and succession. Let us recall in this context that Q2 also fails to include (whether because of revision, negligence, or censorship) the passage about the child actors and the Wars of the Theaters. In wishing to know how the "little eyases" thrive, Hamlet in the folio asks incredulously whether the children will not, once they have grown into "common players," have already been made by their writers to "exclaim against their own succession." Hamlet's question betrays his identification with their plight. Theatrically occupying a contestatory space, the prince seems always to have to exclaim against the succession which is his due; he lives the irreconcilable contradiction of revenger and candidate, caroming between childish impulses and adult responsibilities. He is not unlike King James in this, an heir presumptive who had, as best he could, to remain silent about (if not to exclaim against) his own succession.

Questions of political inheritance or consequence cause the second quarto to suffer bouts of amnesia or incoherence. I want to insist on these dysfunctions as significant: they are textual arrows aimed at the historical blank of failed or perplexed—diseased—succession. Just at the moment in Q2 when Hamlet's revenge seems most imminent, most replete with reasons and emotions, it is edited out, unstated and imprecise—and at just that moment, as if to further disburden the play of its impulses and justifications for king killing, Osric enters with Laertes' swordfight challenge. An exceedingly odd plot contortion then occurs: after finally speaking his clear desire for kingship ("th'election and my hopes"), after hinting that his conscience would be not only untroubled but satisfied by taking arms against a sea of cultural imperatives, Hamlet suddenly forgets, or allows himself to be diverted from, his own intense emotions. He abdicates his newly focused desires at the prospect of the sword fight with Laertes. When Hamlet seems ready to prosecute his right to the throne by taking the long-pondered revenge, the play introduces one more distraction from the purpose—the final, mortal distraction.[31]

The second quarto's *conspicuous* avoidance of the succession question shadows similar, contemporary historical indirections. For James's long incumbency also had to navigate cultural reticence—the silence of interested courtiers, the Elizabethan Parliament's suppression of debate on the question (1602). And as the play closes toward death and a new regime, its relationship to its cultural contexts becomes at once more intimate and more turbulent.

III

Unlike the histories in which it partakes, *Hamlet* seems present to us in full—more than full, in fact, for three whole and separate versions (Q1, Q2, F) exist. But in toto these versions intolerably complicate the question of history's functional interpretability in literary production. *Hamlet*'s variants are a visible if aphasic report of untold other drafts, accidents, influences, choices, replete with meaning across their range of gaps, consistencies, and contradictions. Despite the obvious volubility of the *idea* of *Hamlet*, the three divergent textual manifestations of the play impair claims to completeness that any one of them might ordinarily make. Each text is fragmentary by reason of the others' presence: none can be *the* authoritative *Hamlet*. To try to determine historical operations in a collated version of the play presents an insuperable challenge because of the grossly indeterminate chronology that such a version introduces; our only chance at making such determinations rests in analyzing one of the variants—in this case, the second quarto—whose historical indicators are clearly marked and, at times, just as clearly erased.

The textual conundrum of *Hamlet* produces all sorts of methodological and interpretive pitfalls, but even more vexing is the vigorous, multiform, and refractory presence of the past in the drama. By way of introducing another stage in my argument about the possible operations of history in Shakespearean texts, I begin with this caveat: not only is what we call *Hamlet* an unstable object of inquiry in itself, but its reservoir of historical referentiality overflows, flooding semantic containment. In an attempt to delimit some of the signifying possibilities of history's operation in the text, I return to the distant past: specifically, to one possible prehistory of the *Hamlet*s. However, this prehistory is itself rippled with confusion, secrets, propaganda, and scandal. I cannot then use it as an interpretive template so much as a companion example—a marvelous analogue and potential source of the dramatic texts which I think it helped form. I shall interject historiography here to help qualify Q2 *Hamlet*'s strained attitudes toward cultural supersession—to offer an account of that text's nervousness about its own succession plot. I wish now to rehearse the tale of James's first ascent to the throne, the throne of Scotland, circa 1566. The events of this period establish, on one level, the foundation for that brief moment of *genera mista*, the glorious and tragic arrival at kingship suffered by James and the English nation in the spring of 1603. On another, obviously related level, the tale prepares *Hamlet*'s most basic theatrical interests—its plot formation and its character set.

To feed early Jacobean history into the machinery of a *Hamlet* reading might seem a risky enterprise. Even local analyses, I would suggest, can suffer from tenuous connectedness: historical analogues to literature too often seem at best suggestive, at worst deceptive or immaterial; most often, resonant but coincidental. So an interpretation of a work grounded on a context some four decades distant and a national border removed dangles simultaneously on two frayed ropes: if one should snap, the other will be likelier to detach because of the added downward force. Nonetheless, *Hamlet* itself thematizes the infectious influence of much earlier events; I can thus align my central interpretive gesture here with the text's own premises. Just as the significance of a present moment in an individual's life can arc back to an event or idea several decades prior to that moment—such as a psychological trauma that leaves a permanent residue in subsequent affect and relations—so too can we find the significant antecedents of a culture's present practices and anxieties in its own preadolescence or even nativity. A text's most pressing concerns, too, can be traced back to a time that it (or its author, or its culture) can hardly recall. The notion of a ghostly, virtually unremembered past that jostles the present time takes center stage in *Hamlet*'s (and Hamlet's) constructions of meaning.

The topic of political succession likewise carries within it theoretical and methodological appropriateness about the material relevance of the past to the present. How do we decide where the history of a current moment meaningfully begins? Since claims to the throne typically extend back many generations, legitimacy itself is often an interpretive fiction in which *significant* ancestry is determined from political expediency; monarchs, like meanings, are made and not born. The principle of monarchical selection can seem nearly as arbitrary, and certainly as fraught, as that of interpretive choice among a field of contending and contradictory data. Here I shall reread James's first perilous transit into power, a horrifying movement into succession that reappears as one group of essential contexts for Denmark's political scene.

The tale in brief:

Mary Queen of Scots married her cousin, the young Henry Stuart, Lord Darnley, in July 1565. Described by the historian J. E. Neale as arrogant, inebriated, vicious and despicable, Darnley in time was regarded even less highly than that by Mary.[32] Although she soon became pregnant, the queen quickly grew estranged from her dissolute husband, and she "absolutely refused to grant him the Crown Matrimonial which would have made him King of Scotland for his lifetime as well as hers"; indeed, the unborn child meant, for Darnley, permanent exclusion from succession "to both the crowns he coveted" (McElwee, *Wisest Fool*, 20). Darnley sought to rectify this situation with the aid of lords who had long opposed Mary. He helped hatch a plot to kill the queen's French secretary, David Rizzio, with whom she had allegedly become intimate; the murder was to be performed at dinner in the presence of the queen, then six months pregnant. The plot's primary aim was to force a miscarriage, but some of the rebel lords, including Darnley, probably meant to dispatch the queen as well in the ensuing confusion. Although the unfortunate Rizzio was butchered, Mary and her unborn child managed to escape the bloody fray, escorted through the havoc by the earl of Huntly and James Hepburn, fourth earl of Bothwell. (The prince was born in relative peace and safety three months later, on June 19, 1566.) James's father could not even remain true to his co-conspirators in the Rizzio plot; he attempted to betray them to Mary after she survived the episode, but they countered by revealing his written complicity in the murder, after which point she could not, understandably enough, forgive him, whether because of his iniquity or his stupidity. Following recovery from childbirth and the coup attempt, Mary reconsolidated her power and superficially reconciled with her husband. But she soon turned her affections toward her savior, Bothwell—an ambitious, bold noble who desired that crown matrimonial which eluded Darnley. Bothwell knew that Darnley represented a continuing danger and obstacle, and had to be removed; the earl did not hesitate long, and Mary apparently did not disdain to help him.

For several months after James's birth, foreign reports circulated of Darnley's renewed plots; the most alarming involved kidnapping the infant prince and using him as a bargaining chip for privilege and favor. Meanwhile, Bothwell and possibly Mary advanced plots of their own. The queen brought Darnley—now badly disfigured and recuperating from a bout of smallpox—to a house in Edinburgh, the basement of which had been packed with barrels of gunpowder in anticipation of the royal husband's stay there. Mary visited him on the evening of February 9, 1567, and left around midnight. Two hours later, the house exploded. Henry Stuart, Lord Darnley, "was found naked in the garden, unmarked by powder" (McElwee, *Wisest Fool*, 26); there was speculation that he had been strangled after the explosion failed to finish him off, but no one knows exactly how he died or even the full extent of Mary's complicity in his death. Bothwell came under immediate suspicion for the crime. The queen's subsequent actions did not allay the nation's doubts about her role in the incident: after a scandalously short mourning period, and in the teeth of her in-laws' cries for revenge against the widely suspected Bothwell, she married the earl on May 12. David Harris Willson notes that through this alliance "Mary not only abandoned James but placed his life in dire peril. Bothwell sought at once to gain possession of the Prince, and Mary was ready to yield" (*King James*, 18). The Protestant nobility, "though they had all been implicated more or less in Bothwell's band against Darnley . . . had the brazen effrontery to march out under a banner depicting his naked body crying for revenge" (McElwee, *Wisest Fool*, 29). Their concern was as much to preserve James as to punish the usurping lord; the child, they feared, would be jeopardized by his stepfather's desire for the crown and fear of inevitable revenge. Worse came to worst, and facing nearly unanimous opposition, Mary was forced to surrender to the Scottish lords. She was lucky (maybe not the best word for it) to survive; Edinburgh mobs blistered her with invective, calling her whore and adulteress. By the end of July, she was made to abdicate the throne to the infant James, and a protectorate was installed. Within a year of the assassination Darnley's parents, the earl and countess of Lennox, commissioned a memorial painting which presents a compellingly slanted version of the death of James's father. Darnley appears as a martyr (unmarked by smallpox) in the work, which depicts among other things a plaque that reads: "If they, who are already old, would be deprived of this life before the majority of their descendent, the King of Scots, he may have a memorial from them in order that he shut not out of his memory the recent atrocious murder of the King his father, until God should avenge it through him."[33]

The Darnley episode, from one perspective, is this: a tale about the murder of the pocky, disfigured father by the stepfather—a tale inextricably bound with the queen mother's disgrace, culminating in the son's conscription to revenge. This history so thoroughly anticipates *Hamlet*'s central storyline that we may be sure that the play eyes, even stares straight at, James. But the angle of vision, as always, is somewhat bent. Henry Stuart's death and the clarion call to remember and avenge it occurred in James's infancy, when the events could not have imprinted themselves directly on the prince's consciousness. Hamlet, by contrast, arrives at sentience in the play virtually *as a result of* mourning his father and pondering the injunction to avenge him. The dead king is, for the first few acts of the play, ever present to Hamlet's mind ("My father, me thinkes I see my father," he says even before the Ghost appears to him), claiming an immediacy that Darnley could not have had for the infant James. Hamlet's self-consciousness, and what I have called his knowledge, seem declined almost entirely from information about his namesake's disfiguration and demise, Queen Gertrude's "adultery," and

Claudius's ambitious lust, all of which make (as Hamlet thinks) a wreck of the nation.

Despite these alterations, *Hamlet* uncannily remembers the family violence and scandal that punctuated James's infant accession.[34] By resurrecting nightmarish events from the new king's early life, the drama draws heavily on the material presence of history and on the question of memorial pressure upon the present. Just as the Lennox family made sure to establish "a memorial . . . in order that [James] shut not out of his memory the recent atrocious murder of the King his father," so the Ghost repeatedly expresses its concern that Hamlet recall what he has heard; but Hamlet, like James, cannot quite remember. The problem is that memory, like history, proves infinitely corruptible from within or without—subject to narrative contamination, ideological whitewash, psychological evasion, wish fulfillment, and any number of other interpretive and perceptual deformations. Indeed, the Darnley painting shows just this tendency through its simple act of calling James's father "King" ("the King his father"), which he patently was not. Darnley, son of Henry VII's granddaughter Margaret Douglas, actually had a legitimate if oblique claim to the English crown, but he was called "King Henry" during his lifetime only as an honorific title; his power in Scotland depended on Mary, and never was he a crowned or proclaimed monarch.[35] The Darnley memorial also, more manipulatively, depicts Henry Stuart's martyrdom while (of course) excising all of his considerable duplicity and greed. Pollutions of memory with respect to events— fictional choices, factual exclusions—nicely analogize the relationship of the literary to the historical. Art reassembles cultural trauma and historical crux; the very anxiety of the moment pressures, interrupts, and distends the representation.

James's unremembered past provides, then, a constitutive history for the play; central events of the monarch's life are reanimated as foundational plot elements in Shakespeare's Denmark. At or near the point of James's full political maturation—his ascent to England's throne— *Hamlet* appears, and induces a dramaturgic rebirth of his infant trauma. The play thus participates *bifocally* in history. It merges two stages of the king's life story, each of which is occupied, in a radically different way, with immense succession anxiety: the past horror of Darnley's murder and Mary's disgrace; and the contemporary crisis of James's blocked ascent to the throne. What further complicates the play's inscriptive processes is that the present succession crisis, circa 1603, can by no means be regarded as a monad, a unity; it too separates into two stages, before and after Elizabeth's death. The queen's sustained prevention of James's kingship (through longevity and her unyielding refusal to name a successor) and the epidemic disease that scotched James's happy entry into kingship are both, I believe, inscribed in *Hamlet*. Both disease and female power are reconfigured as barriers to (Hamlet's, James's) succession in the second quarto of 1604.[36] Hamlet's intense political and sexual angst about Gertrude, as well as the theatrical efflorescence of contagion imagery, allude to succession histories. James's seemingly interminable displacement from England's throne thus finds a correlate in the drama's obsessions with history's returns: the text deploys a prior story about the new king's infant accession *at the historical moment* of his mature, frustrated, and long-delayed assumption of rule.

What point does such a divided inscription make? It may have an unconscious ideological function, alleviating a certain pressure from the monarchy—and from the patriarchy. James cannot, the play suggests at a slant, be held accountable for his own succession woes. Despite the extraordinary coincidence of the arrival of a new regime with a brutal onslaught of plague, the new king cannot reasonably be charged with bringing on the epidemic any more than he, as a newly crowned toddler, could have been blamed for the commotion of Scottish politics in 1567. The structural presence of contagion in the play suggests that individual anguish is contiguous with national pain in the life of royalty: ailments cease to become individual property, and paradoxically lose their damning, their *particular* taint. *Hamlet* emphasizes that one man's infections can come to corrupt national health. While I have blamed Hamlet for this corruption, in that he disperses a mutated form of what he absorbs from the father, there is another sense in which he is thrown into a history whose conditions are most profoundly not of his own choosing. He is infected unawares, and although he amplifies and exacerbates the illness, he cannot be held fully accountable for it. The play, that is, tries on one level to liberate the royal subject from the burden of personal responsibility in history. *Hamlet*'s recollection of the nuclear family nightmare that ushered James into premature kingship (and Mary into captivity) suggests the considerable extent to which the monarch *is* a subject, imperiled by uncontrollable, external forces.

The particular subjugating forces take considerably different form in the theater than in history. Note, for example, that James's biological father plotted heinously against his mother (and probably against the infant king himself) to seize royal power. But Shakespeare's plot inscribes history to redeem—at least on the surface—the male ancestor.

Frequently, especially in the second quarto, this redemption occurs at the expense of the queen; and, of course, it operates wholly in opposition to the usurping stepfather. In one reading of the play's employment of its contexts, then, *Hamlet* is a screen memory, a fantasy produced on behalf of the new monarch to occlude both an intolerable present social reality and an equally stressful personal history.[37] *Hamlet* submerges plague into interpersonal structure, and it translates Stuart debauchery (Darnley's wickedness) into fatherly martyrdom. The play summons so as to transform and partly inter an historical trauma of what amounts to child abuse: not a sexual exploitation but a political one. Turbulent early events effectively foreclosed James's agency in his own political fortunes while placing on him a dual burden he could not, in his infancy, have understood: kingship and revenge. *Hamlet* also, on the ideological plane, sets up a cultural screen on behalf of a reprobate but *legitimate* patriarchy. The text makes insubstantial or ghostly the father's historical culpability—Darnley's despicable character—and displaces it onto the illicit male, the stepfather, now written as a justifiably reviled brother and patriarchal interloper.

But *Hamlet* is far from being an apology for a sullied history (James's) or a compromised ideological structure (patriarchy). Indeed, the drama almost obsessively replays the depredations of fathers upon families; the hero's active hostility toward the father constantly makes itself felt: in the Pyrrhus tale, in Hamlet's behavior toward Polonius, in his daft rage at Claudius. On one level, the play exculpates dissolute fatherhood and reverses historical, parental culpability: the villainy of the (legitimate) father is obscured and urgently transferred onto the wicked stepfather; and the blame attached to the mother in history is never, in the second quarto, relinquished. But the text also *refuses* to prettify—indeed, I believe it highlights—the father's monstrosity. It also in turn problematizes the stepfather's supposed rascality. Along these lines, we should recall that the Lord Darnley–Mary Stuart marriage was a union of cousins, both grandchildren of Henry VII; if this is not incestuous, it is at least highly endogamous. The Jacobean line was founded on preexistent family ties. Here lurks a sub rosa Shakespearean irony of reversed identification: Claudius's supposedly terrible act of "incestuous" adultery recalls the *original* marriage between James's father and the queen and may represent a kind of genetic, inscriptive memory in which the alleged villain moves instinctively toward historical legitimacy. When Claudius refers to his nephew as "my Cosin *Hamlet*, and my sonne" (B4v), he speaks what are properly Darnley's words, not

Bothwell's. *Hamlet* works as a valve to release the pressures of disgraceful, embarrassing historical reality—James's verminous, unkingly father and reckless mother—but the valve clogs with the complexities of that reality. The contaminations of context cannot be purged.

A text illuminates its historical correlates most when it diverges from and only intermittently overlaps with them, revealing difference rather than sameness; perfect parallels can measure only a level semantic space between lines that never touch. Intersections, though, produce positions and orientations. Another compelling but screwy parallel in the James-Hamlet nexus is a reversal of power and gender conducted in the movement from history to theater. If we accept that King James occupied a subject position closely but problematically replicated by Hamlet's, and that the king inherited a buried history in his infancy that Hamlet must consciously live through, we cannot fail to note that the location of monarchical power shifts dramatically from historical past to theatrical present. In the years prior to King James's birth, Queen Mary embodied the recognized, dynastic power of Scotland. Yet in Shakespeare's Denmark, Hamlet the Elder is every inch the king—and Gertrude seems not to have much to do with any of the practicalities of rule. The play does hint, as I have proposed, that Claudius owes his crown to his speedy marriage to Gertrude. Thus sexually, and only thus, could he have "pop't in" between the election and Hamlet's hopes; so the second king's privilege may derive from a woman, even as Darnley's did, and just as James's monarchical privilege flowed from Elizabeth's alleged deathbed proclamation. But the queen in Q2 *Hamlet* remains passive and powerless. Gertrude does not function politically much like either Mary or, to be sure, Elizabeth, her possible historical antecedents. Instead, her resemblance to Mary is erotic, not political. This inscriptive alteration affects the play's other representations of the past. For in the wake of Shakespeare's erasure of historical female power and prerogative, in the portrayal of a queen who is the oblivious prize of violent male contention rather than the engineer of or participant in it, the play allows for the possibility of considerable moral differences between the men who vie for her—between the prior (supposedly exalted) husband and the subsequent (allegedly debased) cutpurse of the realm. But Mary's active hostility to Darnley, and her subsequent league with Bothwell, point to an immense rift in the royal marriage and remind us of Darnley's undeserved status as martyr. The historical record suggests that Henry Stuart was a victim not only of the usurping villain but more centrally of his own plots and unsteady alliances. Yet in repeatedly recalling the silent scandal of the queen's remarriage to a murderer—that is, a scandal about which only the son speaks and against which the mother is powerless to defend herself—*Hamlet* eliminates all trace of female *choice*. Historically, this choice of husbands was in Mary's case founded on the huge characterological deficiencies of James's biological father. The play suppresses the mother's potency and will so that it may salvage the father's virtue.

Even though the worst features of Lord Darnley are resuscitated theatrically in Claudius, the stepfather, not in the image of the biological father where they belong; even though the play thus historically demonizes Bothwell through analogy as a drunken lecher who murders a righteous and legitimate king; even if Bothwell was something of a military hero and apparently cared far more for Mary than Darnley did—despite all of these translated character formations, neither the play nor Hamlet can fully prevent the seepage of contrary, suppressed signals from the past. As the furious, ugly, and profoundly unclear recitation of the Ghost suggests, the victimized father cannot play the martyr or even the noble father role without great strain. And while the Ghost, like the second quarto text as a whole, actively participates in the myth of the queen's culpable passivity, this fiction cannot convincingly authorize *all* of Hamlet's antifeminism. That is, Shakespeare's evacuation of female agency does not entirely turn back the onslaught of historical indicators; Hamlet himself must repeatedly block out the strong possibility that Gertrude, too, has made a *choice*, one which threatens to damage the pristine status of his suddenly anonymous father. "What iudgement," he asks his mother rhetorically while comparing pictures of King Hamlet and Claudius, "Would step from this to this?" (J3). Guilt slides: the queen must have *inertly* enabled the stepfather's iniquity and aggression, must not have used "iudgement." Hamlet at this moment can only misogynistically interpret the possibility of his mother's choice as the product of passive female delusion, not lust or "loue, for at your age / The heyday in the blood is tame" (J3). Yet the referential ambiguity of "this to this" underlines precisely the leveling of difference between father and stepfather that the prince cannot stand to admit may justify his mother's behavior. If there is not a great distance between "this" and "this"—not even so great as between "this" and "that"—the possibility arises that Gertrude's remarriage and her failure to mourn Hamlet's father are not perverse but rather *rational*. The further, all but unspeakable possibility is that the wrong "this" may actually be preferable. Indeed, for the Lennox clan, the bulky embarrassment of Mary's choice amounts to an erasure of Darnley and necessitates the memorial painting, in which the queen is, unsurprisingly, not represented.

But *Hamlet* contaminates, even as it reconfigures, the historical and fictional father's memorial: the suppressed history of James's vile sire has a defiant presence in the play. On one level, the queen's lack of volition may be seen to excuse retroactively some of Mary's darker deeds. Ultimately, however, the off-kilter parallel between Darnley and the elder Hamlet submerges the historical trace of Queen Mary's monarchical strength and pleasure, and instead catapults into memorial prominence only the sexual scandal of her inadequate mourning and sprightly remarriage. Hamlet, after swearing to remember the Ghost's commandment, exclaims, "O most pernicious woman," a good gauge of how perceived passivity excuses women from male judgment. The play's evocation of James's history vaporizes the image of Mary Queen of Scots as a potent sovereign and instead only augments her fame as the adulteress of the realm, whose outrageous behavior seemed constantly to hinder her son's access to power. But Mary is twice scapegoated then—for her foolish, o'erhasty marriage to Bothwell accidentally *enabled* James's ascent in that it led to her premature abdication. The mother's infidelity and downfall were, as it happened, preconditions of James's succession. In the theater, it is not until Gertrude falls that Hamlet can be king; not until the queen's unlamented demise does the dying prince pronounce Fortinbras.

The text's process of symbolic or displaced Mary-bashing becomes clearest during Hamlet's wild accusations against Gertrude in the closet scene. He admits that his butchering of Polonius is "a bloody deede, almost as bad, good mother / As kill a King, and marry with his brother" (J2v). The queen leaves the gross, baseless charge intact, undenied in Q2: "As kill a King" is her stunned reply, save for her following uncomprehending questions: "What haue I done, that thou dar'st wagge thy tongue / In noise so rude against me?" and "Ay me, what act?" The play stays cagey about the extent of Gertrude's complicity in the murder, as Hamlet levels nearly exactly the same charges against his mother as those which ended Mary's reign in 1567. The difference is that in *Hamlet*, awareness of the mother's infamy is entirely cocooned in the prince's mind, never to be dislodged nor revealed to anyone other than Gertrude and the audience—while the kingdom remains unaware of any hint of wrongdoing. Mary Queen of Scots was jettisoned by the nobility, friend and foe, but Gertrude never fields any opprobrium from anyone other than her son (and very indirectly, Ophelia: "How should I your true love know . . . ?"). So Q2 etches an intaglio of Mary with Gertrude's features: in one respect the not-to-be-dishonored mother of the king, with the evasive evidence about her guilt providing partial exoneration; in another respect the fountainhead of years of anti-Elizabeth plots and violence, the Catholic whore of Babylon ("O most pernicious woman").

The historical currents are exceedingly rough and hard to navigate here. As a Jacobean (post-Elizabethan) text, the second quarto discredits Queen Mary as a ruler through analogy with Gertrude, reducing female power solely to sexuality, pointedly segregating the son's nobility from the mother's taint. Yet mitigating this position is the fact that the queen's taint resides mainly in the son's mind and in her ambiguous role in preventing his access to kingship. It is true that Mary's Catholic and foreign status helped problematize James's claim to the English throne. But she was also specifically enabling in a way that the play does not permit Gertrude to be. What is more, Mary, like Darnley, was the unremembered past: James grew up, in effect, without her; and while she was nationally demonized, she may have been personally almost negligible.[38] James's first and second kingships were achieved only through the fact of female *absence* and ruin: through Mary's scandal and abdication, through Elizabeth's death.

The drama's neurotically oscillating treatment of female integrity bespeaks its strained relationship to the politics of its contexts.[39] The queen, like the stepfather, is on balance a negative figure. But Gertrude, an inscriptive complex of Marian and Elizabethan attributes, absorbs residual antifeminist energies that *ought* to have dissipated by the time of *Hamlet*. On the one hand, the testimony of none other than the demonized stepfather, James Hepburn, exculpates Mary. The murderous earl of Bothwell (whose marriage with the queen was annulled in 1570) fled Scotland in James's infancy, and he died abroad when the king was just twelve years old. But he supposedly made a full deathbed confession that exonerated the queen of Scots for any guilt in the Darnley murder plot. "Thereafter there was no more vengeance to exact, and for the rest of his life James remained convinced that his mother had not been involved in the initial murder."[40] Yet *Hamlet* confounds or ignores this testimony, and refuses to endorse the idea of the queen's innocence until the very end. This refusal makes Shakespeare's succession tragedy vaguely accusatory, but uncomfortably enough, the accusation applies to more than one queen. In 1601, a theatrical proclamation against a queen's integrity would sound raucously seditious; in 1603, in the post-Elizabethan play that I posit, it could seem *explanatory* of James's elusive political fortunes.

Hamlet's variations from the historical record protect patriarchy, Stuart family history, and male legitimacy from the possibility of arbitrary female choice and power. They also offer, more generally, a way to understand mythographic processes—the imaginary patchwork or the integument over the real. At best, literature positions itself asymptotically near the axes of history: it approaches those axes extremely closely at some points, but it always keeps an actual and theoretical distance. *Hamlet* and its prehistory's confusing parallels, accretions, crossings, and separations tempt a blanket statement of the historicist's creed: the play reproduces in moral and symbolic ambiguities and evasions several analogous historical complexities. The multiply articulated convergence between Hamlet, Claudius, and the Ghost complicate the neat categories of hero and villain that all historical and psychological mythologizing tries to construct. The consequences of such selective constructions can emerge in rhetorical strain. As stubbornly as Hamlet clings to the desire to differentiate his mother's supposedly malignant new husband from her unparagoned old, his own disordered language betrays the impracticability of the task:

> what deuill wast
> That thus hath cosund you at hodman blind;
> Eyes without feeling, feeling without sight,
> Eares without hands, or eyes, smelling sance all,
> Or but a sickly part of one true sence
> Could not so mope: o shame where is thy blush?
> (J3)

Eyes without feeling? Ears without hands or eyes! He sounds like Nick Bottom here, emerging from a discombobulated dream of his own potency and virtue; his discourse flies out of its frame of reason, inadvertently comic in its catalogue of Gertrude's misperceptions while ruthlessly exposing his own. But through Hamlet's operose attempts at differentiating father from stepfather, the play inspires a look back at the rivalry between Darnley and Bothwell. Since Mary risked so much, so rashly for Bothwell, we ought not to suppose that the earl was unmistakably inferior in charms or virtues to the legitimate, the initial husband. The odious Darnley was no sainted grace, no "forme indeede, / Where euery God did seeme to set his seale / To giue the world assurance of a man" (J2v). Darnley defies representation as Hyperion, as the

Ghost does; similarly, the unquestionably criminal Bothwell had his heroic attributes. The central historical pressure here—the father's iniquity, the stepfather's integrity—is up to Hamlet to misunderstand.
With his stubborn refusal to process the copious evidence in the
Ghost's narrative about his father's extensive flaws, Hamlet yields to
and conducts a passionate misreading of history. And in this misprision,
he also loses a chance to read his own predicament as (like James's)
something of a fortunate fall, politically speaking. The temporary triumph of the alleged villain creates a viaduct of power for the true heir.
But Hamlet is so reluctant to claim royal privilege that he seems almost
an imaginative reconstruction of the *infant* James, vulnerable and innocent—"I am set naked on your kingdom"—who obliviously suffered
what Hamlet must consciously endure and mend. In other respects,
Hamlet wishes to reside for as long as he can between the positions of
revolt and rule—to live in political adolescence. He misinterprets this
liminal posture as reluctance to commit violence, which we know is not
his problem; critics mistake the delay for high moral objection or cow-
ardice; but his inability to act may have more pressing historical than
psychological sources. James Stuart, while awaiting Elizabeth's death
and throne, had to downplay his own eagerness for the English kingship
and remain silent about, or at least inactive concerning, the succession
(although he could not, as we shall see, fully manage to do so); Hamlet
can take a more aggressive tack against a monarchy he never feels is
within range of his possessing, but his position is similar to James's in
1603. He is adjacent to royal prerogative and obstructed from it; as he
draws ever closer to kingship, he seems to broadcast a poisonous threat,
nearing death in the process and leaving bodies in his wake.

   Hamlet can be read as a fugue on James's two successions, on two
disparate historical moments. The chaotic prehistory of James's infant
kingship comprises the burden of the tragic Danish plot: a tale about the
impossibility of escape from the father's historical nightmare of murder,
adultery, and revenge, a nightmare further compounded by prolonged
subjection to, or inability to emerge from, a fixed perception of the
mother's shame. The second moment, configured nonspecifically across
the entire expanse of the 1604 quarto text, is James's second accession:
the botched progress of the king's arrival in England in the spring of
1603. This second story may provide the imagistic *substructure* of *Hamlet*'s plot, but it is a structure that undoes plot. The language and action
of contagion so infect the play that narrative coherence continually
breaks down. In the *relation* of the two Jacobean successions lies the

connection between Hamlet's story and that of England's new king. For like Hamlet, James's first entry into royal prerogative was an entry into a familial disaster and a revenge oath; his second accession was a movement into the threat of deadly contamination—the moral morass of Elsinore's court, the poisonous atmosphere of plaguy England. Hamlet, in his *royal* identity, contracts corruption: the contaminations of memory and desire, educed by the ghost of the past; the immersion in a pollution he must try to cleanse. For both Danish prince and Scottish king, mortal vulnerability comes into being at the moment of monarchical responsibility.

Shakespeare's textual origami—the creation of clefts, folds, new figures and depths from a flat material history—reconstructs an intricate image of Jacobean succession trouble. James's prechildhood induction into monarchical pressure takes new form in the shock of Hamlet's unwilled conscription to avenge a murder he knows too little about; and the Danish prince's many subsequent impediments to rule inscribe James's several barriers to English kingship, which culminated in the plague's impassable presence. The outbreak of 1603 displaced an authority that did not have a chance to arrive. All the same, Hamlet, unlike James, is not merely deflected or discouraged from kingship; he actively avoids for the longest time his own interest in it. He only assaults and momentarily assumes monarchy once he is dying—indeed, once he is sped ("I am dead, Horatio"). Thus we may suppose either that he has not desired kingship or that it is *all* he has desired, all along.

IV

In the Shakespearean theatrical consciousness, plague and the succession are intertwined through the operational dysfunctions of compromised, transitional authority. Shakespeare's early Jacobean opus displays diseased power that frequently behaves like the plague. This power is Macbeth, bestowing death madly and trying to murder the future; it is Duke Vincentio, sparing people unaccountably, irrespective of their morality or capacity for virtue; it is Timon, retreating arbitrarily to cast poisonous curses on Athens from outside the city walls, where plagues customarily began; it is Coriolanus, an anger raging unabated, without mercy. By these examples I mean to suggest that the subliminal and structural presence of plague in *Hamlet* is scarcely anomalous in Shakespeare's text.

Let us take the less obvious case of Vincentio. The often observed parallels between James's character and reign, and those of the Duke in *Measure for Measure*, should include both rulers' response to the presence of disease in their realms. In Vienna, contagion takes venereal and metaphoric form as a sexual license whose only putative cure is a proliferating legal repression. Angelo, the substitute ruler, is engaged to mend this disorder. But he almost immediately exposes himself as infected with what he has been installed to cure—desire—and his election by Vincentio comes quickly to seem increasingly arbitrary, even cruel, possibly deliberately incriminating. The Duke's reasons for choosing Angelo are unconvincingly or, alternatively, too lushly motivated. Does he wish to demolish or test the man's virtue, to get someone else to perform his political dirty work, to cure the corruption his own leniency has allowed, to play puppetmaster, or simply to dress up like a monk and take confession? In Vincentio's contradictory, multiple motives to abdicate we can discover an historical intervention that shapes, compels the plot. The play (circa 1604) extends from the circumstance of plague, which has as deep a foundational presence in Vienna as it does in Denmark, or in England. The Duke, for instance, is paranoid about crowds; King James's own tense entry into the mobbed and infected outskirts of London in 1603 might rationalize this feature of theatrical personality. More significant, Vincentio's conscious abandonment of his ruling position figures Shakespeare's resourceful transformation of Jacobean necessity into royal prerogative. The absolute need to abandon place in the presence of that terrible plague which still reigned when *Measure for Measure* was written becomes the stage absolutist's intentional (if confused) production of his own provisional, manipulative abdication. But the epidemic irony bleeds through: The Duke's fantastical plotting, and the arbitrary justice he imposes on his sick state, ultimately suggest that physical infections have political sources and are incurable either by tainted rulers *or* by the abandonment of rule. *Measure for Measure* pictures the infections of power, the contagions of which operate across potentates and regimes. The disease and James were not in any rational way equatable, but they may have been subliminally congruent when the epidemic hit so quickly after Queen Elizabeth's death and the Scottish succession. In fact, the Stuart reign not only began but also ended (in 1625) with especially grim outbreaks of the sickness. Not surprisingly, some Englishmen accused James of bringing down plague from the north.[41]

My brief hypothesis about the plaguy plot origins of *Measure for Measure* is meant to suggest the analogy of epidemic disease to history: it acts on Shakespearean texts as it acts on the culture at large. It repeatedly infiltrates, occupies, structures, and destabilizes meanings. In this respect, plague, like history, figures unpredictably but finally irresistibly; we know it is there, but we cannot always tell in what form, what phase, or what signification. Other important historical contexts for *Hamlet* will demonstrate this thesis further. The simple point is that many English and Scottish histories are arrayed in theatrical Denmark; the more difficult notion is that *Hamlet* absorbs these histories incontinently, to indiscriminate, often shifting and incoherent ends. Past or local contexts appear in the play like cloud formations: now a camel, now very like a whale, now merely the ceiling at Elsinore, the limit of the imaginative horizon. History exceeds the text's use or organization of it, extending beyond paraphrase—or cogency. I shall conclude my treatment of the play with further explorations of this idea. But first I would like to darken (intensify, and obscure) further traces of the past in the second quarto.[42]

It is time once again for that strange ghost Devereux, the earl of Essex, to put in an appearance; any talk about the Jacobean succession in England and its relationship to *Hamlet* ought to include a mention of his machinations. Essex took active part not only in James's project but also in elements of Hamlet's personality: in the madness, vacillation, and melancholy, in the subversive energy and cultural representativeness of the Danish prince. Similarities of character and behavior abound; at least one parallel between the fictional and historical figures throws Hamlet's political interests into relief. John Harington, Queen Elizabeth's "saucy godson," perceived that Essex, a former benefactor, suffered from severely frustrated desire:

> It restethe wythe me in opynion, that ambition thwarted in its career, dothe speedilie lead on to madness; herein I am strengthened by what I learne in my Lord of Essex, who shyftethe from sorrowe and repentaunce to rage and rebellion so suddenlie, as well provethe him devoide of goode reason or right mynde. . . . His speeches of the Queene becomethe no man who hathe *mens sana in corpore sano*.[43]

Hamlet's speeches of the queen are none too rational either, and Harington's thoughts about Essex illuminate Hamlet: they bolster the possibility that Hamlet's unrestrained fury at Gertrude, and much of his other madness besides, *is* explicitly thwarted ambition. Almost anything is easier than acknowledging political neuroses and exclusions. Like James, Essex suffered the sustained embarrassment of political frustration; unlike James, the earl reacted intemperately.

That both Essex *and* James may contribute to the figure of Hamlet was first suggested by Lillian Winstanley:

> At the period when *Hamlet* was written [circa 1600, according to Winstanley], the two great subjects of universal interest were the question of the Scottish succession and the fate of the Essex conspirators; moreover, these two subjects were so intimately connected that they formed but one in the popular mind and, therefore, in treating them as one, Shakespeare would simply be working to a unity already existing in the minds of his audience. The fate of Essex and the fate of James have been blent in one destiny.[44]

I am not sanguine about engaging in a critical practice that finds a single historical figure, even one so potent as Essex, in work after work of contemporary fiction—in *Troilus and Cressida*, in *Henry V*, in *Hamlet*. Still, as a cynosure of national interest, Essex could reasonably be supposed to exert an abiding pressure on the theatrical imagination. Winstanley's argument is smartly post-old-historicist, which is to say, it moves beyond the reflective hypothesis: she says, to her endless credit, "It would be, I think, unfair to say that Hamlet is the portrait of anyone" (176). But she does say, with some warrant and only a slightly disappointing breach of decorum, that "Hamlet is mainly James I, but there are certainly large elements in his character and story taken from Essex" (173). This idea has a certain luster because of its built-in alibi for the character's incoherence: Hamlet can be forgiven for not making sense because of his multiple origins in different historical subjectivities. But if this alibi seems a flimsy justification for inscriptive reading, the method has other advantages; it does, for instance, follow representational logic. Because we know that Devereux worked sedulously to secure the Scottish succession, which could have brought him and his faction, had he survived, to the greatest prominence in the new regime, the characterological alliance with James seems plausible. James and Essex were intertwined on the stage of history before they fused, however complexly, in the literary form of Hamlet. And James's pardoning of the Essex conspirators in his first official act as new king also seems suggestive, a kind of debt payment to the man he later called his martyr.[45]

But historically and figurally too, there are substantive divisions as

well as convergences between Devereux, James, and Hamlet. In the summer of 1599, Lord Mountjoy, of Essex's faction, felt it necessary to reassure James that the earl was not a *rival* for the succession to the English
throne but was rather trying to support and promote the Scottish
claim.[46] James, like many government officials in England and abroad,
became suspicious of Essex's soaring ambition, his busy self-aggrandizement—and thus even of his advocacy. When the earl was killed, James
grieved for him, and he held a long, brutal grudge against Sir Walter
Ralegh for his opposition to Devereux; but in light of Robert Cecil's
silky political stewardship after the Essex affair, James realized that he
had originally made a poor choice of English allies. Hamlet does in certain ways contain and combine the two historical figures of Essex and
James; the most interesting, perhaps, is his contradictory (specifically
Elizabethan) position as both heir apparent (or pretender) and active
threat to the monarchy. In the second quarto, Hamlet deflects his overt
desire for political place, but he never voluntarily removes himself from
the neighborhood of rule. The conflicting activities of the Danish prince
vis-à-vis the throne may reproduce two historical vectors of desire for
kingship, each in alternating unity and conflict. Essex, for all his dili-
gence on James's behalf, would not have been averse to recognition as
most potent, as kingmaker; at his trial for treason, however, he proclaimed, not wholly believably, "For the crown, I never affected it"
(McManaway, "Elizabeth, Essex, and James," 226). And while James
never hid his wish for the English crown, he had to tiptoe around this
desire very carefully, lest a subversive noise alarm his cousin Elizabeth,
as it had already alarmed other Englishmen who heard invasion rumors
from the north. In 1599, James announced to the Scottish parliament
that he "was not certain how soon he should have to use arms" to gain
the English crown; "but whenever it should be, he knew his right and
would venture crown and all for it."[47] He would have dared damnation,
but (unlike Essex) he fortunately did not. In Prince Hamlet, two mingled
and historically implicated relationships to monarchy are played out—
repeated, and exhausted.

Eventually revealed or constructed as an enemy to the state, Essex
lived but could not outlive the consequences of a sustained competition
with royalty. He became an insurgent, as both Elizabeth and James
feared: a threat to power from within, like Hamlet, like Claudius before
him—like plague. Hamlet performs some of Essex's ambitions and disruptions, and in the transfigured form of the prince, the earl is obliquely

granted (perhaps as another debt payment) a wished-for prerogative he never quite attained: the chance to pronounce and thereby apparently control the succession. Essex's image penetrates several representations in the play; as with *Troilus and Cressida*, some of the *Hamlet* doors unlock with the Essex skeleton key. But Essex is historically constrained to the Elizabethan era, and so he has limited usefulness in a Jacobean reading of *Hamlet*. Let us return to the play's involvement in the form and fate of James's early succession struggles and its mutations of Jacobean history.

After Polonius's murder, Claudius sends Hamlet off to die. The voyage to England is supposed to culminate in the prince's execution, but instead he manages, through fortune and fortitude, to escape, as he writes to Horatio:

> Ere wee were two daies old at Sea, a Pyrat of very warlike appointment gaue vs chase[;] finding ourselues too slow of saile, wee put on a compelled valour, and in the grapple I boorded them[;] on the instant they got cleere of our shyp, so I alone became theyr prisoner[;] they haue dealt with me like thieues of mercie, but they knew what they did, I am to doe a turne for them. (L2v).

Hamlet's boarding the pirate ship—the crucial interruption in the journey—brings him back to Denmark with far greater celerity than a smooth voyage to England would have allowed. Just as important, the events of the voyage bring him a momentary salvation, to which his ironic Christ references point (thieves of mercy who do know what they do). Along with its peculiarity as a plot device, the intervention of the pirate ship performs a weird, marvelous displacement of historical figuration. For in his exiled and marginalized phase, Hamlet briefly ceases to resemble James, or even Essex for that matter. Instead, he takes on the trappings of a different, an antithetical figure—that of the supposed villain of the historical piece. Roland M. Frye briefly chronicles the escape of Darnley's murderer:

> Bothwell first fled from the mainland to the outer islands, pursued by the Confederate Lords, whom he escaped by sailing to Scandinavia as the leader of a group of pirates. For several years he appears to have prospered ... but in June, 1573, he was imprisoned by the king of Denmark for crimes real and reputed. In solitary confinement ... he declined into insanity and died on April 4, 1578. Efforts to bring him back to justice in Scotland had all failed.[48]

Pursued by the Scottish authorities for the murder of Henry Stuart, Bothwell embraced criminality, put on a compelled valor as a pirate, sailed to Scandinavia and was eventually imprisoned and died a madman in . . . Denmark. This miniature history shimmers with enticements for a reading of *Hamlet*. What the theatrical pirate episode (delivered from a distance, by letter) begins to suggest is the extraordinary capaciousness of the play as a vessel for historical inscription. For the prince's temporary piracy, not to mention the threat of his madness and imprisonment, absorbs and transfigures yet another nodule of the past—not James's history, exactly, but the history that eluded him: that of Bothwell, the murdering stepfather. Certain restrictions (reversals, transformations) apply. For Hamlet, imprisonment and the threat of death come in the process of *leaving* Denmark; more important, Hamlet's pirate phase, unlike Bothwell's, is a success, actually enabling his safe and defiant return to the shores of his homeland. In marking the pirate episode as a positive point in Hamlet's biography, Shakespeare reroutes historical meaning; he analogically recuperates the Stuart failure of Bothwell's escape *as a necessary, lifesaving stage* in Hamlet's trip toward kingship. Absorption into and salvation by piracy allow Hamlet to appropriate the last stage of Bothwell's career, an apparently unabashed sequence of criminality coming to no good end. Ironic, then, that the pirate episode manages Hamlet's symbolic rebirth, a prelude to his arriving on the shore "naked." Noteworthy too is that the episode signals *political* rebirth; from having lain "worse than the mutines in the bilbo" (N1), he announces his presence to Claudius, who (as we have seen) takes it as a sign of Hamlet's probable royal leanings: "If he be now returned / As the King at his voyage. . . ."

Hamlet hereby incorporates and triumphs over a traumatic stage of James's history; as a consequence of his identification with James and his subsequent imitation of Bothwell's escape, one frustrating episode in the Stuart royal narrative is contained, revised, and put to redemptive use. Historically, James could not commit revenge against Bothwell even had he wanted to because of Denmark's refusal to extradite (and because, as noted, Bothwell died when James was twelve). Thus at one juncture of the text, Prince Hamlet can be construed as a fantasy Jacobean construction: he passes through Bothwell's elusive villainy as if it were a chrysalis. This history is not, however, entirely redemptive; indeed, we could interpret Hamlet's habitation of the Bothwell piracy as effectively contaminating. After all, the episode marks the avenger's most precipitous moral decline in the drama, for he adorns his escape from Claudius's plot with the gratuitous execution and attempted damnation of his former friends: he alters the commission so that Rosencrantz and Guildenstern will be killed "not shriving time allowed," their souls forfeit to his anger. The enabling past—the Bothwell legacy—also, inevitably, becomes corrupting; the Ghost of metahistory haunts every present occasion. Despite his characterological deformations, Hamlet completes a deficiency in James's biography, or at least knits up a frayed, unfinished end in the fabric of regicide and revenge that wrapped the king's young life. This reading gives historical warrant to a literary process: Hamlet must fully absorb wickedness to correct the depredations of the stepfather; he must become like Bothwell to secure a proper succession—one sanctioned by royal pronouncement and legitimized by the self-revelation of depraved, criminal monarchy.

Having capitalized on luck and wit, Hamlet survives the usurper's plot against him. Because Claudius's scheme is overcome through a chance event which Hamlet turns to mastery, we may be invited to read the exile portion of the plot as a sign that inherited history is actually conquerable and can lead to a new self and a new story. Nobody chooses his or her own past—we selectively summon and rephrase our histories so that we may continue living unappalled—but the question in all endeavor is how best to deal with one's inherited options. To make part of the Bothwell plot (the exile, escape, and foreign capture of the murderer) a stage in Hamlet's own successful return and temporary triumph *against* the murderer is briefly to sustain hope that time can be rejointed, the past rewritten. Hamlet's voyage into death ends in a brief reprieve by reason of chance, craft, courage (compelled and put on), brutality, deceptiveness—and not in the least by piracy. Carried back to Denmark on a "Pyrat," Hamlet seems a James figure miraculously borne by the shadow of Bothwell, James's familial bogeyman. The threatening Jacobean past merges with Hamlet's fictional present, receiving representation as serendipity in the gloomiest circumstance.

But Hamlet's and James's imaginary victory over history does not last. The play runs the reel of time backwards: Hamlet's return to the court marks the beginning of the end, foretelling not a birth but a being-borne-into: death. History's nightmare can seem to dissolve into new beginnings, but those look none too rosy. For the return to Denmark can mean only regicide, the last remaining corridor through which Hamlet may enter the monarchy.

V

GUYL: Good my Lord, voutsafe me a word with you.
HAM: Sir a whole historie.

There may be such a thing as a whole history—but *Hamlet* will neither vouchsafe it nor increase a reader's confidence in its possibility. Instead, the play insistently arrays history in fragments. One of the vital scraps of history that surely belongs in a reading of the play involves the idea of revenge as a political doctrine. The historical contexts of *Hamlet* suggest that vengeance can be understood as having a dynastic function, not just a theatrical, affective, or symbolic one. Revenge was actually put into play by James and his men near the end of Queen Elizabeth's reign as a *strategy*, a mode of acquiring the throne and securing the succession. James McManaway has pointed to the fascinating mechanism by which the Scottish king in 1599 deployed a public revenge oath to secure both his safety and his rights to the English crown. This bond among the Scots nobility restates and even quotes an earlier, better-known document: Queen Elizabeth's 1584 Bond of Association. The original bond was the Tudor privy council's crafty response to the seemingly endless Catholic plots against Queen Elizabeth's life, which were almost exclusively aimed at replacing her with Mary Stuart. The document enlisted its signers—presumably the Protestant aristocracy, but perhaps also ordinary, obedient citizens—to pledge "their lives, their fortunes, and their sacred honors . . . to pursue implacably anyone who might attempt to assassinate Elizabeth or remotely benefit by such an attempt" (McManaway, "Elizabeth, Essex, and James," 220). One obvious, not remote beneficiary of a successful attempt would have been James VI of Scotland, conspicuously next in the royal line after Mary, but one who, by the terms of the precautionary bond, "would be disabled in his claim" in the event of a successful plot against Queen Elizabeth. ⋅
But in 1599, McManaway shows, the Scots revived and reconfigured the Elizabethan bond, with considerable overlap in phrase and meaning and with a potent sense of irony, for the worthy twin expedients of James's bodily defense and insurance for his succession. John Chamberlain heard of the deed and dryly describes it thus: "The Scottish nobilitie find themseves greeved that theyre king is no more respected, and have lately made an association among themselves against all those that shall hinder his right and succession."[49] Their clever redaction transformed a document earlier meant to inhibit the Stuart claim to England's throne

into a bold assertion of Stuart royal prerogative. The headnote to the "generall band" explains it succinctly: "made by the good subiects of the kings Matie for the preseruation of his highnes person, & pursuit of his vndoubted right of the Crowne of England and Ireland" (McManaway, "Elizabeth, Essex, and James," 228). This simple sentence exemplifies the Bond's larger purpose: its remarkable, really seismic shift from an oath to defend the king of one sovereign nation into an oath to secure that king's right of succession to the throne of another:

> we solemnelye vowe and promise before the great god . . . to serve, and humblye obey our said soueraigne against . . . all sortes of persones . . . as shall attempte or vndertake by deede, counsell, or concealment, to any practise that may in any respect tend to the harme of his Maties most Royall person. . . . And by cause almightie god . . . hath established the vndoubted right of the Crownes of England & Ireland . . . next to his dear sister Elizabeth nowe Queene of England . . . we . . . solemnly swear and protest . . . to maintaine & defend our soueraigne in his vndoubted right and title to the crowne of England and Ireland against all other pretenders whatsoever, but like wise shall . . . bestowe our selves, our lives, children, . . . what sowuer else in the persuite there of against what soeuer person, that shall after the death of the Queene of England, hinder impugn or with stand his Maties heires or successors, in the peaceable getting and enioying, or possessing of the said crownes of England and Ireland. And shall by forceable meanes take the vttermost revenge vpon them . . . and neuer desist till we haue established our dearest soueraigne . . . in the Royall Kingdome . . . without preiudice All wayes to his Maties dearest sister Queene Elizabeth, during all the dayes of hir life tyme.
> (McManaway, "Elizabeth, Essex, and James," 229)

The great care taken in this document to exclude the possibility of James's ascending Elizabeth's throne in her lifetime may be intended to defuse the contemporary rumors about a Scottish invasion to secure that succession. Rhetorically, however, the Bond's promise to await the death of Elizabeth only underscores the clenched-fist claim James makes on her throne. But most significant for our purposes is the notion that Jacobean legitimacy comes not from an unequivocally established hereditary right, an argument the bond neglects to make; rather, legitimacy stems from its own forceful assertion and from the willingness, even the passionate dedication, to the extremities of revenge should that right be abridged. James's council in 1599 reversed a history of his exclusion and propelled his monarchy into yet another revenge oath—but this time it was an adult oath of choice, not a child's unknowing inheritance. The bond of 1599, unlike the one sworn for him by his grandparents against Bothwell, makes revenge the sign of monarchical privilege, and establishes revenge as a possible foundation upon which succession will be achieved. And in its way, of course, the document itself is a form of revenge—condign retribution, perhaps, against the person who had kept James so long from the apex of authority.

In Hamlet's case, revenge and the succession weirdly seem both interdependent *and* mutually exclusive. The throne will not be available until Claudius is forcibly removed from it; but any open act against the king would be treason. Thus, to open a position in the monarchy requires seditious violence that disqualifies Hamlet from candidacy, if it does not kill him first. As it happens, the play gives revenge ideological sanction by thrusting it upon Hamlet in a context and at a moment *apparently* not of his own choosing—but this illusion of nonchoice, of chance or random opportunity, is Hamlet's chosen vehicle throughout his descending orbit to the throne.[50] His impulsive act produces a seemingly fortuitous, inculpable vengeance. But before this point, the prince has begun to link (in a poorly articulated way) the two issues of revenge and election or succession as complementary motivations: "Dooes it not thinke thee stand me now vppon? / He that hath kild my King . . . / Pop't in betweene th'election and my hopes,/ . . . ist not perfect conscience?" James's Scottish bond of 1599 feeds into this crucial turn in *Hamlet*'s plot: it enunciates a move from oppression by the idea and doctrine of revenge (Elizabeth's 1584 Bond of Association) to active empowerment through that selfsame idea and doctrine. James's bond, like Elizabeth's before him, was intended to discourage attempts at regicide by announcing the inevitability of retribution; but at the same time, his open declaration of the right to succession may well have had a dampening effect upon the queen's already limp impulse to nominate a successor.

Hamlet, too, must negotiate a narrow walkway of disclosure and concealment, but as the *Gonzago* scene shows, he is unable to do so, revealing in the ambivalent figure of Lucianus a desire for both murder and rule. The conflation of the morally discredited motive of personal, murderous rage with the more ideologically justifiable interests of political privilege and familial oath retards Hamlet's expeditious move into kingship. So on the monarchy's behalf the final swordfight scene makes an astonishing turn: Hamlet completes the long-intended revenge, but for a different crime than the one that has fueled the energy of the rest of the play. *That* energy is clearly dissipating, heading elsewhere. When Laertes' accusation of Claudius unequivocally exposes the king's guilt, Hamlet leaps into regicidal action as a result of the rigged swordfight and his mother's death—*not* as a way of obtaining either the kingship or vengeance for his father. Hamlet becomes defender of exogamy, taunter of his perverted uncle: "Heare thou incestious damned Dane, / Drinke of this potion . . . / Follow my mother" (O1). The murder of Claudius deflects any royalist anxieties about a regicide undertaken *only for the sake of* a succession, and so it accords nicely with the threats and restraints of James's 1599 bond. Thus Hamlet, unlike Claudius before him, can kill a king without formally or lastingly becoming one. And James can become a king, as his bond promises, without having killed one, while nonetheless having used the revenge mechanism to ensure his right.

One other restriction on Hamlet's acts should draw our attention outward from the play to the environing history. Gertrude's swoon precedes and facilitates Hamlet's realization of his revenge. Theatrically, to establish the succession, however brief and abortive, the death of the queen must occur. This death, more than any other, enables the subsequent act of regicide and catalyzes Hamlet's last push toward what limited power he can obtain. In the morbid Gertrude, images of Mary and Elizabeth *as predecessor monarchs* again converge: power is drawn from a female source. The Jacobean Hamlet demonstrates that "power" should not be misunderstood as "office." Hamlet is no crowned king, but he can name the next one; conversely, during his plaguy ascension to the throne, James had the name of king without the full complement of privileges. But the power could not have been granted him without the death of queens.

It is safe to say that the more recent death, Elizabeth's, had been long awaited. Indeed, the Scottish king had endured a vexed relationship to his English cousin since at least the mid-1580s—from the time that James's mother lived under the threat of execution for plots real and imagined. Elizabeth carried out the execution in 1587 with her customary mixture of reluctance and plausible deniability. Just as she had been urged to eliminate the threat Mary posed, James was pressured to respond to the outrage of his mother's death; he was challenged, in fact, to take vengeance on England for the murder of the Scots queen.[51] After Mary's execution, the possibility lingered that James might well carry a grudge against Elizabeth, even to the point of forming a potentially disastrous alliance with Spain against England.[52] The fears never panned out, but Elizabeth and James maintained a delicately antagonistic relationship throughout the 1590s; she took the role of nettled instructor and defender of all things Protestant, while her student-cousin had to remain vaguely apologetic about his monarchical deficiencies and his tolerance of Catholics. Even when, late in the century, James's English succession began to look more and more likely, he came close to ruining his chances by backing the increasingly antiauthoritarian earl of Essex. This relationship flirted with disaster when James seriously considered Essex's plea to invade England to save the earl and the nation. Such an act would have marked James as more an enemy of the state than its savior, one who "would attempt to gather fruit before it is ripe."[53] Essex wanted James to strong-arm his enemies at court—to take revenge on the nation's slighting of the Scots king and (closer to the mark) on the treacherous Cecilian faction.

The more we see of politically motivated acts of revenge in history, the less intelligibly revenge functions as a measurable quantity, a rational object of inquiry. On one side, through the Scottish Bond of Association, the possibility of group vengeance may have helped authorize and thus secure a new king for England. But alternatively, any aggressive Jacobean act of revenge against England would have demolished what prudent delay facilitated. James's succession was the fruit, in a real sense, that he did *not* attempt to gather before it was ripe—the fruit of not having avenged his mother's death when he might have, of not having militarily, at Essex's request, jumped the gun for love or honor. In the literary space, retribution against the king (which the play takes great pains to disguise as revenge) clears a path for a new king as well— but it is not the king we should be pleased to have. The cynical replacement figure Fortinbras, previously an enemy to Denmark, achieves the monarchy by capitalizing on Hamlet's belated actions against Claudius. (It is this belatedness that ensures Hamlet's *failure* to ascend and possess the throne.) Because Hamlet's flawed, unpremeditated vengeance is taken virtually posthumously, it seals and stamps his last act as tragic. Revenge is good, revenge is not good; it briefly gratifies, and permanently demolishes.

The complications proliferate. James's own revenge document, the second Bond of Association, suggests that the specter of retribution can protect a monarch whose revenge oath amounts to a national vote of confidence; thus can an odd sort of legitimacy be compelled through a promise of retaliatory violence. The bond never amounted to much, as far as I know, but it never had to, and so it did its work: it sufficiently proclaimed support for James as the only *enforceable* candidate for the English crown. It was a calculated threat. At the same time, James's right to succeed to the throne depended, conspicuously if not entirely, on the "dying voice" of the queen, and not on revenge at all. (Perhaps this right depended merely on the *fiction* of her approving vote; the succession actually hung upon Robert Cecil's craft and efficacy. We cannot know what, if anything, the queen expressed when she lay dying; but Cecil and historians after him deemed significant the story of the explicit nomination of James.) It is curious that Hamlet, so complexly Jacobean all along, achieves *Elizabeth's* prerogative in his final moments alive; the rights of his monarchy become last rites, as he performs the naming of kingship in the presence of death. At once he seems fractionally James-like again, caricaturing the king's 1603 arrival into death-surrounded rule: the coroner is the crowner.[54] Much of Hamlet's experience throughout the play has involved being shut out of kingship. His entry into power mimics James's: it comes too late, and it smells of mortality. The long-postponed revenge to which both figures were consigned shows at the last as an attenuated thing: it's hard to know, with all the bodies strewn everywhere, what the fuss was about.

In the first quarto, published in 1603, Hamlet never does establish the succession or voice the best candidate. Indeed, he has no inkling, prophecy, or preference concerning Fortinbras's takeover. In other words, until 1603, he and Shakespeare remain unimplicated in the politics of the arriving regime. But in the second quarto, Hamlet helps legitimize a succession that names the son of a former enemy of state: symbolically, James himself, the invading son from the north, has been elected. The later text thereby offers an exquisitely complicated Jacobean fantasy: James, although having been excluded for so long, finally metaphorically establishes *himself* in his own succession after the queen's death and after having guiltlessly rid himself of the ancestral obligations of revenge. Hamlet naming Fortinbras is a translated version of James naming James.

The historical identifications here may seem to veer toward arithmetical parody, requiring something akin to a transitive law of inscriptive relevance: "If James equals Hamlet and Hamlet equals Fortinbras, then James equals Hamlet plus the sum of characters A and B such that . . ." Any reasonable critical investigation would seek to avoid such parodic potential. Yet, as *Troilus and Cressida* suggests, Shakespearean representations of high-level politics repeatedly deploy multiple vessels for the portrayal of single, immensely complicated historical subjects, and these vessels are often, and justly so within the logic of the plot, *antithetical* forces, or complementary versions of opposing internalities. James, no less than Essex, can be figured as a conflictual entity whose divisions unify representationally in unpredictable convergences—such as in the odd respect Hamlet and Fortinbras accord one another. Thus the literary text can *avoid* parody, can reproduce the historical person not as a caricature but as an ethically complex, ideologically torn personage, at once more and less attractive than he or she appears in either official or underground historical discourse. At the same time, however, this theatrical reconstitution of subjectivity tends potentially toward the uncomfortably schematic; as arrayed in *Troilus and Cressida*, for instance, the single subject Essex splits neatly into two tight, corollary personae, each of which rather coldly metonymizes one version of Devereux's psychic discords. But I hope to have shown by now that Shakespeare's inscriptive procedure varies from play to play; it even varies substantially within individual texts. The immense range of *Hamlet*'s major historical referentialities—the second quarto's subliminal enactment of epidemic disease, its more overt but not more simplistic delineation of Jacobean history—defies pure schematization. And just as the play reenacts without sanitizing Stuart family scandal and succession taint, so does it offer only partial settlements and further confusions in the ideology of revenge. By evoking James through the marginally successful, accidental avenger Hamlet and the politically opportunistic, nonavenging, best-remaining-candidate Fortinbras, the play insolubly problematizes the meaning of the Jacobean succession and the discourse of revenge that helped, however indirectly, to secure it.

As the history of *Hamlet* criticism demonstrates, revenge cannot cohere as *both* a dramatic and an historical fact. The idea can be rationalized as a cathartic theatrical principle—villains should be punished by wronged avengers who ought to prevail—but that position stands against both a dominant cultural sentiment (the Christian prohibition that "God will repay") and the recent events of succession politics. Good doctrine does not generally support or produce good theater. Conversely, revenge may be a functional part of the pragmatic state intelligence (we shall avenge the death of our future sovereign), but such a corporate plot falls flat in the theater, which tends to privilege and anatomize individual agon.[55] From any angle, however, the problematic topic is huge, overdetermined. Revenge's historical polysemy is magnified by its literary complications. No single political valence, no moral or religious argument about what "Shakespeare's audience would have felt" (always a desperate interpretive gambit), can possibly unify the conflicted subject of revenge in the play, just as no interpretation can satisfactorily and completely respond to the politics of *Hamlet*'s and Hamlet's last act. For instance, it does us no good to think that in some Calvinist political theory, citizens had the duty, the perfect conscience, to take vengeful action against tyrants when Hamlet *himself* displays so many features of the tyrant. Is this to suggest that Hamlet ought to commit suicide? On the other hand, however, could the prince really suffer meekly throughout the play, waiting for falling sparrows, while Shakespeare's company sold no tickets? The play is trapped in the interstices of political, moral, and theatrical imperatives. The audience is blocked, finally and frustratingly, from responding to the issue of vengeance in an unconflicted way.

The conditions under which the prince finally secures his tantalizing objects of desire—revenge, the throne—are precisely conditions which preclude any conceivable gratification in the event: Hamlet himself is dying and can inherit nothing except the (superficially considerable but actually supererogatory) power to control the election, to name Fortinbras. By the beginning of the swordfight, Hamlet has, unbelievably, forgotten about the revenge plot of the play; by the end, that plot has become extraneous. Revenge occurs as the result of chance, in the midst of a scuffle. Hamlet's acts have long since become scattershot, finally unintelligible in terms of the traditional vengeance story that has meant so much to him. Killing the king becomes merely another movement of sword and cup in a frenzy of stage business. What is more, once Claudius's crimes have been revealed (but not, significantly enough, by Hamlet), the king does not have much of a career left. So an audience is robbed of even the perplexed pleasure of a dramatic climax to Hamlet's bloody and vengeful premeditations. The other reward that has been promised, Hamlet's assumption of authority, also vanishes. The investiture of Fortinbras with Hamlet's voice may give the cherished illusion of monarchical power to the moribund prince, but even in elected kingships, might makes right, and the entry of Norway's prince into the now defenseless, depopulated Danish court makes it clear that the voice vote was a gratuity, a self-flattering dream or at best (as Hamlet says) a prophecy. What Hamlet's political influence really amounts to is a derisive recycling of history that dismantles all of the previous real-estate gains of his father. So revenge's final irony is that the Ghost's fiat ultimately sacrifices the entire kingdom to the national enemy. And we must not forget that young Fortinbras's own *deflection* from revenge by his supposedly impotent uncle has essentially guaranteed the restitution of his ancestral properties, his tenebrous rights of memory to all of Denmark, without his having to fire a shot in anger, only in triumph—the play's final sounds. Fortinbras's determination *not* to attack the state, not to actively avenge his father's defeat, has brought him a far deeper, more unconventional revenge: the gratification of the winner. He has gained a much more extensive empire than the *lex talionis* could have ensured.

So where can we stand in relation to the question of vengeance? We cannot orient ourselves to it in any one way, because it is such a skittery signifier, a political, intellectual, and moral will-o'-the-wisp. Revenge is obviously justified and gratifying in rare cases, a cynical expedient in many, finally stupid and self-defeating in most; but it is utterly necessary to the dramatic structure, however deformed and postponed, of this tragedy. Vengeance cannot be theorized completely and coherently as *both* a philosophical and a literary phenomenon, especially when that theory bounces off of historical reference. In the last years of Elizabeth's rule, and in the brisk activity surrounding the succession of James, "revenge" was a presence (as it was in James's reign) of intense but finally indeterminate importance.[56] In forebearing from avenging his mother's death, James enabled his own succession; but by reconfiguring the Bond of Association, he subscribed to a national promise of vengeance, thus helping to clear a path to that succession. The play and its historical inscriptions orbit the revenge question erratically at best, fluctuating weirdly within the mysterious apogee and perigee of choice and chance; in *Hamlet*, vengeance finally shows as an ambivalent and, again, indeterminate accident. Because retributive violence, regnant at the end of the play, passes from human will into happenstance, which some call providence, it cannot be judged as an intention. Thus, Shakespeare can dramatistically both bless and criticize revenge without embracing or being held responsible for its bloodthirsty and globally destructive doctrine.

Literature may record a fissure of ambivalence or confusion where a correlative incoherence exists in history, and to ask of *Hamlet* something that Tudor-Stuart culture cannot provide—a clear valence to revenge—is to ask an unanswerable question. We should instead ask, in our final phase of analyzing *Hamlet*'s historical conditions, how revenge's semantic irreconcilability functions in a play that seems to forget the issue entirely by the end. I believe that the question of vengeance is simply the most renowned conundrum in a text whose every aspect points in multiple directions. A pocket of incoherence in itself, revenge also spreads (like compost on weeds) a chaos of contradictory cultural signifiers. It functions as an irony machine.

One of the more peculiar of revenge's produced ironies is that, as I have suggested, Fortinbras resembles in his nonavenging, unprotested succession no one so much as King James. The similarity produces further foreboding about the nature of both the Scottish and the Norwegian successions: the man with some "rights of memory" comes to preside over a court of the dead. If both Fortinbras and Hamlet represent possibilities of Jacobean inscription, the play's ambivalence about succession shades into doomsaying. The most positive prognosis the play allows for Denmark is that the state's recovery from Hamlet's actions will come at great cost. That cost is Fortinbras, who eerily evokes in his memorial claim to the throne an image of invasion-turned-legitimate succession; of plague-become-cure. As the play's most cynical flourish on the whole topic of succession, the triumph of Fortinbras cannot help but negatively color James's inheritance, throwing shadows on the son of England's enemy. Something goes badly wrong not only with plot at the end of *Hamlet*, in that the entire revenge theme becomes a weak afterthought, but also with the connections between the text and its historical referents. One of these referents, the cultural upheaval produced by the plague, achieves dramaturgic, eidetic prominence at the moment of Fortinbras's glory, as bodies lie scattered in a tableau of sudden, caught catastrophe. But the phenomenon of pest, like the problematic of revenge, calls forth more questions of identification and value than it answers. The complex figuration of plague in *Hamlet* articulates the palsied plot of cultural conditions circa 1603, when James's long-awaited succession resulted not in the serene occupancy of the throne but rather in his mortifying flight from it. James could not prevent the burgeoning of fatal disease on his accession any more than Hamlet can finally prevent the entry of a strong-arming conqueror. But Hamlet does not merely prophesy Fortinbras; he sanctions and virtually conjures him, laying waste to the state in a way that even plague could not. Hamlet and Fortinbras together shut down the whole Danish dynastic line.[57] The problem of inscription becomes pressing at this point; we witness not only a succession but a demolition. And James is the figure in the carpet, the lurking, still unclear image of succession and destruction.

VI

This jigsaw of history and theater might usefully be reassembled in the frame of plague. Epidemic illness corrupts and compromises not only the political but also the aesthetic process. Because contagion by definition erases boundaries, it produces multiple likenesses; in the context of the sickness, every threat to stability becomes alarmingly similar, a disease of the state. Fortinbras and Hamlet fall into a historical pool of resemblance. They enter a similarity with the physical and psychological operations and effects of pestilence, miming its depredations upon culture.

But while it seems reasonable enough to suppose that one or two fictional personages represent or evoke, in part or in whole, an historical figure, it must ring false to argue that a character or even a cast of characters can function as simulacra for epidemic disease—a *transhistorical* force. Interpretive ethics should harness the impulse to map such an intensely complicated, formidable presence as the plague onto dramatic characters, no matter how complex they are. For while Hamlet's language partakes of the marvelous, infused with the amperage of a transcendental, murderous energy, he remains a figure of a man, finally subject in his world to the fragility of the flesh. Despite the strong hint that he linguistically surpasses his own physical limitations—three times he states his death as a fact ("I am dead *Horatio* . . . *Horatio* I am dead . . . I die *Horatio*" [O1–O1v]), yet each time he survives his own sentence and continues to speak—he does expire at last. His mortality casts doubt on his ability to represent an essentially transcendent, historically unbound disaster. Likewise, his mighty opposite Claudius, while certainly capable of wickedness, never passes much beyond the human motivations "for which I did the murther; / My Crowne, mine owne ambition, and my Queene" (J1). Finally, Fortinbras, king of the dead, lacks either Hamlet's pestilent inhumanity or the disease's harsh motivelessness; he is middle management, not an obvious bearer of supernatural destruction.

There is of course a credible, inhuman inscription of the disease in the play: the Ghost. The image of King Hamlet can be regarded as the founding infestation; it hexes the language and health of the state. The Ghost certainly emblematizes plague's key attributes: a disembodied, corruptive energy, the pivotal effect of which is to set death in motion and to overthrow a king. Hamlet himself tells us that when the Ghost first appears—in "the very witching time of night"—is also when "hell it selfe breakes out / Contagion to this world" (H4v). But the surest analogy between the Ghost and the plague lies in the fact that both are recurrent phenomena. The idea of "haunting" now used mostly in reference to poltergeists and other spooks is based etymologically not so much on occupation as on repetition, on habitual action or location.[58] And "to haunt" in one Renaissance usage referred to "unseen or immaterial visitants" *including* disease, such hauntings being especially "causes of distraction or trouble" (*OED*, "haunt," s.v. 5.a). This sense

of haunting links Hamlet's diseased distractions to plague's unique character in the Renaissance as a *common* supernatural event. When James's
entourage was being followed by (and, seemingly, endlessly producing)
the disease, Thomas Edmonds wrote that "the Court hath been so continually haunted with the sickness . . . as we are forced to remove from
place to place."[59] For all the catastrophic alteration signified by plagues,
they more frighteningly meant *recursion*: the same death was replayed
on a national scale, the same books of cures were translated and reprinted, the same laws against vagrancy and vagabondage were resurrected, and terribly familiar demographics prevailed. The plague was an
episodic crisis of the past now present: a crisis of history's return.

A ghost *always* represents and ushers in historical crises. This Ghost's
many (indirect) victims signify that a submission to the imperatives of
the past can demolish entire cultures as well as individuals. However,
King Hamlet's haunting is particular, not general: the spirit pours its
worst poison directly into the son. The myriad relationships of sickness
to history are conducted through Hamlet, not the Ghost. By adopting
the father's infective mode and transmitting the ancestor's disease,
Hamlet seizes what the present time has denied him: he seizes power, if
only the terminal power to undo the present. Ironically, when he attempts to put his power into use at last, he calls forth as the successor to
the throne a *past* name, the name of the father's vanquished enemy.
Burdens of history convect in Hamlet's character, and he always makes
of these pressures something contagious and destructive. The effect of
the Ghost on Hamlet is, in a like but tortuous way, replayed through the
sphere of inscription, in the effect of history on the text of the second
quarto. Temporal borders rupture; the imaginative plague that is the
past overtakes the theatrical present, absorbs and disperses Jacobean
history. The defeated elder Bothwell is recalled in redemptive piracy;
Darnley dies again and returns newly disfigured, seeking vengeance;
Mary reappears as the target of Hamlet's most misogynistic imaginary
accusations. And with this reemergence of Stuart history, present identifications grow strange. Claudius is unaccountably like James, insofar
as both are victims of subversive diseases; Fortinbras, opportunistic infection that he is, also figures the new king; and Hamlet throughout
forms homologies and displacements among several Tudor and Stuart
personages and forces, including Essex (in his advocacy of and danger
to the succession), Elizabeth (through his dying voice), and the much-
troubled James.

One more example will suffice to sketch the uprooted, fragmentary

historiography of the play and suggest the plaguy destruction of categories in which *Hamlet*'s histories engage. As a kind of coda to the Bothwell legacy, another, identically named nemesis pestered King James in
his maturity. Mary's second husband was James Hepburn, fourth earl of
Bothwell; his nephew was Francis Stewart-Hepburn, fifth earl of Bothwell, who became one of James's most dangerous enemies. Just as Fortinbras junior returns at the end of *Hamlet* to visit (or perhaps redeem)
the sins of the fathers upon the nation of the son, so the second Bothwell
returned, with the name of the past, to haunt King James. The complex
source of the younger Bothwell's hostility was a mixture of personal
ambition, religious outrage at James's conciliatory stance toward rebel
Catholic lords, and fiscal fury at the king's appropriation, throughout
the early 1590s, of many of the nobility's lands and powers. The short
version of the story is that Bothwell fought back, inflicting several out-
rages upon the dignity and person of James with minimal royal retribution; finally, in 1593, he apprehended and detained James under a brief
house arrest. The king managed to escape, eventually arresting the
younger Bothwell in turn and finally working the exile of his enemy—
but not before young Stewart-Hepburn had driven a wedge between
James and Elizabeth.[60] The queen objected to her cousin's continued
leniency to, and inaction concerning, the rebel lord; James for his part
was furious that Elizabeth repeatedly refused to apprehend his energetic
young enemy.

Looking to this complicated history, Lillian Winstanley has excavated another wing in the subterranean archive of *Hamlet*'s representational processes:

> An excellent drama can . . . be made by combining in one the parts played by
> the two Bothwells. There is nothing difficult in such a conception: the two
> belonged to the same family, they were uncle and nephew, they held the same
> title. . . . [E]ven modern Scottish historians have remarked that the younger
> Bothwell seemed like a reincarnation of the elder.
>   The device of putting the two in one is quite simple and obvious . . . : the
> crimes committed by Claudius are the crimes of the elder Bothwell which are
> far more striking and dramatic than the crimes of the younger Bothwell; but
> the relation of Hamlet to Claudius is the relation of James to the younger
> Bothwell. Why not?[61]

Here is why not: because to be so admirably tidy about the conduct of
history in this drama is assuredly to be wrong—although Winstanley is
not, I think, on the wrong track. Her favorite combination-inscription
formula opens up further interpretive possibilities for, but also disjunc-

tions between, the text and the Jacobean story. Added bits of information seriously compromise her historical identifications—such as, for
example, James's conviction that the younger Bothwell was dabbling in
witchcraft. The king's paranoia about the occult was keen after he returned from his wedding trip to Denmark in 1590, where, as Christina
Larner notes, "Witch-hunting was endemic. . . . [James] is likely to have
been impressed by the fact that the learned and important in that country took the terrors and menace of witchcraft seriously."[62] The intense
interest he took in the subject was, as Larner makes clear, an interest in
treason; the two topics were necessarily enmeshed in his mind. He determined to implicate the younger Bothwell in conspiratorial witchery as a
way to demonize, exorcise, and apprehend (seize, understand) him.
Winstanley does not discuss the possible ramifications of the younger
Bothwell's suspected sorcery; once the question of the paranormal is
brought into the discussion of *Hamlet*, historical identifications once
again become confoundingly sloppy. True, Claudius is referred to as
"that incestuous, that adulterate beast, / With witchcraft of his wits"
(D3). So far, so good: the younger Bothwell might thus be said to help
constitute the figure of Claudius. But it is Hamlet who speaks with the
Ghost and who announces, after *Gonzago*, that "Tis now the very
witching time of night." If there is converse with the supernatural, if
there is magical treason staged by the play, Hamlet performs it.

It is not my intent to fault Winstanley's critical approach, because I
am obviously much in its debt; I only question its simplifications. The
problem with reading historical inscription in *Hamlet* is that end points
to identification are elusive; as soon as the reader finds a secure historical purchase, just one more fact or a differently perceived resemblance
causes a landslide of semantic slippage. What seems extraordinarily suggestive but unresolvable in the colloquy between the drama and its
Jacobean-Bothwellian connections is the perplexing chiasm between the
uncle-nephew relationship in history—the Team Bothwell as Jacobean
nemesis—and the same relation, also converging on a unity, between
Hamlet and Claudius in the text. What spirograph is traced here? We
must abandon the notion of single or dual historical correspondence in
favor of a multidimensional constellation of references: the two Bothwells variously confounded James, who has been victimized like Hamlet, who seditiously hounds the king, who in turn is like the two Bothwells in both his villainy and frustrating power to evade punishment.
Uncle and nephew of the past, the criminal, witchy, treasonous (but not
unquestionably wicked) Bothwells, and uncle/nephew of the textual pre-

sent, Claudius and Hamlet, diverge structurally, but at key points they are disturbingly similar in the threat they pose to political order.

If the writing-in of the past in *Hamlet* has a gnomic point, it is that theater can reconstitute history without reducing or caricaturing it. But can the text represent its contexts coherently? Can it construct, out of the widely signifying past, a moment of meaning and resolve? The play displays, reanimates, but does *not* cleanly anatomize or limit historical energies that tend toward the entropic; the writing-in yields a hermeneutic opening out. Contentious participants in culture, over time, resemble one another; disordering influences are analogized with infection; notions of cause, justification, ideological difference slip away. In *Hamlet*, layers of similitude among characters break down categorical boundaries between them, foisting interpretive uncertainty not only upon an audience, but also upon the history glancingly represented. Shakespeare's alarming convergences of Hamlet and Claudius, Hamlet and Fortinbras, Hamlet and any other producers of discord call forth an unwelcome contagion between categories that most audiences (and certainly the characters themselves) wish to keep separate: uncle/father, winner/loser, ruler/subject, hero/villain, present/past, structure/chaos. Neat layers of significance blend into one another, as when the Bothwell earls receive theatrical life as an antagonistic but convergent division (Hamlet/Claudius), not a unity, as Winstanley would have it. Determination of historical codes or references in the play must be provisional: Hamlet only haltingly, intermittently represents the put-upon and succession-starved King James; and it seems that every twist in the plot introduces another possibility for the aesthetic return of *some* aspect of the new king's past. For instance, I have placed the intrusion of young Bothwell into James's life in the same referential frame as the intrusion of young Fortinbras into Denmark. The return of Fortinbras figures an historical rerun of precisely the sort that Francis Stewart-Hepburn must have seemed: the frights of memory. Yet this inscription juggles with us. For Fortinbras as a type of Young Bothwell coexists with Fortinbras as James, the northern ruler and potential invader feared by some Englishmen. If we take the possible reverberations of history seriously here, then the self becomes its demonic other as James and young Bothwell funnel into the figure of Fortinbras. A fractured mirage of Jacobean images begins to assemble. Just like a dream in which the dreamer plays every role and suffers each character's triumphs and handicaps, *Hamlet* sutures intimate scraps of James's history into a patchwork body of personal figurations that are also topical, *cultural* figurations—because when the dreamer is the king, his portents are national. If the figure of James lends some conceptual unity to the baffling historiographical imbrications and discontinuities in *Hamlet*, the play, as a displaced dream of someone else's anxieties, still cannot deploy those inscriptions in an entirely rational, unified manner. History becomes random Jacobean anthology in the text. Unlike the operative mimetic coherence of contemporary contexts in *Troilus and Cressida*, Denmark's referential fragments are dysfunctional *as* representations: their sheer multiplicity, their dubious genealogy, makes them poorly matched pieces, yoked by theatrical violence in a plot whose dream logic never quite gels.

Hamlet establishes the endless complexity of persons in history, and this establishment depends on the play's refusal, or rather inability, to schematize persons and history, to isolate a group of histories and distinguish among them. In this incompetence lies a vast disorganizing potential. Stuffed with orts out of joint from the Jacobean past, the second quarto of *Hamlet* absorbs immense cultural and historical incoherence without completely digesting it.

There are two ways to take the drama's internalization and decomposition of its contexts. The first is to assign full aesthetic intentionality to the author and the text: to say that Shakespeare has a conscious mimetic program which produces the cracked histories I have traced. If this program is intentional, however, it is also a theatrical failure: it results in huge disruptions in plot and psychology that have long bothered critics of *Hamlet*. These critics have labored for centuries under the despotism of an assumption that the play makes sense. One would have to conclude from the contextual reading that the text is disturbed by its own mimetic process, its inscriptional procedure, a procedure it cannot manage given the range and variety of materials enfolded in the stories of James, the succession, and the bubonic plague.

But another way to read the presence of history in the text would take the plague as a model, not merely an example, of historical intervention. King Hamlet's demise inevitably evokes memories of the Darnley murder, and creates an aperture for history to enter the text; from that point, "history" cannot be kept out, and its effects as well as its boundaries spread. It becomes an infectious pressure on and a pollutant in the interpretive and mimetic function. Here is the problem: once we see the foundation of the plot as materially derived from historical fact—the Darnley murder, say, or James's ongoing problems with the Bothwells—the drama cannot easily be read except through the filter of that controlling story; that story becomes the text's touchstone, its stable meaning. This hermeneutic trap is the accidental but necessary consequence of the work's having admitted *any* clear and pivotal topicality into the theater. A piece of history that contributes, for instance, a crucial plot twist, a primary image cluster, or the likeness of a major character also dangles a lure for readers—a promise of accessibility. More often than not, Shakespeare makes good on this promise; only rarely do his histories lead nowhere. His plays are *typically* choosy repositories of reference. But when the social and cultural fields that surround the text infiltrate it apparently at random, the structures on which literary form traditionally depends can break down. Any art must deploy its cultural referentiality with care if it hopes to arrange the scatterings of the past and present; if, that is, it hopes to derive sense from temporality. A text which draws promiscuously on or helplessly absorbs the contradictions and multiplicities of history will suffer hermeneutic disruptions, nonproductive polysemy, dysfunctional theatrics. In *Hamlet*, history becomes an unwholesome influence that the text can neither resist nor contain.

Plague, as a model of the aesthetic process of historical intervention in *Hamlet*, replaces sociological or psychological sense with contagion patterns that gesture toward but frustrate design. The disease's multiple manifestations and interventions rationalize (if anything can) the second quarto's radically discontinuous acts of referentiality, in which several characters variously configure a single historical fact, or one character absorbs osmotically but fractionally several historical features, identities, or relations. But even a flexible theoretical understanding of the text's interplay with disease has limited usefulness. Plague, after all, is not historically an effete structure or an aesthetic object; it is a thuggish fact, an agonizing assault on the body. Its torque and sudden danger exceed stability; it cannot be fully controlled or transformed into something the imagination can stand and use. When Shakespeare's artistic tools are sharp, the sickness in Denmark appears to metaphorize a dynamic, contagious process of epistemological, moral, and social dissolution. But the play cannot sustain a single coherent image of the disease. A culture contains but is also described by its illnesses; just so, the play is tainted by the pathological environment it describes.

I cannot say with certainty that the second quarto of 1604 represents a postaccession and postplague revision or therefore that the play definitively acknowledges the recent national horror. Its precise dates of composition, redaction, and performance will remain elusive. No matter. What is clear is that *Hamlet* draws on the interregnum imagination, one which included the presence of sickness. The play stages a threat to monarchy from an antithetical energy; it pictures a cavern where force falls and tosses about. Like the second tetralogy, *Hamlet* considers the transitional, contingent nature of monarchy and the corkscrew trajectories of an ambition that has been blocked from its plotted ascent. The text's primary subliminal energy—the frustrated desire for political success, for succession—charges a place that has been blasted from within by a mysterious corruption.

The presence of James's past in the text ought to dictate certain plots and organize certain theatrical experiences, but it actually undoes and disorganizes plot and experience: partly because it was a past that was never satisfactorily resolved (the murderer of the father escaped, the murderer's nephew returned like a ghost to pester James); partly because the history itself was contradictory (the stepfather in many ways was at least morally comparable to the reprobate father); and partly because James was haunted by tragedy in his succession. The second quarto, rattled by its indiscriminate absorption of the king's troubling and suspended past, has made itself vulnerably subject to *too many* histories. The play compounds history's unreadability by linking James and Hamlet, the dramatis personae and the contexts of the drama, in a unity of intellectual misgiving; *Hamlet* imitates the plague's style of category disturbance by implicitly engaging dramatic subjectivity in acts of contagion so that everything means everything. Its sometimes deliberate, often slurred construal of the past results in overdeterminations that take their toll on the interpretive potential, the knowability, of the play.[63] No chart of historical figures, currents, or quadrants can stabilize this work.

The text further blocks interpretive maneuvers by depicting not only national histories but also minutely personal connections to the past, and not all of these are James's connections. As everyone knows, the very name "Hamlet" echoes that of Shakespeare's son Hamnet, who was buried in 1596. The boy was, suggestively enough, a twin—his sister, Judith, survived. In Shakespeare's theatrical transformation of tragic familial fact, the twinning phenomenon becomes nightmarish, memorializing a past that *cannot* be buried: the son calls the father-Ghost by his own name ("Ile call thee *Hamlet*" [D1v]) and so levels the differences between them, between then and now, death and life. The scene of the son calling out to the dead father mirrors the biographical scene that the play actually performs: the living father Shakespeare calling out to his dead son who bore the name the father bestows again on a play, a tragical history of father and son. In this context the play becomes a personal mourning ritual, encoding the author's own difficulty in processing the terrible knowledge of the past, the death of his child. Of course, Hamlet's severe imperfections complicate this touching elegiac tableau. And as with the drama's more political histories, the complications proliferate, for the name has further ramifications evoked but unresolved by the text. A young woman named Katherine Hamlett, one of Shakespeare's childhood neighbors, drowned in the Avon in 1579. Not only did she meet Ophelia's fate, but, like Ophelia, she was the subject of a coroner's inquest.[64] Shakespeare writes a play around a name besmirched by doom: "Hamlet" is attached in history to two morbid destinies that converge, temporally and semantically out of sync, in the author's life. The fate of Ophelia, because it remembers Katherine Hamlett's demise, obliquely recalls the name of the son; and although the fictional Hamlet is conspicuously absent from the scene of Ophelia's death, her funeral brings him, poorly led, into the grave.

These twinnings typify the opaque and garbled referentiality in which the play engages at every turn. *Hamlet* comprises, with indecipherable complexity, buried histories: cultural and monarchical remembrances fused with those even more elusive and painful memorial reconstructions of the author. The play's myriad cultural influences have a nonlogical, unstructured relationship to one another. And I have not even touched on the influx of "ideas of the time," prominent histories in their own right—accounts of what it was possible to think and thus to mean or not to mean.[65] The figure of Hamlet and his intercourse with his burdens reify some central political and philosophical struggles of the high Renaissance: conflicts of spiritual piety versus worldly business; tension between improvisational rashness and cautious rationality; sympathy to a politically oppositional Catholicism versus loyalty to reformation structures and ideologies (a conflict contained in the purgatorial Ghost and in the predestinarian convictions of Claudius *and* Hamlet). The prince enacts all of these conflictual relations and also bears the immense representational burden of Jacobean history that I have labored to unpack. But finally, Hamlet's figuration as a repository of Renaissance culture cannot secure human status. He is a portrait of unification without unity, of collocation without coherence.

What can we make at last of the play's rewriting of James's life, of Hamlet's polyvalent intake and dispersal of contemporary and foundational Stuart contexts? The convolutions of the inscriptive process suggest that even *particular* histories are uncontrollable or chance elements, impervious to literary management—that history is an intellectual banquet whereby "a little more than a little is by much too much." The theatrical text will always, as Quince says with inadvertent brilliance in *A Midsummer Night's Dream*, come "to disfigure, or to present" a reality external to itself; it inevitably presents a disfigured approximation, an amended shadow of impinging shapes of the real. However, theater's deformation and reformation of its historical material need not signify incapability or failure. It may instead betoken triumph over the intractable elements of workaday life. In theater, the alternatives of the past and the potentialities of the present can be laid beside one another, remembered and processed, forming new semantic relations. Theater construes the *possibilities* of history, the nearly lived and barely avoided. Certainly, *Hamlet* does not passively receive inchoate contexts. At its best, the play marvelously deploys cultural referentiality to intensify theatrical experience. What I wish finally to suggest, however, is that *Hamlet* cannot contain its histories as themes or influences. If the play is a virtual anthology of historical coordinates, it also necessarily becomes a repository of illogic, its contexts frustrating form and the instrumentality of the past.

I have been discussing the relationship of succession anxieties to the concerns of the second quarto, but it should be noted at last that the idea of succession is integral to all literary plot—if by "succession" one means a sequence of events that comes to semantic fruition. The happy succession saga is a model story, really, a narrative perfection: one event follows causally on another until tension resolves in the denouement of a new regime, logically consummating the old. A prior story is now superseded, and ideally, order prevails; whatever treason occurred in the tale functioned merely as the plot obstacle, so satisfying and necessary to overcome. In *Hamlet*, however, failed succession is narratively self-referential as well as historically situated: the story of frustrated inheritance and ironic takeover stages its own metafiction of narrative incoherence. The prince's experience of prolonged political disappointment, and the play's obstructed catharsis and revenge, are perfect examples of fictional anticlimax; plot fails to provide cumulative understanding. Plot in Denmark conspicuously and repeatedly trips, interrupts itself, dawdles, and postpones to the point of tragedy the achievement of royalty: as everyone knows, *Hamlet* makes belatedness and delay the very condition of its form. These features do resonate with the history of James's successions, the past and present historical contexts, but they structurally exaggerate the character of those contexts. The least pleasant features of Jacobean succession history, including the disturbing adjacency of monarchy and disease, become the most prominent elements in *Hamlet*'s antisuccession plot. Historically, the epidemic only momentarily wrecked the plot of succession; plague was but *temporarily* inimical to the story of English rule that had been uninterrupted for forty-four years.[66] But theatrically, disease takes dominion everywhere; the political structure and the form of the narrative are both shot through with illness. And treason in the plot is not merely a brief interruption before the denouement, but rather the constant activity of the rightful heir, whose aggressive self-consumption causes the story of succession to make less and less sense.

Hamlet's illogicalities arise in part because the play and its wide, dark river of referents share a chaotic flow; in the turbulence, text is put profoundly into question as a meaning-bearing object. If the historically overburdened second quarto fails to synthesize itself, or even to allow the possibility of synthesis, at least it acknowledges the world that formed it, the contexts that stress its present meanings. *Twelfth Night*, by contrast, avoids such acknowledgments.

FOUR

"A twenty years' removed thing"

Twelfth Night's Nostalgia

Twelfth Night does not directly express or refer to its contexts, circa 1601, in anything like the way *Troilus and Cressida* and *Hamlet* stage their own contemporaneousness.[1] Instead, the play complexly insulates the text from the current time. In keeping the real at bay while restlessly calling to and echoing it, *Twelfth Night* performs on a large scale what its characters repeatedly enact: the sustained delusions of mediation; and the construction of a reality which fools rather than mends.

The central theatrical target of such activity is Malvolio. Any historical reading of the text must treat this character carefully, for he is the figure most densely involved in the workaday world of status, obligation, and accounts.[2] He has a special gravitational force in the constellation of the self-concerned: he embodies a principle of boundedness and weight. But instead of offering solid temporal markers, Olivia's steward makes and is made an unsteady indicator of the history he apparently configures.

On the way into *Twelfth Night*'s inscriptions, let us begin with Malvolio and his representational aptitudes. These are, I shall claim, constantly formed through the interventions of other characters. The actions of Malvolio's enemies help to disgrace him, but the nature of that disgrace is historically coded. Malvolio's "character" is thus constructed by his competitors through a set of mediated temporal and cultural references. In Shakespeare's Illyria, what happens to Malvolio both produces and challenges the historicity of the text.

I

Archbishop Whitgift's counterblast to the early Puritan manifesto *An Admonition to Parliament* (1572) helped set the tone for many subsequent commentaries on the church reform movement:

> This name Puritane is very aptly giuen to these men, not bicause they be pure no more than were the Heretikes called *Cathari*, but bicause they think them selues to be *mundioris ceteris*, more pure than others, as *Catheri* did, and separate them selues from all other Churches and congregations as spotted and defyled.[3]

This sounds like a response not to some newfangled irritant but to an entrenched threat. Puritan self-exaltation, Whitgift believes, is unearned, unfounded in any moral superiority or in real spiritual or hermeneutic merit. Most subsequent popular (i.e., Anglican) response to Puritans involved just this Whitgiftian assertion of the distance between "precisian" self-image and actual worth. Thomas Nashe levels dishonest time-pleasers with his claim that it is "not amisse" that "they are commonly called Puritans," but only because "they take themselues to be pure, when they are filthy in Gods sight."[4] In *Pierce Penniless*, Nashe further subscribes to the dominant cultural stereotype of Puritans as hypocrites: "Vnder hypocrisie [I comprehende] al Machiavilisme, puritanisme, & outward gloasing with a mans enemie."[5] Shakespeare fills in this common outline with his portrait of Angelo in *Measure for Measure*, the demonic "precise" man whose sadistic virtue hides severe moral deformities. And in *All's Well That Ends Well*, Lavatch opines that "though honesty be no Puritan, yet it will do no hurt; it will wear the surplice of humility over the black gown of a big heart" (1.3.90–93). This complicated reference glances back at the vestiarian controversy which began the Puritan movement in England, and mocks contemporary reformers' face- and neck-saving hypocrisy in donning priestly robes while wearing "the black Geneva gown, the Calvinists' natural garb, under it."[6] Puritans may have seen the surplice as popish, but some of them apparently knew how to cloak a controversy. So honesty could be no Puritan, and no Puritan honest, no matter what he wore.

This hackneyed verdict of hypocrisy against the strict moralists unfairly reduces a vast range of persons, a flexible theology, and an awesomely complicated sociopolitical movement to a single attribute.[7] Satire, we know, need not be fair. But neither is it completely reductive: in addition to the image of a hypocrite, the portrait of the Puritan in the English Renaissance commonly pictured a secretly ambitious, proud, and, most important, covertly subversive reformer.[8] Depending on one's inclination, it is possible to fit Shakespeare's Malvolio into that frame as a deserving comic target, a two-faced, threatening social climber who gets what's coming to him.

Of the many critics who have taken Malvolio to task for his moral flaws, one of the harshest has been Paul Siegel, who has called him a "comic Puritan automaton" embodying Bergsonian psychic rigidity. The steward, according to Siegel, deserves the abuse he suffers at the hands of the misruling revelers.[9] Thus, Malvolio is "the Puritan spoilsport in the midst of gaiety" (217), a criticism echoing J. L. Simmons's identification of the character as "an enduring representation of the anticomic spirit."[10] While it is safe to equate "Puritan spoilsport" and "anticomic spirit," it is less certain that Malvolio ought to be associated unequivocally with Puritanism. For the original charge against him does not come from a disinterested observer: it comes from Maria, who has a potent animus against the annoying servant.

In ascribing Puritanism to Malvolio, Maria is not explaining his spiritual affiliation or practice. Discourse about religion occupies the play, but Maria's comment about Malvolio, like other theological or scriptural reference in Illyria, tends to nullify or drain the referent of spiritual content. For instance, Feste lives "by the church," but when pressed, he revises this statement to mean that he lives *near* the church, and not necessarily by its precepts (3.1.3–7); and his later impersonation of a curate is designed to torment, not enlighten, thus confirming the point.[11] More broadly, the general shape of the fable, whereby shipwreck leads to further tribulation and finally reward, gently parodies the Christian redemptive story with the comedy of gender transformation and social mobility. So it should not seem peculiar that the play's treatment of Malvolio has a religious register; but what does run counter to expectation is that the demonized figure is himself subjected to demons. Maria, the "most excellent devil of wit," will lead Sir Toby "To the gates of Tartar" (2.5.206) for the jest against the steward. Perhaps any scheme which results in a duped man's imprisonment in hideous darkness could be labeled demonic, but Shakespeare is explicit about Maria's deviltry; asking for information about Malvolio, Toby implores her, "Possess us, possess us, tell us something of him." Maria's response to the request does possess her listeners, onstage and off, with an idea that is hard to exorcise:

MARIA: Marry, sir, sometimes he is a kind of Puritan.
SIR AND: O, if I thought that, I'd beat him like a dog. . . .
MARIA: The devil a Puritan that he is, or anything constantly but a time-
            pleaser, an affectioned ass, that cons state without book, and utters
            it by great swarths: the best persuaded of himself, so crammed (as
            he thinks) with excellencies, that it is his grounds of faith that all
            that look on him love him: and on that vice in him will my revenge
            find notable cause to work.

                                                              (2.3. 140–53)

In a way, Maria preempts all subsequent commentary on Malvolio's
Puritanism by asserting that he does not even have enough integrity or
constancy to be "a kind of Puritan." Instead, she suggestively offers,
"the devil a Puritan that he is, or anything constantly," which seems to
deny the charge ("the hell he is") even as it subliminally affirms it. For
"the Devil is a Puritan" was a standard Anglican cant phrase.[12] So the
hint has been dropped, like a note to a longing lover, and critics have
lunged for it. Maria's verbal artillery in this passage strikes Malvolio on
several fronts, and the charge of "Puritan"—an all-purpose Elizabethan
term of abuse—is only one of the most potent. The claim with more
extensive implications, at least for the "love theme" in the play, is that
against Malvolio's conceit. Called "the best persuaded of himself," the
accusation chimes with Olivia's earlier reproof, "you are sick of self-
love, Malvolio, and taste with a distempered appetite." But if Maria
thinks this charge sets Malvolio apart from his fellows, she is sorely
mistaken; the description rather sets him a place alongside *most* of the
other Illyrians and their hungry, self-obsessive personalities.[13] Let us try
to read further into Maria's half-retracted hint.

    The maidservant's reluctance to call Malvolio a Puritan outright sug-
gests that he both is and is not Puritanical. This ambivalence does not
bother some of Malvolio's more dedicated opponents. For instance, in
reference to the epithet "time-pleaser," Siegel comments: "Maria . . . is
merely making the charge that was made against Puritans generally:
they are concerned with their religion only insofar as it serves their
profit" ("Malvolio," 218).[14] The critic seems untroubled—he freely admits—that the supposedly common accusation does not jibe with Malvolio's function in the play: the servant, after all, never professes *any*
religion, let alone one from which profit or position follows. He practices nothing more than a snooty manner, a prim but essentially secular
court style. But Maria's equivocation about her enemy's Puritanism
should not be erased, because it figures crucially in her effort to catego-

rize and thus to scapegoat him. Maria, in other words, has a vague idea about what Malvolio is, but a more certain notion of what she would like to make him, and she sets about to do just that—to transform him. Her efforts, and those of her co-conspirators, have been broadly successful.

Siegel demonstrates this success through his definition of the abusive epithet "niggardly rascally sheep-biter" (2.5.4–5) which Sir Toby levels at Malvolio. To gloss the phrase as Siegel does—"miserly, cheating Puritan"—one must claim that "miserliness and cheating in business [were traditionally] associated with Puritans." Siegel admits that "Malvolio is not shown as either a miser or a cheat"; still, though, he continues, "Sir Toby, in speaking of him as a Puritan, makes use of the stock epithets for Puritans" ("Malvolio," 219)[15]—which, however, do not quite apply. If the argument seems insufficient from the available evidence, how can we account for the fairly widespread acceptance of the Malvolio-as-Puritan view? In partial answer to this question, let us have another look at Sir Toby's derisive term for the steward. What *is* a sheep-biter? Perhaps it describes an aggressive, low-postured animal: wolves bite sheep (but surely Toby does not identify himself as mutton?), and dogs can herd sheep by nipping at them and following close behind. Following behind, actually, may be the operative insult here. For "sheep-biter" could refer to the custom of orally castrating farm animals[16]—a custom which would reveal Malvolio not only as wolfish (one who bites sheep) but more directly as sexually deviant, a person of abject posture and bestial or possibly homoerotic orality and inclination.[17] The *OED* (def. 2b) sheds some light on "sheep-biter," although in a post-Shakespearean context. The supporting quotation for the definition "a shifty, sneaking, or thievish fellow" comes from Peter Heylin's *A Full Relation of Two Journeys . . . Into the Mainland of France* (1656), yet it alludes not to a thief but to an epicene: "I was fain sometimes to put on a little impudence, that I might avoid the suspicion of a gelding or a sheep-biter." If the two terms are synonymous, "sheep-biter" would be Renaissance pejorative code for an unmasculine male. The paranoia about perceived masculinity that we see in Heylin's quotation can be projected back into Toby's wishes: the drunken schemer asks Fabian, "Would'st thou not be glad to have the niggardly rascally sheep-biter come by some notable shame?" The shaming of Malvolio, however, could not involve the revelation of his parsimony; for a steward, that is no shame at all. Instead, it involves the exposure of his sexual desires. Here the insulting term becomes significant. For if "sheep-biter" is imaginatively associable with

"gelding" or an insufficiently impudent (masculine) male, as the Heylin
quotation suggests, Toby's epithet betrays a wish to emasculate or feminize his rival. The put-down could then be aligned with his later comment that "Malvolio's a Peg-a-Ramsey" (2.3.76) or even with Andrew
Aguecheek's sputtering insult: "Fie on him, Jezebel!" (2.5.41). Indeed,
the "sheep-biter" charge discloses Toby's own fantasies of oral and sexual violence, perhaps in retaliation for having been metaphorically bit-
ten: hiding on the side of the stage, he later says to Malvolio, "And does
not Toby take you a blow o' the lips then?" (2.5.68). However we understand the peculiar insult, and there are several ways to do so, it seems
as though clichés of Puritanism—miserliness, hypocrisy, and so on—
have little to do with it.

   This discursus on sheep-biting is meant to suggest that the process of
evaluating Malvolio has crucially to do with the desires and agendas of
the characters who practice on him. Rather than expose the steward's
essential Puritanism (if there is any such thing), the low-comic figures set
about to construct his character and then subject him to the consequences of this construction. To better understand this operation and its
radii to religious and historical discourse, we need to examine Maria's
letter, the central vehicle of mediation between Malvolio, his sense of
self, and the audience's understanding.

   The note from Maria paints Malvolio into a cornered idea of his
place in several ways. These include the striking imitation of Olivia's
handwriting; "her very phrases"; and even more convincingly, Olivia's
wax letter seal, a central bait in the identity trap at which the steward
snaps:

MAL: By my life, this is my lady's hand: these be her very C's, her U's, and her
        T's, and thus makes she her great P's. It is in contempt of question her
        hand. . . .
        To the unknown beloved, this, and my good wishes.
        Her very phrases! By your leave, wax. Soft! and the impressure her
        Lucrece, with which she uses to seal: 'tis my lady! To whom should this
        be?

                                                                      (2.5. 87–96)

In this disturbing comic moment, Olivia's alleged billet-doux substitutes
for Olivia herself: "this is my lady's hand" becomes, a few lines later,
" 'tis my lady!" But this substitution can be made only once Malvolio
breaks the letter's seal. The juxtaposition of "the impressure her Lucrece" and " 'tis my lady" suggests an identification between the presumed author of the letter and the famous literary victim of violation

with whose image, strangely, Olivia seals her mail.[18] The implications of this identification, cognate with the play's general practice of serial metamorphoses, are resident in Malvolio's courtly tearing of the feminine letter—"By your leave, wax"—a reminder of the fate of Lucrece. Indeed, with its alluring lacunae and riddles, Maria's letter presents a subliminal invitation to a rape, drawing Malvolio further into his invasive interpretation. Once he begins to reconstruct his lady from the evidence of her hand, the leering humor of his response to the graphology, to her *c*'s, *u*'s, and *t*'s, secures a point about the material presence of language in this play.[19] The missive substitutes word for body, linguistic for physical presence. The Fool's wish that his sister had no name, because "to dally with that word might make my sister wanton" (3.1.18–19), can come true in the theatrical world, where language calls several kinds of "character" into being.

The seal is a forgery no less than the imitated handwriting, a signature in the absence of the most important marker of identity: presence, the countenance close up. Olivia's absence ensures the note's persuasiveness, for the "fortunate unhappy" is too embarrassed to make a more direct avowal of love. The document seduces precisely because of its implied disguise, and thus the letter is a perfect mediator: a text without an underlying, authentic voice. Maria, invisible behind the words, impersonates the (supposedly concealed) Olivia, whose coy riddles are meant to seem a transparent disguise. But the anonymous note deceives chiefly because it paradoxically stabilizes the absent author's identity as it surprisingly throws the *reader's* into doubt. The source, like the "hand," remains "in contempt of question," but the recipient is "the unknown beloved," and Malvolio, with growing excitement, wonders to whom the letter should be addressed. By dislocating the identity of the reader, by excerpting, deleting, and rearranging letters from his name—*M, O, A, I*—the note opens a psychological space for the implantation of an identity *in* the reader, a process to which Malvolio eagerly submits.

As he reads the letter aloud, a motif of secrecy and silence emerges that further disestablishes the secure identity of the recipient: "*Jove knows I love; / But who? / Lips, do not move, / No man must know.*" (And since the communiqué has its source in feminine power, no man *will* know.) The words recall Lucrece as the letter continues with its inviting quatrains: "*I may command where I adore; / But silence, like a Lucrece knife, / With bloodless stroke my heart doth gore; / M.O.A.I. doth sway my life*" (2.5.106–9). The only lines Malvolio notices or mentions in this verse are the first and fourth, thus reenacting the silence of the Lucrece story. He wonders about "M.O.A.I." and then speculates:

> "I may command where I adore." Why, she may command me: I serve her, she is my lady. Why, this is evident to any formal capacity. There is no obstruction in this. And the end: what should that alphabetical position portend? If I could make that resemble something in me!
>
> (116–22)

An object lesson on the dangers of exegesis, this scene supposedly reveals the worst tendencies of the megalomaniacal reader who tries to find his or her own image in every text. Yet this scene shows precisely what a good reader Malvolio is—until his enticed desire, the mediated message, and the fractured image of the self in language get the better of him: "M.O.A.I. This simulation is not as the former: and yet, to crush this a little, it would bow to me, for every one of these letters are in my name" (2.5.139–41). This brilliant account of an aggressive close-reader's desire tropes in miniature on the play's own enticing anagrams, its unreadable diddling with the olivia-viola-malvolio alphabetical mix.

But Malvolio cannot remain comfortable with the lexical incompleteness of "M.O.A.I."; the graphemes must be crushed and made to bow to his frustrated, interpretive violence. He is drawn into thinking he is penetrating and mastering a text that has actually penetrated him. The sexual implications of the reading, and of Malvolio's position as object rather than agent of the assault—the sheep, not the biter—are played out by Maria's surveillance team:

MALV: "M"—But then there is no consonancy in the sequel; that suffers
                under probation: "A" should follow, but "O" does.
FABIAN: And "O" shall end, I hope.
SIR TO: Ay, or I'll cudgel him, and make him cry "O"!
MALV: And then "I" comes behind.
FABIAN: Ay, and you had any eye behind you, you might see more detraction
                at your heels than fortunes before you.

(2.5.130–38)

The positional change of "A" and "O," the "I" that "comes behind," and Sir Toby's angry desire to make the steward "cry 'O' " all reduce the missive's alphabetical dalliance to a sex joke. We can locate one meaning of the incomplete anagram in the commentary that the eavesdroppers make about it. They turn the scene into the rape of Malvolio: he is linguistically sodomized here, with an "O" where his "A" should be, and an eye/I that "comes behind" the "A" at his end.[20] The anagram of his name predictably obsesses him, as does the possibility that Olivia adores the person she rules, not the office—even though the note says she may command where, not whom she adores. Malvolio, it is clear, ought to have considered the lines he passes over; the silence that gores recalls not only Lucrece but Philomel, two models of the imposition of others' will. The tableau of Malvolio's reading is a scene of identity slippage: Lucrece metamorphoses from a figure for or signature of the letter's supposed author (Olivia) to a figure for or image of the reader, as Malvolio suffers a rapine seizure of his identity. The silence behind the riddle and the defective anagram of the steward's name reify gaps or openings for the implantation of another version of the self: the willing reader becomes the container for an artificial, formed desire. Malvolio willingly participates in this construction because he believes himself to have been blessed by the fraudulent vessel, the empty text.

Malvolio, then, undergoes substantial alteration because of the interpretations he is lured into. His identity becomes the product of intermediaries—the letter, the observers, and their commentaries—and so the steward's "personality" or his "Puritanism" seeps through the filter of the unreliable narrators who create him. Our preconceptions about Malvolio are largely Maria's doing; and Sir Toby's funny, angry ejaculations in response to the steward's fantasies ("Bolts and shackles! . . . Fire and brimstone! . . . O for a stone bow to hit him in the eye!") help intensify the anti-Malvolio effect. But the eavesdroppers to Malvolio's reading are, in fact, interpretive interlopers, altering what might otherwise be seen as a hardworking servant's reasonable reaction to the promise of receiving, at long last, favor. This trap has been a long time in the making: "Maria once told me she did affect me, and I have heard herself come thus near" (2.5.23–25). Yet, an audience's suspicions that Malvolio is a sexually repressed Puritan type who cannot harness the body's energies of misrule (Belching and other explosive celebrations) have, like his own wants, been seeded by someone else, the terribly clever Maria. We should not blame Malvolio for feeling the way the false letter seeks to make him feel. We can only blame him for submitting too readily to the suspicious interpretive conditions that transform him. Malvolio, man of letters, has been mis-taken.

The letter's seal and its inviting quatrains destabilize the identity of "the unknown beloved," making Malvolio a vulnerable Lucrece figure. But this operation is merely an envoy to the letter's darker purpose: to *replace* the steward's identity with another one, a monstrous mélange of disunified features comprising conflicting materials. This effect makes the "Puritan" label particularly hard to justify. It is true that as Siegel says, the letter causes Malvolio to act "an exaggeration of the way he has already behaved in sternly admonishing Sir Toby and speaking sourly to Feste" (221), but that is its rhetorical, confidence-woman genius. To draw in the "trout that must be caught with tickling" (2.5.22), Maria dangles this dazzling bait: she endorses Malvolio's ordinary behavior. "Be opposite with a kinsman, surly with servants" (2.5.149), the note says trapically. The letter cannot enjoin a complete turnaround in his affect, for that would derationalize the attraction that Olivia supposedly feels for her servant, who is so good at what he does. But neither can it simply order him to "keep up the good work," for then there would be no mark to distinguish Malvolio's change in status; there would be no comic payoff. So Maria, in scriptive disguise, pushes Malvolio to behavioral extremities once he delusionally and ecstatically believes that his lady loves him. The letter finally and devastatingly makes Malvolio act *opposite* to the way he usually behaves. The cause of this change is the promise of recognition: Olivia will now reward actions which Malvolio would *never* perform under ordinary circumstances.

The letter's most memorable instructions urge Malvolio to alter his behavior in a specifically Puritanical direction: they encourage "a kind of Puritan" oppositionality. For instance, the note counsels, *"Put thyself into the trick of singularity"* (2.5.150). As Siegel points out, the word "singularity" was frequently and negatively applied to Puritans "who with their 'new-fangleness' and 'innovations' were already . . . rocking the precariously settled order of the established church."[21] A classic example postdating the play is Jonson's archetypal Zeal-of-the-Land Busy, who "affects the violence of singularity in all he does." But Malvolio has not yet affected this violence; he has been separate, but not particularly singular.[22] He must be made to behave more singularly. To that end, the letter inspires its gull to act more like an irritating stage Puritan than he ever has before. But irritating to whom? To Olivia, of course. The forgery creates a forgery: Malvolio will behave Puritanically, which behavior, as Maria knows, Olivia will hate: "I know my lady will strike him: if she do, he'll smile, and take't for a great favour" (3.2.79–80).

Let us look at the renowned fashion request in the letter: *"Remember who commended thy yellow stockings, and wished to see thee ever cross-gartered: I say remember"* (2.5.152–54). Furness's *Variorum* cites W. A. Wright: " 'yellow stockings' were apparently a common article of dress in the 16th century. . . . They had apparently gone out of fashion in Sir Thomas Overbury's time, for in his *Characters* he says of 'A Country Gentleman,' 'If he goes to Court, it is in yellow stockings'; as if this were a sign of rusticity." The point of this request, then, is to make Malvolio look like a rube, like one who emphatically does not belong at court. While Olivia has no court exactly—only Orsino does—she is a great lady, and her house acts as the play's center of social and cultural activity. Malvolio is made to appear constricted, ill-fitting, especially for courtly movement. As for the garters, the same point may obtain; another *Variorum* note quotes Barton Holyday "speaking of the ill-success of his play called *Technogamia* [1618]," where the implication seems to be that the play would have done better if there had appeared "some sharp cross-gartered man, Whom their loud laugh might nickname Puritan" (*Variorum*, 174). This quotation suggests that crossed garters are a cheap sight gag denoting a person well out of step with fashion. Malvolio is ordered to affect such an appearance; he does not customarily dress this way. But Siegel argues that the steward must be a Puritan because the phrase "remember who commended thy yellow stockings" means that "[Malvolio] wore them previously . . . [which] is borne out by his statement: 'She did commend my yellow stockings of late, she did praise my leg being cross-gartered' " (222). His possession of the fussy garb is not the issue here; rather, we should consider his inclination to don it. We miss much if we overlook Malvolio's desperate attempt to believe what he has just read: "I do not now fool myself, to let imagination jade me; for every reason excites to this, that my lady loves me. She did commend . . . " (2.5.164–66). His language hints at subliminal doubt for which he is rarely given credit: he says, in fact, that he does not now fool himself to let his imagination fool him. His recollection of Olivia's praise is patently delusional, and he shows that he has no predisposition to wear such uncomfortable stuff: "I could be sad: this does make some obstruction in the blood, this cross-gartering; but what of that?" (3.4.19–21).[23]

The quotations from the *Variorum* suggest that Malvolio's new clothes were, at least by 1618, recognizably those of the Puritan, but the point of his cross-dressing is lost unless we apprehend its goal from Maria's point of view: to alienate him from the powerful mistress of the house, or to put him out of place at the symbolic court. This project bears political and erotic inscriptions. Olivia's female servant seeks to oust her higher-placed male rival by setting him against the lady of the house in a way he cannot understand: "he will come to her in yellow stockings, and 'tis a color she abhors, and cross-gartered, a fashion she detests" (2.5.194–96).[24]

II

The sartorial Puritanizing of Malvolio is part of a project to remove him from the favor of the most powerful woman in Illyria, and this project has pointed historical overtones. Leslie Hotson offers a choice gloss on Maria's hate couture: "Like Olivia, Queen Elizabeth (whose own personal colours were white and black) abhorred yellow. For six years yellow had been the colour of danger in her Court—being flaunted by the faction of the Duke of Norfolk until his attainder and execution in 1572. And the flag of her arch-enemy, Spain, was yellow."[25] The connection between Olivia and Elizabeth has a certain amount of strain built in, but this is the strain of every representation of the queen near the end of her reign. I shall return to the question of the play's inscriptive tremors, but there is an alluring connection between Olivia and Elizabeth in light of Maria's activity: the witty "piece of Eve's flesh" baffles Malvolio by turning him into a yellow-clad, Catholic-tinged Puritan. He becomes a living standard-bearer of two poles of Elizabethan religious subversion.

The ideological construction of Malvolio incorporates forged historical signs as characterological indices. After her triumph has been achieved, the letter read and its partly veiled meanings completed by the desirous reader, Maria announces its effects:

MARIA: Yond gull Malvolio is turned heathen, a very renegado; for there is no Christian that means to be saved by believing rightly can ever believe such impossible passages of grossness. He's in yellow stockings!

SIR TO: And cross gartered?

MARIA: Most villainously; like a pedant that keeps a school i'th'church. I have dogged him like his murderer.

                                                                (3.2.66–74)

That last line conjures alarming images of the horrible Richard Topcliffe hunting down Jesuits, pursuing them to their hiding holes, and eventually hounding them to their state-sponsored deaths.[26] In fact, Malvolio becomes a baffling confluence of religious types in Maria's gleeful description. He bears literal colors and symbolic echoes of Catholicism (and Catholic persecution), but the designation "renegado" is, provoca-

tively, the Spanish word for a "deserter of his faith."[27] Malvolio thus
alters descriptively from a nonbeliever ("heathen"), to a heretic from
Catholicism ("renegado": a Protestant apostate?) to a virtual idolater
who believes in "impossible passages" or corrupt, apocryphal writings.
This last accusation, ironic given its source, attacks textual grounds of
belief and seems to look back at Elizabethan controversies over Puritan
hermeneutics. Let us consider the implications of Malvolio's misguided
study.

Calling him one who does not believe "rightly," Maria mocks the
"impossible passages of grossness" of her own scripture that have led
Malvolio to his present absurdity. Implicit in his reverential response to
the letter—which is of course primarily an erotic, not a spiritual document—may be, in fact, a critique of Puritan theological practice, a slam
against an overreliance on the received text. Puritan reading was (to
Anglicans) overly precise and even demonstrably false in its bristling
insistence on the authority of the word. As J. L. Simmons has written,
"Like a Precisian, Malvolio determines to follow the letter 'point de-
vise.' . . . But his exegesis exemplifies, in the symbolic action, a Puritan's
approach to scriptural interpretation in the spirit of self-love, of Bad-
Will" ("Source for Shakespeare's Malvolio," 182). To Maria, Malvolio
is a deceived worshiper. By precisely following the letter of the letter, he
can be "no Christian that means to be saved" but is instead one who will
suffer a descent from which only a paid fool can (gracelessly) deliver
him. Interpretation factors salvation.

Richard Bancroft imputed to Puritans the desire to "impose a meaning uppon [the Scriptures] . . . not to deliver the true sense of them, but
to bring a sense of their owne: not a yeelding to the wordes, but a kind of
compulsion, inforcement, or violence offered: to make that to seeme to
be contained in them . . . which they presumed should be understood by
them, before they read them."[28] Malvolio does offer the letter some hermeneutic violence, but it is as I have suggested a coerced, invited assault—a lure to a preprocessed interpretation. The dual drama of the
scene is thus that it *reminds* us of the Puritan interpretive habit of mind,
one that does not take either the autonomy or the corruption of the
word (Feste, Maria) into account; but it measures at the same time quite
a distance from the scene of actual Puritan reading precisely because this
text is fraudulent, an engineered trap. Maria's writing is *designed* to
deceive. In fact, there is a logical problem with the claim critics make
about Malvolio's misprision. The scene is supposed to entertain us with
the tableau of a reader misreading in a way that the writer controls, but

it cancels that supposed meaning with another ironical one: Malvolio is actually reading *correctly*, insofar as he responds exactly as the source of the script intended. The interpretation is right; the text is wrong. Thus, the allegorical take on Malvolio as the typically mistaken Puritan produces this heresy: Scripture can be false, and it can be damning. If disguise throws identity and meaning into doubt, Maria's forgery implies that biblical text, too, is customarily in disguise, interpretively unstable—that it is strewn in our path, and merry devils chuckle at us while we interpret. Not only can Scripture gauge one's access to salvation, but it can actually be designed to entrap.

Perhaps the point is simply that the steward is led into self-entrapment, the way Puritans supposedly were. But Malvolio's reception of the message is almost completely respectable. He does not rush to judgment (he does not instantly say, for instance, "I am the man!" as Viola comically, if correctly, does); he notices that "this simulation is not as the former"—or, in other words, the representation of the signified "Malvolio" by "M.O.A.I." does not resemble him in the same way as previous signs in the message did. If Malvolio's interpretation is meant to parody the flaws of Puritan reading, the parody has limited range, because the reader's response is shown to be much in tune with the author's intent. Along these lines, we might consider that when Maria asserts, "There is no Christian that means to be saved by believing rightly can ever believe such impossible passages of grossness," the "impossible passages" *could* refer to the entire stage business of Malvolio's makeover. If so, the question of identification in the passage becomes, as often in Shakespeare, unclear. "No Christian that means to be saved by believing rightly" then would point equally to the dupe and the duper, the person laboring under the illusion and the one beholding the incredible event, "an improbable fiction," as Fabian says. Maria confesses her own implication in disbelief or apostasy.

Because Malvolio is incapable of disguise, he cannot imagine that text deceives; he trusts in the letter, the word. He is, in fact, the polar opposite of the culturally demonized image of the Puritan: he is a nonhypocrite, a person of pained limitations and pinched ambitions, but so without guile or subversive potential that his every deviation from his fixed self shows like madness.

However, despite her contribution to his altered character, Maria still wants to blame Malvolio for his adoption of Puritan attributes. She seems, that is, increasingly certain about what she has made him. For instance, by saying that Malvolio appears "like a pedant that keeps a school i'th'church," she depicts her rival as a particular type of rustic ideologue who spread religious education wherever he could. This description of the translated servant is about as technical a taxonomy of Puritanism as the play permits. One of the radical reformers' abiding premises concerned the need for the intense and widespread instruction of each congregation of worshipers. John Knox, the Scottish Calvinist, asserts in his "Book of Discipline" that "every several church" must

> have a Schoolmaster appointed, such a one as is able, at least, to teach Grammar and the Latin tongue. . . . If it be upland, where the people convene to doctrine but once in the week, then must either the Reader or the Minister there appointed, take care over the children and youth of the parish, to instruct them in their first rudiments, and especially in the Catechism. . . .
> And [so] must discreet, learned, and grave men be appointed to visit all Schools for the trial of their exercise, profit, and continuance.[29]

The idea, of course, is that "within [a] few years," the "whole Realm (we doubt not) . . . shall serve the self of true preachers" (Porter, *Puritanism in Tudor England*, 200). The pedants that keep school in the church—concerned, as Knox says, to teach students "to read perfectly"—were recognizably Puritan preachers. In the reformers' program, schoolmasterly divines were the crucial vehicles of doctrinal dissemination. Maria claims that her letter has sparked in Malvolio a recognizable and potentially radical conversion: he has been translated into a proselytizing Puritan schoolteacher.

It does seem, as we watch Malvolio process the discovered letter, that he overcomes his subliminal doubts to respond as would a Calvinist to an unequivocal sign of his own justification: "I thank my stars, I am happy" (2.5.170); and later, "Jove, not I, is the doer of this, and he is to be thanked" (3.4.83). He exhibits the Calvinist's characteristic self-abjection and sense of received, not achieved merit; in the words of the *Institutes*, "We must now recognize that our salvation consists in God's mercy alone, but not in any worth of ours, or in anything coming from us. Accordingly, on this mercy we must establish and as it were deeply fix all our hope, paying no regard to our works nor seeking any help from them."[30] Malvolio behaves strikingly as if he were the direct beneficiary of grace descending—as if he were a committed Puritan who only now knows himself to be one of the very few elect. But as Maria's description of him makes plain, the steward bears mixed sectarian marks more complex than this; Malvolio's conversion is not simply to reform Protestantism. Even his Puritan-style garters are crossed, which may imply the kind of popish crucifixion worship that Calvinists particularly detested. How can we account for this referential mixedness? One way is to recall that Puritans, Catholics, and various heretical sects were readily if unfairly lumped in the same oppositional camp by Anglicans. As the title page of Oliver Ormerod's *Puritano-papismus* (1605) asserts, "The Puritanes haue in sundry things ioyned with the Pharisies, Apostolickes, Aerians, . . . Catharists, Enthusiasts, Donatists, Iouianists, Brownists and Papists."[31] Ormerod's thesis is that Puritans have the same effect on the official state church as does the official state enemy. In this dialogic text, his character the "Protestant" (i.e., an Anglican) flings fighting words at the "Puritan": "euen . . . though ye be at enmitie with the papists; though you impugne their Doctrine; . . . though ye call for their punishment; yet, in defacing & deprauing of this Church of England, you fully ioyne with them against vs" (*Puritano-papismus*, M3). In the dialogue itself, the Protestant insists he can show "that there was scarce any Heresie inuented by olde Heretickes, which eyther the *Papistes* or the *Puritanes* haue not reuiued and renewed with fresh and new colours" (*Puritano-papismus*, N2v).

Puritans, to Ormerod, are not only heretics but are as bad as Catholics in their idolatry: *'Those that worshippe their owne opinions, conceits and fancies, and yeelde not to the truth, though neuer so plainly demonstrated, are idolaters'* (*Puritano-papismus*, P2). These damning words might describe any number of characters in Illyria, but they seem especially apt for Malvolio the "renegado," basking in the deceptive glow of Maria's letter. His own opinion does become a sort of worship, but it is a false idol which he mistakes for justification. Ormerod continues:

> That it is Idolatrie to worshippe a mans owne opinions, and not to yeelde to truth: I prooue it by this speech of the Apostle: *"couetousnes is idolatrie.["*] From which saying of his, I dispute thus: If the Apostle held those to bee idolaters, that did set their hearts vpon their ritches, and were so wedded vnto them, as that no perswasion could bring them from the loue of them: the consequence is not to be rebuked that we inferre vpon it; that we may as well tearme them idolaters, that doe set their hearts vppon their opinions.
>
> (*Puritano-papismus*, P2)

There is irony in this apostolic demolition of the Puritans, whose central theology was (at least supposed to be) Pauline.[32] Paralleling the love of "opinions" and "riches" as forms of idolatry, Ormerod strafes the Puritan heathen who *"worshippe their owne opinions."* But, he points out, papists are no better, "for Popery is (as a one truely saith) *an hotch-*

potch and miserable mingle-mangle of all Sathans forgeries and diuelish heresies" (*Puritano-papismus*, 9). Malvolio becomes just such an image of this hodgepodge in complying with Maria's satanic forgeries.

This Anglican radicalizing of both Puritans and papists takes *Twelfth Night* into the referential area of religious controversy. Comprising but dividing the house of Olivia—a house fortified against amorous assaults—are the followers of Maria ("Mistress Mary") and, opposed to them, the solitary steward, made into a faux Puritan and encouraged through Marian plots to mount an assault of sorts on the ruling woman. Olivia, that is, has a governance problem, and it is far more of a problem than she knows; it becomes clear only when a costumed Puritan/Catholic assaults her in the guise of service, pretending to an imagined favor. This scenario reproduces, in an ironic and misshapen way, Elizabethan religious tensions. As J. E. Neale has argued, "The men who pressed most relentlessly for the execution of Mary Queen of Scots and urged ruthless legislation against Catholics were also earnest Puritans. In this curious world of conflicting ideologies, Queen Elizabeth found herself . . . fighting a triangular duel and suffering from the shots of the other two duellists, Catholics and Puritans."[33] But Neale also notes—it is the point of his essay—that both opposition parties, and especially the oppressed Puritans, were surprisingly loyal to Elizabeth: "Her Puritan fanatics had no more obstinate opponent: she, in turn, had no more devoted worshippers. It is the strangest paradox of her reign and the supreme tribute to her greatness" (124). By molding Malvolio into "a kind of Puritan," really a Puritano-papismus, Maria projects onto her despised fellow servant a complex of Elizabethan hostilities that effectually marginalize one whose "grounds of faith" are alien to right-thinking, socially rising Anglicans.

It may be that Maria plants on fertile ground, for even prior to her scriptive transformation of him, Malvolio does bear some subtle Calvinist shadings. He disdains the ring, for instance, which (he thinks) Olivia seeks to return to Cesario: "Come sir, you peevishly threw it to her: and her will is, it should be so returned. If it be worth stooping for, there it lies, in your eye: if not, be it his that finds it" (2.2.12–15). Puritans objected to Anglican matrimonial ritual and in particular the sacramental overtones of the ring ceremony; although this is no marriage scene, doctrinal objections may echo distantly here.[34] But there are sharper outlines of Malvolio's leanings toward reform religion, and these are etched on the background of the play's status obsessions and Malvolio's own employment. I have already mentioned his Calvinist reaction to signs of his election, his sense that good fortune is purely the matter of divine grace. But to the extent that this fortune primarily means his ascent in class status, the reward seemingly confirms a common Calvinist suspicion that all fortune, material and spiritual, can be ascribed to divine intervention. (In this respect, the antipredestinarian axiom *'Some are born great, some achieve greatness, and some have greatness thrust upon 'em'* is a thoroughly anti-Calvinist sentiment, and the fact that Malvolio accepts it may confirm Maria's claim that he cannot be a constant Puritan.)

This is not to say that Puritans were unconflicted about material profit. In the exquisitely dull diary of Richard Rogers, for example, a constant nervousness about property intrudes, and he often thanks God for steadying his thoughts about the fiscal world: "Since my last writing god hath continued his kindness to me, for I have had a comfortable and sensible feeling of the contempt of the worlde. . . . I have not meanly thought of earthly peace or provision, nether of any increasing of our commodities, although godes hand is not shortned to us that way."[35] Rogers's last clause might explain why he has not meanly thought of earthly provision: provided with plenty, he has not had to worry about his bounty. But throughout his diary, severe temptation does come primarily in materialist guise: "I saw that the love of worldly things cleaveth so neer to my hart that I must purge it out strongulier than yet it hath been" (65). Referring to some unspecified social advancement, Rogers writes, "In deed I did not a litle reioice before in the late preferrment which the lorde had brought uppon me, and least I shoulde have been too ioyfull the lord did show me my weaknes that I might still be holden under with it" (67). The paradox of Calvinist success—the godly person thriving in the secular world that should be strange and hollow to him—leads to a constant regulation of pleasure in the midst of thriving, but also to a redoubled if constantly denied focus on the material world. Even as Malvolio crows about his good fortune after receiving the confirmatory letter, he must almost superstitiously remind himself that "Jove, not I, is the doer of this, and he is to be thanked" (3.4.83–84).

Part of the problem in making a secure identification of Malvolio's social or religious position before his conversion is that his very occupation has a spiritual potential that neither he nor his tormentors understands. Embodying contradiction which the other characters misread as hypocrisy, Olivia's serving man actually comprises tensions between emergent and residual ideologies or historical presences. Malvolio, taken as a composite of pre- and post-transformation selves, embodies the notion of the incipiently capitalist Puritan, a Weberian figure described best by R. H. Tawney in *Religion and the Rise of Capitalism.* Tawney's not universally rejected thesis is that Puritan theory validates the capitalist profit motive (or, more to the point of this discussion, social mobility) through the "doctrine of stewardship," which holds that men must shepherd one another, and the world, to try the best they can to establish a godly kingdom on earth; socioeconomic maneuvering by that small segment of humanity known as the elect would then be merely one of the forms such stewardship could take. Much as this view has come under attack, and much as it recreates the image of Puritan as money-grubbing hypocrite, it does open up the semantic possibilities of Malvolio the steward.[36]

The doctrine or theology of stewardship, as Tawney frames it, is an integral part of Protestant theory, and although the idea flowered in the late seventeenth century, it was nevertheless implicit in the work of the early reformers and in Scripture. The doctrine argues from the New Testament (especially 1 Corinthians 4:1, Galatians 4:2, Luke 12:42, and Ephesians 3:2) that "all Christians are . . . stewards of God's mysteries" and that "stewardship before God involves time, talents, possessions and self."[37] In its domestic or secular sense, the Greek *oikonomos* refers to "a superior slave or a freed man who was placed in complete charge of the household" (*Encyclopedia*, 2264)—Malvolio's position exactly. But Olivia's man obviously takes his job a little more seriously than that, and he delivers with ringing clarity his sense not only of his own superiority but of his fellows' profligacy: " 'Cousin Toby,' " he imagines himself saying, " 'You must amend your drunkenness. . . . Besides, you waste the treasure of your time' " (2.5.70–76). He sounds like an early Puritan diarist or minister—an insufferable yet potentially indispensable presence. But even as we recognize that Malvolio represents the possibility of a more serious spiritual orientation to things, it becomes clear how far short he falls of his potential. In the New Testament metaphor, Christians are "stewards of God's varied grace" (1 Peter 4:10); each person must be responsible for the spiritual and physical well-being of his fellows. Stewardship in the Gospel "can be nothing less than a life reflecting the whole-hearted response of love and gratitude to God for his immeasurable mercy in Christ. . . . [The] totality of life, oriented towards the neighbor, responding to God's love" (*Encyclopedia*, 2264–65). As expressed, this doctrine wholly counters Malvolio's customary relationship with the world. Even before receipt of the letter—but most particularly afterwards—Malvolio casts himself as a privileged man, set off against those who "are not of my element," as he says. In harboring suspicions of his own election, Malvolio unknowingly records his unworthiness. He is no Christian steward, no doer of God's business; he wishes not to take care of, but rather to lord it over his housemates. Yet his opposite numbers likewise lack a sense of these principles, a point the play frequently makes. Sir Toby misses the ironies of his own scathing question to Malvolio: "Art any more than a steward?" Toby cannot imagine, from his besotted, class-driven perspective, that stewardship models one relation to God and fellow on which Christianity could be said to found itself.

Malvolio, granted stewardship of Olivia's prosperous household, is finally in most ways an unlikely candidate for Puritan leanings—especially insofar as Elizabethan Puritanism signified active subversiveness, the threat to order. Maria seeks to ruin Malvolio by finessing the removal of this newly altered, fractious churl. But neither Maria *nor* Malvolio sets about to demolish the Olivia regime; indeed, they both want to rise quietly in power within it. To do so necessitates that they both establish "uniform, godly and quiet order within [the] realm, to avoid all controversies, schisms, and dissensions that may arise"—the words of an Elizabethan proclamation of June 1573 against the Puritans.[38] Maria herself is quite committed to the maintenance of household order; as Elliot Krieger has written, she, like Malvolio, wants to rein in the unruly aristocrats:

> Against Maria's involvement in the Malvolio-plot balances her serious concern for the maintenance of order—not, as may be the case with Malvolio, because of any personal predilection for decorum, but because her mistress wants the house to remain sad and civil. . . . As a result, Maria encourages a particular *kind* of revelry: she transforms Sir Toby's drunken carousals and midnight catches into a sport that requires silent observation and, for the most part, non-interference. (*Marxist Study*, 118–19)

In other words, she succeeds where Malvolio fails—and on two counts. First, she manages to delimit the disorder that he cannot; and second, she ascends in rank through an aristocratic marriage, a goal that also escapes her fellow underling. Maria and Malvolio are locked in a struggle for social mobility and favor from Olivia, and therefore neither can be emphatically radical. Krieger understands a crucial point about the maidservant: "Maria is hardly a proto-bourgeoise, in that her aspiration supports and confirms rather than challenges the continued validity of aristocratic privilege, but . . . only Maria in *Twelfth Night* indicates the bourgeois and Puritan emphasis on independence, competition, and the association of stature with merit" (*Marxist Study*, 121).[39]

This notion of Maria as a de facto Puritan fruitfully complicates my argument. The idea is supported by her opprobrium against Malvolio: "The devil a Puritan he is, or anything constantly, but a time-pleaser, an affectioned ass, that cons state without book, and utters it by great swarths" (2.3.146–48). Juxtaposed to her ambivalent rejection of Malvolio's worthiness to be a *real* Puritan is Maria's conviction of his phony, staged recitations—the fact that he "cons state without book," that he speaks only rehearsed, preinterpreted text. Maria here repeats a pivotal *Puritan* critique against the "popishe abuses yet remaining in the Englishe church." In *An Admonition to the Parliament*, the first loud shot in the long skirmish between English reformers and the official ecclesiastical establishment (and, therefore, Elizabeth's government), the author complains about the Anglican ministry:

> By the word of God, it is an offyce of preaching, they make it an offyce of reading. . . . In the scriptures there is attributed unto the ministers of God, the knowledge of the heavenly misteries, and therfore as the greatest token of their love, they are enjoined to fede Gods Lambes, and yet with these, suche are admitted and accepted, as onely are bare readers that are able to say service, and minister a sacrament. . . . Reading is not feeding, but it is as evill as playing upon a stage, and worse too. For players yet learne their partes wythout booke, and these, a manye of them can scarcely read within booke. These are emptie feeders, darcke eyes, ill workemen.[40]

To the English Puritan, mere reading of the Scripture to a congregation, as opposed to improvisational and heartfelt preaching, has the taint of theater about it.[41] Those evil stage players who can "yet learne their partes wythout booke" are marginally better, even in their actor's infamy, than Anglican priests who can scarcely read at all. To Maria, Malvolio *merely* learns his part without book, merely spits out what he has memorized by rote and not digested: he has not, that is, been nourished by true feeding, and he is incapable of the kind of inspired improvisation that she undertakes. Given her project to construct him as a parody of religious and especially Puritan excesses, her objections to him are distinctly, oddly, Puritanical. In exclaiming against his being a not very good Puritan, against his inconstancy and his Anglican style, *she* sounds the ideological note of rebellion; he represents the insincere authority figure against whose oppression she labors. The main effect of her efforts is the production of a single moment of disorder—the moment when Olivia will discipline the upstart servant: "I know my lady will strike him: if she do, he'll smile, and take't for a great favour" (3.2.79–80). Maria's letter encourages an aggressive overture from a parody of a Puritan hopeful that results in his imprisonment. Her central project, to Puritanize or at least to transform her rival into a self-alienated religious farce, expresses a firsthand knowledge of Puritan ethos; she seems to have absorbed, from personal knowledge of this ethos, the sense that particular religious trappings can produce discord, can attract authority's attention, and can therefore incur punishment.

Maria thus overlays, on the palimpsest of Malvolio's character, an *historical* narrative: a version of the early Puritan movement's relations with the establishment. These relations were constantly strained through reformers' brash and sometimes unfathomable defiance. In 1573, Bishop Edwin Sandys wrote to Lords Leicester and Burghley, complaining about a truculent preacher, "one Mr. Wake, of Christs Churche in Oxforde, who this last yeare made a good sermon at the Crosse," but who, more recently, "beinge sett on and provoked therunto . . . by suche as are authors and maynteynors of theise newe and seditious fansies, his whole sermon was consumed in raylinge against this present state. . . . Such men must be restrained if the state shall stand saffe. . . . There is a conuenticle or rather conspiracie breedinge in London" (Frere and Douglas, *Puritan Manifestoes*, xxii–xxiii). Typically, the official response to such effrontery was, as Sandys suggests, restraint or imprisonment—Malvolio's fate. The alarm in the bishop's report stems from the literal conversion of formerly good sermon-givers to unabashed railers against the English church. But the bishop also offers a psychological reading of the movement that sheds some light on the converted Malvolio:

> Suche as preached discretelie the last yeare now labour by raylinge to feede the fansies of the people. Selfe likinge hath intoxicated them, and the flatterie of the fantasticall people hath bewitched them. Bothe seeke dangerous alteration, thinking that their state cannot be impaired, hopinge that it may be betared. (Frere and Douglas, *Puritan Manifestoes*, xxii)

Malvolio, bewitched by the flattery of "the fantasticall people" (whom he rightly dubs "the lighter people"), and intoxicated with or sick of "Selfe likinge," certainly seeks dangerous alteration for the purposes of social ascent. But we must remember that he is an agent of order *until* his latent urge for power is teased out by what he takes as an invitation to rise. In other words, he resembles a Puritan most in his disruption of his own formerly valued role as power's operative, a maintainer of control. Driven by the thought that, as Sandys puts it, his state "may be be-tared," he becomes useless to Olivia ("Smil'st thou? I sent for thee upon a sad occasion" [3.4.18]) and even an active affront to the woman who relies on him.

Interestingly enough, Malvolio's metamorphosis is not *politically* ramified in the play. Despite Maria's crafty exhortation to "let thy tongue tang arguments of state" (2.5.150), the steward never gets the chance to do so, largely because there *are* no arguments of state: Illyria is virtually without politics. Malvolio's political reticence is certainly a good thing: had he the chance to "read politic authors," as he says he will, he might well have further alienated Olivia through inappropriate religious or diplomatic commentary, which doubtless was Maria's in-tent. Such arguments of state were famously characteristic of Puritans, whose attack on Anglican church practice was always, directly or not, a critique of the monarch and her policies.[42] Because Elizabeth's church settlement was a compromise formation, the queen's ecumenical control involved, like her court affairs, delicate political negotiation, a perilous balance; in this case, the balance lay between Catholic and more vigor-ously reformist ideologies and practices. So to the queen, the sustained doctrinal recalcitrance of Puritan ministers, their insistence on a congre-gational as opposed to a rigidly hierarchical form of church government, and their commitment to the individual as opposed to the collective sense of spiritual responsibility—all these represented a dangerous, con-trary political intervention.[43]

Maria's removal of her rival through Puritanized alienation makes historical sense because of Elizabeth's long-standing hostility toward the radical Protestant movement. What infuriated the queen most about the reformers was neither their social or class pretensions, nor their (real or imagined) piety, but specifically their potential for political divisiveness. As early as 1565, Elizabeth had hit upon and partly created the traits of stereotypical Puritans in decrying their "diversity, variety, contention and vain love of singularity"; she asserted that England must maintain "one rule, form and manner of order."[44] As the minister of this order in the Illyrian great house, Malvolio seeks to constrain riot of any sort, and stands as the barrier against just those characteristics with which Eliza-beth identified Puritanism. But his interpellation by Maria—what we might call his Marian persecution—leads him to imagine himself be-longing in, not to, the system he protects, which in turn leads to the status threat and social alienation of his disguise in Catholic-colored

Puritan attributes. Maria makes Malvolio into a type of the disorder that Elizabeth feared, the image of crazed, desirous singularity that represented an assault on her government and her person.

The fear was not the queen's alone; the most resolutely anti-Puritan character in Illyria is none other than that model of holiday wit, Sir Andrew Aguecheek. Sir Andrew would beat Malvolio as a dog if he thought the man were a Puritan (2.3.141), and would "as lief be a Brownist as a politician" (3.2.30). A Brownist, well out of favor and business by 1600, was a Puritan separatist—one of the few truly revolutionary Elizabethan Puritans, a member of a sect whose disagreement with the Church of England was severe enough to cause schism and to incur an active Anglican persecution—which, for the most part, mainstream Puritans escaped.[45] Sir Andrew must hate politicians because, presumably, they need a sharp wit to make their way in the world. But why is he so against Brownists, the Puritans with the most extreme convictions? Perhaps because an old-money, landed aristocratic type such as Sir Andrew would have much to fear from those persons who most clearly represented contestatory politics and social as well as religious reform. Andrew, clinging desperately to a fading idea of his own privilege, would find threatening any departure from established structure or procedure. Thus, he is the central carrier of the play's nostalgic impulse, its regret for a past moment that was not fully enjoyed: "O, had I but followed the arts!" (1.3.92); "In sooth, thou wast in very gracious fooling last night" (2.3.22); "I was adored once, too" (2.3.181). It is not an accident that this figure, amusingly stupid and kind of sad, is so hostile to Puritanism. The problem for Andrew and his sympathizers is that the movement he fears was hardly a marginalized belief or practice; Calvinist theology (though not the complete presbyterian program for church reform) had penetrated even Whitgift's consciousness, influencing the Lambeth articles and drawing the queen's ire. What is more, there was long a great sympathy for the Puritan program, especially in its militant anti-Catholicism, among the queen's flashier and more influential nobles: Essex and Leicester were Puritan sympathizers, subscribers to the international doctrines of radical Protestant reform. (Essex, it might be added, had both Puritan and Catholic hopefuls about him.) Sir Andrew's animus against Puritans illuminates some of the play's darker corners, insofar as the silly Aguecheek fears effective change—which Puritans always represented in the Renaissance, however absurdly or threateningly the representation was made.[46] Andrew, of course, would dread any organized movement because he is intimidated by competence. But his protest against both Brownists and politicians is ideological: what works (succeeds and labors) is past his ken, or out of his element. If the play relives a past oppression of the Puritan by the upper (and even the lower) classes, it also ends with a tableau of damaged aristocrat dissolutes quarreling as they exit; Toby and Andrew have *both* been bloodied. As for Malvolio, he retains at the end some power to hurt, but can do none in the confines of the text. His political impotence follows on his romantic frustrations; Olivia's unavailability erases his handmade dreams of power. Although Malvolio makes his erotic interest in Olivia painfully clear, she interprets his behavior as either fatigue or illness; she simply doesn't know what he's talking about:

OLIV: Wilt thou go to bed, Malvolio?
MAL: To bed? Ay, sweetheart, and I'll come to thee.
OLIV: God comfort thee! Why dost thou smile so . . . ?
(3.4.30–32)

It is too much to say that Elizabeth found Puritanism unintelligible, but she did find it profoundly alienating. Malvolio, after his transformation by Maria, figures a complexly convected and historically improbable threat: a Catholic-like Puritan who has long wished to, and who now thinks he can, erotically master the most potent woman in the land. The absurdity of this figure is unparalleled in any serious historical context; recusants tended not to think or be thought of in these terms. But, as I shall suggest, there was an historical context for Puritan intervention in Elizabeth's amorous affairs. And this intrusion did not aid the Puritans' cause or increase their favor.

Through Maria's devices, comedy remakes history. But in the form of Malvolio, the construction of "history" is incoherent. His garb is an effect of opposites yoked by violence, two subversive strains becoming a comic costume, ideological motley. Since he *does* suffer a sort of Marian persecution, Malvolio can thus be aligned with the cultural dominant— not the Puritan so much as the anti-Catholic Anglican. More perplexingly, the Puritanical Catholic "Mistress Mary" assimilates quietly into the domain of the "fair princess" (3.1.99) Olivia. Her peaceful disappearance into the lady's extended family and her scourge of the oppositional figure she has created conceptually pocket *two* highly vexing problems of the early Elizabethan era: the repeated Marian (Tudor and Stuart) plots against the peace of the queen; and reform Protestant disorders, which were almost as threatening to the realm from within as was the Scottish or Spanish Catholic menace from without. But even in this political fantasy, the central figure cannot escape unscathed: for the deft demolition of Malvolio centrally involves and disguises an assault against Olivia, however abortive. To succeed, Maria must rig a trap and bait it with her employer. It is not enough that Malvolio be ousted; he must, pricked by the spurs of Maria's intent, attempt to possess the woman of the house, the great lady of the land—and this is the real Marian assault on the central female figure. But in encouraging the flurry of confrontational erotic activity, Maria correspondingly *distances* from Olivia the sectarian implications of Malvolio's change, because the steward asks for erotic, not religious recognition. In fact, the episode marginalizes all doctrinal controversy: spiritual questions are confined to Feste's prison-house catechism of Malvolio. The discourse of eschatology and transmigration occurs well out of Olivia's earshot. This episode, in figuring a scourging of spiritual controversies, encodes a wished-for *distance* of these controversies from the queen; Olivia is completely unaware and inculpable of Malvolio's inquisition and humiliation, and so she is diplomatically protected from (most of) the blame for the Puritan's expulsion.

To imagine that a Marian plot would actually help the court, as Maria claims of Malvolio's ouster ("The house will be the quieter," she says counterintuitively, for his removal should *liberate* noisy Sir Toby), is to participate in an historical delusion whereby anti-Elizabeth plots ultimately strengthened the nation. Mary Stuart's endless treasonous schemes, which featured enciphered letters and secret-agent mediators, are defused in *Twelfth Night*, recalled on a symbolic bias; they imaginatively become the topic of entertainment, the theatrical display of *comic* religious persecution.

Malvolio functions as a symbolic locus for multiple but largely frustrated religious interests over which Elizabeth's Anglican compromise grimly triumphed. But Puritanism, Catholicism, *and* the eroticism of Elizabeth worship were largely vestigial (though dormant and emergent) influences on the reign in 1601. Why then are they represented in this play? If we take "Twelfth Night" as an historical or secular rather than a sacral allusion, the play's topicality signifies both an act of *remembrance* and the awareness of cusp, of ending. In the historical reading, this somewhat somber comedy becomes nostalgia: a melancholy vision on the eve of momentous change and lenten entertainment.

The keenest Puritan "threats" began in the early 1570s and continued, with some interruptions, through the mid-1580s.[47] By 1601, Puritans and Catholics were dispirited, and both eagerly looked north to James of Scotland's succession for greater tolerance, if not for spiritual and political succor.[48] *Twelfth Night's* specifically political inscriptions seem to frustrate the endeavors of topical reading, because no pressing adjacency, no really charged contemporary cultural agon of 1601, can be read into (or beside) the events of the play. Shakespeare's vision seems rather more prescient than present: Malvolio's promise to revenge himself on the whole pack of revelers has the uncanny resonance of an abused, newly made Puritan warning a dissolute aristocracy of the revolution to come.

This promise actually extends in two directions at once: Malvolio does look eerily forward to the revolution of 1642, as many critics have said. But if we cannot credit Shakespeare with extraordinary foresight, we may at least allow that his memory is good. For the revenge of the hostile Puritan represents a vengeance that had *already* been taken, one which the play deflects and displaces, but which has a firm dramatic consequence. The play is careful not to let the Puritanized or radicalized Malvolio interfere with Olivia's erotic project, for the match with Sebastian (whom she thinks Cesario) has already occurred; the Elizabeth figure has wed with remarkable and uncharacteristic alacrity, incaution, and hopefulness. But historically, the Puritan faction of the nation had something significant to say about the queen's nuptials, and did indeed take its revenge, in a manner of speaking, against the persecuting figure to whom they were, however, resolutely loyal. The publication of the Puritan John Stubbs's *A Discoverie of a Gaping Gulf Whereinto England is Like to be Swallowed by an other French Marriage . . .* (1579) helped fuel the firestorm of local and international anger about the proposed match between Elizabeth and the heir presumptive of France; the work pestered the queen's plans by publicizing and reviling them. For Elizabeth, the Puritan threat had surprising force, magnified in the nexus of politics and erotics. In *Twelfth Night*, the specter of a Puritan revenge on matrimony is not erased; it is merely displaced. For Malvolio will have the chance to forestall another alliance—the Viola-Orsino marriage—through his imprisonment of the sea captain who holds Viola's clothes and her gender identity.[49] Viola must depend on the now Puritanical Malvolio's good graces if she hopes to wear her woman's weeds again. But since the Puritans, in Jonas Barish's words, famously "rehearse, ad nauseam, . . . the supposed scriptural injunction against men in women's dress, with its implicit threat to the proper division between the sexes,"[50] we may suppose that the newly Puritanized Malvolio would have—should he need one—a ready excuse to frustrate the proper resolution to the marriage. So the Marian plot may have a lasting effect after all: the play holds out small hope of Malvolio's mollification.

Even as inscriptions of Catholic and Puritan oppositionality converge in Malvolio, his lady's romantic affairs reimagine a critical historical episode two decades past: the courtship of Queen Elizabeth and François Valois, duke of Alençon and Anjou. Elizabeth's storied entertainment of the French match has important points of contact with *Twelfth Night*. For Puritans were not the only vigorous opponents of the marriage. Catholics, whom the alliance directly threatened, were none too pleased about it either. And the queen's own men in the pulpits and presence chamber, standing on quarrels of faith and safety, sturdily opposed it; by throwing enough public relations obstacles in the way, they managed to make the marriage prospect seem more troublesome than advantageous. Consider this literary condensation of historical fact: because Olivia weds in secret speed, neither Malvolio nor anyone else in her house can disrupt her marriage; and because Maria herself has trundled off to wed Sir Toby, the Puritanized and Catholic-coded impediments to the marriage have been quelled before they can arise. In this daydream of sectarian political impotence, an Elizabeth figure escapes factional intrusions in her marital progresses. Indeed, prior to act 5, the only difficulty in Olivia's course of true love is her erotic choice: she favors a romantic mediator over the official suitor. To better understand this plot intervention, it will help to have a closer look at the Anjou episode.

III

Catherine de' Médicis had proposed a marriage between Elizabeth and her younger son, François Valois, then Duke of Alençon, around the time of the St. Bartholomew's Day massacre of 1572. Understandably, occasions were inhospitable for an Anglo-French union; still, Elizabeth toyed with the idea for several years before letting interest in the match lapse around 1576. But toward the end of her second decade in power, the possibility of the union with Valois, now Duke of Anjou, was resurrected. It may have been Anjou's aggressive confrontation of the Spanish forces in the Netherlands that made the marriage seem worth pursuing and the duke worth controlling. But as J. B. Black has suggested, other factors commended the renewed overtures:

[T]here was a seriousness about this courtship of Anjou in 1578 entirely absent from all previous manoeuvres of a similar nature. Apart altogether from the French danger in the Netherlands, a marriage with Anjou seemed to offer a means of egress from many of the fears that haunted the queen's mind. . . . It might, for example, get rid of the otherwise insoluble succession problem by providing an heir to continue the line of Henry VIII—a matter that troubled Elizabeth more acutely as she grew older. It would greatly strengthen the Anglo-French alliance. . . . It would go far to dispose of the danger from Mary Stuart.[51]

Obstacles included the religious and, not incidentally, age differences of the prospective lovers: Elizabeth was already forty-five, Anjou some twenty years her junior. But the high-level alliance promised substantial advantages, and so preparations for marriage negotiations began in the summer of 1578.[52] Preliminary envoys were sent from France, but they received little satisfaction and made little progress. In the absence of the duke himself, the queen refused to negotiate seriously; she was distrustful of an absent suitor.[53] France had to find a more persuasive intermediary to keep the negotiations alive while Anjou arranged his inevitable visit. The candidate: Jean de Simier, the duke's closest counselor and master of his wardrobe. William Camden calls him "a most choice courtier, exquisitely skilled in love-toys, pleasant conceits, and court dalliances."[54] The moral reproof beneath this assessment has filtered down to the twentieth century; Black names him, with less subtlety and civility, "the most accomplished philanderer of the period."[55] Black seems to think it a scandal that the queen should have had anything to do with Simier. In fact, scandal became the keynote of the emissary's employment.

Jean de Simier proved both a more and less propitious choice for amorous diplomacy than previous ambassadors had been: he caused the marriage negotiations to proceed apace, but his presence and efficacy sent alarms through Puritan and hard Anglican hearts in England. Elizabeth's long indifference to the French affair softened in the presence of this man, Anjou's "chief darling."[56] The queen's relations to the love ambassador quickly became the subject of much court gossip, not to mention some sinister activity; the earl of Leicester, for one, plotted to kill him, for he regarded Simier as a threat to achieve a union which he and other militant Protestants reviled.[57] Elizabeth, in turn, grew increasingly vehement in defense of Anjou's servant, banishing Leicester from court for two months when the plot against Simier was discovered. Such

was the growing fondness between Elizabeth and the French courtier
that it became necessary to reassure Valois that his servant was not playing him false, that her "ape" (her pet name for Simier) was behaving
impeccably, as some of the rumors of sexual impropriety had sped
across the channel. In a letter to her French ambassador, Amias Paulet
(circa February 1579), Elizabeth pointedly praised the mediator's dedication to the duke:

> And as for the gentleman himself, De Simyer . . . we [have] found in him
> otherwise so great fidelity towards his master, so rare a sufficiency and dis-
> cretion in one of his years in the handling of the cause, and so great devotion
> towards the match itself, as we had both great reason to like of him, as also to
> wish that we had a subject so well able to serve us.[58]

Simier's presence, however, continued to elicit much discussion. "It
is not unknown to every estate and degree," writes Henry Howard,
earl of Northampton, "how that Monsieur d'Anjou, brother and heir
apparent to the King of France, for this year's space almost, by his
ledger-ambassador here (a gentleman of good note and credit about
him and of a goodly wit and great dexterity in managing of affairs)
hath continually solicited a marriage to be had between our gracious
sovereign and himself." Thus begins Howard's defense against
Stubbs's *Discoverie of a Gaping Gulf.*[59] The earl intends to provide
"sufficient and invincible arguments," as he later says, on behalf of the
courtship, but he must begin by validating Simier's presence. For
Stubbs had assailed the go-between as a professional deceiver and an
epitome of continental Catholic untrustworthiness: "Yea, unless we
ourselves close our own eyes, we may see that it is a very French Popish wooing to send hither smooth-tongued Simiers to gloss and glaver
[flatter] and hold talk of marriage" (Berry, *Stubbs's "Gaping Gulf,"*
80). But even defenders of the marriage revealed suppressed doubts
about the form of the courtship. Howard, for one, strains a bit to defend Simier's part in the yearlong surrogate wooing. To praise Simier,
as he does, for possessing "a goodly wit and great dexterity in managing of affairs" sounds like a tongue-in-check indictment. The "marriage to be had between our gracious sovereign and himself" seems to
refer either to Anjou *or* to his proxy as the groom in question. Simier
has intervened grammatically between "Monsieur d'Anjou" and "a
marriage to be had." Everyone knew that the proposed alliance was a
mediated affair; Anjou's absence and the wooing by his "ledger-
ambassador," however, was suspect, because "unless the master were

the man," as Olivia says (1.5.298), the queen may have been developing an attachment to the wrong person.

Such confusion was inherent in the mediator's role. Like Viola in her surrogate courtship of Olivia, the embassy to Elizabeth received liberal negotiating prerogatives. Here is Simier's official commission from his master:

> We make it known to all that being assured of the fidelity, capability, prudence and dexterity of our trusty Jehan de Simier, lord of that place, Baron of St. Mary, etc., our councillor and master of our wardrobe, we have chosen him as our commissioner to the said Queen, . . . giving him hereby full powers to negotiate, resolve, and conclude marriage with the said Queen, according to the articles we have given into his hands.[60]

To negotiate, resolve, and conclude a marriage is virtually to marry; and the exceptional range of privilege the mediator enjoyed came to encroach on the courtship proceedings.

In a royal proclamation against Stubbs's "lewd, seditious book" and against the Puritan "libelers" who opposed the match, the queen praised Anjou vis-à-vis Simier, even at the risk of protesting too much; the courtier not only lacked any "manifest token of any evil condition as wherewith he is charged; but, contrariwise . . . there hath appeared singular wisdom, modesty, and great temperance in all his embassy, to the allowance of the wisdom of his lord and master in making choice of such a servant."[61] We cannot know whether the queen's interest in Simier was more than diplomatic. As for the courtier, deliciously dedicated to the task of surrogate wooing, he may not, at first, have been deliberately untrue to his master's political and erotic project. On April 12, 1579, he wrote that, having begun to "treat of the articles of marriage" between Elizabeth and Anjou, "I have every good hope; but will wait to say more till the curtain is drawn, the candle out, and Monsieur in bed. Then I will speak with good assurance" (*CSPF 1578–79*, 487).[62] But the negotiations ran aground on several points. The queen kept adding conditions and responding testily when Anjou added some of his own. She balked at his demands for an allowance and generally objected to his fiscal interests. The most important early condition, however, was her insistence on seeing her intended face-to-face. This point caused Simier the greatest anxiety: "This interview . . . can only serve to hinder this happy negotiation and put off the entrance into a haven so desired."[63]

When the disguised Viola insists on speaking to an unveiled Olivia, the lady slyly replies: "Have you any commission from your lord to

negotiate with my face? You are now out of your text: but we will draw
the curtain and show you the picture" (1.5.234–37). Olivia's riposte
both highlights the mediator's independent initiative and alters the historical identifications of wooer and wooed: the *woman* is now the coveted and rare sight. The revelation of Olivia's countenance allows the
mediator an intimacy that the master should have attempted. This is a
decisive moment in the play's romance, and it carries within it both historical critique and fancy: Anjou's inappropriate distance, passivity, and
coyness are overcome on stage by two assertive women in dedicated (if
half-knowing) flirtation. As a fanciful but pointed historical commentary, the scene suggests that Elizabeth's courtships could have been ex-
pedited considerably had there been no men—or only a mediator—involved. Such come-hither maneuvers as Viola makes in her interview
with the lady are well past Orsino's narcissistic and imaginative limits.
Viola's overture has unquestionably transcended her "commission,"
which Orsino defines thus: to "unfold the passion of my love," and
"surprise her with discourse of my dear faith" (1.4.24–25). (It bodes ill
that the discourse of Orsino's "faith" would come as a surprise.) When
Viola had performed only the commission, the result was as always:
Olivia's indifference. In response to the lady's query "How does he love
me?" the go-between speaks Petrarchan boilerplate: "With adorations,
fertile tears, / With groans that thunder love, with sighs of fire" (258–
60). Small wonder that the duke has been unsuccessful. Only when
Viola leaps "all civil bounds," only when she enters a subjectivity that
Orsino could not possibly inhabit, does Olivia fall. For the romance to
occur, a youthful, attractive, female mediator must take sexy initiative.
The new homoerotic courtship has acquired an edge and a possibility
which the nonnegotiated relationship never had.

The complications of homoeroticism and disguise have only oblique
relations to the recorded facts of the French affair. Shakespeare's homosexual subtext has a vibrant life of its own, and inscriptively its burdens
are inconsiderable. But it *is* clear that Simier's mediator function perfectly describes Viola's life in Illyria: "All the occurrence of my fortune
since," she tells the deceived at the end of the play, "Hath been between
this lady and this lord" (5.1.255–56). It is also plain that the drama
translates an historical mediation into the sexual and characterological
in-betweenness that Viola forms.

Both real-world and theatrical courtships suffer injuries from the go-
between. After the ultimate collapse of the French negotiations, Anjou
did not blame the official object of his desire; instead, he slapped his

frustrations on a single scapegoat: Simier, the darling intermediary. Rumors of Elizabeth's flirtations with her "ape" and others persisted throughout the Anjou courtship, and so the duke might well have felt betrayed when the trifling vessel of his marriage negotiations began to sink. We cannot know the extent to which these rumors functioned as an excuse for a long-foundering affair. Certainly Catherine de' Médicis did not hesitate to blame her son's failed betrothal on Elizabeth's morals; she wrote defiantly about Anjou and the queen to her ambassador, La Mothé Fenelon: "My son has informed me through the King that he will never marry her even if she wishes it, especially because he has always heard so poorly of her honor; and he has seen letters written by all the ambassadors who have been there, such that [if he were to marry] he would believe himself dishonored, and would lose the reputation he thinks he has acquired."[64] Mary Queen of Scots also accused Elizabeth of sexual incontinence in the context of the French match and claimed, in a famous missive to her rival, to have heard reports that the queen "had not only engaged your honor with a foreigner named Simier . . . [but that] you coupled with him and studied various immodest liberties together."[65] Such charges do not, of course, explain the collapse of the marriage negotiations. But the accusations against Simier prepare for a Shakespearean plot development: Orsino's turn against his favorite. The Illyrian duke compensates for his romantic misfortune with this ugly, embarrassing display of ego and homoerotic bravado before Olivia:

> Since you to non-regardance cast my faith,
> And that I partly know the instrument
> That screws me from my true place in your favour,
> Live you the marble-breasted tyrant still. . . .
> Come, boy, with me; my thoughts are ripe in mischief:
> I'll sacrifice the lamb that I do love
> To spite a raven's heart within a dove.
>   (5.1.119–29)

He would like to kill Olivia (at 5.1.115–17), but the attack on the powerful woman, the "marble-breasted tyrant," cannot be made, not at least in Elizabeth's time; and so Orsino settles for a powerless victim: "Come, boy, with me; my thoughts are ripe in mischief." The man who once reveled in the phallic dream of the "rich golden shaft" killing "the flock of all affections else" in Olivia, who imagined himself filling Olivia's "sovereign thrones" with "one self king" (1.1.35–39) and thus producing a version of Anjou's political desires, reveals himself at last as a passionate thug. If Orsino's homosexual leanings can be read into the violence toward his beloved boy, the instrument he "partly knows," so too can an historical allusion.

Bernardino de Mendoza, the Spanish ambassador to England in the 1580s, reports a remarkable scene between the French duke and his mediator. Elizabeth, having informed Anjou of her desire to reestablish an "ancient alliance" with Philip II of Spain, noticed that Simier had entered the room "by the private stair"; she withdrew, "saying that she did not wish to stand between master and servant," and the following exchange took place:

> Alençon asked him whether his tarrying here was caused by a fear that he would have him killed when he arrived in France. He replied that, for his part, this was not the reason, although there was some ground for the fears that his enemies might attempt it. Alençon answered throwing upon him the whole blame of the present hopelessness of the marriage negotiations.[66]

Anjou followed the veiled death threat with misguided charges against Simier, blaming him for the alienation of numerous political affections. Actually, Simier might reasonably have been accused of greater intimacy with the queen than his commission allowed. In 1581, as the duke pressed Elizabeth for a marital commitment, she responded by trying gently to convince him to leave her court and go to Flanders, enlisting Burghley and others to offer money and citing the obvious reasons for a strong anti-Catholic presence there. "When the Queen had done this," Mendoza wrote, "she sent secretly for Simier, who apparently for a long time she has had in her interest, and has been entertaining here. To him she complained greatly of the annoyance she felt at Alençon's pressing her so closely, saying that she could not get rid of him without danger, or entertain him further without inconvenience" (*CSPS*, 243–44). Indeed, the only way to remove Anjou from her court was to promise him substantial wealth, a promise which greatly cheered him. Somehow Mendoza learned that the queen "dwelt at length with Simier on the point, and the colloquy ended with great merriment as they said that Alençon was a fine gallant to sell his lady for money" (*CSPS*, 245).

In the Anjou match, the messenger, sent as political grease for the diplomatic machine, became (in John Lennon's memorable pun) a Spaniard in the works, or if not quite so threatening, at least something of a double agent crossing his master's interests. The rift between Anjou and his mediator became serious enough to eventuate not only in death threats but in Anjou's depriving Simier of all property and possessions.[67] While Cesario shares no *overtly* oppositional intimacy with Olivia, the young wo/man certainly encroaches on the duke's romantic prerogative in the guise of suing for it. To put the noble lady into a holiday humor, "like enough to consent," requires delicate maneuvering, especially insofar as the amorous instrument must eventually forego his or her place as the erotic surrogate. Neither Simier nor Viola seems entirely willing to relinquish this role.

Historical inscriptions in *Twelfth Night* recall mediational problems in the French affair; they also devastatingly undermine Orsino through similitude with the rejected Valois. Anjou's unstable character finds several echoes in Orsino's deeply flawed person. As the newly favored Cesario asks Valentine about the duke, "You . . . fear his humour . . . that you call in question the continuance of his love. Is he inconstant, sir, in his favours?" (1.4.5–7). Although Valentine answers in the negative, Illyria's duke appears wed to inconstancy. His love, he claims, is all-encompassing, but whatever enters the ocean of his affections instantly drowns, falling "into abatement and low price, / Even in a minute" (1.1.13–14). Anjou himself was, as Amias Paulet wrote, "not ignorant of the 'alarums' (as he called them) and sinister impressions which had been given . . . of his treating for marriage in other places, protesting with oaths that he was guiltless therein" (*CSPF 1578–79*, 462). Even more serious than these rumored dalliances, and causally related to them, was the question of the duke's vacillating stance on religion—initially a selling point for the marriage in England, insofar as Anjou was for many years a staunch Huguenot defender. But he was also a Huguenot betrayer: in 1575, "Alençon deserted the Protestant cause entirely, and became suddenly a devout Catholic" on the premise of a projected marriage with Philip II's eldest daughter, and the attainment of government over the Spanish Netherlands. "He even accepted the command of a force against the Huguenots, upon whom he was implacable in his severity."[68]

Besides their characterological similarity, the critical link between Anjou and Orsino is erotic failure of a particular type. Illyria's duke is constantly undermined not only by his behavior but more seriously by a woman he cannot understand or control. Specifically, he cannot grasp the idea that Olivia, like Elizabeth, lacks interest in a romance she does not master. One of Sebastian's most charming features (besides his interchangeability with Viola) is the easy, sweet way he allows himself to be drawn under the contessa's yoke; this yielding, an interesting counterpart to Viola's aggression as Cesario, makes him the perfect romantic object:

OLIV: Thou shalt not choose but go:
         Do not deny.
         Nay, come, I prithee; would thou'dst be rul'd by me!
SEB: Madam, I will.

                                                          (4.1.56–64)

Sebastian, unlike Orsino, seems aware that Olivia inscribes the figure of
Elizabeth. Olivia, for her part, sees a figure very much like Anjou in
Orsino. Her refusal of the Illyrian ruler—"I cannot love him"—has
something of an historical rationale. But Orsino's failure and Olivia's
choice—like Viola's cross-dressing—do not completely yield to historical understanding. They are in effect derived from a theatrical impulse
that effaces the specificities of the past.

                                IV

Twelfth Night conceptually repairs a vast formal if not historical deficit:
the play marries off the unmarried queen. Through Olivia's person,
Shakespeare rewrites the unfulfilled history of Elizabeth's frustrating
Anjou courtship. The text indulges a retrospective political fantasy
amidst its portrayal of female erotic *initiative*: the great lady circum-
vents unwieldy, public, mediated romance to privately choose and wed
her own husband—who is, she thinks, the mediator of the political
match. Olivia cares nothing for a high-level diplomatic alliance. The
sovereign woman of Shakespeare's comedy splices Elizabeth's formidable political control onto a complicated fantasy of impulsive aristocratic
courtship, female erotic aggressiveness, and social ascent through marriage.[69]

    For genre's sake, the text must endorse the powerful woman's wed-
ded condition, but it does not escape ambivalence in doing so. Olivia has
in no uncertain terms married the wrong person, one she did not fall in
love with: a man. What can it mean historically that Olivia's first, most
intense object of desire is a disguised woman?[70] Although topicality in
Illyria is laxly mimetic and underdetermined ("What you will"), at a
distance from *Hamlet*'s or *Troilus*'s overwrought systems of reference,
we can venture that some cords bind text and past. Elizabeth's lifelong
aversion to marriage is mastered, in the plot of *Twelfth Night*, by lucky
ambisexuality: female power is "betroth'd both to a maid and man"
(5.1.261). The play effects, through erotics, a theatrical variant on the
queen's political androgyny. Olivia's desires, like Elizabeth's public per-

sonae, span a biological divide as *Twelfth Night* lets the queen figuratively woo and marry herself.[71]

Specific operations of inscription drop out here. It is true that the transvestite theater may ironically encode and approximate certain historical facts—such as that of Elizabeth's rhetorical androgyny—but *Twelfth Night*'s sexual plot sacrifices referentiality for a representational surplus of selves and desires.

The fantasy of Olivia's marriage is paid for and abetted by its nonnormative eroticism. The play strongly insinuates, well before its shaky heterosexual climax, that Olivia's "real" desires, on which Viola's wooing capitalizes, are lesbian. At the same time, as I shall argue, this particular homoeroticism grounds itself in a complicated appeal to narcissism—a decidedly different appeal than Patroclus makes to his sweetheart Achilles in *Troilus and Cressida*. One might claim that such eroticism has the effect of neutralizing historical questions of surrogacy and mediation, and of canceling politics entirely: Olivia prefers a vigorous female servant to an enervated male ruler. But another, more satisfying claim about *Twelfth Night*'s homoeroticism interprets it not as a way of escaping politics but as a way of affirming affect. In a play full of replacement objects of desire—letters, songs, and money for lovers, jests for passion, Sebastian for Viola—homoerotic love seems *authentic*, the thing for which (as Olivia and Antonio both show) undisguised risk is undertaken. The play's baseline, indelible passion may well be homosexual. Even if this textual impulse mutes specific historical signals, Olivia's and Viola's eroticism can be taken as *generally* descriptive of the play's relationship to its contexts: yearning but distant; an intimacy enticed by separation.

Patriarchal norms do not overwhelm *Twelfth Night*. The central prenuptial moments in the play are circuits of specifically female eroticism and aggression: when Viola woos Olivia; when Olivia easily masters Sebastian and leads him off to marry, following (he must think) the world's shortest courtship; when Maria so entices Malvolio through her disguised letter that the steward tumbles from his place, "in recompense whereof [Toby] hath married her" (5.1.363). The betrothal game which usually reduces a woman to a possessed object is played in Illyria inside the lines of female prerogative. It is within Viola's power to win and reject the objects of her love; in Maria's power to lure and baffle the contingent man (and make him a Lucrece, a Jezebel, a Peg-a-Ramsey); in Olivia's power to refuse, to choose, and to excuse the objects, convey-

ances, and victims of desire. Female erotic hegemony achieves its pinna-
cle near the end of act 1, where Viola performs a miraculous seduction
of the hitherto unobtainable Olivia. The page entices, perhaps produces,
lesbian desire through the lure of a specifically female narcissism.

After some coy badinage in her first embassy to Olivia, Viola/Cesario
tells the great lady about the fiery love that Orsino bears; but her language dangerously substitutes herself for the master: "If I did love you in
my master's flame, / With such a suff'ring, such a deadly life, / In your
denial I would find no sense, / I would not understand it" (1.5.268–71).
Viola posits herself as the hypothetical wooer here and finds much virtue
in "if": specifically, she finds a voice of magnetic intensity. Her fictive
longing soon generates a twin—Olivia's genuine desire. Drawn inside
Viola's "if," the lady queries, "Why, what would you?" Viola then delivers a speech that comprises both mournful vocalic distance and passive sexual aggression:

> Make me a willow cabin at your gate,
> And call upon my soul within the house.
> Write loyal cantons of contemned love,
> And sing them loud, even in the dead of night.
> Halloo your name to the reverberate hills,
> And make the babbling gossip of the air
> Cry out, "Olivia!" O, you should not rest
> Between the elements of air and earth
> But you should pity me.
>
> (1.5.273–79)

Coded as the Echo figure to whom she refers, Viola vocally bestows an
already solipsistic Olivia upon herself by delivering a speech that is a
rhetorical mirror of desire. In this scene and for the rest of the play,
aspects of Echo and Narcissus shadow the two women. Here, the soul
that Viola would call upon unwittingly reproduces the morbid desires
Olivia has been harboring: the willow, contemned love, dead of night,
hallowed name, and ghostly echo all suggest the great lady's practiced
sorrow, and irresistibly entice her with an image of her own emotional
fancies. Olivia, concerned as she has been to appear in mourning, receives from Viola an echoic image of love like deathly sorrow.

In this speech, Viola inducts a complicated, plastic self in which the
grammatical subject—the "I"—drops out and becomes improbably an
active object, a "me" *hypothetically* busy as a recipient of courtship.
The grammatical trick lies in Viola's response to Olivia's query "what
would you?" Implying (but not saying) "I would do the following,"

Viola puts forth a list of activities that, removed from context, sound like imperatives, not subjunctives—that is, not things *she* would do, but things she would have the auditor do. Even in its final lines ("O, you should not rest . . . "), the speech posits the listener as the active participant; the speaker occupies the passive or receptive position.[72] "Make me a willow cabin," she orders. The grammatical surprise of the lines accords with a psychological and theatrical one: Viola is improbably both taking control and disappearing. By effecting a reversal of the subject and the object, Viola/Cesario enacts a mythic paradigm: she becomes the vocal expression of an unfulfilled, dislocated desire that destabilizes speaker and listener. She becomes, that is, an echo to something that has not quite been expressed, an elaborate reflection of a narcissist who, in the course of the scene, loses her place. Imaginatively collapsing the distinction between speaker and auditor, Viola, in the best courtly tradition, obviates the other. The soul she would "call upon . . . within the house" is "my soul," which need not even refer to the beloved; it may be a self-reference. Yet Viola's discourse wheels around a speaking self that has broken off from subjectivity. As some critics have noted, it is hard to tell who, exactly, speaks and seduces so effectively here.[73]

The hook of the speech occurs with Viola's allusion to the babbling gossip Echo. If we can bypass for a moment the pronominal ambiguity, Viola avers that she will make Echo call out Olivia's name. At first, this association between Echo and Viola seems apt. Throughout the play Viola emulates Ovid's mythic Echo by harboring a futile desire for her own unobtainable Narcissus, Orsino. And like Echo, Viola is invisible, elusive; Olivia cannot guess who she is or to what purpose she speaks ("What are you? What would you?"). The uncertainty of Viola's identity, pronominal or otherwise, is a constant fact of the play, a fact that enables the willow cabin speech. But the correspondence between Viola and Echo is not seamless. For if Viola can make Echo, the "babbling gossip of the air," cry out "Olivia," then it is Viola who positions herself, however briefly, as Narcissus—the one who calls. Almost all of the romantic activity Viola imagines in the lines is linguistic: she would call, write, sing, hallow, and make the air cry. She becomes the image of a love that has turned completely bodiless, into discourse; however, this image perfectly describes *Echo's* ontological reality, her metamorphosis from flesh to derivative word. Echo's repetitions of Narcissus's cries dislodge language from subjectivity, signification from identification; just so, Viola's speech, a beautiful whirl of referent, becomes an odd conflation of echoic and narcissistic elements. She plays a Narcissus crying out the name of a lover she does not perfectly desire. At the same time, simply by naming Olivia, Viola performs the echo function she said she would make Echo perform, returning an aural image of the beloved (" 'Olivia!' ") even as she returned a moral image earlier ("I see you what you are, you are too proud, / But if you were the devil, you are fair").

What sets this scene apart from conventional romantic interviews is that the language of desire emanates from a fictive, surrogate voice of the "wrong" gender. The willow cabin passage is not innocent of desire; indeed, it overflows with longing—but locating that desire is another matter. Viola's motives for delivering such a seductive account of her own passion are themselves Echoic in that she cannot explain them and that they are opaque to psychologistic analysis.[74] The erotic tide of this scene ripples through the rest of the play.

When he calls Viola "thou dissembling cub!" near the end of *Twelfth Night*, Orsino, we can see, quite literally doesn't know the half of it. He does not know Viola's biological femininity; he does not know her love for him; he thinks he divines but cannot imagine her flirtatious returns to Olivia, which had long ceased to be theatrically convincing as courtship embassies solely on his behalf. Necessary to the plot, but also psychosexually suggestive, Viola's returns to Olivia are like echoes to the lady's needs: whenever Olivia calls, Viola comes, and answers. Her visits to Olivia at 2.4 ("Sir, shall I to this lady?"), 3.1, and 3.4 limn a subconscious desire that seems magically to materialize, in socially acceptable form, when Sebastian reappears in act 4. Given what we know that Viola knows about her effect on the great lady, Orsino cannot imagine how right he is to suspect Viola of faithlessness; yet it is a deception she does not necessarily control.[75]

The lesbian subtext of the willow cabin scene challenges ideas of psychological unity and linear or coherent sexuality. Aspects of role playing, master serving, and lesbian longing all operate here. However, these notions describe only part of the complexity of the surrogate courtship. Viola's discourse inserts itself in the nexus of homosexuality (desire for the same) and narcissism (desire for the selfsame), a *collapsible* space on the Shakespearean stage which Viola, as Cesario, literally crosses in her transit from the master narcissist Orsino to the master-mistress Olivia. The page appeals to the narcissism of her female erotic target; but fed as it is by a woman in disguise, this narcissism is indistinguishable from lesbian eroticism. Olivia hears from the masked page a promise to vault her name into the reverberating canyons of echo; since it is Olivia's *own* name that thrillingly will give her no rest, the precise axes of her desire are hard to locate. Much of the problem is the person to whom she responds. Like the hybrid Narcissus-Echo that she is, Viola has absence—a missing or diminished subjectivity—at her heart. John Hollander, giving a brief history of the Echo trope, notes that "Ovid's nymph vanished into voice; the natural fact of disembodied voice vanishes, in a later stage of things, into text."[76] Viola's self-absence, apparent in the grammar of her erotic overture, is a matter of fact: she later tells Olivia "I am not what I am," speaking not one but two "I's" which, Iago-like, cancel each other out. Speaking for someone else, projecting a desire that may and may not be her own, effectively expunging herself from her romantic syntax, Viola is a kind of nothing: a curtain of resonant words over "a blank," the word she uses to describe her history.

So this scene, charged by lesbian desire, is also insulated by the very indeterminacy of the conductor. In Golding's Ovid, Echo pursues Narcissus through the forest even as he searches for her; in frustration, "he looketh backe, and seeing no man followe, / Why fliste, he cryeth once againe: and she the same doth hallowe."[77] Narcissus, "seeing no man followe," does not even look for a woman or consider the possibility that the answering voice is actually female. This gender blindness may work subtextually in the Olivia-Viola scene. And Viola's promise to "hallow your name to the reverberate hills" probably recalls Golding's translation.[78] If so, Shakespeare remembers a moment when Echo and Narcissus are indistinguishable ("she the same doth hallowe"): who is calling, who is called? This confusion amplifies the unsteady eroticism of the Narcissus myth. Golding describes his Narcissus the same way Viola appears: as Cesario is "in standing water, between boy and man," so Narcissus "seemde to stande beetwene the state of man and Lad"; and the sixteen-year-old Narcissus has the same bisexual appeal that Viola and Sebastian enflame: "The hearts of divers trim yong men his beautie gan to move, / And many a Ladie fresh and faire was taken in his love" (Golding, *Metamorphoses*, 3.438–40).[79]

One arresting moment in the courtship scene comes just after the interview, when Olivia, stupefied, recalls what has taken place:

OLIVIA: "What is your parentage?"
           "Above my fortunes, yet my state is well;
           I am a gentleman." I'll be sworn thou art.
                (1.5.293–95)

In quoting what has just taken place, Olivia, the "too proud" beauty and object of all desires, has suddenly, materially been transformed into Echo, the abject repeater. She soon pursues her reluctant unknown quarry, trailing after the now proud Narcissus/Viola: "O what a deal of scorn looks beautiful / In the contempt and anger of his lip!" (3.1.147–48). The implicit complications in the willow cabin speech take shape in the plot: wooer and beloved, seeker and sought are reversed. Viola, who had assured the lady no rest "But you should pity me," will herself be forced to discourage the smitten Olivia, saying, in a self-echo, "I pity you" (3.1.125). The reversal of suitor and love object is mythographic as well as theatrical. Olivia becomes the lovelorn voice, destined for unrequited passion until Viola's own biological echo (or reflection) appears.[80]

Intimations of Echo and Narcissus run gracefully through the play. These figures help define the Illyrians' erotic and social possibilities. The person in control of echo, in control of the voice's source, has relatively greater power than one who is made to echo and who thus becomes contingent, subjected. For instance, the movement of echo from a referent in Viola's speech to an enactment in Olivia's recollection of the conversation marks a shift in erotic dominance: Olivia soon abandons her aloof station, stepping down from admired to importunate.[81] Other characters try to deploy echo for the illusion of control, but the figure often reverberates their weaknesses. The hopeless Sir Andrew becomes—pitifully, as Olivia is not—another Echo to Viola, quoting in asides Cesario's dashing speech:

VIOLA: Most excellent accomplished lady, the heavens rain odours on
           you!
ANDREW: That youth's a rare courtier: "rain odours"—well.
VIOLA: My matter hath no voice, lady, but to your own most pregnant
           and vouchsafed ear.
ANDREW: "Odours," "pregnant," and "vouchsafed": I'll get 'em all three
           ready.
                                                                  (3.1.86–93).

Despite Viola's claim that her matter "hath no voice" but to Olivia's ear, Sir Andrew is really the voiceless one here. His echoic behavior, unlike Olivia's, registers a mental deficit; he repeats what he's heard in an attempt to appropriate a style he has been practicing to no noticeable effect. Olivia echoes her conversation with Viola in an erotic reverie; Andrew echoes in a tense pitch of envy.

While Viola's invocation of echo proves seductive, and Andrew's impotent, the trope can have darker consequences. When Malvolio employs the figure, it redounds disastrously. In echoing Maria's letter, he endeavors to secure complicit identification with sounds that were never made. The echoing steward seems quite mad because of his unintelligible quotations:

MAL: "Be not afraid of greatness": 'twas well writ.
OLIVIA: What mean'st thou by that, Malvolio?
MAL: "Some are born great"—
OLIVIA: Ha?
MAL: "Some achieve greatness"—
OLIVIA: What say'st thou?
MAL: "And some have greatness thrust upon them."
OLIVIA: Heaven restore thee! . . .
          . . . Why, this is very midsummer madness.
                                              (3.4.38–55)

Malvolio's echoes are supposed to reveal the secret history of a desire that does not exist; instead, his fatuous parroting dooms him to Toby's rotten care. He suffers the Ovidian Echo's fate: desire-laden playback produces not consummation but solitude. Malvolio loses his dignity through the verbal mirror of Maria's forgery, which not only illuminates his desires but magnifies his inclination to serve. He is made to mime behavior that, literally, no one requests: his response to the forged letter is an echo to a vacuum. He responds to a gap where text ordinarily stands for voice, and where voice stands for selfhood. What allows or furthers Malvolio's subjection, then, is that echoic trope which gives Viola such erotic power in the play.

Curiously, his humiliation is itself echoed. At the end of the play Feste speaks his lines again (" 'Some are born great' ") when Malvolio's victimization has become public and palpable. But the Fool does not confine his echoes to the letter:

CLOWN: Why, "Some are born great, some achieve greatness, and some have greatness thrown upon them." I was one, sir, in this interlude, one Sir Topas, sir, but that's all one. "By the Lord, fool, I am not mad." But do you remember, "Madam, why laugh you at such a barren rascal, and you smile not, he's gagged"? And thus the whirligig of time brings in his revenges.
                                              (5.1.369–76)

What the whirligig brings in, here at least, is history, the verbal past— echo's revenge. With peculiar doubleness in his roles as both controller and conduit of sentiment, Feste betrays his own vulnerability. He shows how Malvolio's earlier obloquy wounded him, how the echo of that insulting language has lingered; he has been waiting the whole play to bounce those words back to the speaker. Feste's quotations reveal echo's lability as a trope: it can enlarge or diminish the social presence of the speaker, underscoring his or her weakness or power, sometimes (as here) both at once. As if to prove the point, Feste's mention of revenge is itself echoed immediately by Malvolio—"I'll be reveng'd on the whole pack of you!"—and this cry represents *both* his threat to festivity and his present inability to make good on that threat. A last reverberation further complicates echo's meanings. Olivia delivers, in response to her steward's plaint, a statement of apparent sympathy: "He hath been most notoriously abus'd." But because, as several readers have noticed, this too echoes Malvolio ("Fool, there was never man so notoriously abused" [4.2.90]), the trope functions ambivalently as either parodic anaphora or sincere confirmation. Repeating Malvolio's cries of injustice either neutralizes or legitimates them. The echo chamber in which the steward finds himself humiliated may eventually answer to his purpose: the whirligig could bring in another set of revenges, depending on the sincerity of the female echo, Olivia's response.

Echo traditionally manifests a defective version of linguistic selfhood in that it is discourse narrowly determined by another speaker. When Feste, as Sir Topas, tells the imprisoned Malvolio to "leave this vain bibble-babble" (4.2.100), the phrase recalls Viola's "babbling gossip of the air"; both Malvolio's and Viola's language serve poorly as self-representations (which in Illyria are always "vain"—impotent or conceited). But as deployed by Olivia and Feste, and as enacted in Viola's willow cabin speech, echo erases the passivity that Ovid writes in the figure. Ovid's Echo is an aural replication of a male vocalic self. But the plot of *Twelfth Night* reconsiders this tradition, as masculine narcissistic lassitude in Illyria (Orsino) gives way to feminine echoic and not incidentally *erotic* potency (Viola, Olivia). That is, echo in the play enacts a countermythography of female agency. Even in the *Metamorphoses*, though, this possibility is latent. As Caren Greenberg has said of Ovid's figure, "Echo still performs linguistically; she is able to choose how much of the end of an utterance she wants to repeat. She remains a speaker because she can produce language which is in relation to her desires."[82] Perhaps, as a female appropriation of perplexed male utterance, Echo has *always* signaled a gendered redistribution of power: her language serves a desire different from that which produced it. But echoic language also represents a kind of impotence, and that is *relational*: a failure of interlocutors to connect. In Shakespeare's subtle adaptation, echo figures a discourse that both acknowledges the force of the excluded speaker and simultaneously marks his or her deficiency. Even so, as Greenberg suggests, echo does provide a way to appropriate sound or sense from—to alter the meanings of—another speaker. The traditionally contingent figure gathers, in the course of *Twelfth Night*, force and meaning.

V

It's a poor sort of memory that only works backwards.
    Lewis Carroll, Through the Looking Glass

The transformations of echo in *Twelfth Night* expose an important fact about this trope of similarity: it alters signification through repetition. Just as Olivia's echo of Malvolio's language twists it into a new statement, the valence of which is left to an actor to determine, so does every echo ring changes on its originary utterance. Echo is not, like emulation in *Troilus and Cressida* or contagion in *Hamlet*, a figure for the *dissipation* of significance. When, for instance, Diomedes mimics Troilus's chivalry and pays court to the captive Cressida, he exposes through emulation the hollowness of the chivalric code and its potential for coercive, antifeminist violence; he does not fundamentally alter the meaning of that code. Likewise, Hamlet's infective psychic turbulence becomes horrible precisely because of the way it reduces several intellects to a semantic flatline, to the same kind of dysfunction. Contagion in Denmark and emulation in Troy are both historical referents and processes of hermeneutic depletion. By contrast, when Olivia echoes to herself a bit of conversation with Cesario, she signifies mainly an emotional and erotic shift: the felt presence of the beloved's language is *positively* disorienting. Having the same words spoken by another person in another place entirely changes their sense. Echoes of language show how temporal and spatial changes reconfigure meaning. Echo turns on, becomes a trope of, context.

It thus has consequences for a theory of historical inscription and, like emulation and contagion, can emerge as inscription's metaphor. A textured repetition of prior language, echo embroiders meanings on history by dint of time alone. In highlighting new speakers and contexts, it confounds the supposition that a later, derivative discursive form will faithfully replay an earlier, foundational one. In the terms of this study, echoic recontextualization decisively changes and so problematizes historical meanings. We should not imagine that the Elizabeth or the religious controversy reverberated by *Twelfth Night* in 1601 has a perfectly mimetic relationship to historical fact; the echo of history in the play proffers the *simultaneous* presence and absence, voice and silence, of the utterance that is the past. Because echoes jar contextual certainty, they tell a semantic distance between the speaking (historical) voice and its present vibration.

In its standard poetic form, echo figures a structure of call-and-immediate-response. But in *Twelfth Night* Shakespeare delays the echoic loop such that repetitions often occur with a substantial lag between speech and speech. This delay, this temporal gap, schematizes the play's relation to its contexts. *Twelfth Night*'s historical inscriptions have the kind of simplicity and elusiveness, the echoic distance, that enfranchise nostalgia about the remote past. But while the inscribed events are a long way from the text that echoes them, their dissonances can still be heard. By recalling the Anjou affair through the unappealing Orsino and the messy mediation of Viola, the play forestalls regret about a failed, finally inconsequential episode which strained diplomatic and fiscal resources. If any nostalgia remains over Elizabeth's last chance at marriage, *Twelfth Night* scuttles it. Nostalgia is an unencumbered access of history; once facts and doubts make the voyage back, landfall in the past seems less desirable.

After nearly a year of Simier's surrogate wooing, François Valois finally arrived in England for his first meeting with Elizabeth on August 17, 1579. Unfortunately, only about ten days before the widely and publicly anticipated visit, John Stubbs's raging antimarriage pamphlet appeared. Because of this development, the queen took care to conceal Anjou's visit; interestingly enough, he came ashore in disguise.[83] He stayed two weeks, and Elizabeth reportedly liked him well; but according to ambassador Mendoza, the visit mainly inspired the more resolute Protestants in the court, especially Leicester and Walsingham, to plot ever more fervently against the marriage. And the aristocrats were not the only ones stirred; supposedly, Mendoza claimed, the general population was on the verge of open revolt over the issue. Of all the antimarriage constituencies, however, the Puritans were the most agitated. According to a French ambassador, they thought that this match would spell their demise, and as Conyers Read notes, "They did not lose an hour of time to preach, write and incite the people of England to oppose it. . . . [T]he Queen was much shaken by these tactics and . . . at one time she thought of adding to her Council four Catholics of influence in order to counterbalance the rest."[84]

Puritan outrage at the prospective marriage causes the historical referent on the margins of *Twelfth Night* to crowd the thematic center, and rationalizes the notorious abuse the constructed scapegoat suffers. A neat inscriptive irony makes the play's affecter of Puritanism the unwitting original pandar for Olivia's romance. It is Malvolio's enticing, bisexual description of Cesario that causes the lady to bring him in ("One would think his mother's milk were scarce out of him" [1.5.163]); it is the steward who delivers the ring to the messenger. Later, after Malvolio's transformation into oblivious oppositionality, he postures and preens for his lady when she calls; but again unbeknownst to him, Olivia eagerly awaits *Cesario's* visit and wants Malvolio there only for the company of someone "sad and civil" (3.4.5). The culmination of this irony comes in the steward's last appearance in the play: because of when he enters and exits, he remains in darkness about Olivia's marriage. All that he knows for certain is that his lady does not love him.[85] Had Malvolio known of the gaping gulf into which his hopes were about to fall, he surely would have objected as strenuously to Olivia's marriage as Stubbs did to the French match. Stubbs, though severely punished—notoriously abused, we might say—by Elizabeth for his pamphlet, nonetheless recovered from his wounds and infamy well enough to achieve a post from which he could serve as judge and jury in civil and criminal cases: he ended his career as steward of Yarmouth, a position he attained in 1585.

Malvolio's sufferings bring a generic disruption to this historically dislocated play. Formally the comedy is off-kilter; Viola does not return to the female gender, Orsino and Olivia do not end together, Antonio remains shut out of pleasure. It would be wrong to assign all the generic glitches to the steward's ill treatment, but it is not wrong to insist that the pain he bears revives tonal dissonances and historical ironies of the Anjou affair and its aftermath. One of these is that the supposedly radical Puritans were, in their objections to the Catholic-Anglican match, articulating a *mainstream* sentiment whose most ardent supporters were the queen's own ministers and counselors. Another, gloomier irony is that the queen's scapegoating of Stubbs and his printer (whose right hands were chopped off in a grotesque exhibition of state power) put under color of treason what was really a fiercely nationalist desire to maintain English Protestant integrity. And worse still: Elizabeth's own feelings about the marriage ultimately came awfully close to those of the men she punished.

In topical terms, the defeat of the constructed Puritan and the theatrical presence of the mediator reproduce essential features of Elizabeth's last significant courtship, which took place, from the perspective of *Twelfth Night*, long ago: Viola and Malvolio play strains of a fantasia about the politico-erotic history of the English queen. The figures also signal a simultaneous distance from, *and* an echoic, yearning return to, a prior moment in history. The play thus at once erases and reconstitutes historical distance. Just as Simier and Viola stand in for other lovers, so too does the text offer itself as an estranged surrogate for history, positing and disfiguring foundational meanings. The play's (im)position between history and its own time is a mediation, representationally unstable—and thus a model for the literary deployment of the past. Actively re-forming a reality from which it stands well removed, *Twelfth Night* behaves like one of its own interlopers, connecting what is widely separate—theatrical characters and historical implications—while disturbing an order that it establishes from the materials of history and wish. And just as Cesario is both a mediator and the product of a mediation or intervention (Viola's disguise), so is the play a product and process of the disguising of history I have called inscription.

For a story so radiant with the allure of the faulty or false image, *Twelfth Night* cannot offer anything like an undisguised history. The unusually fluid boundaries within the play's categories of gender and identity, and even within a single character's notions of himself or herself, conspire to doom mulish hopes about representational mimesis. In spite of the inscriptive model that Echo would seem to supply, the play's reverberations are never perfectly consonant with the past; they are rather necessarily distorting. One example of this point comes amidst Maria's observations about the events at Olivia's house:

MARIA: Since the youth of the Count's was today with my lady, she is much
           out of quiet. For Monsieur Malvolio, let me alone with him.

                                                                    (2.3.131–35)

Viola's surrogate wooing and Malvolio's imminent woe are juxtaposed to produce an historically suggestive glissando, and it is the kind of sound that disrupts allegorical reading. The thought of the (disguised) mediator leads Maria directly into one of the truly peculiar epithets of the play: she registers snide disrespect for her fellow servant by naming Malvolio "Monsieur," glancing at the exalted position she knows the steward would like to occupy. But "Monsieur" is not merely a title of respect; it was the common name for Anjou throughout England during the courtship. In 1580, there was a single, universally recognized "Monsieur" in the nation. What could it mean that Maria anticipates her Puritanizing expulsion of Malvolio by labeling him with the epithet for Elizabeth's famous suitor? Of all the figures in the play, it would seem that the conscientious domestic resembles the Duke of Anjou least. Perhaps by naming Malvolio "Monsieur" before she turns the steward into a frustrated lover, Maria evokes what in 1601 looked like the historical *inevitability* of the failure of the French match. Or perhaps she merely tosses a barb at Malvolio's aristocratic aspirations. But Olivia's maidservant also causes an ironic collapse of inscriptions, for by granting Malvolio the sarcastic title of Elizabeth's official wooer, Maria subversively draws Anjou and the soon-to-be-made Puritan into comparison. Maria's mention of "Monsieur Malvolio" prepares us for a fused image, two wrecks of the 1580s: the hopeful French lover and the rejected Puritan.

Favor flows to the protean, not the Puritan—to the one whose self or desire sustains convincing change or admits of flexibility. In the psychological rules of the play, not only Malvolio but also Antonio must suffer, because they fool no one. Antonio is, as Leo Salingar points out, "the only character in the main plot who tries to establish a false identity and fails"; this occurs when, apprehended by Orsino's officer, he pretends to be someone else: "You do mistake me, sir." "No sir, no jot," replies the officer; "I know your favour well" (3.4.336–37).[86] Malvolio's and Antonio's opposites are Orsino, the changeable taffeta and opal; disguised Viola, an O without a figure; Olivia, lady of volatile passions; and Sebastian, "which I called Roderigo" (2.1.16), a bisexual stranger who does not at all mind being called Cesario. Like its characters, the text partakes of a formal and historical shape-shifting that slips the bonds of constraining temporality, the cramped seams of its own culture. Thus, the particular past to which *Twelfth Night* refers, circa 1580, seems to offer a retreat from current, unhopeful conditions. But the paradox of the play is that this past was every bit as fraught and insecure as England's late-Elizabethan present. The text cannot intervene between its lived present and this history without reproducing dissonances that comedy fails to contain. A final glimpse at the most haunting of the play's historical representations may illuminate the difficulty that texts have in metamorphosing history into nostalgia.

Contemporary with and politically related to the machinations of the

French match—which, we will recall, had as one of its goals the curtail-
ment of Spain's power throughout Europe—was the struggle over the
Portuguese succession. Six claimants for the throne of Portugal vied
after the death, in 1578, of King Sebastian. The clearest title belonged to
England's nemesis, Philip II of Spain; and after Sebastian's death, the
Portuguese ambassador made Elizabeth realize, as Conyers Read writes,

> how dangerous it would be for England to allow her secret enemy to add
> Portugal and all the wealth of the Portuguese Indies to his resources. . . . The
> increasing enthusiasm for the match on both sides of the Channel which led
> up to the secret visit of Alençon to England in August 1579 was clearly stimu-
> lated by the Portuguese question.[87]

Chief among the alternatives to Philip was Don Antonio, prior of Crato,
King Sebastian's illegitimate nephew. Antonio was proclaimed king by
popular voice; but Portugal's monarchy was definitively nonelective,
and the vote carried no political weight. When he was driven out of the
country by the Spanish in September 1580—Antonio went first to
France, then to England—the necessity of Elizabeth's alliance with
France (and support of Anjou in the Netherlands) became inescapably
clear.

Given *Twelfth Night*'s obsessive gamesmanship with names of vary-
ing significance, the presence of a man named Antonio pursuing another
named Sebastian summons one more reference that accords with the
periodic frame in which I read the text. Antonio's romantic fixation on
Sebastian in Illyria historically recalls the political pretender's passion
for Sebastian's *place*, not his person.[88] By claiming legitimacy to inherit,
Don Antonio attempted to secure the same mistaken testament to political recognition that his theatrical namesake attempts for affective and
spiritual reasons:

> ANTONIO: This youth that you see here
>   I snatch'd one half out of the jaws of death,
>   Reliev'd him with such sanctity of love;
>   And to his image, which methought did promise
>   Most venerable worth, did I devotion.
> FIRST OFFICER: What's that to us? The time goes by. Away!
> ANTONIO: But O how vile an idol proves this god!
>   (3.4.368–74)

This scene of Antonio's betrayal by Viola (not, as he thinks, Sebastian)
and the officer's response strikingly echoes Judas's guilt over the con-

demnation of Christ: "Then Judas, which had betrayed him, when he saw that he was condemned, repented himself, . . . Saying, I have sinned in that I have betrayed the innocent blood. And they said, What is that to us?" (Matthew 27:3–4). It is of course the Christlike Antonio who has been twice betrayed by the vile idol Viola, but the dramatic scene cleaves closer to the historical tale than the biblical. Antonio, figured as a former threat to Illyria ("Thou notable pirate, saltwater thief," Orsino calls him), is quietly neglected at the last, bereft of support. *Twelfth Night* records his defeat and observes his final solitude; his beloved Sebastian fails, with whatever good intentions, to provide for him.

Such was the fate, too, of the historical Don Antonio, left without hereditary provision and seeking always his place to rule, or at least a place to reside. His sorry treatment by several foreign potentates, including alleged allies like Elizabeth, was underpublicized in the reign. In 1582, he languished in unpleasant quarters in London, terribly ill, "desolate not only of necessaries, but of comfort"; he sent for the aid of one of the queen's physicians, who never arrived (Nicolas, *Life of Hatton*, 202). Antonio survived that indignity, but others followed hard upon. He remained, for the rest of his life, poorly attended and ill fated; this "bastard of the royal line" spent the decade of the 1580s moving between France and England, "a forlorn suppliant."[89] His later career is a history of lost sea battles, failed uprisings, and frustrated piracy. Even his voyage to the Portuguese coast in 1589 with Sir Francis Drake failed expensively; a year later he retired to France, impoverished, and died there after five years of penury in 1595.[90]

For the Antonio who finds himself in Illyria, in love with a man he rescued, without fiscal, sexual, or emotional gratification at the last, ruin is finally the upshot of erotics, not politics. Indeed, this transformation of history is vitally characteristic of *Twelfth Night*: the play metamorphoses struggles of ideology and history into intimate emotional confrontations, traumas, and restitutions. In substituting affective or sexual entanglements for the political past that representationally underwrites them, the play imitates Viola by obscuring its own origins. But weary and defeated figures, the oppositional or incompetent, the dissolute and the disappointed on the borders of the Elizabethan story, filter into Shakespearean representation here with their contaminating histories. *Twelfth Night*'s putative nostalgic project thus constantly undermines itself through the mnemonics of the marginal.

The Antonio/Sebastian references, Anjou/Simier allusions, and glimpses of a reconstructed, ousted Puritanism set the significant referential moment of the play two decades prior to its accepted date of performance, making it, as Antonio feels himself to be, "a twenty years' removed thing" (5.1.87) from the present historical reality. But just because topicality is retrogressive does not mean that it is retrospective; the play smudges a collective and already faded cultural memory to salvage what carelessness and pleasure it can. Nostalgia cannot, will not, clarify the past. And like narcissism, it cannot return a completely satisfying image of the self. The recollection of the French match purposely obscures one of the most tumultuous periods of the queen's career, when the nation, in the absence of a recognized heir, stepped at last into the downward spiral of succession struggles so complexly figured in *Hamlet* and in virtually every parliamentary debate from the mid-1580s on. So *Twelfth Night* provides what the marvelous reign of Elizabeth could not: miraculously speedy, successful courtship shorn of political implications, in which erotic failure or error is gracefully overcome; and, most important, a venue in which echoes of the past evoke admired and unresented female mastery.

The past is always constructed from the materials of the present. Our understanding of history does not just move backwards; it reproduces current experience and anticipates what's next. If Shakespeare's play recalls an era when Elizabeth had a real, practical chance at marriage, it also manages to recall obliquely that, even in 1580, an heir to the throne was on the outer regions of physical probability. Viola informs the queen figure of Illyria, "Lady you are the cruellest she alive / To lead these graces to the grave / And leave no copy." This sonnetlike request for the beloved's self-reproduction through offspring momentarily causes the tensions of the factual present to disturb the fantasy courtship scene. But Olivia buries the recommendation for progeny by turning the meaning of "copy" from "child" into something else entirely:

> O sir, I will not be so hard-hearted: I will give out divers schedules of my beauty. It shall be inventoried, and every particle and utensil labelled to my will. As, item, two lips indifferent red; item, two grey eyes . . .
>
> (1.5.247–51)

This, clearly, is a copy the woman can form without help from a man, a reproduction that can be *self*-made. The question of an heir never ceased to be uncomfortable, even in 1601. But Olivia deflects the discomfort with Elizabethan grace and egotism, as if to say, in her temporally disjunctive manner: "such a one I was this present" (1.5.237–38), *this* one, is and always has been sufficient.

On the last night of festivity, epiphanies are to come. One can hope for the best: "This shall end without the perdition of souls" (3.4.294). Two choices remain: look back, grateful and bleary eyed; or wake to nervousness.

Notes

INTRODUCTION

1. My chronologies have, with the conspicuous exception of *Hamlet*, relied on received scholarly wisdom about the most plausible compositional dates for the plays. The earliest assured terminus ad quem for any of the works would be for *Twelfth Night*, seen and recorded by John Manningham in 1601. *Hamlet* and *Troilus* have consecutive Stationer's Register (SR) entries (in 1602 and 1603, respectively), but both of these works exist in quartos that should complicate our certitude about their final composition dates. *Troilus and Cressida* may have been revised at any time before its first textual appearance in the quarto of 1609. Convenience, the SR entry, and certain formal features argue for 1602, and so I set it in that year; but other aspects of the work, such as its fixation on venereal disease, could well justify a later date (the curses of Thersites, Lear, and Timon seem contemporaneous). Further discussions of my dating of Q2 *Hamlet* will be found in chapters 2 and 3.

2. J. E. Neale, *Essays in Elizabethan History* (London: Jonathan Cape, 1958), 113.

3. Frankie Rubinstein's note on the "good years" makes clear how the peculiar term applied to disaster, particularly to bodily disaster such as plague and venereal disease. See "They Were Not Such Good Years," *Shakespeare Quarterly* 40, no. 1 (spring 1990): 70–74.

4. Wallace Stevens, "Anecdote of the Jar," in *The Palm at the End of the Mind: Selected Poems and a Play*, ed. Holly Stevens (New York: Vintage Books, 1972), 46.

5. Fredric Jameson, *The Political Unconscious: Narrative as a Socially Symbolic Act* (Ithaca: Cornell Univ. Press, 1981), 81; hereafter cited in text. Jameson's influential policy statements about context and its relation to Marxist readings of class struggle have been the founding ballast for (less political) new-historicist readings of the relations between social and literary forms. True to the

political deracination of historicism, my readings evade a class-conscious aesthetic by emphasizing historical forms that are not specifically or inevitably economic and by studying ideological extensions in culture that are not necessarily masks of class struggle and domination.

6. Stephen Greenblatt, "Murdering Peasants: Status, Genre, and the Representation of Rebellion," *Representations* 1 (1983): 1–29; Greenblatt, "Fiction and Friction," in his *Shakespearean Negotiations: The Circulation of Social Energy in Renaissance England* (Berkeley: Univ. of Calif. Press, 1987), 66–93. For a potent criticism of Greenblatt's use of the tangentially related fact or story, particularly regarding the story of Marin le Marcis and *Twelfth Night*, see Joel Fineman, "The History of the Anecdote: Fiction and Fiction," in H. Aram Veeser, ed., *The New Historicism* (London: Methuen, 1990), 49–76.

7. Walter Cohen, "Political Criticism of Shakespeare," in Jean E. Howard and Marion F. O'Connor, eds., *Shakespeare Reproduced* (New York and London: Methuen, 1987), 34. See also Jean E. Howard, "The New Historicism in Renaissance Studies," *ELR* (1986): 13–43.

8. The commitment to narrow topicalities has, I think, produced some of the most consistently interesting new-historical work: Renaissance readers Patricia Fumerton, Richard Helgerson, Leah Marcus, Louis Montrose, Maureen Quilligan, and Don E. Wayne come to mind as exemplary practitioners of the local. My indebtedness to their studies will be apparent throughout.

9. *The Random House Dictionary of the English Language*, unabridged ed., s.v. "tell" (New York: Random House, 1971). The word derives from the Arabic *tall*, a mound or hill.

10. "In effect, fiction plays on the stratification of meaning: it narrates one thing in order to tell something else; it delineates itself in a language from which it continuously draws effects of meaning that cannot be circumscribed or checked." Michel de Certeau, "History: Science and Fiction," in *Heterologies: Discourse on the Other*, trans. Brain Massumi (Minneapolis: Univ. of Minnesota Press, 1986), 202.

11. Lee Patterson argues (on political grounds) for restoring *intentionality* as an interpretive term; see the excellent chapter "Historical Criticism and the Claims of Humanism," in his *Negotiating the Past: The Historical Understanding of Medieval Literature* (Madison: Univ. of Wisconsin Press, 1987), 41–76, esp. 65ff.

For one account of the multiplicity of the text and its compound authorship, see Roland Barthes, "Theory of the Text," in Robert Young, ed., *Untying the Text: A Poststructuralist Reader* (London: Routledge, 1981), 31–47.

12. Quoted in J. E. Neale, *Elizabeth I and Her Parliaments, 1584–1601*, 2 vols. (London: Jonathan Cape, 1957), 2:119.

13. Spenser, *The Faerie Queene*, ed. Thomas P. Roche, Jr. (Midddlesex: Penguin, 1978), 16. For a directly relevant analysis of Spenser's Elizabethan inscriptions, see Louis Adrian Montrose, "The Elizabethan Subject and the Spenserian Text," in Patricia Parker and David Quint, eds., *Literary Theory/Renaissance Texts* (Baltimore and London: Johns Hopkins Univ. Press, 1986), 303–40.

14. *Endymion: The Man in the Moon*, in Charles Read Baskerville, Virgil B.

Heltzel, and Arthur H. Nethercot, eds., *Elizabethan and Stuart Plays* (New York: Holt, Rinehart, and Winston, 1934), 171–204.

15. "The Prologue at Court," in *Old Fortunatus*, in vol. 1 of *The Dramatic Works of Thomas Dekker*, ed. Fredson Bowers (Cambridge: Cambridge Univ. Press, 1953).

16. Alan Liu, "The Power of Formalism: The New Historicism," *ELH* 56 (1989): 721–71.

17. René Girard, *Violence and the Sacred*, trans. Yvonne Freccero (Baltimore: Johns Hopkins Univ. Press, 1977).

18. James Gleick defines "self-similarity" as "symmetry across scale. It implies recursion, pattern inside of pattern," and he gives as an example the "infinitely deep reflection of a person standing between two mirrors." Gleick, *Chaos: Making a New Science* (New York: Penguin, 1987), 103.

19. I am indebted to the lucid and suggestive discussion of relations between chaos theory and poststructuralism in N. Katherine Hayles, *Chaos Bound: Orderly Disorder in Contemporary Theory and Science* (Ithaca: Cornell Univ. Press, 1990), esp. chaps. 7 and 8; hereafter cited in text.

20. Sontag, *Illness as Metaphor* (New York: Random House, 1979), 66.

21. Alvin M. Saperstein, "Chaos—A Model for the Outbreak of War," *Nature* 309 (May 1984): 303.

22. W. H. Auden, *"Musée des Beaux Arts,"* in *Selected Poetry*, 2d ed. (New York: Random House, 1971), 49.

The major upheavals of history may have no demonstrable effect on imaginative documents: the more traumatic the occasion, the more likely it is to short out metaphorical circuits. Cultural disaster disturbs not only the psyche but language and all social ritual and practice; words slip, playhouses close, an inability to organize sets in. To some extent I am writing about the tyranny of the absent, about the thing that dominates by reason of its being underground; it is a Freudian historicism that interests me. The repressed thing, the deflected or marginalized historical referent, drives these plays. Historical pressures, like personal traumas, exert disarmingly complicated force on the Shakespearean text.

23. See Elaine Scarry, *The Body in Pain: The Making and Unmaking of the World* (New York: Oxford Univ. Press, 1985); Gail Kern Paster, *The Body Embarrassed: Drama and the Disciplines of Shame in Early Modern England* (Ithaca: Cornell Univ. Press, 1992); and Frank Whigham, *Seizures of the Will in Renaissance Drama* (Cambridge: Cambridge Univ. Press, forthcoming). See also Peter Stallybrass and Allon White, *The Poetics and Politics of Transgression* (Ithaca: Cornell Univ. Press, 1986).

24. For Kaposi's sarcoma as the early mass-media indicator of the disease, see Loren K. Clarke and Malcolm Potts, *The AIDS Reader* (Boston: Branden Publishing, 1988), 84–88, and Gerald M. Oppenheimer, "Causes, Cases, and Cohorts: The Role of Epidemiology in the Historical Construction of AIDS," in Elizabeth Fee and Daniel M. Fox, eds., *AIDS: The Making of a Chronic Disease* (Berkeley: Univ. of California Press, 1992), 49–83. I am indebted to Mark Condon for these references.

25. For an interesting critique of this media-sponsored view, see Douglas

Crimp, "How to Have Promiscuity in an Epidemic," in Crimp, ed., *AIDS: Cultural Analysis/Cultural Activism* (Cambridge: MIT Press, 1989), 237–71.

26. Quoted in Randy Shilts, *And the Band Played On: Politics, People, and the AIDS Epidemic* (New York: Viking Penguin, 1987), 352.

27. One exception is Edward Guerrero, "AIDS as Monster in Science Fiction and Horror Cinema," *Journal of Popular Film and Television* 18, no. 3 (fall 1990): 86–93.

28. The antitechnological bias of the movie should not be overlooked, especially insofar as that, too, plays into the AIDS thematic. After all, in a hideously real way, Brundle has absorbed into his body a *computer* virus. The threat is figured as unnatural not only because of nonnormative sexual associations but because Brundle is the first human to contract what only integrated circuits could get: a virus transmitted through digital technology. In an infected age, neither flesh nor mind is safe. But the final grotesquerie of the film, Brundle's fusion with the telepod itself, is not more appalling than the decomposing half-man—an image of the aged, broken body—that is the movie's tragic nightmare. Technology, it seems, only accelerates agonizing natural processes, making them seem unnatural.

29. Linda Bamber, *Comic Women, Tragic Men* (Stanford: Stanford Univ. Press, 1982).

30. Michel de Certeau, "The Freudian Novel: History and Literature," in *Heterologies*, 31–32.

CHAPTER 1.
EMULOUS FACTIONS AND THE COLLAPSE OF CHIVALRY

1. Thomas Wilson, *The State of England, Anno Dom. 1600*, ed. F. J. Fisher, Camden Miscellany, vol. 16 (London: Camden Society, 1936), 34; hereafter cited in the text.

In 1596 an envoy of the Venetian ambassador wrote of his reception in England: "I noticed that in this country they are in great alarm about the enemy; they will not allow anyone to enter who is not quite well known and who has not been thoroughly examined." *Calendar of State Papers, Venetian, 1592–1603* (London, 1897), 236; hereafter cited as *CSPV*.

2. Some of England's rare attacks were conceived as preventive, defensive measures. Thomas Birch quotes a state paper (*The advantages, which her majesty hath gotten by that, which hath passed at Cadiz . . . 1596*) which begins: "Her majesty being threatened to be invaded, hath like a mighty and magnanimous prince sent her navy and army to offer her enemy battle at his own door." Birch, *Memoirs of the Reign of Queen Elizabeth*, 2 vols. (London, 1754; rpt. New York: AMS Press, 1970), 2:47. Subsequent references will be to volume 2 of this edition.

3. Quoted in George P. Rice, *The Public Speaking of Queen Elizabeth I* (New York: Columbia Univ. Press, 1951), 96.

It is likely that the speech was not delivered in this precise form; its textual origins are rather shady. See Susan Frye, "The Myth of Elizabeth I at Tilbury," *Sixteenth Century Journal* 23 (1992): 95–114.

4. R. B. Outhwaite asserts that "almost every year after 1588 produced fears of invasion." "Dearth, the English Crown, and the 'Crisis of the 1590's'," in Peter Clark, ed., *The European Crisis of the 1590s* (London: George Allen and Unwin, 1985), 24.

5. All quotations from *Troilus and Cressida* are from the Arden edition, ed. Kenneth Palmer (London: Methuen, 1982). Quotations from all other Shakespeare plays are from G. Blakemore Evans, ed., *The Riverside Shakespeare* (Boston: Houghton Mifflin, 1974). Cressida's defense of her "belly," like Elizabeth's, is a defense of the womb; see *O.E.D.*, s.v. "belly."

England's invasion neurosis potentially figured a vast cultural paradox: it let soldiers and courtiers imagine that the collective body they constituted was penetrable, not penetrating—female, not male. A widescale (historical) identification with the feminine threatens masculine identity, a threat which the play variously inscribes. One of the most memorable instances of profound male insecurity in these terms occurs when Troilus witnesses Cressida's betrayal; he describes his horror as his own reason's self-separation, division, penetrability, and dissolution (5.2.145–59.).

6. Wilson, *State of England*, 41. He may have been referring to the sumptuary laws as those that discourage emulation between the peers and gentlemen.

7. See John Neale, "The Elizabethan Political Scene," in his *Essays in Elizabethan History* (London: Jonathan Cape, 1958), 59–84, and Conyers Read, "Factions in the English Privy Council under Elizabeth," *American Historical Association Annual Report* 1 (1911): 113–19.

This is Neale's view, but G. R. Elton takes a more cautious stance: "Whether Elizabeth took care to maintain the factions simply to prevent herself being overwhelmed by any one of them must remain a matter for doubt; the effect, however, of her refusal to allow total victory to this or that group was to provide all political ambition with a platform at the very centre of affairs. In her reign, and in her father's, too, conflict took place within the Court." Elton, *Studies in Tudor and Stuart Politics and Government*, 4 vols. (Cambridge: Cambridge Univ. Press, 1983), 3:52. Elizabeth felt it was better to suffer internal divisions that could remain under surveillance than to lose containment of those disturbances and find them gathering strength outside the court, in the city, the church, the country.

8. [André Hurault, sieur de Maisse], *De Maisse: A Journal of All that was accomplished by Monsieur de Maisse, Ambassador in England . . . 1597*, trans. and ed. G. B. Harrison and R. A. Jones (Bloomsbury, Eng.: Nonesuch Press, 1931), 18. Hereafter cited parenthetically in the text as de Maisse, *Journal*.

9. Robert Naunton, *Fragmenta Regalia*, in Walter Scott, ed., *Somers' Tracts* (London, 1809; rpt. New York: AMS Press, 1965), 253. I have also benefited from the edition of John S. Cerovski (Washington, D.C.: Folger Books, 1985). Naunton refers here to the early factions in the queen's reign.

For an opposing view of the importance of early Elizabethan factions, see Simon Adams, "Eliza Enthroned? The Court and Its Politics," in Christopher Haigh, ed., *The Reign of Elizabeth I* (London: Macmillan, 1984), 55. Adams elsewhere admits that factions profoundly influenced Tudor rule in the 1590s:

"Faction, Clientage, and Party: English Politics, 1550–1603," *History Today* 32 (December 1982): 33–39.

10. Anthony Esler, *The Aspiring Mind of the Elizabethan Younger Generation* (Durham: Duke Univ. Press, 1966), 87–164, has a thorough exposition of this point.

11. Quoted in Neale, "Elizabethan Political Scene," 79.

12. Adams mentions the indirection of the Whitehall plot in "Faction, Clientage, and Party," 39. Sir Henry Wotton, who fought beside Essex in Ireland, later wrote of the Cecilians' "strong and subtile faction, which cared and consulted for [Essex's] ruin, as a foundation they must build upon"; the Cecilians "were intent to betray him abroad, and mis-interpret him at home." *Reliquae Wottonianae*, 4th. ed. (London, 1685), 188.

13. Neale asserts that Essex's spectacular demands left Elizabeth little choice but to back the Cecilians: "At the time of Essex's fall Robert Cecil was Secretary, Chancellor of the Duchy of Lancaster and Master of the Court of Wards—a unique combination of offices; and if we reflect on the power and patronage they conferred . . . we can appreciate how near to creating a rival monopoly Elizabeth was forced to go." "Elizabethan Political Scene," 81.

14. George Chapman, preface to the *Seauen Bookes of the Iliades*, in *Chapman's Homer*, ed. Allardyce Nicholl, 2 vols. (New York: Pantheon, 1956), 1:503; hereafter cited in the text as *Chapman's Homer*. For a fine, cogent reading of the place of Essex in the careers of both Chapman and Shakespeare, see Richard Ide, *Possessed with Greatness: The Heroic Tragedies of Chapman and Shakespeare* (Chapel Hill: Univ. of North Carolina Press, 1980), 3–33, 98–101.

15. *CSPV*, 384. The ambassador makes this claim in the context of Essex's recent arrest for insubordination. Subversiveness made Essex seem all the more heroic.

16. Ide, *Possessed with Greatness*, 23.

17. Cedric Whitman, *Homer and the Heroic Tradition* (New York: Norton, 1958), 182.

18. The threat was to Essex as well. Departures from the affairs of state did nothing to better his fortunes; if anything, they only harmed him and intensified factional unrest. His withdrawals blended elements of self-indulgence and self-sabotage. De Maisse knew well that the earl's absence "gives occasion to his enemies to calumniate him, and to make him suspected by the Queen as if he wished to make a separate party and withdraw himself, favored by the nobility and the people" (*Journal*, 67–68). However, Joel Hurstfield contends that Robert Cecil's undoing of Essex was not intentional or at least did not represent a systematic program; see "The Succession Struggle in Late Elizabethan England," in his *Freedom, Corruption, and Government in Elizabethan England* (Cambridge: Harvard Univ. Press, 1973), 127. Cecil frequently claimed to bear Essex no ill will and even allegedly sued on his behalf to the queen during Essex's disgrace; Birch, *Memoirs*, 438, 442. On this point, see P. M. Handover, *The Second Cecil* (London: Eyre and Spottiswoode, 1959), 153–57.

As Ulysses warns the immured Achilles, "To have done is to hang / Quite out of fashion, like a rusty mail / In monumental mockery" (3.3.151–53), and Essex certainly knew the advantages of presence: "My Lord of Essex did lately want

Sir George Carew to be Lord Leiutenante of Ireland, rather than his owne unkle, Sir William Knollys, because he had given him some cause of offence, and by thus thrusting him into high office, he would remove him from cowrte." John Harington, in *Nugae Antiquae*, ed. T. Park, 2 vols. (London, 1809), 1:173.

19. A perceptive commentary on these lines, and on the ways in which the figure of Henry reconceives Essex, can be found in Jonathan Dollimore and Alan Sinfield, "History and Ideology: The Instance of *Henry V*," in John Drakakis, ed., *Alternative Shakespeares* (London: Methuen, 1985), 206–27. "Henry is both general and ruler, and therefore the structural problem of the over-mighty subject . . . does not present itself" (220).

20. My debt to Louis Adrian Montrose will be increasingly clear throughout this chapter; this particular formulation of a textual and cultural interrelationship is adapted from his comments about *A Midsummer Night's Dream*. See Montrose, " 'Shaping Fantasies': Figurations of Gender and Power in Elizabethan Culture," *Representations* 2 (spring 1983): 61–94. In terms of method I have also found useful his "Renaissance Literary Studies and the Subject of History," *English Literary Renaissance* 16 (winter 1986): 5–12; and in the same volume, Jean Howard, "The New Historicism in Renaissance Studies," 13–43.

21. Note Ulysses' warning to Achilles about the providence in a watchful state (3.3.195–205), long taken to be a reference to the Elizabethan spy network. See Harry Berger Jr., "*Troilus and Cressida*: The Observer as Basilisk," *Comparative Drama* 2 (summer 1968): 122–36, on the play's tendency to conduct extensive observations of its characters.

The faction system fostered voyeurism and paranoia because, as Thomas Wilson notes, each noble had "his enemyes eye to overlooke him" (*State of England*, 42). All actions were accountable simply because nothing could remain hidden. Such watchfulness was the constant weight under which the courtiers labored—observed of all observers. The strain was particularly great on Essex. In 1599, during his confinement at York House, the earl was repeatedly warned by friends such as Sir Thomas Egerton that "sharp eyes were upon him, that his actions, public and private, were observed." See Laura Hanes Cadwallader, "Career of the Earl of Essex 1597–1601," Ph.D. diss., Univ. of Pennsylvania, 1923, 62. Cadwallader's work is an indispensable account of the events leading to Essex's demise.

22. Quoted in G. B. Harrison, *The Life and Death of Robert Devereux, Earl of Essex* (London: Cassell, 1937), 261.

23. See Virginia Crocheron Gildersleeve, *Government Regulation of the Elizabethan Drama* (New York: Columbia Univ. Press, 1908), 98–99.

This reading of Essex's theatrical intent must be qualified by the remarkable resonance between the earl's career at this point (1601) and Richard's—not Bolingbroke's—political fortunes in Shakespeare's *Richard II*. Scholars traditionally assume that the earl and his men commissioned the performance to foster sympathy for rebellion against an unjust monarch; in this reading, Henry Bolingbroke would "stand for" Essex, who wishes to be the ambitious noble riding a wave of popular acclaim. To this extent, Elizabeth's reported gloss on the performance—"I am Richard the second, know ye not that?"—has been entirely influential. But it may be shortsighted. Rather, Essex may have thought of himself as Richard: not the usurper but the mistreated and displaced man. For King Richard finds himself supplanted, his power upended, after returning from a rash trip to Ireland. This situation, as I discuss below, echoes the situation in which Essex found himself in 1601 following *his* Irish journey. Certainly it is only once he is out of power, after his return from Ireland, that Richard becomes a sympathetic and attractive figure. And it is Essex, not Elizabeth, who in 1601 is impotent, who has been imprisoned by rivals, who broods over and bewails his sorry state. Thus the "meaning" of the historical performance of *Richard II* in 1601 may have more to do with manipulating sympathies and dramatic identifications—Essex as the sorrowful, bereft man—than with the naked grab for power that, it has been thought, the deposition scene was supposed to support. This is not to say that the commissioning of the performace was *not* a challenge to the queen, only that it was contestatory in a different way—more passively or resignedly so (thus, perhaps, more Achillean). If the earl theatrically identified himself as Shakespeare's Richard, it was an attempt to redefine his persona as misunderstood, newly thoughtful and, in a way, repentant ("I wasted time, and now doth time waste me"). The public gathering of sympathy is in itself an insurrection, a revision of the queen's view of her former favorite.

Richard II shows how unlikable, how robotic a successful usurper can be. Henry, though he has history on his side, is not a figure to inspire an overthrow if the affective reading—Shakespeare's character study—is taken seriously. It is more likely that, by 1601, Essex saw himself through the play as the man who *once* had a king's prerogative—"the greatest personage in England," as Contarini had called him—rather than as the man who would or could be king ("For you have but mistook me all this while" [*Richard II*, 3.2.174]). It is almost intolerably optimistic, given the state of his fortunes and resources at the time, for Essex to have supposed that any play could have secured him power.

24. Shakespeare's mimetic politics of sickness are an unmetaphored version of the conventional wisdom that strife between the peers diseased the nation. Laurence Humphrey wrote in 1563 that "Nothing plageth England but the many breaches and ever unsure, never faithfull, frendshyppe of the Nobles." Quoted in Lawrence Stone, *The Crisis of the Aristocracy, 1558–1641* (Oxford: Clarendon Press, 1965), 179. It is worth noting that 1563 was a particularly terrible plague year; to say that the greatest plague in England was the infighting of the nobility was, then, to make quite a claim.

25. Joel Fineman, "Fratricide and Cuckoldry: Shakespeare's Doubles," in Murray M. Schwartz and Coppelia Kahn, eds., *Representing Shakespeare: New Psychoanalytic Essays* (Baltimore: Johns Hopkins Univ. Press, 1980), 94; hereafter cited in text. René Girard's application of the concept of emulation to the play has influenced my reading greatly; see "The Politics of Desire in *Troilus and Cressida*," in Patricia Parker and Geoffrey Hartman, eds., *Shakespeare and the Question of Theory* (New York: Methuen, 1985), 188–209.

26. "What we call 'competition' is better described as men's attempt to *outimitate* one another." Kenneth Burke, cited in Frank Whigham, *Ambition and Privilege: The Social Tropes of Elizabethan Courtesy Theory* (Berkeley: Univ. of California Press, 1984), 78. See also Esler, *Aspiring Mind*, 51–86.

27. René Girard, "The Plague in Literature and Myth," in his *"To Double*

Business Bound": Essays on Myth and Literature (Baltimore: Johns Hopkins Univ. Press, 1978), 136–54. The idea of undifferentiated disruptive rivals is central to much of Shakespeare's (and Girard's) work, but rivals are not quite doubles in this play; they are complementary members of a single disjunctive political and sexual system.

Francis Bacon's understanding of factional undifferentiation was similar to Girard's: "Shepherds of people had need know the calendars of tempests in state; which are commonly greatest when things grow to equality; as natural tempests are greatest about the *Equinoctia.*" "Of Seditions and Troubles" (1625), in *The Works of Francis Bacon*, ed. James Spedding, 7 vols. (London, 1890), 6:406. Bacon had long been chary of factious alliances and probably sought to warn Essex against them. In "Of Followers and Friends" (*Essays*, 1597), he notes: "Factious followers are worse to be liked, which follow not vpon affection to him with whome they raunge themselues, but vpon discontentment conceiued against some other, wherevpon commonly insueth that ill intelligence that wee many times see between great personages." *Works*, 6:528.

28. The play repeatedly enacts this difficulty of differentiation as a difficulty of recognition. On this matter, see Rosalie Colie's splendid chapter on the play, "Forms and Their Meaning: 'Monumental Mock'ry,' " in her *Shakespeare's Living Art* (Princeton: Princeton Univ. Press, 1974), 317–49.

29. In writing *Troilus and Cressida*, Shakespeare answered the contemporary vogue of Trojan war dramas by emulating them. The last years of Elizabeth's reign saw a proliferation of staged versions of the Troy story. See J. S. P. Tatlock, "The Siege of Troy in Elizabethan Literature, Especially in Shakespeare and Heywood," *PMLA* 30, no. 4 (1915): 673–770.

30. Conon de Béthune, *Lyrics of the Troubadours and Trouveres*, trans. and ed. Frederick Goldin (New York: Anchor Books, 1973), 346–47.

31. Stone, *Crisis*, 255. For the phrase "purse and person," see *The Merchant of Venice*, 1.1.138, and *2 Henry IV*, 2.1.116.

32. Edward Said, "The Text, the World, the Critic," in Josué V. Harari, ed., *Textual Strategies: Perspectives in Post Structuralist Criticism* (Ithaca: Cornell Univ. Press, 1979), 184.

33. Frances Yates, *Astraea: The Imperial Theme in the Sixteenth Century* (London: Routledge and Kegan Paul, ARK, 1985), 50.

34. William Camden, *Britain; or, A Chorographicall Description of . . . England, Scotland and Ireland*, trans. Philemon Holland (London, 1637), 7. It must be mentioned that the myth of Trojan origins dies hard. Camden's boldness is temporized by this ironic afterthought: "For mine owne part, let Brutus be taken for the father, and founder of the British nation; I will not be of a contrary mind" (8).

35. For Shakespeare, the foundations of the Troy story are medieval; his most important sources, with the important exception of Chapman's Homer, are Lydgate, Chaucer, and Caxton. Caxton is particularly prominent in the literary history of Shakespeare's *Troilus and Cressida*, given his status as the bearer of chivalric culture into print. Indeed, an important source text for the play was also the first book printed in English: Caxton's *Recuyell of the historyes of*

Troye (1474), a compendium of knights and courts, tournaments and challenges.

36. Maurice Hugh Keen, "Chivalry, Nobility, and the Man-at-Arms," in C. T. Allman, ed., *War, Literature, and Politics in the Late Middle Ages* (Liverpool: Liverpool Univ. Press, 1976), 33, 45. Keen's convincing arguments about the chivalric ethic, which he develops more fully in *Chivalry* (New Haven: Yale Univ. Press, 1984), have helped shape my understanding of the Renaissance chivalric code and its transgressions.

37. "Caxton's Preface," in *Malory: Works*, ed. Eugene Vinaver, 2d ed. (Oxford: Oxford Univ. Press, 1971), xv.

38. See Norman Council, "Ben Jonson, Inigo Jones, and the Transformation of Tudor Chivalry," *ELH* 47 (summer 1980): 261.

39. Malcolm Vale, *War and Chivalry* (London: Duckworth, 1981), 167.

40. On the changing atmosphere of later Elizabethan chivalry, see Roy Strong, *The Cult of Elizabeth* (London: Thames and Hudson, 1977), 117–62, and Stephen Orgel, "Making Greatness Familiar," *Genre* 15 (spring/summer 1982): 41–48.

41. Montrose, " 'Shaping Fantasies,' " 85. Professor Montrose has skillfully charted the overlapping trajectories of politics and sexuality in the Elizabethan court, and often it is best simply to recontextualize his insights, as I do here. My reading of *Troilus and Cressida* is in part an attempt to extend the chronological and thematic field of his observations to show the increasing ineffectiveness of the sexual and political mechanisms by which the Elizabethan court maintained its dangerous balance.

42. Orgel, "Making Greatness Familiar," 41.

43. Early in the reign, in a speech to Parliament, she said to the Commons, "Though after my death you may have many stepdames, yet shall you never have a more natural mother than I mean to be unto you all." Quoted in Louis Montrose, " 'Eliza, Queene of shepheardes,' and the Pastoral of Power," *English Literary Renaissance* 10 (spring 1980): 156. This pronouncement was both reassuring and somewhat defiant in 1563, because for several years advisers had already been urging marriage and motherhood for the sake of the succession; at the beginning of Elizabeth's career, then, the maternal metaphor was exculpatory. But when the queen was older and without hope of a direct heir, there was less stake in seeming motherly than unconquerable, as she does in the Tilbury speech. In her last address to Parliament she rephrased her early devotion, excising the maternal trope: "And though you have had and may have many mightier and wiser Princes sitting in this Seat, yet you never had nor shall have any that will love you better." "Queen Elizabeth's Speech to Her Last Parliament," in Arthur Kinney, ed., *Elizabethan Backgrounds* (Hamden, Conn.: Archon Books, 1975), 335.

It would seem that the only subjects who could still be receptive to the queen's erotic maternalism were generational contemporaries. In William Cecil's last letter (July 10, 1598), the bedridden counselor wrote to his son of the queen's recent solicitude: "Let her Majesty understand how her singular kindness doth overcome my power to acquit it who, though she will not be a mother, yet she showed herself by feeding me, with her own princely hand, as a careful nurse.

And if I may be weaned to feed myself I shall be more ready to serve her on the earth." Quoted in Conyers Read, *Lord Burghley and Queen Elizabeth* (New York: Knopf, 1960), 545. The royal distance from sexual and maternal roles is apparent, but so is the abiding power of those roles. Cecil's caution about the mode of feeding quietly betrays his own undying hopes for Elizabeth's maternality ("though she will not be a mother") even as it recognizes the need to be weaned from such intimate and unconsummated hopes back into a position of subordination and service.

44. Strong, *Cult of Elizabeth*, 112: "The strength of the Elizabethan image lay in its capacity to be read and re-read many ways and never to present a single outright statement which left no room for manoeuvre, as did its successors in the new style." Montrose also notes that "as virgin, spouse, and mother, Elizabeth gathered unto herself all the Marian attributes." " 'Eliza,' " 156.

45. "Elizabeth's self-mastery and mastery of others were enhanced by . . . the sublimation of her temporal and ecclesiastical authority into a nurturing maternity." Montrose, " 'Shaping Fantasies,' " 79–80.

46. George Peele, *Anglorum Feriae*, in *The Life and Minor Works of George Peele*, ed. David H. Horne, 3 vols. (New Haven: Yale Univ. Press, 1952), 1:265–75, ll. 332–33.

47. Ralegh is given as the source of this quotation in the *Dictionary of National Biography*, ed. Leslie Stephen and Sidney Lee, 22 vols. (New York: Macmillan, 1908), 5:881; hereafter cited as *DNB*.

48. Montrose, "Gifts and Reasons: The Contexts of Peele's *Araygnement of Paris*," *ELH* 47 (fall 1980): 440.

49. The court included a very few other women, and Elizabeth insisted on veto power over all of her favorites' marriages. Essex circumvented this power when he wed secretly in 1590, and he temporarily fell from favor because of it; Ralegh was imprisoned in 1592 for his covert marriage to Elizabeth Throckmorton. And, as Neville Williams has said, "If marriage was being entered because the lady was pregnant the Queen's temper knew no bounds." Williams, *All the Queen's Men: Elizabeth I and Her Courtiers* (New York: Macmillan, 1972), 21.

50. Lawrence Stone describes these delaying tactics as the "policy of masterly inactivity and politic temporizing [which] was a brilliant success insofar as it staved off the civil wars which were tearing apart large areas of contemporary Europe." *The Causes of the English Revolution 1529–1642* (New York: Harper and Row, 1972), 78.

51. For a useful introduction to some of the recurring themes and tropes of the tournament and tilt performances, see Frances Yates, "Elizabethan Chivalry: The Romance of the Accession Day Tilts," in *Astraea*, 88–111.

52. Richard McCoy has argued convincingly that the earl of Essex's spectacular chivalric self-presentations at Queen's Day events were threateningly contentious. Essex's 1595 tilt device, an extraordinarily self-aggrandizing (and thus self-canceling) argument for his outstanding capacity for service, so upset Elizabeth that she walked out of the performance. See " 'A Dangerous Image': The Earl of Essex and Elizabethan Chivalry," *Journal of Medieval and Renaissance Studies* 13 (fall 1983): 313–29. See also section IV, below, for further discussion of Essex's 1595 tilt.

53. Hector's challenge, unlike its antecedents in the Troy legends, is utterly superfluous to the war. At the beginning of book 7 of the *Iliad* the gods impel Hector to deliver an offer of single combat to stop the bloodshed for one day. In Caxton's *Recuyell of the histories of Troye*, ed. H. Oskar Sommer (London, 1894), 603, Hector and Achilles consent to single combat to prevent any further loss of life. The *chivalric* challenge and defense of the lady are Shakespeare's inventions, as Robert K. Presson notes in *Shakespeare's Troilus and Cressida and the Legends of Troy* (Madison: Univ. of Wisconsin Press, 1953), 33.

54. See E. K. Chambers, *Sir Henry Lee* (Oxford: Clarendon Press, 1936).

55. Sara P. Watson, "The Queen's Champion," *Western Reserve Bulletin*, n.s., 34 (1931): 65–89.

56. Eric Partridge does not cite these lines, but he does say that *come* suggested orgasm in Shakespeare's day. However, he confirms my sense of the passage with his definitions of *lance* and *sunburnt*. *Shakespeare's Bawdy* (New York: Dutton, 1960), 138, 198.

57. See Paul Fussell, *The Great War and Modern Memory* (Oxford: Oxford Univ. Press, 1975), 270–309.

For an insightful reading of represented homosexuality in Troy, see Linda Charnes, " 'So Unsecret to Ourselves': Notorious Identity and the Material Subject in Shakespeare's *Troilus and Cressida*," *Shakespeare Quarterly* 40 (1989): 413–40.

58. I owe this point to M. M. Burns's fine analysis in *"Troilus and Cressida*: The Worst of Both Worlds," *Shakespeare Studies* 13 (1980): 105–30.

59. Partridge, *Shakespeare's Bawdy*, 198.

60. This point is made by Neil Powell in "Hero and Human: The Problem of Achilles," *Critical Quarterly* 21, no. 2 (summer 1979): 17–28.

61. Girard, "Politics of Desire," 199. He is referring here to Helen.

62. Arthur Percival Rossiter first noticed this "knavish device of aural ambiguity." *Angel with Horns*, ed. Graham Storey (London: Longmans, 1961), 133.

Many commentators have eloquently decried the flagitious antifeminism in the play. See Katherine Stockholder, "Power and Pleasure in *Troilus and Cressida*, or Rhetoric and Structure of the Anti-Tragic," *College English* 30, no. 7 (April 1968): 539–54: "Troilus and Pandarus equally enjoy the masculine joke which derives from the un-courtly tendency to treat women only as sex objects. ... [T]heir banter forms a kind of inverted Restoration Comedy; rather than mask tender feeling with worldly cynicism, it uses the tender courtly role to mask cynical detachment" (541). See also Grant Voth and Oliver Evans, "Cressida and the World of the Play," *Shakespeare Studies* 8 (1975): 231–39.

63. Girard seems several times on the verge of acknowledging the homoerotic as a central element if not a goal of the proceedings: "Troilus needs the admiring look of other men. ... It always takes other men to make an erotic or a military conquest truly valuable in the eyes of the conqueror himself." "Politics of Desire," 193. But he seriously underestimates the potent homoerotic nature of jealousy in this text.

64. Eve Kosofsky Sedgwick, *Between Men: English Literature and Male Homosocial Desire* (New York: Columbia Univ. Press, 1985), 20. See also Sedg-

wick's criticism of Girard's mimetic desire model as insufficiently accounting for gender differences in its account of triangulation (21–25).

65. For the homosocial frame around heterosexual relations, see Gayle Rubin, "The Traffic in Women: Notes Toward a Political Economy of Sex," in Rayna Reiter, ed., *Toward an Anthropology of Women* (New York: Monthly Review Press, 1975), 157–210.

66. See Sigmund Freud, "On Narcissism: An Introduction," in *The Standard Edition of the Complete Psychological Works of Sigmund Freud*, ed. and trans. James Strachey, 24 vols. (London: Hogarth, 1957), 14:73–102. Freud allows for a "normal" narcissism that is not a perversion but rather "the libidinal complement to . . . the instinct of self-preservation" (31). Elsewhere he emphasizes the homoerotic character of the disorder (if in fact it is a disorder). Denis de Rougemont explicates the entire courtly romantic ethos as a transformation of self-love, although without the homoerotic overtones: "The passion of love is at bottom narcissism, the lover's self-magnification, far more than it is a relation with the beloved. . . . Passion requires that the *self* shall become greater than all things." *Love in the Western World* (New York: Harper Colophon, 1961), 260.

67. Quoted in J. E. Neale, *Queen Elizabeth I* (New York: Doubleday, Anchor, 1957), 334.

68. Sir John Markham noted sharply that Essex was going to Ireland not "to serve the Queenes realme, but to humour his own revenge" against Mountjoy, another court rival. Harington, *Nugae Antiquae*, 1:241.

Essex did not go to Ireland without hesitation; he knew the strong possibility of failure there. About his Irish campaign, see Cadwallader, "Career of the Earl of Essex," 34–57; and Harrison, *Devereux* (supra, n. 22), 211–47.

69. Quoted in Birch, *Memoirs*, 415.

70. Quoted in Harington, *Nugae Antiquae*, 1:356; italics in original. Harington's letters and remembrances repeatedly record the turmoil that Essex's Irish excursion wrought in the queen. See *Nugae Antiquae*, esp. 1:178–80; 303; 313–14; 317–19; 322.

71. McCoy, " 'Dangerous Image,' " 316.

72. John Speed, *History of Great Britain* (London, 1611), 1190; cited in Palmer, ed., *Troilus and Cressida*, 142.

73. Quoted in James E. Savage, "*Troilus and Cressida* and Elizabethan Court Factions," *Univ. of Mississippi Studies in English* 5 (1964): 50. See also *DNB*, 5:877, and Thomas Coningsby, *Journal of the Siege of Rouen*, ed. John Gough Nichols (London: Camden Society, 1847).

74. For the Philautia tilt speeches, see James Spedding, *The Life and Letters of Francis Bacon*, 15 vols. (London, 1861), 1:369–91.

75. Rowland White to Robert Sidney, Nov. 22, 1595, quoted in John Nichols, *Progresses and Public Processions of Queen Elizabeth*, 3 vols. (London, 1823), 3:371. See McCoy, " 'Dangerous Image,' " 323; Strong, *Cult of Elizabeth*, 141.

76. Note, for instance, the many readers who have seen Essex in Achilles (as well as a host of other Elizabethan parallels in the play), in the *Variorum* edition of *Troilus and Cressida*, ed. Harold N. Hillebrand (Philadelphia: Lippincott, 1953), 375–82. See also Harrison, *Devereux*, 347: "Reflections of the anxieties

and disillusions of these years can be seen in many contemporary books and plays. No one, for instance, at the time could have failed to notice the striking parallels between Essex's story and much of Shakespeare's *Troilus and Cress-ida.*" The most judicious and perceptive treatment in the "old" historicist mode is C. F. Tucker Brooke's seminal article, "Shakespeare's Study in Culture and Anarchy," *Yale Review,* n.s., 17, no. 3 (April 1928): 571–77. For another consideration of the place of Essex in the play, see E. A. J. Honigmann, *Myriad-minded Shakespeare* (New York: St. Martin's, 1989), 112–29.

77. Savage, *"Troilus and Cressida,"* 50. I am much in debt to this suggestive article, although I do not share its view of a single reflective manifestation of Essex or its tendency to allegorize the play in strict correspondences: "If Hector reflects Essex, then Troilus reflects Southampton" (51).

78. De Maisse writes, "The Queen is put in fear of him, and they tell her that he wishes to be always in arms." *Journal,* 17.

79. Essex to the Lords of the Privy Council, 1599, quoted in Lacey Baldwin Smith, *Treason in Tudor England: Politics and Paranoia* (London: Jonathan Cape, 1986), 231.

80. Howard, "The New Historicism in Renaissance Studies," 25.

81. Francis Henry Cripps-Day, *History of the Tournament* (London, 1918; rpt. New York: AMS Press, 1982), 125. See also Johan Huizinga, *The Waning of the Middle Ages,* 3d ed. (London: Edward Arnold, 1937), 72: "The nobles like to throw a veil of mystery and melancholy over the procedure. The knight should be unknown. He is called 'le blanc chevalier,' 'le chevalier mesconnu.' "

82. Strong, *Cult of Elizabeth,* 141.

83. "It is the English usage for eminent lords or knights at their decease to bequeath and leave almost the best of their clothes to their serving men, which it is unseemly for the latter to wear, so that they offer them then for sale for a small sum to the actors." Thomas Platter (1599), quoted in Andrew Gurr, *The Shake-spearean Stage, 1574–1642,* 2d ed. (Cambridge: Cambridge Univ. Press, 1980), 178.

84. The fine phrase is Montrose's, which he uses in reference to Queen Elizabeth: "her pervasive cultural presence was a condition of the play's imaginative possibility." " 'Shaping Fantasies,' " 62.

85. For another treatment of similar court dynamics, including the relationship of Machiavellian politicking to chivalry and "residual male discontent" about female power, see Peter Erickson, "The Order of the Garter, the Cult of Elizabeth, and Class-Gender Tension in *The Merry Wives of Windsor,*" in Jean E. Howard and Marion F. O'Connor, eds., *Shakespeare Reproduced: The Text in History and Ideology* (New York and London: Methuen, 1987), 116–40.

86. See James McManaway, "Elizabeth, Essex, and James," in *Elizabethan and Jacobean Studies Presented to F. P. Wilson* (Oxford: Clarendon Press, 1959), 219–30. This article is a crucial resource for information about politics at the end of Elizabeth's reign; I employ it further in chapter 3.

87. Cressida is abandoned not only by Troilus but, more surprisingly, by Shakespeare: by the end of the play she becomes unknown, unknowable, her last words a letter we never hear because Troilus destroys it ("no matter from the heart," he presumes for us [5.3.108]). The playwright thus conspires to abscond

with the captive Cressida's selfhood. It is the soldier's mode to deny the woman her motivational dimensions and sympathetic claims; but in *Troilus and Cressida* it is ultimately the authorial mode to do so as well. On this point, see Janet Adelman, " 'This is and is not Cressid': The Characterization of Cressida," in *The (M)other Tongue: Essays in Feminist Psychoanalytic Interpretation,* ed. Shirley Nelson Garner et al. (Ithaca: Cornell Univ. Press, 1985), 119–41.

88. Like most assertions about individual characters in this perplexing drama, this one must be qualified: Diomedes later adopts the chivalric style. On the widespread characterological inconstancy in the play, see Colie (supra, n. 28).

89. For a fine reading of the fissures in Elizabethan ideology exposed by one long-standing problem, the Irish wars, and the Shakespearean representation of those gaps, see Dollimore and Sinfield, "History and Ideology": "The play offers a displaced, imaginary resolution of one of the state's most intractable problems" (225). By the time of *Troilus and Cressida,* no resolution, imaginary or otherwise, seemed possible.

90. "It is . . . the attempt of ideologies to render otherwise incomprehensible social structures meaningful, to so construe them as to make it possible to act purposefully within them, that accounts both for the ideologies' highly figurative nature and for the intensity with which, once accepted, they are held." Clifford Geertz, "Ideology as a Cultural System," in *The Interpretation of Cultures* (New York: Basic Books, 1973), 220.

CHAPTER 2.
WORD AND PLAGUE IN THE SECOND QUARTO *HAMLET*

1. Most of my information about the beginning and progress of the plague of 1603 is drawn directly from an indispensable reference on the subject: F. P. Wilson, *The Plague in Shakespeare's London* (Oxford: Clarendon Press, 1927); hereafter cited in text and notes as Wilson, *Plague.* See 85–113 for the plague of 1603. See also the *Calendar of State Papers, Venetian, 1592–1603,* 527 (hereafter cited as *CSPV*), and *Calendar of State Papers, Domestic 1601–1603,* 301.

2. Paul A. Slack, "Mortality and Epidemic Crisis, 1485–1610," in Charles Webster, ed., *Health, Medicine, and Mortality in the Sixteenth Century* (Cambridge: Cambridge Univ. Press, 1979), 22. Slack notes that the plague of 1603 caused a 20 percent depopulation of London.

Plague was endemic in England for so long after the first horrible Tudor outbreak of 1563 that we cannot say the conditions had actually grown more favorable. It had been possible for the Venetian ambassador to say in 1545 that the English "have some little plague . . . well nigh every year, for which they are not accustomed to make sanitary provisions, as it does not usually make great progress." Quoted in C. Creighton, *A History of Epidemics in Britain,* 2 vols. (Cambridge: Cambridge Univ. Press, 1891), 1:312. The ambassador reveals the economic bias of this indifference: "the cases for the most part occur amongst the lower classes, as if their dissolute mode of life impaired their constitutions." But that was before the great outbreak of 1563, which took upwards of thirty thousand lives.

3. Quoted in John Nichols, ed., *The Progresses and Public Processions of King James the First*, 5 vols. (London, 1828; rpt. New York: Kraus Reprint, 1980), 1:190; hereafter cited in text and notes as Nichols, *Progresses*. I have modernized the spelling in quotations from this text.

4. William Camden, *Annals of the Reign of Queen Elizabeth*, quoted in Nichols, *Progresses*, 1:228 n. 1. Those numbers, modern scholars believe, are low. As Wilson notes, a figure that included the liberties and outparishes must have been considerably higher. See Wilson, *Plague*, 93–94, and Paul Slack's crucial study, *The Impact of Plague in Tudor and Stuart England* (London: Routledge, 1985), 144–72.

5. See E. K. Chambers, *The Elizabethan Stage*, 4 vols. (Oxford: Clarendon Press, 1923), 4:349–50, for the theater closings of 1603–4.

6. See Paul Werstine: "The Textual Mystery of *Hamlet*," *Shakespeare Quarterly* 39, no. 1 (spring 1988): 1–26. Werstine summarily ignores Q1 in his account of "mystery," but he does usefully show that alternative texts are not merely versions of a single work but, rather, demonstrably and radically different works.

7. Eric Sams cunningly tracks the textual controversy over revision, memorial reconstruction, and origin while leveling devastating criticism at those editors who reject the first quarto out of hand. "Taboo or Not Taboo? The Text, Dating, and Authorship of *Hamlet*, 1589–1623," *Hamlet Studies* 10 (summer/winter 1988): 12–46. Another review of the possibilities of date and textual genesis, which examines recent editorial choices, is MacD. P. Jackson, "Editing *Hamlet* in the 1980's: Textual Theories and Textual Practices," *Hamlet Studies* 11 (summer/winter 1989): 60–72. Jackson, who does not refer to Sams, casually repeats in a footnote the notion that Q1 must represent a later state of *Hamlet* than does Q2 because "it perpetuates so many of F's modifications to Q2" (67 n. 3). He does not, unfortunately, say what these modifications are, nor does he mention, as Sams tells us, that there are "177 Q1 agreements with Q2 against F and 173 with F against Q2" ("Taboo or Not Taboo?" 28).

8. I shut the folio *Hamlet* out of consideration here because of its contradictory and perplexing historical signals. Obviously, it cannot sensibly be extrapolated from or interpolated into the contexts of *its* publication in 1623. We might argue on ambiguous evidence that F represents an earlier or later manuscript than either Q2 or Q1, but such speculations, while often interesting for their ideas about theatrical and textual revision, tend to be historically occluded. The folio is a theatrically superior version, and I do not think it should be ignored as a copy text or abandoned for analysis just because its publication history obscures its relation to contemporary contexts. But contentions about F's or Q2's probable composition date that depend on the passages absent from one or the other text always strain to provide notoriously elusive authorial or theatrical rationale for the discrepancies. There are flies in every ointment of textual dating. For examples of these problems, see Joseph Loewenstein, "Plays Agonistic and Competitive: The Textual Approach to Elsinore," *Renaissance Drama*, n.s., 19 (1988): 245–66; and David Ward, "The King in *Hamlet*," *Shakespeare Quarterly* 43, no. 3 (fall 1992): 280–302. Ward's argument resembles mine in regarding the second quarto's relevant referential frame as Jacobean, but our

views of the underlying relation of the text to its histories diverge widely. A later version of *Hamlet* than most scholars have so far entertained, and one related to the presence of plague, is posited by Willem Schrickx, "The Date of Dekker's *The Meeting of Gallants* and the Printing of *Hamlet*," *Hamlet Studies* 5 (summer/winter 1983): 82–86.

It may seem perverse to ignore F in favor of a comparison between the "bad" first quarto and the "good" quarto. However, recent revaluations of Q1 have helped rehabilitate its tarnished reputation. See Stephen Urkowitz, "Good News about 'Bad' Quartos," in Maurice Charney, ed., *"Bad" Shakespeare: Reevaluations of the Shakespeare Canon* (Cranbury, N.J.: Associated University Presses, 1989), 189–206; and for an argument against ignoring the autonomy of separate texts, see Urkowitz, " 'Well-sayd olde Mole': Burying Three *Hamlets* in Modern Editions," in Georgianna Ziegler, ed., *Shakespeare Study Today* (New York: AMS Press, 1986), 37–70. Unquestionably, Q1 has its problems as a Shakespearean artifact; it contains blemishes and lacunae that suggest its status as a draft copy and perhaps its hasty assembly. But the edition has a unique claim on our attention: whatever its source or quality, it is the first printed *Hamlet* to which Shakespeare's name is attached. We do not need to determine the authority or validity of the text to see that, even if it is a poorly recalled reconstruction of a performance based on the second quarto, its representation of that performance contributes significantly to an historical view of what *"Hamlet"* meant in 1603.

9. Caroline Spurgeon shows that Shakespeare's disease imagery peaks conspicuously in *Hamlet. Shakespeare's Imagery and What It Tells Us* (New York: Macmillan, 1935). In chart 7 (appendix), Spurgeon tallies twenty disease images for the play. For arguments about the date of the play, see the Arden edition, ed. Harold Jenkins (London: Methuen, 1982), 1–13.

10. We do not need to posit that the outbreak produced the imagery of the second quarto text, of course; the thematics of disease in the play draw from a variety of sources, including medical discourse, political metaphor, and theological suspicion.

From 1603 to 1609, London remained almost constantly under attack from bubonic plague, and the years 1610 and 1611 had several plague-ridden months. J. Leeds Barroll has noted that the period between 1603 and 1611 held "very few possibilities for public performance of the plays at . . . the Globe" because "in these nine years, there were available to Shakespeare not more than twenty-eight months . . . of public performance" because of the endemic plague and the consequent theater closings. Barroll, "Shakespeare and the Plague," in Wendell M. Aycock, ed., *Shakespeare's Art from a Comparative Perspective: Proceedings of the Comparative Literature Symposium*, vol. 12 (Lubbock: Texas Tech Univ. Press, 1981), 26. Including the plague years 1592–94, then, about eight years of Shakespeare's twenty-three-year career were interrupted by the epidemic. For a fuller treatment of the chronology and theatrical history of the disease, see Barroll, *Politics, Plague, and Shakespeare's Theater: The Stuart Years* (Ithaca: Cornell Univ. Press, 1991), a fine account of the sociological and practical effects of the first Jacobean plague.

11. I have used the collotype facsimile edition of both the first and the second

quartos, published for the Shakespeare Association (London: Sidgwick and Jackson, 1940), nos. 7 and 4, respectively. I have modernized obsolete typographical conventions. Spelling and punctuation have been retained, except where otherwise noted in brackets. Because the facsimile text is unlineated, quotations from this edition are cited parenthetically by signature leaf, with the verso page indicated by "v."

12. Derek A. Traversi, *An Approach to Shakespeare*, 2d ed. (New York: Doubleday, 1956), 94.

Many commentators have emphasized *Hamlet*'s general dependence on ideas of disease; I am indebted to, among others, Robert Grudin, *Mighty Opposites: Shakespeare and Renaissance Contrariety* (Berkeley: Univ. of California Press, 1979), and Maynard Mack, "The World of Hamlet," *Yale Review* 41 (1952): 502–23. Grudin notes that *Hamlet* treats human passions "as base, unwholesome things which resemble diseases" (122). This remark even understates the case a bit: passions, actions, words, and indeed all human practices in the play are diseases in that they corrupt or undo a supposedly pristine prior condition and in that they are irresistible to other persons. Mack likewise sees that for Hamlet, the "character of the world" comprises a "deep consciousness of infection" that inevitably sullies the hero (518).

In "Why Hamlet Dies," Joseph J. Romm comments on the contagion imagery in the play and concludes that the disease with which Hamlet is infected is the *same* as the Ghost's sickness: "Has not the Ghost infected Hamlet with Hell's contagion—his all-consuming desire for revenge, which leads Hamlet to commit foul murders?" *Hamlet Studies* 10 (summer/winter 1988): 82. I discuss the similarity of the infections below, but suffice it for now to say that the Ghost's desire for revenge is not the *only* ailment that Hamlet contracts.

For an exemplary reading of the textual and theatrical presence of death in the play, see Margaret Ferguson, "Letters and Spirits in *Hamlet*," in Patricia Parker and Geoffrey Hartman, eds., *Shakespeare and the Question of Theory* (New York: Methuen, 1985), 292–309.

13. In an early plague tract, for instance, Gilbert Skene writes of the "corrupt venum" that "occupeis the hart" in a plague patient. Thomas Lodge, in 1603, sees the plague carbuncle as a crucible full of "contagious and pestilent venime . . . infected by the euil quality of the aire, which maketh such pustules ouer and aboue their naturall malitiousnesse more maligne, dangerous, & deadly." In *The Wonderfull Yeare 1603* Thomas Dekker addresses—with overtones suggestive for *Hamlet*—"the ghosts of those more (by many) than 40000. that with the virulent poison of infection haue been driuen out of your earthlie dwelling." Later, in *Worke for Armorours* (1609), Dekker describes the emotional effect of the disease on Londoners: "The poyson of the Lingering infection, strikes so deepe into all mens harts, that their cheekes (like cowardly Souldiers) haue lost their colours." Writing also in the plague year 1609, John Davies of Hereford imagines "Th'Almighties hand" breaking a vial of poison, and "a plague out-flees / That gluts the Aire with Vapors venemous, / That putrifie, infect, and flesh confound, / And makes Earthes breath most contagious, / That in the Earth and Aire but Death is found!" Gilbert Skene, *Ane Breve Descriptiovn of the Pest* (Edinburgh, 1568; rpt. Amsterdam: Theatrum Orbis Terrarum, 1971

[STC 22626.5]), A7v; Thomas Lodge, *A Treatise of the Plague* (London, 1603; rpt. Amsterdam and Norwood, N.J.: Theatrum Orbis Terrarum, 1979 [STC 16676]), J4; Thomas Dekker, *The Wonderfull Yeare 1603*, in *The Plague Pamphlets of Thomas Dekker*, ed. F. P. Wilson (Oxford: Clarendon Press, 1925), 26 (hereafter cited as Dekker, *Plague Pamphlets*); Dekker, *Worke for Armorours*, in *The Non-Dramatic Works of Thomas Dekker*, ed. Alexander B. Grosart, 5 vols. (New York: Russell and Russell, 1963), 4:95; John Davies, "The Triumph of Death, or The Picture of the Plague: According to the Life, as it was in *Anno Domini 1603*," in *The Complete Works of John Davies of Hereford*, ed. Alexander B. Grosart, 2 vols. (New York: AMS Press, 1967), 1:42.

I have used these sources for their chronological range, but with the exception of Dekker, whose concerns are more broadly literary than medical, there is not much diversity to be found in the contemporary approach to or theory about the disease. The fact that authority rather than originality was, in the Renaissance, still the best selling point for a medical treatise may help explain the continuity in the conception of the epidemic.

14. Stephen Bradwell, *Physick For the Sicknesse, Commonly Called The Plague* (London, 1636; rpt. Amsterdam, Theatrum Orbis Terrarum, 1977 [STC 3536]), 3; hereafter cited in text as Bradwell, *Physick*.

15. Harold Goddard was the first to emphasize the parallel between the Ghost's speech and King Hamlet's death as two versions of aural poisoning. Goddard plays many variations on the theme, especially stressing Polonius's virulent speech acts throughout; Hamlet's own verbal venom, however, receives less attention. See *The Meaning of Shakespeare*, 2 vols. (Chicago: Univ. of Chicago Press, 1953), 1:331–86. One of the best early commentaries on Hamlet's infective potential, central to Goddard's work and my own, is G. Wilson Knight's classic reading "The Embassy of Death: An Essay on *Hamlet*," in *The Wheel of Fire: Interpretations of Shakespearean Tragedy*, 5th ed. (New York: Meridian Books, 1957), 17–46. For later commentaries that treat the auditory theme, see Terence Hawkes, *That Shakespeherian Rag: Essays on a Critical Process* (London and New York: Methuen, 1986), 92–119; Malcolm Evans, *Signifying Nothing: Truth's True Contents in Shakespeare's Text* (Athens: Univ. of Georgia Press, 1986); James Calderwood, *To Be and Not To Be: Negation and Metadrama in Shakespeare's "Hamlet"* (New York: Columbia Univ. Press, 1983), esp. 67–72, 204 n.12.

16. The general pattern has been sketched insightfully by Lee Sheridan Cox, who also reads the conjunction of poison, plague, and language as central to the (second-quarto based) text:

> That talk can take on the property of poison is again implied by the use of forms of the word *blast* to describe both. . . . There is simply no doubt that the speech/ear figures repeatedly say that as hebenon "blasted" the wholesome blood, so speech may contaminate, that as poison brought on a "leperous" death, so words may infect and destroy. . . . The movement of the pattern . . . leads to the possibility that . . . the original method and means of murder informs an ironic but logical process wherein a poisoned man's speech becomes a potential poison and a victim a latent poisoner.

Cox, *Figurative Design in Hamlet: The Significance of the Dumb Show* (Ohio: Ohio State Univ. Press, 1973), 41–43. Cox points to a pattern of "chain reaction" whereby "the pestilential nature of evil" (43) turns all listeners into victims and those victims into future potential infectors. This crucial schematic has explanatory force for much of the play. But the power of language in the second quarto, its startling material effect, extends even further than Cox implies. His fine work, which was called to my attention after this chapter was complete, anticipates many of my observations here; and although Cox does not historicize his insights, his close reading of disease in the play confirms some of my conclusions.

17. *The Complete Essays of Montaigne*, trans. Donald M. Frame (Stanford: Stanford Univ. Press, 1958), 74–75.

18. Giralomo Fracastoro, *De Contagione et Contagiosis Morbis et Eorum Curatione*, trans. Wilmer Cave Wright (New York: Putnam's, 1930); hereafter cited in text and notes as Fracastor, *Contagion*.

19. René Girard, "The Plague in Literature and Myth," in *"To Double Business Bound": Essays on Myth and Literature* (Baltimore: Johns Hopkins Univ. Press, 1978), 136. For Girard, the actual or referential presence of epidemics in imaginative texts signals or alludes to a social upheaval that can be resolved only through the culture's deployment of the scapegoat mechanism. In other words, cycles of reciprocal violence, metaphorized by the undifferentiation of plague effects, can be broken only by the arbitrary selection (carefully rationalized through plot dynamics and internal logic) of a sacrificial victim.

My interest in *Hamlet's* operative and generally subtextual plague—that is, there is no actual *physical* epidemic—has been sparked in many ways by Girard's work, but it leans away from the sociological and mythographic aspect of sickness toward the play's aesthetic inscriptions of its intercourse with history.

20. The Ghost evokes an extensive, ambiguous language of *similarity* that is insufficiently differentiated (and differentiable) from the discourse of *identity*. When, for example, Horatio tells Hamlet that he saw a ghost, he calls it "the King your father"; claiming that the specter is the dead king, he says "I knewe your father, / These hands are not more like" (C2–C2v). Not more like each other than the Ghost is like the King (i.e., reverse or mirror images)? Or not more like *themselves* than the Ghost is like the elder Hamlet? In one case the issue is a likeness figured paradoxically in a left-right reversal; in the other, the issue is identity. We can also see the opening crises of self-naming and identification in these terms ("*Bar.* Say, what is *Horatio* there? *Hor.* A peece of him.") as linguistic and ontological problems generated by the experience of the Ghost, a figure that traditionally puts such questions front and center. I thank Gena K. Hooper for her insights about these issues.

21. Ophelia is (at least) twice victim of horrific aural contamination. Early in the play, Polonius darkens Ophelia's mental landscape with (self-revelatory) warnings about Hamlet's probable bad intents: "I doe knowe / When the blood burnes, how prodigall the soule / Lends the tongue vowes" (C4v), he informs her. These loveless words literally change her mind. She is made susceptible to infection—the rational disjunctions of the sort that Hamlet later obscenely communicates during *The Murder of Gonzago*—through the father's metalanguage.

Explicit reference to the contagious or toxic effects of language is not unusual in the Shakespeare canon. Iago tells us of his plans to ruin Othello: "I'll pour this pestilence in his ear" (*Othello*, 2.3.356); and Lady Macbeth says something similar when she ponders how her husband lacks the "illness" that should attend ambition, to remedy which, "I may pour my spirits in thine ear" (1.4.19–20, 26). (References to Shakespeare's plays other than *Hamlet* will be to the versions in *The Riverside Shakespeare*, ed. G. Blakemore Evans [Boston: Houghton Mifflin, 1974].)

Iago's plan aligns sexuality with epistemological doubt, the assertion that Desdemona is trying to reinstate Cassio as lieutenant "for her body's lust." Iago's verbal poison is a figurative pestilence that spreads within the Moor's imagination, seemingly of its own accord, contaminating what was susceptible but less corrupt. His demolition of Othello, wrought almost entirely in language ("It is not words that shakes me thus," Othello incorrectly notes), indicates the extent to which Shakespeare understands communicative acts as capable of huge destruction.

22. Thomas Lodge also described the plague as an impairment of character: "an euil, malignant, venemous, or vitious disposition . . . may be imparted and bestowed on an other by touch." Lodge, *A Treatise of the Plague* (1603), B3.

23. *2 Henry IV* (5.1.75–77). This clever social diagnosis spins off of a visual rather than a verbal spool of *imitatio*; Falstaff's assumption that diseases are spread specularly is replaced by *Hamlet*'s knowledge that the transmission is always auditory.

24. "Seminarum" is Fracastor's term. In his remarkable, seemingly clairvoyant treatise on infection, he anticipates by several centuries the modern discovery of bacterial and viral vectors of epidemic disease.

25. Laertes may be citing a received Polonian wisdom about the dangers of plague; Bradwell *(Physick, 9)* sees as particularly susceptible to infection

> *Women*, especially *women with childe*; for their bodies are full of excrementitious humors, and much heat withall. . . . Also *Virgins* that are ripe for marriage, are apt to receive infection, and being once stricken, seldome or never escape without great meanes.

Note that the susceptibility of pregnant women calls for an explanation along the lines of humor theory, but that of virgins does not; the quarantine around expectant mothers requires justification, but the already present mental and moral quarantine around maids needs no ideological reinforcement.

26. Claudius, like the Ghost, commits an aural assault which is also figuratively a sexual assault, a pouring of fluid into an unguarded receptacle. The incestuous homoeroticism of the attack complicates the horror with which the Ghost reacts to its own story. Claudius's designation as "that incestuous . . . beast" may refer both to his affair with Gertrude and to his rapine murder of the king his brother.

27. Marina Warner, *Alone of All Her Sex: The Myth and Cult of the Virgin Mary* (New York: Knopf, 1976), 37: "Origen . . . suggested that Mary had conceived Jesus the Word at the words of the angel. He intended perhaps to make a characteristic Alexandrian point, about the conception of wisdom in the soul by the power of the spirit, as expounded by Philo Judaeus' school of mystical philosophy. But Origen's idea quickly acquired a literal stamp." Warner also quotes

a thirteenth-century English dancing song that is relevant here: "Glad us maiden, mother mild / Through thine ear thou were with child / Gabriel he said it thee."

The Christian auditory conception is obviously designed to avoid sexuality, to preserve the possibility of Mary's physical virginity. In Hamlet's case, however, the message from the Ghost is so deeply fraught with sexual and criminal tones that it can function only as divine parody, not as genuine replica.

28. Hamlet is repelled by corporeality, yet he never fully wishes or manages to escape from it. A fine recent reading of the hero's obsessive concerns with physicality and its consequences for the play's plot is by John Hunt, "The Catastrophic Body in *Hamlet*," *Shakespeare Quarterly* 39, no. 1 (spring 1988): 27–44. See also Francis Barker, *The Tremulous Private Body* (London: Methuen, 1984), 25–41.

29. The line "Most Lazarlike with vile and loathesome crust" is unique to Q2; the emphasis on the king's leprous demise is thus highlighted here. Q1 does mention the "leaprous distilment" and how the elder Hamlet's "smoothe body" was "barked, and tetterd ouer" (C4v). But the infectious overtones of the murder are underscored in the later text.

30. S. N. Brody, *The Disease of the Soul: Leprosy in Medieval Literature* (Ithaca: Cornell Univ. Press, 1974). See also Steven Mullaney, *The Place of the Stage* (Chicago: Univ. of Chicago Press, 1987), 31–40, for an interesting reading of the theatrical significance (in terms of ritual and margin) of the lazar houses in Renaissance England.

31. William B. Ober, "Can the Leper Change His Spots? The Iconography of Leprosy," in his *Bottoms Up!: A Pathologist's Essays on Medicine and the Humanities* (New York: Harper, 1988), 99–152.

32. Thomas Dekker, in "Newes from Graues-ende" (1604), identifies moral corruption as the cause of epidemics and aptly describes its lazarlike symptoms: "For euery man within him feedes / A worme which this contagion breedes; / Our heauenly parts are plaguy sick, / And there such leaprous spotts do stick, / That God in anger fills his hand / With Vengeance." Dekker, *Plague Pamphlets*, 85–86. Plague was a subsuming illness that absorbed—categorically and perceptually—other forms of sickness. On "the various skin manifestations accompanying plague," Barroll comments: "the individual poxlike irruptions often covering the body affected by general plague were known as blains. The carbuncles, which may also accompany plague, ... were quite painful and, in fact, the excruciating pain of plague was understood by physicians of the time as coming not from the rupturing of the bubo ... but from the unbearable burning of the carbuncles." *Politics*, 80. We ought to keep this description in mind when considering the full horrific force of Pyrrhus, to be discussed below.

33. There is another precise appropriateness in the Ghost's symptomatology of the king's demise. Whereas plague was acute and highly morbid, leprosy was *chronic*—survivable for long periods. In fact, lepers were often regarded as the living dead, their state a death-in-life. In this way, the ailment fits a ghost's obsessions. William Ober believes that this may be the true origin of the term "Lazar"—in other words, one who has returned from the dead, and not merely

one who is isolated and physically decrepit. "Can a Leper Change His Spots?" 111.

Janet Adelman notes (in *Suffocating Mothers: Fantasies of Maternal Origin in Shakespeare's Plays, "Hamlet" to "The Tempest"* [London: Routledge, 1992], 254–55 n. 33) that "skin eruptions of the sort the ghost describes were one of the symptoms of syphilis"; she cites James Cleugh, *Secret Enemy: The Story of a Disease* (London: Thames and Hudson, 1954), 46–50. Scabs, crusts, and excrescences "harder than bark" (Josef Grunbeck, in Cleugh, 49) were the topical symptoms. Syphilis, like leprosy, was a chronic, incurable ailment. The diseased sexuality implied in the association further marks the Ghost as debased, and adds another complication to Hamlet's dilemma about whether to trust what he hears.

34. This is a telling departure from Q1, where the Ghost answers Hamlet's outburst of realization—"my vncle! my vncle!"—with a direct affirmation: "Yea he, that . . . wretch." But in the second quarto, the Ghost seems to be accusing itself in answering Hamlet about the source of the crime: "I that incestuous . . . "

35. Cedric Watts has an admirably concise treatment of the Ghost's several contradictions in *"Hamlet": Harvester New Critical Introductions to Shakespeare* (New York and London: Harvester, 1988), 32–39.

36. King Hamlet's life seems not to have been retrospectively illuminated quite enough, but the Ghost owns a veritable treasure trove of reliable information compared to the knowledge possessed by another revenging Ghost—Don Andrea of Kyd's *The Spanish Tragedy*. Andrea is markedly underexercised about what he knows and, incredibly, does not even know what he knows. Transformation into a Ghost seems to cause epistemological deficit; or perhaps it is only because of such transformations that deficits become clear.

37. Was Gertrude complicitous with or seduced by Claudius? Did she love or at least sleep with him before the murder? Was King Hamlet a creature of virtue, and who preyed on whom? As Alvin Kernan has remarked about the play, "The *dramatis personae* are curious about and determined to find answers to exactly the same questions that inevitably occur to readers and critics." Kernan, "The Plays and the Playwrights," in J. Leeds Barroll et al., eds., *The Revels History of Drama in English*, 4 vols. (London: Methuen, 1975), 3:382.

38. If we take "honest" to mean "truth-telling," the jury is still out on the Ghost at this point in the play. If "honest" means "sober or sexually chaste," as it so often does in Shakespeare, Hamlet truly has been disturbed by the narrative.

39. See Harry Levin, "An Explication of the Player's Speech," in *The Question of Hamlet* (New York: Oxford Univ. Press, 1959), 138–64. On "disowning knowledge" as a typical tragic mode in Shakespeare and in *Hamlet*, see Stanley Cavell, *Disowning Knowledge in Six Plays of Shakespeare* (Cambridge: Cambridge Univ. Press, 1987), 179–91.

40. Ophelia's comparable report in Q1 emphasizes Hamlet's disordered appearance but contains only this embryonic idea about Hamlet's similarity to the Ghost: "He . . . parts away / Silent, as is the mid time of the night" (Q1, sig. D2v).

41. The pronominal referent problem here is more than routinely annoying: all the third-person masculine pronouns in this passage *could* refer to Claudius without straining the sense of the lines. Such a reading would show Hamlet merely bolstering his hateful opinion of his uncle and still not acknowledging any of his father's flaws: Claudius's broad-blown crimes and heavy heavenly audit must not be meliorated by a happy death. But the very fact that the referent *is* ambiguous or imprecise points to the more plausible reading. Q1, predictably, lacks ambiguity at this point; coming upon Claudius at prayer, Hamlet reflects: "he tooke my father sleeping, his sins brim full, / And how his soule stoode to the state of heauen / Who knowes" (G1v). The potential unclarity of "his soule" is quickly resolved with the past tense verb "stoode": the dead King Hamlet must be the subject of the sentence.

42. As Janet Adelman interestingly suggested to me, plague fear may manifest a terror of *biological* reproduction, which requires sexual (not just linguistic) intercourse.

43. Lodge, *Treatise of the Plague* (1603), B2v.

44. Montaigne provides a typical atmospheric reading of the plaguy miasma:

> Both outside and inside my house I was greeted by a plague of the utmost virulence. For as healthy bodies are subject to graver illnesses because they can be overcome only by these, so the very salubrious air of my place, where in the memory of man no contagion, even though in the neighborhood, had been able to get a foothold, became poisoned and produced strange results.

The language of plague, poison, and dangerous air collects in an imaginative capsule. Montaigne goes on to describe, with characteristic incisiveness, the paranoia that settles on social groups under the rule of the disease: "I, who am so hospitable, had a great deal of trouble finding a retreat for my family: a family astray, a source of fear to their friends and themselves, and of horror wherever they sought to settle, having to shift their abode as soon as one of the group began to feel pain in the end of his finger. All illnesses are taken for the plague; people do not give themselves time to recognize them. . . . your imagination meanwhile [works] you up in its own way and [turns] even your health into a fever." "Of Physiognomy," in *Complete Essays*, 801–2. Alain Courbin discusses the homeopathy of aromatic fumigation as a popular defense against atmospheric plague putrefaction in *The Foul and the Fragrant: Odor and the French Social Imagination* (Cambridge: Harvard Univ. Press, 1986), 61. For more on corrupt air as a commonly perceived cause of several diseases ancient and modern, see Claudine Herzlich and Janine Pierret, *Illness and Self in Society*, trans. Elborg Foster (Baltimore and London: Johns Hopkins Univ. Press, 1987), 98–109. For corrupted air and the "stinks" in London, see Cheryl Lynn Ross, "The Plague of *The Alchemist*," *Renaissance Quarterly* 41, no. 3 (autumn 1988): 439–58.

Thomas Lodge states confidently that "all pestilential sicknesses . . . are ingendered from the ayre," but this cause creates an alarming vacuum of possible cures, because "men hauing a necessitie to sucke in the ayre, together with the same sucke in the infection and venome" (*Treatise of the Plague*, B3v, B4). Or as

Bradwell says, "Ayre is that which we draw in with our breath continually, and wee cannot live without it one minute . . . therefore we had need take heed that the ayre we draw be pure and wholsome" (*Physick*, 12).

45. John Davies, too, employs this language in a similar way: "The babe new born [plague] nipped straight in the head, / With air that through his yet unclosed Mould / Did pierce his brains, and through them poison spread." "The Triumph of Death," in *Complete Works*, 1:46.

46. Francis Hering, *Certaine Rules, Directions, or Advertisements* . . . , sig. B2 (London, 1625); quoted in Wilson, *Plague*, 10.

47. Lodge, *Treatise of the Plague*, K4v.

48. Davies, "The Triumph of Death," 1:46.

From such an atmosphere, we might expect the written to take prominence over the oral, script over speech, if only for safety's sake. But no language was a haven, as Thomas Dekker makes clear in his preface to *The Wonderfull Yeare 1603*:

> If you read, you may happilie laugh; tis my desire you should, because mirth is both *Phisicall*, and wholesome against the *Plague*, with which sicknes, (to tell truth) this booke is, (though not sorely) yet somewhat infected. I pray, driue it not out of your companie for all that. (Dekker, *Plague Pamphlets*, 3)

The possibility of his own text's infection articulates Dekker's awareness of the disease's omnipresence and of the threat inherent in any communicative act.

49. So, towns fear'd towns, and men each other fear'd;
     All were at least attainted with suspect,
     And sooth to say so was their envy stirr'd
     That one would seek another to infect:
     For whether the disease to envy mov'd,
     Or human nature's malice was the cause,
     Th'infected often all Conclusions prov'd
     To plague him that from them himself withdraws.

Davies, "The Triumph of Death," in *Complete Works*, 1:47. Note the way in which "envy" works opposite to the expected mode of mimetic desire in this quotation: the envious person seeks to spread or bestow, not contract or imitate, diseases. Wilson mentions the depraved multitude who, "afflicted with running sores recklessly thrust themselves into company." *Plague*, 95, citing J. Bamford's *A Short Dialogue* (1603).

50. For a different semiosis of disease indicators, see Eugen Baer, "The Medical Symptom," in John Deely, Brooke Williams, and Felicia E. Kruse, eds., *Frontiers in Semiotics* (Bloomington: Indiana Univ. Press, 1986), 140–52.

51. Roger Fenton, *A perfume against the Noysome Pestilence, prescribed by Moses unto Aaron, Num. 16: 46* (London, 1603 [STC 10800]), sig. A5.

52. Eric Partridge cites the Latin *pestis* and admits it "of obscure origin"; he calls up the Hittite *pasihati*, "to crush" or "to trample," for comparison. S.v. "pest," in *Origins: A Short Modern Etymological Dictionary of Modern English* (New York: Greenwich House/Macmillan, 1983). Consultation with Hebraists and relevant textual sources about the passage in Numbers has failed to uncover or illuminate the etymological basis for Fenton's assertion.

53. Henoch Clapham, *Epistle Discoursing upon the present Pestilence*, 2d ed. (London, 1603), sig. B1v; quoted in Slack, *Impact of Plague*, 233–34.

Apparently, the sense of having been struck was not unusual. Stephen Bradwell, writing in 1636 of the last great plague year (1625), observed, "Some felt themselves manifestly stricken, being sensible of a blow suddenly given them on the head, neck, back, or side: Sometime so violently, that they have been eyther almost, or altogether over-turned" (*Physick*, 2).

54. In speculating with terror on the infinite tortures in the arsenal of a god who could rain down such pestilence, John Davies of Hereford summons the inexpressibility topos:

> what be [those tortures] that deuised are
> By Wisedome that of Nought made all this All,
> That stretch as farre past speach, as past compare:
> Surmounting Wonder; supernatural!

"The Triumph of Death," in *Complete Works*, 1:48. Scarcely a paean to divine goodness, these lines hint that the vast misery of the present plaguy world ("all this All") inhered in the chaos, the Nought, that spawned it. "Of nought" means "out of nothing," but it just as well could mean "all for naught, for no consequence or purpose" because the world may return to nothing with such large mortality.

55. Ironically, this fear was unfounded except in the case of the rare and almost always fatal pneumonic plague, which was (unlike the bubonic and septicemic varieties) transmitted aerially by patients' sneezing or coughing. For a summary of the disease's epidemiology, see Barroll, *Politics*, 73–96.

56. Gilbert Skene's early vernacular plague tract, *Ane Breve Descriptioun of the Pest*, contains a suggestive clinical note that may be relevant: "The principall signis of dethe in pestilentiall personis," Skene avers, "ar . . . imperfectioun of speche and stinkand [stinking] breithe." Skene, *Ane Breve Descriptioun*, cap. 6 (cited supra, n. 13). The second of these attributes is clear enough; the writer refers to the putrid exhalations of the dying, a halitosis which pestered individuals and whole cities in the olfactory mess of epidemics. But Skene provides no further clinical definition of "imperfectioun of speche." He probably has in mind the plague victim's crippling shortness of breath and pain-induced dementia, both of which would allow only abbreviated or unintelligible utterances. However, the writer may be describing, as so many did, the plague's injurious impact on social relations. Imperfect (unintelligible) speech and reeking breath compel intractable isolation, issuing as they do from one who can be neither approached nor understood—the paradoxical upshot of suffering from a disease anyone can get. In Hamlet's case, verbal "imperfection" amalgamates linguistic impotence and pointed if elusive functionality.

57. Michel Foucault, "The Order of Discourse," in Robert Young, ed., *Untying the Text: A Post-Structuralist Reader* (Boston: Routledge and Kegan Paul, 1981), 51; hereafter cited in text. This essay was also published in English as "The Discourse on Language," an appendix to Foucault's *The Archaeology of Knowledge* (New York: Pantheon, 1972), 215–37. The piece was an inaugural lecture for the College de France in 1970; Foucault's wish to slip surreptitiously into discourse countervails the institution's need for a demarcated, ceremonial

presentation. His lecture centers on "the order of discourse," or the nature, control, conditions, and political complications of the interlocutive act. As the pure, disembodied speaker (paradoxically obsessed with his former body), the Ghost does to an extent project Foucault's desires: to hover on the borders of the living world without corporeality, without suffering the indignities that bodies always suffer. The Ghost, as a form of plague, becomes an image of language. Useful Lacanian speculations on the Ghost have been made by Marjorie Garber, "*Hamlet*: Giving Up the Ghost," *Shakespeare's Ghost Writers* (London: Methuen, 1987), 124–76.

58. I have borrowed the lovely phrase "horizon of surmise" from Professor Allen Grossman.

59. For this principle—that there is no textual interpretation without alteration of what constitutes the text—see Stanley Fish, "Wrong Again," in *Doing What Comes Naturally: Change, Rhetoric, and the Practice of Theory in Literary and Legal Studies* (Durham: Duke Univ. Press, 1989), 103–19.

60. The obvious analogue here, to our *own* intrusive understanding, our own inability to interpret without alteration, constantly emerges in the experience of attempting to process the second quarto text. But since it is awfully hard to know what Hamlet *is* from the beginning, it becomes impossible to know what he becomes unless we, the interpreters, enter into the process of his becoming—which, in the infectious space of theater, we all certainly do. For more on theater as a particularly contagious space for literary language, see Antonin Artaud, *Theater and Its Double*, vol. 4 of *Collected Works*, trans. Victor Corti (London: Calder and Boyars, 1974); and Jacqueline Rose, "Sexuality in the Reading of Shakespeare," in John Drakakis, ed., *Alternative Shakespeares* (London: Methuen, 1985), 95–118.

61. Thomas Nashe, *Strange Newes, of the Intercepting Certaine Letters* (1592), in *The Works of Thomas Nashe*, ed. Ronald Brunlees McKerrow, 5 vols. (London: A. H. Bullen, 1904), 1:287.

Shakespeare would likely have been aware of this passage; he was aware of much of Nashe's work. J. J. M. Tobin, "More Elements from Nashe," *Hamlet Studies* 5 (summer/winter 1983): 52–58, notes that '*Strange Newes* . . . provided Shakespeare with some turns of phrase or pieces of diction unique in the canon for use in *Hamlet*" (52).

62. The famous dumbshow crux was the interpretive nemesis of W. W. Greg and J. Dover Wilson, and it has recently been recalled but elaborately evaded by Terence Hawkes in his account of the play in *That Shakespeherian Rag*, 92–119. Hawkes gives an interesting account of one history of this crux; he explicates Wilson's extensive avoidance of a politically implicated critical position on *Hamlet*. But surprisingly, Hawkes then reiterates avoidance by retreating interpretively from the text, even from a deconstructive reading; we cannot return to *Hamlet*, he says, because "there is no unitary, self-presenting play for us to turn back to." The critic renders himself as silent on the dumbshow as Claudius had been.

For a survey on the dumbshow problem, see Jenkins, *Hamlet*, 501–5.

63. Looking at the two quartos, however, we can get a fair idea about what pesters Claudius in each text. In Q2, the king feels compelled to depart immedi-

ately after Hamlet announces: "You shall see anon how the murtherer gets the loue of *Gonzagoes* wife" (H3). But in the first quarto, it is the image of the purely political, not sexual, power grab that forces the king out of the room; Hamlet's last line before the king rises is "He poysons him for his estate" (F4v). As I discuss in the next chapter, the second quarto is insistent on the intertwined corruptions of sexuality and politics in a way that Q1 is not.

64. Nigel Alexander, *Poison, Play, and Duel: A Study in "Hamlet"* (London: Routledge and Kegan Paul, 1971), 20.

65. George Puttenham, *The Arte of English Poesie*, ed. Gladys Doidge Willcock and Alice Walker (Cambridge: Cambridge Univ. Press, 1936), 260.

66. The play's shifting patterns of sense and nonsense have been elegantly explicated by Stephen Booth, "On the Value of *Hamlet*," in Norman Rabkin, ed., *Reinterpretations of Renaissance Drama* (New York: Columbia Univ. Press, 1969), 137–76. However, neither Booth nor any other reader that I know of regards Hamlet's certitude after the Gonzago performance as a problem.

67. Knight, *Wheel of Fire*, 38; see also 32.

68. If Hamlet becomes the metaphorical ailment afflicting Denmark, Fortinbras might be the curative the state has needed—someone external to the nation's ills, even if he has participated indirectly in them. Although doubts will surely remain that the man who has "sharkt vp a list of lawelesse resolutes / For foode and diet to some enterprise / That hath a stomacke in't" (B2v) is the best man for the job of king, he is virtually the only one left.

69. Philippe du Plessis-Mornay, *Vindiciae Contra Tyrannos* (Defense of liberty against tyrants), trans. and ed. Julian H. Franklin, in *Constitutionalism and Resistance in the Sixteenth Century: Three Treatises by Hotman, Beza, and Mornay* (New York: Pegasus, 1969), 190; hereafter cited in text.

See Kenneth Rothwell, "*Hamlet*, Duplessis-Mornay, and the 'Irenic' Vision," *Hamlet Studies* 3 (1981): 13–31, and his later "Hamlet's 'Glass of Fashion': Power, Self, and the Reformation," in Luther H. Martin et al., eds., *Technologies of the Self: A Seminar with Michel Foucault* (Amherst: Univ. of Massachusetts Press, 1988), 80–98. Rothwell takes Shakespeare's use of the Huguenot antityrant tract unironically, and as a key to character: "Hamlet's reformist tendencies often parallel the discourse of . . . Duplessis-Mornay. . . . Of primary interest here is the ideology of Duplessis and the French reformers, which might account for Hamlet's shift from perturbation to serenity, a shift that parallels in many ways the 'irenicist' attitudes that made the French reformers the most tolerant of the dissenters." "Hamlet's 'Glass of Fashion,' " 90–91.

70. G. Wilson Knight saw Hamlet many years ago as "the ambassador of death walking amid life":

> But it is to be noted that the consciousness of death, and consequent bitterness, cruelty, and inaction, in Hamlet not only grows in his own mind disintegrating it as we watch, but also spreads its effects outward among the other persons like a blighting disease, and . . . insidiously undermines the health of the state, and adds victim to victim until at the end the stage is filled with corpses. . . . Thus Hamlet is an element of evil in the state of Denmark.

Knight, *Wheel of Fire*, 32, 38.

71. Opinions about the relative moral and ethical rectitude of Hamlet and Claudius are as diverse as the critics writing about them. On "complementarity," see Norman Rabkin, *Shakespeare and the Common Understanding* (Berkeley: Univ. of California Press, 1967), 1–15, and *Shakespeare and the Problem of Meaning* (Berkeley: Univ. of California Press, 1981). Howard Mumford Jones makes an interesting defense of Claudius in *The King in Hamlet*, Comparative Literature Series, no. 1 (Austin: Univ. of Texas, 1918). The contrary and predominant view of Claudius's wicked tyranny, and the play's abundant historical signs thereof, is provided by, among others, Roland Mushat Frye in *The Renaissance Hamlet* (Princeton: Princeton Univ. Press, 1984), esp. 131–40. Some aspects of the king's depravity are unarguable. But Hamlet matches him, *cap a pé*.

72. A heartbreaking example of this failure is Nehemiah Wallington's account of his spiritual consolation over the deaths of his children in plague; in Ralph Houlbrooke, ed., *English Family Life, 1576–1716: An Anthology from Diaries* (London: Basil Blackwell, 1988), 141–44.

73. For a sustained treatment of the convergence theme, see Eileen Jorge Allman, *Player King and Adversary* (Baton Rouge: Louisiana State Univ. Press, 1980). See also Ferguson, "Letters and Spirits," for a sharp discussion of this matter.

74. Virgil, *The Aeneid*, trans. W. F. Jackson Knight (Harmondsworth: Penguin, 1956), 108.

Harold Jenkins also notices the Virgilian connection here, but I believe he misreads it: "Hamlet's slip of memory thus stresses the savagery of Pyrrhus from the start." *Hamlet*, 263 (note to 2.2.446).

75. Aeneas, incidentally, is not so terribly heroic in the medieval *historiae destructionis Troiae*, having in some versions betrayed the city so that the prophecy of his founding the next great civilization could be assured. And in Lydgate and Caxton, the Trojan is also (along with Antenor) largely responsible for the city's downfall.

76. Hamlet also wants a corrective model of *maternal* mourning, which is why he recalls that Gertrude had formerly followed his "poore fathers bodie / Like *Niobe*, all teares" (C1v); Niobe mourned *not* for a husband, however, but for her children.

77. True to his contagious spirit, Hamlet beseeches Horatio to "drawe thy breath in paine / To tell my story" (O1v). In his final verbal gambit, the prince charges his beloved companion to reproduce and transmit a narrative that Horatio could not possibly retell accurately. (In the first quarto, Hamlet more modestly asks not to be individually represented, but rather to be part of a collective representation: "What tongue should tell the story of our deaths, / If not from thee?" [I3v].) The second quarto Hamlet's injunction to Horatio is a remarkably Ghost-like maneuver, enjoining an auditor to prolong the infectious discord that death promised to end. Although the physical circuit of poison closes, a narrative contagion will endure.

78. In Q1, finally, it is Hamlet himself who calls out, in response to the queen's swoon, "Treason, ho, keepe the gates" (I3v); in the earlier text he is not the threat to order, but its defender.

CHAPTER 3. SUCCESSION, REVENGE, AND HISTORY

1. John Harington pithily anticipates this point: "Treason dothe never prosper;—what's the reason? / Why; if it prosper, none dare call it Treason." Norman Egbert McClure, ed., *The Letters and Epigrams of John Harington* (Philadelphia: University of Pennsylvania Press, 1930), 255.

2. Thomas Dekker, *The Wonderfull Yeare 1603*, in *The Plague Pamphlets of
Thomas Dekker*, ed. F. P. Wilson (Oxford: Clarendon Press, 1925), 21, 25.

3. William McElwee, *The Wisest Fool in Christendom: The Reign of King
James I and VI* (New York: Harcourt, Brace, 1958), 109; hereafter cited in text
and notes as McElwee, *Wisest Fool*.

4. "The True Narration of the Entertainment of his Royal Majestie from the
time of his Departure from Edenbrough till his Receiving at London," in John
Nichols, ed., *The Progresses and Public Processions of King James the First*, 5
vols. (London, 1828; rpt. New York, Kraus Reprint, 1980), 1:113; hereafter
cited as Nichols, *Progresses*.

5. Quoted in F. P. Wilson, *The Plague in Shakespeare's London* (Oxford:
Clarendon Press, 1927), 94–95; hereafter cited in text and notes as Wilson,
Plague.

6. Quoted in Paul Slack, *The Impact of Plague in Tudor and Stuart England*
(London: Routledge, 1985), 304. But elsewhere (258–59) Slack notes that such
rebellions as the mayor feared were remarkably rare.

7. Wilson, *Plague*, 95–96. Wilson also quotes a proclamation from the Lord
Mayor issued at the height of the plague on September 17, 1603:

> The people infected and whose houses are infected (against all honesty, human Civility
> and good conscience seeking as it were rather the desolation of the City and of this
> kingdom by dispersing of the infection than otherwise) do daily intrude themselves into
> all Companies both private and public . . . and do flock and follow the dead to the
> grave in multitudes one still infecting another to the displeasure of Almighty God and
> great grief of his Majesty.

In this vision of plaguy society, the human impulse toward self-preservation
becomes perverted, and the only community exists as death-centered, flocking
(literally and figuratively, I take it) to the grave. Slack notes that most incidents
of willful dissemination of plague were unconfirmed hearsay; but he rightly observes that "rumours and threats are sufficient in themselves to show the divisive
impact of plague in social relationships at every level" (*Impact of Plague*, 293).

8. In 1606 Lord Dunfermline, the lord chancellor of Scotland, wrote to
Thomas Egerton, Lord Ellesmere, to tell him of the devastating tenacity of the
disease:

> The onlie truble we haiff is this contagious sicknes of peste, whilk [which] is spread
> marvelouslie in the best townes of this realme. In Edenburght it hes bene countinuall
> this four yeares, at the present not werie wehement, bot sik [such] as stayes the cow-
> moun course of administration off justice, whilk can not be weill exercised in naa other
> plaice. Air and Striveling ar almoste overthrowin with the seiknes, within thir twa
> monethes about twa thowsand personnes dead in ane of them. The maist of the peple
> fled, and the tounes almost left desolat.

The Egerton Papers, ed. J. Payne Collier (London: Camden Society Publications,
1840), 406–7. To the magistrate's aristocratic chagrin, even "the best townes of

this realme" cannot defend against the epidemic, as if class boundaries should be impenetrable to illness. Dunfermline goes on to describe the frequent council meetings in which "we tak the best ordour we may for mantenance of his Majesties peace and obedience." Although he mentions the deaths of the townspeople, the lord chancellor seems most concerned with upholding order. Not only does the disease prevent the administration of justice everywhere it goes, but it more threateningly figures active revolt: two towns "ar almoste overthrowin with the seiknes." Such language discloses the symbolism of the pestilence as treason in the Renaissance.

9. The history of the disease in the English Renaissance is a history of monarchy on the run; every ruler from Henry VII to James I fled an outbreak of the disease at least once. See J. F. D. Shrewsbury, *A History of the Bubonic Plague in the British Isles* (Cambridge: Cambridge Univ. Press, 1970), 127–35. See also Philip Ziegler, *The Black Death* (New York: John Day, 1969), 157.

10. Howes's *Chronicle* testifies to the kingly attributes of the disease, in specific contrast to James and his progress into the city: "By reason of God's Visitation for our sins, the Plague and Pestilence there reigning in the City of London and Suburbs . . . the King rode not from the Tower through the City in Royal manner as had been accustomed." Here the "reigning" of the plague suggests a divine sanction against England, and pictures the disease as a proxy ruler; but the point of the passage is to compare the customary "Royal manner" with the way James's own royalty has been compromised. Quoted in Nichols, *Progresses*, 1:227.

Indeed, a "reign" of plague seems to have been a standard locution. In *Romeo and Juliet*, Friar John explains that he was unable to convey Friar Lawrence's message because, while he was in Verona, "the searchers of the town, / Suspecting that we both were in a house / Where the infectious pestilence did reign, / Seal'd up the doors, and would not let us forth" (5.2. 8–11).

11. Wilson, *Plague*, 106–7.

12. Nichols, *Progresses*, 1:271. The second letter, also from Woodstock, is dated September 17.

13. Sir John Davies, "The Triumph of Death, or The Picture of the Plague: According to the Life, as it was in *Anno Domini* 1603," in *The Complete Works of John Davies of Hereford*, ed. Alexander B. Grosart, 2 vols. (New York: AMS Press, 1967), 1:45.

14. Proclamation no. 967, in Robert Steele, ed., *A Bibliography of Royal Proclamations of the Tudor and Stuart Sovereigns . . . 1485–1714*, vol. 1, *England and Wales* (1910; rpt. New York: Burt Franklin, 1967), 110.

15. Joel Hurstfield, "The Succession Struggle in Late Elizabethan England," in S. T. Bindoff, J. Hurstfield, and C. H. Williams, eds., *Elizabethan Government and Society: Essays Presented to Sir John Neale* (London: Athlone Press, 1961), 369–96: "Finally, at the time of the parliament of 1601, a bill was drafted to prohibit the writing or publishing of books about the succession on the grounds that they bred faction and inspired traitorous acts against the Queen" (372). Nevertheless, Thomas Wilson knew "that the King of Scotland will carry it, as very many Englishmen do know assuredly. But to determine thereof is to all English capitally forbidden, and therefore so I leave

it." *State of England, Anno Dom. 1600* (London: Camden Society Publications, 1934), 5.

16. Conrad Russell, *The Crisis of Parliaments: English History 1509–1660* (London: Oxford Univ. Press, 1971), 256.

17. The joy of ceremony, like most other functions of kingship, was dispensable in the time of an epidemic. John Chamberlain wrote his escalating despair about the matter: "Powles grows very thin, for every man shrinckes away and I am half ashamed to see myself left alone. Our pageants are prettely forward, but most of them are such small timbred gentlemen that they cannot last long and I doubt yf the plague cease not the sooner they will rot and sincke where they stand." *Letters of John Chamberlain*, ed. Norman Egbert McClure, 2 vols. (Philadelphia: American Philosophical Society, 1939), 1:195 (letter of July 10, 1603, to Dudley Carleton).

18. "At the beginning [plague] strooke (like an Arrowe) on the head but of one Citty, but in a short time after, it flewe from Cittie to Citty, and in the end stucke in the very hart of the whole kingdome. Insomuch, that Death came (like a tyrannous Usurper) to the Court gates, & threatned to depose the Emperour himselfe." George Wilkins, *The Three Miseries of Barbary: Plague, Famine, and Ciuill Warre* (London, 1606 [STC 25639]), sig. C2.

19. See Clifford Geertz, "Centers, Kings, Charisma: Reflections on a Symbolics of Power," in his *Local Knowledge* (New York: Basic Books, 1983), 121–46.

20. McElwee points out (*Wisest Fool*, 115) that James's trip to London was made in a closed coach: because of the sickness, the king could not even be seen.

21. It might be mentioned that, by the end of the play, Hamlet becomes exceedingly conscious of rank: "this three yeeres I haue tooke note of it, the age is growne so picked, that the toe of the pesant coms so neere the heele of the Courtier he galls his kybe" (M3). This comment is apropos of the gravedigger's frustratingly precise responses to Hamlet's inquiries; the peasants now speak just as impassably as courtiers, and Hamlet, for once, cannot outwit an interlocutor.

Annabel Patterson discusses Hamlet as a mediator between popular and aristocratic concerns in *Shakespeare and the Popular Voice* (Oxford: Basil Blackwell, 1989), 13–31, 93–106.

22. Note Laertes' assumption here that Hamlet's choice is dependent on *election*—on what the body of people want for him. Laertes' speech corroborates the notion of Denmark's "elective monarchy," a system answerable to the desires of the multitude. Hamlet, at least in his theatrical tastes, resists such democratic systems: he wishes to hear a speech from the player that was caviar to the general.

23. Here I follow E. A. Honigmann, "The Politics in *Hamlet* and 'The World of the Play,'" in *Statford-upon-Avon Studies*, vol. 5, *Hamlet* (New York, 1964), 129–47. He argues that Claudius's first speech "creates a mystery about the succession that is not resolved." Also important is A. P. Stabler, "Elective Monarchy in the Sources of *Hamlet*," *Studies in Philology* 62, no. 5 (October 1965): 654–61. Stabler asserts that "the question as to who is rightfully king . . . would be an example of one more ambiguity, one more 'question' which Hamlet has to

face, and in whose treatment by Hamlet we come to know his character. . . . It is an ambiguous, rather than a clear-cut case of usurpation as the term is generally understood" (660). Contrary views are provided by Harold Jenkins in his "longer note" to Claudius's speech (*Hamlet* [London: Methuen, Arden, 1982], 433–34). Although Jenkins rightly mentions the parallel to Norway's situation, where the brother of Fortinbras the Elder, not the son, succeeded to the throne, we must remember the conditions under which Norway came to rule. There was a clear and public vacancy after the single combat between the elder Hamlet and Fortinbras; with the king of Norway gone, it only makes sense that his adult brother should take the reins, for it seems unlikely that young Fortinbras is much older than Hamlet—and the fight occurred the very day young Hamlet was born. Had King Hamlet *lost* the fight with Fortinbras, it would be reasonable to expect that his brother Claudius would have taken control of the nation, if only until the male heir reached majority, at which point (perhaps) an election *would* occur. So Jenkins's point about the succession is misplaced, because the significant parallel is not in political process but in subject position: Norway, "impotent and bedrid," tames his nephew in a brief power struggle over the issue of foreign policy; Claudius, who seems so much more potent, never can handle Hamlet completely.

24. On this point Stabler agrees with Honigmann's hypothesis that Claudius was never elected in the first place, that he simply "pop't in," as Hamlet later says, with no vote having been made: "Hamlet had hoped, in the normal course of events, for an election, in which he would certainly have stood an excellent chance against Claudius with the electorate; but Claudius has . . . by taking over the government at that time and through such means, come between Hamlet and the realization of the hoped-for election" (659 n. 14).

25. The submerged discourse about birth in these lines—in the words "purse," "seal," "folded," "form," "impression," and "changeling"—suggests that Hamlet's conception and bringing to light produce only death, in the best tradition of autogenetic Shakespearean villains such as Iago: "I have't. It is engend'red. Hell and night / Must bring this monstrous birth to the world's light" (*Othello*, 1.3.403–04). Hamlet did not, we should remember, need to forge the orders to escape his compatriots; his forgery thus highlights the mortality he creatively disperses.

26. The generally erotic character of this passage was first called to my attention by Sharon Berken.

27. *Wilson's Arte of Rhetorique* (1560), ed. G. H. Mair (Oxford: Clarendon Press, 1909), 99.

28. A word about the second quarto's reading of this line. "Though you fret me not" makes as much sense as "though you fret me," the standard editorial choice: it just makes different sense. In Q2, Hamlet suggests that simply because the friends do not actively worry him does not mean that he is relaxed or off his guard around them. The folio reading "though you fret me, you cannot . . . " gives Rosencrantz and Guildenstern a bit more power to aggravate Hamlet. Either reading strikes me as valid, with the folio's "Though *x*, not *y*" having more logical (if not necessarily thematic) integrity than "Though not *x*, not *y*" of the quarto.

29. For an interesting reading of Hamlet's latent femininity, see David Leverenz, "The Woman in *Hamlet*: An Interpersonal View," in Murray M. Schwartz and Coppelia Kahn, eds., *Representing Shakespeare: New Psychoanalytic Essays* (Baltimore: Johns Hopkins, 1980), 110–28.

30. Stabler has made this point: "No matter that here the 'rabble' is in fact 'abusing the custom' and choosing to 'ratify and prop' inappropriately; the point is that they, the people, and not Claudius's cronies of the royal Council, are asserting the elective privilege" ("Elective Monarchy," 659–60).

31. In the folio, just after "is't not perfect conscience / To quit him with this arm?" thirteen lines intervene in which Hamlet (1) further justifies killing Claudius; (2) agrees with Horatio that the king will soon know "the issue of the business" from England; (3) apologizes to Horatio for his disgraceful behavior at Ophelia's funeral, and (4) resolves to "count [Laertes'] favors." Hamlet's eleventh-hour remorse here thus paves the way for Osric's challenge, which Hamlet might well justify taking up as a courtesy to the wronged Laertes. Hamlet's wholesale flight from the revenge on which he was perched thus has a dramatic point in the folio version, and the digression from the prince's intentions may seem less noticeable. But have lines been cut in the second quarto or added in the folio? Neither text will answer.

32. My account of the Mary-Darnley-Bothwell episode is drawn principally from two sources, J. E. Neale, *Queen Elizabeth I* (New York: Doubleday, Anchor, 1957), 130–76 (see p. 135 for the description of Darnley), and William McElwee, *Wisest Fool*, 19–33. (Both works are hereafter cited in the text.) I have also consulted David Harris Willson, *King James VI and I* (London: Jonathan Cape, 1956), 18–19; hereafter cited as Willson, *King James*.

33. Duncan Thomson, *Painting in Scotland 1570–1650* (Edinburgh: Trustees of the National Galleries of Scotland, 1975), 18–19; quoted in Roland Mushat Frye, *The Renaissance Hamlet* (Princeton: Princeton Univ. Press, 1984), 32. Frye reproduces Livinus de Vogelaare's painting *The Darnley Memorial*, and George Vertue's eighteenth-century engraving of the same, on 32–33.

34. Lillian Winstanley was the first to show that many of the essentials of *Hamlet*'s characters and plot derive not from literary source but from Jacobean biography. Winstanley's *Hamlet and the Scottish Succession* (Cambridge: Cambridge Univ. Press, 1921) is the most thorough exposition of the relationship between the Darnley murder and the plot, language, and meaning of the play. James, she argues, resembles Hamlet far more closely than the Scandinavian avenger Amleth does. Winstanley realizes that a convergence of historical events need not be represented perfectly in a literary text. If the parallels she draws are too pat, her conclusions sometimes stretched a bit, she still provides a treasure trove of information and suggestions about the Jacobean *Hamlet*, and her work is indispensable to my reading.

35. It is interesting to note that the marriage of Mary and Darnley united, in the eyes of many contemporary observers, the two people with the strongest claim to inherit England's throne; and when Elizabeth heard of the proposed union, she sent word that the marriage was "dangerous to the common amity" of the English and Scottish nations.

36. Paul Slack provides a suggestive historical footnote about the plague that

unites these apparently disparate issues: "Francis Herring called 1603 'the women's year,' and a thorough study of St. Boltoph's Bishopsgate parish in London has amply confirmed that male deaths vastly outnumbered female deaths in that epidemic." Slack, *Impact of Plague*, 179, citing Herring, *Modest Defence* (1604), sig. A4. The women in *Hamlet* do not fare conspicuously better than the men, but all anxiety, including misogyny, is exacerbated in the context of epidemic outbreaks and further heightened by political upheaval.

37. On "screen memory," see Sigmund Freud, *The Psychopathology of Everyday Life*, trans. Alan Tyson (New York: Norton, 1966), 43–52. Freud supposes that the screen memory covers for or even subconsciously eradicates an unpleasant or threatening primal event.

38. In psychoanalytic theory, this inference would be unacceptable or heretical: the mother always matters, perhaps even more so in her absence than in her presence. But in terms of James's conscious and public anxieties, the lack of parental (and familial) influence was important only insofar as it affected his chances at succession. In the context of explaining why he was heading off to Denmark to obtain his bride in 1589, James describes his childhood: "I was alone, without father or mother, brother or sister, king of this realm and heir apparent of England. This nakedness made me to be weak and my enemies stark. One man was as no man, and the want of hope of succession bred disdain." G. P. V. Akrigg, ed., *Letters of King James VI and I* (Berkeley: Univ. of California Press, 1984), 98. It is noteworthy that James constructs his deprivation of family not as a personal but a political liability and that as early as 1589 he regarded himself unequivocally as next in line to the English throne. Jonathan Goldberg gives an account of James's complex attitude toward Mary in *James I and the Politics of Literature* (Baltimore: Johns Hopkins Univ. Press, 1983), 11–17, 25–26, 119.

39. This oscillation also speaks of the strain Hamlet feels in confronting maternal sexuality. For a fine, extended explication of this point, see Janet Adelman, *Suffocating Mothers: Fantasies of Maternal Origin in Shakespeare's Plays, "Hamlet" to "The Tempest"* (New York: Routledge, 1992), 11–37.

40. Frye, *Renaissance Hamlet*, 34.

41. Shrewsbury, *History of the Bubonic Plague*, 264. Plague was widespread in Scotland just before the major outbreak in England, but it is impossible to tell where the epidemic began. The most likely suspect was the Low Countries; Stow writes in his *Annals* of 1605: "the plague of pest. being great in Holland, Sealand, and other the low countries, and many souldiers returning thence into England, the infection was also spied in divers parts of this realme" (quoted in Wilson, *Plague*, 86).

42. One possible cause for *Hamlet*'s conflicted relationship to its contexts rests in the play's multiple, indeterminate chronology; it is out of temporal joint. In its Elizabethan time frame, the play looks to be wistfully valedictory for an heroic age now faded, one which *Troilus and Cressida* decisively inters a year or two later. Q1 (pre-1603) has a more powerful, affirmative queen than the subsequent quarto; but the plot of royal blockade and the murderous stepfather (i.e., the Jacobean plot) exists there all the same. Straddling two regimes, the *Hamlets* of Q1 and Q2 both belong to both: the play(s) cannot be synthesized, but neither

do they independently seem "characteristic" of an age or a regime. Q1 and Q2 both conduct their most intense referentialities pointing simultaneously in two directions, looking before and after. The supersession of cultures in 1603 and the subsequent supersession of *texts* in 1604—Q2 supplanting and usurping Q1—produces agitations in any attempt to interpret them as if they were fully complementary.

43. John Harington, in *Nugae Antiquae*, ed. T. Park, 2 vols. (London, 1809), 1:179.

44. Winstanley, *Hamlet and the Scottish Succession*, 172. For an extended application of the idea that Essex is inscribed in *Hamlet*, see ibid., 139–64.

45. See Akrigg, *Letters of King James*, 173.

46. James McManaway, "Elizabeth, Essex, and James," in Herbert Davis and Helen Gardner, eds., *Elizabethan and Jacobean Studies Presented to F. P. Wilson* (Oxford: Clarendon Press, 1959), 226; hereafter cited in the text.

47. Quoted in Hurstfield, "Succession Struggle," 393.

During the previous year Essex had made serious overtures to James that indicated an armed Scottish threat would be the best way to compel Elizabeth to declare James as her successor. James cautiously responded to Essex's tempting invitation for support; he wrote that he "would think of it, and put [himself] in a readiness to take any good occasion." This readiness for James, unlike for Hamlet, *was* martial. In June 1600, the Scots king tried to solicit money from his lords for an army to support his bid for Queen Elizabeth's crown. On these issues, and the quotation from James, see John Guy, *Tudor England* (Oxford: Oxford Univ. Press, 1990), 445.

After Cecil's support was offered, James repented of his itchy trigger finger. He realized "what a foolish part were that in me if I might do it to hazard my honour, state, and person, in entering that kingdom by violence as a usurper" (quoted in Hurstfield, "Succession Struggle," 392–93). For a brief but significant moment in history, the moment in which the succession may, in fact, have been engineered, James remarkably resembled—in intention, in desire—not just the prince denied his place but, more tellingly, Claudius, Laertes, and Fortinbras. I discuss further kaleidoscopic possibilities of the royal image, and Hamlet's relation to the same, below. See Hurstfield, "Succession Struggle," for a fine account of Cecil's role in the smooth transition of power.

On English invasion anxiety about James, the *Calendar of State Papers, Domestic Series* [*CSPD*] (1598–1601) contains suggestive summaries and excerpts from the letters of John Petit to Peter Halins. Here is but one dispatch, dated October 11, 1599: "Rumours fly that the King of Scots is preparing to war against England, and that his brother-in-law of Denmark has broken the ice already" (327). References to the *CSPD* letters and John Guy are from Stuart Kurland's essay "Hamlet and the Scottish Succession?" which I was fortunate to see in manuscript. My thanks to Leah Marcus for drawing this essay to my attention.

48. Frye, *Renaissance Hamlet*, 330 n. 87.

49. John Chamberlain to Dudley Carleton, 22 February 1600, in *Letters*, 1:87.

50. Jon Elster perceptively comments that the conditions of what we con-

ceive of as rational choice are often really the selections we make from a set of extreme restrictions. See Elster, *Sour Grapes: Studies in the Subversion of Rationality* (Cambridge: Cambridge Univ. Press, 1983).

51. It is a curious irony that the man leading the charge for revenge was Francis Stewart Hepburn, fifth earl of Bothwell—the nephew of Mary's second husband. The younger Bothwell proved to be a painful thorn in James's side, as I discuss below.

52. See Peter Wentworth, *A Pithie Exhortation About the Succession* (London, 1598).

53. Hurstfield, "Succession Struggle," 391.

54. In the gravedigger scene, the second "clowne" says to the first about Ophelia's death that "the crowner hath sate on her, and finds it Christian buriall" (M1v). That a coroner was a "crowner" seems entirely but elusively significant in *Hamlet*; it does continue a sustained association between kingship and death, but it may also suggest that in death people receive their apotheoses, their crowns or rewards, for their earthly lives.

55. Indeed, the play quickly dispenses with the possible influence that communities might have; Laertes refuses to let the mob that seeks to elect him into the royal presence chamber with Claudius.

56. Even a casual perusal of the multiple murders, betrayals, and treasons that pepper Scottish clan history in the sixteenth century reveals that the revenge code was an integral part of family and political life of the new king's time. James was, in fact, called on frequently to avenge the death of kinsmen and friends—most notably (other than that of his father, Darnley) the death of the earl of Moray. See McElwee, *Wisest Fool*, 70.

57. This outcome may well be pinned to Claudius's deeds rather than Hamlet's, insofar as the king has permitted Fortinbras to use Denmark as a shortcut on the way to Poland and, presumably, on the way back. Imagine the danger involved: Claudius gives free passage through his lands to armed forces which until fairly recently were threatening his kingdom. While it seems improbable that he would make such a broad tactical error, the audience and Hamlet must be allowed to track the progress of Fortinbras the fortunate.

58. As the *OED* notes under the verb "haunt," "From the uncertainty of the derivation, it is not clear whether the earliest sense in French and English was to practise habitually (an action, etc.) or to frequent habitually (a place)." As part of a potentially relevant etymology, note Eric Partridge's intriguing inclusion of the word "hamlet" beneath the stem "haunt" in *Origins: A Short Etymological Dictionary of Modern English* (New York: Greenwich House, 1983).

59. Quoted in Nichols, *Progresses*, 1:258–59.

60. For a closer look into James's foot-in-the-mouth anger with Elizabeth over the Bothwell affair, see Akrigg, *Letters of King James*, 112–28.

61. Winstanley, *Hamlet and the Scottish Succession*, 90–91.

62. Christina Larner, "James VI and I and Witchcraft," in Alan G. R. Smith, ed., *The Reign of James VI and I* (London: Macmillan, 1973), 81. On Bothwell and witchcraft, see also McElwee, *Wisest Fool*, 70–74.

63. Like the end of *Troilus and Cressida*, *Hamlet* evokes an absence of a

dominant ideology, missing from or unavailable in transitional culture. (The crushing but vague object called "patriarchy" must be excepted from this generalization.) It has been suggested that the notion of "dominant ideology" be abandoned, and this abandonment might be appropriate in a plague world, where that which is most contagious and infectious (i.e., persuasive) is also and obviously most unstable and fatal. See Nicholas Abercrombie and Bryan S. Turner, "The Dominant Ideology Thesis," *British Journal of Sociology* 29 (June 1978): 149–70, and T. J. Jackson Lears, "The Concept of Cultural Hegemony: Problems and Possibilities," *American Historical Review* 90, no. 3 (1985): 567–93. I am indebted to Frank Donoghue for these references.

64. "In 1580, the Stratford-on-Avon archives record an inquest on Katherine Hamlett, drowned in the Avon. Verdict—misadventure." Eric Sams, "Taboo or Not Taboo? The Text, Dating, and Authorship of *Hamlet*, 1589–1623," *Hamlet Studies* 10 (summer/winter 1988): 14.

65. I refer the reader to Roland M. Frye's impressive compendium of such contexts in *The Renaissance Hamlet*.

66. The experience of dangerous sequence and design in history brought the word "plot" an actively threatening connotation: James himself publicized the evils of plot, first in the Gowrie conspiracy, then, most fully, in the Gunpowder Plot of 1605. As Peter Brooks suggestively writes: "The fourth sense of the word ['plot'], the scheme or conspiracy, seems to have come into English through the contaminating influence of the French *complot*, and became widely known at the time of the Gunpowder Plot. I would suggest that in modern literature . . . the organizing line of plot is more often than not some scheme or machination, a concerted plan for the accomplishment of some purpose which goes against the ostensible and dominant legalities of the fictional world, the realization of a blocked and resisted desire." Brooks, *Reading for the Plot: Design and Intention in Narrative* (New York: Vintage, 1984), 12. Blocked and resisted desire is the foundation of *Hamlet*'s plot; the play undoes plot without resolving the blockage or resistance.

CHAPTER 4. "A TWENTY YEARS' REMOVED THING"

1. In making this claim, my argument directly opposes that of Leslie Hotson, whose close reading of the play's contexts is based on archival records of Don Virginio Orsino's visit to Queen Elizabeth's court in 1601, where the duke was entertained with dances, masques, and music. Hotson's work is invaluable for its wealth of contemporary excavations and its imaginative textual forays; I have been especially influenced by his treatment of the Olivia-Elizabeth parallel. However, his reading as a whole is based on what seem to me several untenable premises, chief among them this: that Orsino in *Twelfth Night* is meant as a *compliment* to the visiting dignitary. See Leslie Hotson, *The First Night of "Twelfth Night"* (London: Rupert Hart-Davies, 1954), esp. 113–32, for the inscription of Elizabeth in the play.

2. The most thorough treatment of Malvolio's social position is John Draper, *The "Twelfth Night" of Shakespeare's Audience* (Stanford: Stanford Univ. Press, 1950), 86–113.

3. Archbishop John Whitgift, *An Answere to a certen libel intituled An Admonition to the parliament 1572* (London, 1572), 18.

4. Nashe, *Pasquil's Return*, in *The Works of Thomas Nashe*, ed. Ronald Brunlees McKerrow, 5 vols. (London: A. H. Bullen, 1904), 1:94.

5. Nashe, *Pierce Penniless*, in *Works*, 2:100.

6. G. K. Hunter, ed., *All's Well That Ends Well* (rpt. London: Methuen, 1977), and note to 1.3.91–92. Robert Greene complains that even his genuine remorse about past turpitude was mocked as a hypocritical act: "When I had discouered that I sorrowed for my wickednesse . . . they fell vpon me in ieasting manner, calling me Puritane and Presizian." Greene, *Repentance*, in *The Life and Complete Works in Prose and Verse of Robert Greene*, ed. Alexander B. Grosart, 12 vols. (London: Aylesbury, printed for private circulation, 1881–86), 12:176.

For more on the vestiarian controversy, see Marshall Mason Knappen's seminal work, *Tudor Puritanism: A Chapter in the History of Idealism* (Chicago: Univ. of Chicago Press, 1939), 187–216.

7. On this point, see any of the following superb studies: Knappen, *Tudor Puritanism*; Patrick Collinson, *The Elizabeth Puritan Movement* (London: Jonathan Cape, 1967); Michael Walzer, *The Revolution of the Saints: Studies in the Origins of Radical Politics* (London: Weidenfeld and Nicholson, 1966); William Haller, *The Rise of Puritanism* (New York: Harper and Row, 1957); J. E. Neale, *Elizabeth I and Her Parliaments, 1584–1601* (London: Jonathan Cape, 1957); and for the literary response, William P. Holden, *Anti-Puritan Satire 1572–1642* (New Haven: Yale Univ. Press, 1954).

8. So Meredith Hanmer, writing in 1577 a history of the early church, asserts that "Novatus . . . became himself the author and ringleader of his own hereticall sect, to wit, of such as through their swelling pride do call themselves Puritans." In *The auncient ecclesiasticall histories of the first six hundred years after Christ . . .* (London, 1577), VI.43.116.

9. Paul Siegel, "Malvolio: Comic Puritan Automaton," in Maurice Charney, ed., *Shakespearean Comedy* (New York Literary Forum, 1980), 217–30; hereafter cited in text and notes as Siegel, "Malvolio."

10. J. L. Simmons, "A Source for Shakespeare's Malvolio: The Elizabethan Controversy with the Puritans," *Huntington Library Quarterly* 36 (May 1973): 181. Simmons makes the most complete case for Malvolio as a Puritan inscription; Siegel and all subsequent commentators on the issue are much indebted to this article.

11. All citations and quotations from *Twelfth Night* are from the Arden edition, ed. J. M. Lothian and T. W. Craik (London: Methuen, 1975).

12. Paul Siegel, *Shakespeare in His Time and Ours* (Notre Dame: Univ. of Notre Dame Press, 1968), 246.

13. "For a static and deterministic Humour, Shakespeare substituted a kinetic, governing Appetite in the action . . . of his major characters." John Hollander, "*Twelfth Night* and the Morality of Indulgence," in James L. Calderwood and Harold E. Toliver, eds., *Essays in Shakespearean Criticism* (Englewood Cliffs, N.J.: Prentice-Hall, 1970), 292. See also Kenneth Burke's marvelous description of Orsino's "larval feeding," from "Trial Translation

(From *Twelfth Night*)," in his *The Philosophy of Literary Form*, 3d ed. (Berkeley: Univ. of California Press, 1973), 344–49. I thank Frank Whigham for this reference.

14. Siegel makes the leap between Maria's designation "time-pleaser" and one who professes religion simply for his own profit by means of Thomas Wilson's *A Discourse upon Usury* (1572; rpt. New York: Harcourt, Brace, 1925), which may have appeared when it did partly as a counter to *An Admonition to Parliament* (1572). Siegel cites Wilson's argument that "touching this sinne of usury, none doe more openly offende in thys behalfe than do these counterfaite professours of thys pure religion" (178); Siegel, "Malvolio," 218.

15. Siegel cites Holden's *Anti-Puritan Satire 1572–1642*, 42, 114–15, for evidence that Puritans were regarded as misers and business cheats. Siegel, "Malvolio," 219.

16. This custom might sound barbaric and improbable, but in agricultural areas it is (or was) frequent. In one recent American case, "A former agricultural sciences high school teacher who was fired after one of his students castrated a pig with his teeth is asking the Texas Education Agency for his job back." The man, named (this is true) Dick Pirkey, defended his pedagogical method by explaining that "when he was in college, his professor showed him how to orally castrate lambs. . . . Indeed, a textbook used by the Harmony [Texas] school district recommends oral castration of lambs. . . . A lawyer representing Pirkey presented three textbooks that discuss oral lamb castration, including one with pictures." David Elliot, "Pig Castration Teacher Wants Job Back," *Austin American-Statesman*, January 28, 1993, B1.

17. For Toby's own inclination to assume and command such postures, see his orders to Andrew concerning Cesario: "Go, Sir Andrew: scout me for him at the corner of the orchard, like a bum-baily" (3.4.177–78). Lothian and Craik define the term: "a bailiff (sheriff's officer) who comes up *behind* his quarry" (*Twelfth Night*, 102). This positioning is reminiscent of the observation of Malvolio and his discovery of the letter, as I discuss below.

18. For a full-length consideration of the ways in which the Lucrece story functions in the larger context of Western humanism, see Stephanie H. Jed, *Chaste Thinking: The Rape of Lucretia and the Birth of Humanism* (Bloomington and Indianapolis: Univ. of Indiana Press, 1989).

19. See Barbara Freedman, *Staging the Gaze: Postmodernism, Psychoanalysis, and Shakespearean Comedy* (Ithaca: Cornell Univ. Press, 1991), 192–235, and Elizabeth Freund, "*Twelfth Night* and the Tyranny of Interpretation," *ELH* 53 (1986): 471–89.

20. For some other examples of the *I/ay* and *O* puns, see Eric Partridge, *Shakespeare's Bawdy* (New York: Dutton, 1960), 109 and 159, s.v. "eye" and "O." The "A" may stand for "ass" or "arse," a possibility I am less confident about; still, the reading is tempting, in that the "A" and the "O" are said to be in the wrong places in the anagram, and so this scene can stand as a low-comic, parodic version of the Viola plot.

21. See James F. Forrest, "Malvolio and Puritan 'Singularity,' " *English Language Notes* 11 (1973), 260; cited in Siegel, "Malvolio," 221.

22. See Holden, *Anti-Puritan Satire*, for a balanced reading of Malvolio's

Puritan and non-Puritan elements: "Indeed, Malvolio shows no sign of religious eccentricity in the course of the play; it is, rather, in other respects that he gives the impression of being Puritanical. . . . He is too solemn and sad: he talks unnecessarily of decay and death. . . . However, in his speeches in later scenes, Malvolio has no trace of the traditional idiom or phrase of the precisian: he talks as a well-trained servant in a household should" (124–25). See also the note by Rolfe in the *Variorum* edition of *Twelfth Night*, ed. Horace Howard Furness (Philadelphia: J. B. Lippincott, 1904), 130.

Malvolio's interest in decay and death, by the way, invites a comparison between the steward and the fool, who is always singing about the end of festivity. This comparison becomes explicit at the end of the play when Olivia, with measured sympathy, says to her steward: "Alas, poor fool, how have they baffled thee." It should also be noted that Malvolio's description of Viola as Cesario could play as a species of "excellent fooling," although this would not occur to him:

OLIV: What kind o' man is he?
MAL: Why, of mankind.
OLIV: What manner of man?
MAL: Of very ill manner . . .
                                    (1.5.152–55)

We can spy a further convergence between Malvolio and Feste not only in their bitter rivalry but in the fool's own moral pronouncements; he has already made to Orsino the *most* Puritanical commentary in the drama: "Truly, sir, and pleasure will be paid, one time or another" (2.4.70). Malvolio is far from isolated in his constructed convictions. Indeed, Puritanism, verbal precision, and accounting (or attention to money) are all of a piece in Illyria. Shown to be, in the letter-deciphering scene, a "corrupter of words" like Feste (and, more to the point, of nonwords such as "M.O.A.I."), Malvolio does not make wanton with language, as Feste and Maria do, but attempts to make words too accurate, too representational. Summing up the evidence of Toby's behavior that, he thinks, points to his favor, Malvolio asserts that "no dram of a scruple, no scruple of a scruple, no obstacle, no incredulous or unsafe circumstance—what can be said?—nothing that can be can come between me and the full prospect of my hopes" (3.4.79–83). His verbal involutions, shorn of the spirit of foolery, seem like foolishness. But the attempts either to straitjacket language or to disengage it from sense (Feste: "my lady has a white hand, and the Myrmidons are no bottle-ale houses" [2.3.28–29]) have the same degree of moral rectitude, and both serve their corrupters a single purpose: to profit materially ("Come on, there is sixpence for you"). The clown and the steward, the fool and the madman, fight over the same *precise* ground.

23. The obstruction in the blood registers the bodily effect of interpretive blockage; earlier, sifting through the letter's clues, Malvolio commented: "Why, this is evident to any formal capacity. There is no obstruction in this" (2.5.117–19). The culmination of these references comes in act 4, where Feste/Sir Topas paradoxically asserts that Malvolio's prison is and is not dark: "Why, it hath bay-windows transparent as barricadoes, and the clerestories toward the south-

north are as lustrous as ebony: and yet complainest thou of obstruction?" (4.2.37–40). The symbolic subtext of these lines is the claim that Malvolio sees only "through a glass darkly"—that is, not at all: "now I know in part; but then shall I know even as also I am known" (1 Cor. 13:12). But even though revelation and recognition do come to him, they are scarcely spiritual uncoverings. The claim that Malvolio's designed torment has anything to do with his spiritual deficit is itself a morally occluded one, particularly coming from the revenging Fool and his admirers.

24. A perceptive account of this dynamic between servants is in Elliot Krieger, *A Marxist Study of Shakespeare's Comedies* (New York: Barnes and Noble, 1979), 97–130; hereafter cited in text.

25. Hotson, *First Night,* 113.

26. Generally speaking, Puritans (whose Calvinist theology was integrally related to and not far afield from the dominant Anglicans') were not treated in such fashion. For a brief account of Jesuit persecution, see Patrick McGrath, *Papists and Puritans under Elizabeth I* (London: Blandford Press, 1967), 255–58.

27. Lothian and Craik note that the folio spelling, "Renegatho," "reflects the word's Spanish origin and Elizabethan pronunciation" (*Twelfth Night,* 88).

28. Bancroft, *Survay of the Pretended Holy Discipline* (London, 1593), 415–16; quoted in Simmons, "Source for Shakespeare's Malvolio," 184.

29. Quoted in Harry Culverwell Porter, ed., *Puritanism in Tudor England* (London: Macmillan, 1970), 198–99; hereafter cited in text.

30. John Calvin, *Institutes of the Christian Religion,* trans. Ford Lewis Battles (Grand Rapids, Mich.: Eerdmans, 1986), 34. But Malvolio should have read on: "never will we have enough confidence in God unless we become deeply distrustful of ourselves. Never will we lift up our hearts enough in him unless they be previously cast down in us" (34).

31. Oliver Ormerod, *Puritano-Papismus: or A discouerie of Puritan-papisme,* 24, sig. P2; hereafter cited in text. This work is appended to *The Picture of a Puritan; or, A Relation of the opinions, qualities, and practises of the Anabaptists in Germanie, and of the Puritanes in England* (London, 1605; rpt. Amsterdam: Theatrum Orbis Terrarum, 1975 [STC 18851]).

32. John S. Coolidge, *The Pauline Renaissance in England: Puritanism and the Bible* (Oxford: Clarendon Press, 1970), esp. 1–22.

33. J. E. Neale, "The Via Media in Politics: A Historical Parallel," in his *Essays in Elizabethan History* (London: Jonathan Cape, 1958), 120–21.

34. John Field, the stalwart Puritan author and organizer, inveighed against the custom:

> As for matrimony, that also has corruptions too many. It was wont to be counted a sacrament; and therefore they use yet a sacramental sign, to which they attribute the virtue of wedlock. I mean the wedding ring, which they foully abuse and dally withal, in taking it up and laying it down.

Field, "A View of popish Abuses yet remaining in the English Church, for which the godly Ministers have refused to subscribe," quoted in Porter, *Puritanism in Tudor England,* 128–29. For more on Field, see Patrick Collinson, "John Field and Elizabethan Puritanism," in S. T. Bindoff, J. Hurstfield, and C. H. Williams eds., *Elizabethan Government and Society: Essays Presented to Sir John Neale* (London: Athlone Press, 1961), 127–62.

35. Marshall Mason Knappen, ed., *Two Elizabethan Puritan Diaries by Richard Rogers and Samuel Ward* (Chicago: American Society for Church History, 1933), 65.

36. R. H. Tawney, *Religion and the Rise of Capitalism*, rev. ed. (New York: Harcourt Brace, 1937), esp. 226–43. For a vigorous rejection of Tawney's hypothesis on the grounds that "such ideas are utterly unrepresentative of classical Puritanism and even of Puritan economic theory," see A. G. Dickens, *The English Reformation* (New York: Schocken, 1964), 316–17. Dickens argues, with important resonances for those who would see Malvolio in solely Puritanical garb, that the Puritan movement was "an essentially other-worldly religion, dominated not only by an almost morbid moral sensitivity but by a real distrust of 'modern' capitalist tendencies" (317). But David Zaret suggests that the "rhetorical use of contractual themes by Puritan clerics makes sense only in view of their assumption that godly parishioners were familiar with the principles and practices dictated by the rational pursuit of self-interest in markets. Indeed, textual evidence indicates how this assumption explicitly animated Puritan rhetoric." See *The Heavenly Contract: Ideology and Organization in Pre-Revolutionary Puritanism* (Chicago: Univ. of Chicago Press, 1985), 203. The "corrosive individualism that undermined the corporate solidarity and structure of communal life and thus paved the way for capitalist society" (*Heavenly Contract*, 201) that some historians have described Puritanism as fostering well describes Malvolio's solitary (if not "singular") stance and concern with his own status in the play. But I cannot help thinking that the so-called festive community of Illyria, especially the other members of Olivia's house, comprises an aggregate of corrosive individuals whose sincere dedication to producing nothing itself undermines the capitalist enterprise. The structure of communal life in *Twelfth Night* is among the play's most difficult social elements to pin down.

37. See *The Interpreter's Dictionary of the Bible*, s.v. "steward, stewardship." I have also benefited from the citations in *The Encyclopedia of the Lutheran Church*, ed. Julius Bodensieck, 3 vols. (Minneapolis: Augsburg, 1965), 3:2264–65; hereafter cited in the text as *Encyclopedia*.

38. Quoted in Porter, *Puritanism in Tudor England*, 143.

39. It might be argued that these characteristics became distinctly "Puritan" only in the mid to later seventeenth century, and thus that Krieger's claim is ahistorical. But he makes a useful point about the symbolic and philosophical similarity of tormentor and victim, and about their actual divergence in terms of class affiliations.

40. John Field (?), *An Admonition to the Parliament* (London, 1572), in W. H. Frere and C. E. Douglas, eds., *Puritan Manifestoes: A Study of the Origin of the Puritan Revolt* (London: Church Historical Society, 1907), 22; hereafter cited in text.

41. For more on the specific objections of Puritans to theater, see Jonas Barish, *The Antitheatrical Prejudice* (Berkeley: Univ. of California Press, 1981), 80–131.

42. For a stunning early Elizabethan example of a direct critique, see Edward Dering, *A Sermon Preached Before the Queenes Majestie* (1570), in his *Workes* (London, 1597).

43. Neale, "Via Media in Politics": "To Queen Elizabeth, Puritanism was an abomination. She hated and scorned its doctrinaire character, disliked its radicalism, and detested its inquisitorial discipline" (121).

44. Letter to Archbishop Parker, quoted in Porter, *Puritanism in Tudor England*, 141.

45. For a fine summary of the position and status of the Brownists in Elizabethan England, see Samuel Hopkins, *The Puritans and Queen Elizabeth; or, the Church, Court, and Parliament of England*, 3 vols. (New York, 1875), 1:218–33.

46. "The thrust of Puritan doctrine, for all the evasiveness of the ministers, was clear enough: it pointed toward the overthrow of the traditional order." Walzer, *Revolution of the Saints*, 118.

47. Anglican authorities worried openly about and fought vigorously against burgeoning Puritan parliamentary influence primarily in the 1570s to the early 1590s. In *Elizabeth I and Her Parliaments*, Neale asserts that " 'the godly brotherhood'—as they termed themselves—were in process of creating a revolutionary situation" (145) in the parliaments of the mid-1580s.

48. Patrick McGrath confirms that "the Puritans, like the Papists, were not again to enjoy the successes which had been so marked a feature of their history in the 1580s." McGrath, *Papists and Puritans*, 252.

49. This point is emphasized by Stephen Orgel, " 'Nobody's Perfect'; or, Why Did the English Stage Take Boys for Women?" *South Atlantic Quarterly* 88, no. 1 (winter 1989): 27.

50. Barish, *Antitheatrical Prejudice*, 89.

The Puritan critique of ambisexual garb was not the only source for invective against sartorial boundary-crossing. In *The Description of Britaine* (1577), William Harrison writes with ill temper of the growing favor for men's accoutrements in women's clothing:

> In women also, it is most to be lamented, that they do now far exceed the lightness of our men (who nevertheless are transformed from the cap even to the very shoe). . . . What should I say of their doublets with pendant codpieces on the breast full of jags and cuts, and sleeves of sundry colours? Their galligascons to bear out their bums and make their attire to fit plum round (as they term it) about them. Their fardingals, and diversely coloured nether stocks of silk, jerdsey, and such like, whereby their bodies are rather deformed than commended? I have met with some of these trulls in London so disguised that it hath passed my skill to discern whether they were men or women.
>   Thus it is now come to pass, that women are become men, and men transformed into monsters.

In *Elizabethan England*, ed. Lothrop Withington (London: Walter Scott, n.d.), 110. This account of the colorful, shape-changing garments recalls at once Malvolio, whose constricting garters pain him pleasingly, and Orsino, who, according to Feste, should have a doublet made of changeable taffeta.

51. J. B. Black, *The Reign of Elizabeth, 1558–1603* (Oxford: Clarendon Press, 1936), 300–301. The best-detailed study in English of the political ener-

gies and maneuvers around the affair is by Conyers Read, *Mr. Secretary Walsingham and the Policy of Queen Elizabeth*, 3 vols. (Oxford: Archon Books, 1967), 2:1–117.

52. As Burleigh and other lords speculated, the crucial benefit of the match would have been its creation of a potent anti-Spanish alliance, for King Henri III would likely have joined his brother Anjou and Elizabeth in aiding Dutch rebels against the encroachments of Spanish forces. The Netherlands revolt, under Anjou's auspices, was a major selling point for the French match. See Mack P. Holt, *The Duke of Anjou and the Politique Struggle During the Wars of Religion* (Cambridge: Cambridge Univ. Press, 1986), 118–20.

53. Her suspicions may have been fed by a diet of reports about Anjou's appearance. His visage was rumored to have been badly marred by smallpox, and the queen discouragingly instructed his ambassadors that "she could not marry any prince without seeing him, and if Alençon was going to take offence in case, after seeing him, she did not accept him, he had better not come." Cited in Martin Andrew Sharp Hume, *The Courtships of Queen Elizabeth* (New York: Macmillan, 1898), 195.

54. Quoted in Harris Nicolas, *Memoirs of the Life and Times of Sir Christopher Hatton* (London: Richard Bentley, 1847), 106.

55. Black, *Reign of Elizabeth*, 301.

56. The epithet is cited in Neale, *Queen Elizabeth I: A Biography* (New York: Doubleday, Anchor, 1957), 245, but unfortunately he does not give a source for it.

57. See Nicolas, *Life of Hatton*, 106.

58. Quoted in Nicolas, *Life of Hatton*, 108. The letter can also be found in G. B. Harrison, ed., *The Letters of Queen Elizabeth* (London: Cassell, 1935), 130–35. The missive ends with another chafed reference to rumors that may have arisen against the queen and Simier: "Having thus at large laid before you the whole course of our late proceeding with de Simier . . . we nothing doubt but that you will report the same both to the King and to the Duke in that good sort as both they may be induced to see their error, and we discharged of such calumniations as perhaps by such as are maliciously affected towards us in that Court may be given out against us."

59. Lloyd E. Berry, ed., *John Stubbs's "Gaping Gulf" with Letters and Other Relevant Documents* (Charlottesville: Univ. Press of Virginia for the Folger Shakespeare Library, 1968), 156. Subsequent references to Stubbs and Northampton will be to this edition, cited in text and notes as Berry, *Stubbs's "Gaping Gulf."*

60. *Calendar of State Papers, Foreign Series, 1578–1579*, ed. Arthur John Butler (London, 1903), 310. Hereafter cited as *CSPF 1578–79.*

61. Berry, *Stubbs's "Gaping Gulf,"* 149–50. This document is also excerpted in John Strype, *Annals of the Reformation and Establishment of Religion*, 8 vols. (Oxford: Clarendon, 1824), 4:232–38. For further praise of Simier, see *CSPF 1578–79*, 463.

62. The letter, from Simier to Roch des Sorbiers, seigneur des Pruneaux (Anjou's commissioner to the Netherlands), continues with sincere praise of the queen: "I swear to you that she is the most virtuous and honourable princess in

the world; her wit is admirable, and there are so many other parts to remark in her that I should need much ink and paper to catalogue them." *CSPF 1578–79*, 487.

63. Simier to Michael de Castelnau, seigneur de Mauvissiere, French ambassador in England, Nov. 3, 1578; in *CSPF 1578–79*, 260.

64. "C'est que mon fils m'a faict dire par le Roy qu'il ne la veut jamais espouser, quand bien elle le voudroit, *d'aultant qu'il a tousjours si mal oui parler de son honneur*, et en a veu des lettres escriptes de tous les ambassadeurs, qui y ont esté, *qu'il penseroit estre déshonnoré et perdre toute la réputation qu'il pense avoir acquise*." Quoted in Nicolas, *Life of Hatton*, 16 note b; italics in original. No date is given for this letter, but I assume it was written circa 1581–82, when the negotiations were all but finished.

65. "Que vous aviez non seullement engasge vostre honneur auveques un estrangier Nomme Simier . . . ou vous le basiez et lisiez auvec luy de diverses privaultes deshonnestes." In William Murdin, *A Collection of State Papers . . . relating to affairs in the reign of Queen Elizabeth, from the year 1571 to 1596* (London, 1759), 558–60. Concerning the queen's sexual voracity, Mary seems to suggest that Elizabeth's interests ran toward both men and women ("indubitably, you were not like other women"). The letter is partly quoted and translated (with these passages deleted) in Thomas Robertson, *The History of Mary Queen of Scots* (Edinburgh, 1793), 149.

66. *Calendar of Letters and State Papers, Spanish, 1580–1586*, ed. Martin A. S. Hume (London, 1896), 266. Hereafter cited as *CSPS*.

67. Hume, *Courtships of Queen Elizabeth*, 231.

68. Ibid., 186. For more on Anjou's untrustworthiness, see *CSPF 1578–79*, 451; Berry, *Stubbs's "Gaping Gulf"*; and especially the well-known letter from Sir Philip Sidney to the queen. "As for monsieur," he says,

> he is to be judged by his will and power: his will to be as full of light ambition as is possible . . . ; his inconstant attempt against his brother, his thrusting himself into the Low-Country matters, his sometime seeking the king of Spain's daughter, sometimes your majesty, are evident testimonies of his being carried away with every wind of hope; taught to love greatness any way gotten.

Reprinted in John Strype, *Annals of the Reformation and Establishment of Religion*, 8 vols. (Oxford: Clarendon, 1824), 2:644.

69. This fantasy depends on a *limited* disturbance of class structures: the twins are, after all, well-born. But much of the stage business devolves from the obvious favor that the servant Cesario garners from Olivia. Thus does Viola become the target of almost everyone's anger and jealousy. Competition for the great woman is played out in measured compartments of class hostility. Even Sir Toby plots against the mediator, insofar as the prank fight with Andrew targets the new favorite.

Olivia's position at the courtly center of nearly everyone's desires in the play is the surest sign of her participation in Elizabethan inscription. Many of the characters fantasize about possessing her. The motives have often to do with property rights, status, or money, but these do not diminish the sincerity of the passion. Malvolio's smug imaginings of potency, of leaving Olivia sleeping in her day bed, is a dream of power many Elizabethan courtiers indulged; and Sir Toby's overly angry response to the fantasy alludes to the profound personal and cultural investment in this dream. Sir Andrew's interest in Olivia, attenuated as it is (and virtually indistinguishable from his interest in Sir Toby), adds more than a filip to the plot; it rounds out the impression of her universal desirability. And when Feste comes at Viola with this jealous shrapnel, the impression is consolidated:

VIOLA: I warrant thou art a merry fellow, and car'st for nothing.

CLOWN: Not so, sir, I do care for something; but in my conscience, sir, I do not care for you: if that be to care for nothing, sir, I would it would make you invisible.

VIOLA: Art not thou the Lady Olivia's fool?

(3.1.26–32)

With this deft question, Viola uncovers what Feste does indeed care for. The possibility of his lady's marriage brings the clown no pleasure: "She will keep no fool, sir, till she be married, and fools are as like husbands as pilchards are to herrings, the husband's the bigger" (3.1.33–36).

Manningham, significantly, remembered Olivia as a widow: "FEBR. 1601. At our feast wee had a play called 'Twelve night, or what you will'; much like the commedy of errors. . . . A good practise in it to make the steward beleeve his Lady widowe was in Love with him, by counterfayting a letter, as from his Lady, in generall termes, telling him what shee liked best in him." Robert Parker Sorlien, ed., *The Diary of John Manningham of the Middle Temple, 1602–03* (Hanover, N.H.: Univ. Press of New England for the Univ. of Rhode Island, 1976), 48. As an imagined widow, Olivia would be capable of granting the bourgeois wish for social ascent through profitable marriage. In this respect, Olivia may well prefer the lower-ranked suitor, as Sir Toby has suggested—"she'll not match above her degree, neither in estate, years, nor wit; I have heard her swear it" (1.3.106–7)—a reasonable precaution against relinquishing her high station.

70. Such a courtship recalls, as readers have noted, John Lyly's lasting image of two women in love in *Gallathea* (c. 1585). See Leah Marcus's commentary on the fashion for these representations, with potential historical correlates: *Puzzling Shakespeare: Local Reading and Its Discontents* (Berkeley: Univ. of California Press, 1988), 97–104. Marcus's discussion of the wish for Elizabeth's metamorphosis into a man in order to meet and possibly woo Mary Queen of Scots is especially interesting.

71. See Leah Scragg, *The Metamorphosis of Gallathea: A Study in Creative Adaptation* (Washington, D.C.: Univ. Press of America, 1982), and Phyllis Rackin, "Androgyny, Mimesis, and the Marriage of the Boy Heroine on the English Renaissance Stage," *PMLA* 102, no. 1 (January 1987): 29–41. Ellen M. Caldwell argues, somewhat ahistorically, that Lyly's play aims at Elizabeth and suggests a "method for uniting the parts of a woman's divided nature, of her competing urges for separateness and union, or for chastity and love." Caldwell, "John Lyly's *Gallathea*: A New Rhetoric of Love for the Virgin Queen," *ELR* 17 (winter 1987): 23.

72. Freund, "Tyranny of Interpretation," says some pertinent things about

the "I" in Viola's and Olivia's discourse; she regards it as a signifier in crisis: "We expect the speech of self-presentation to situate or contextualize an identity, but if we seek modest assurance of the identity of the speaking "I" we are compelled to unravel a labyrinthine specularity, a tissue of subversive textuality. Who speaks?" (483). About the willow cabin speech she argues, even more sharply, "The tonalities of the speech incorporate voices and echoes to the point where language overextends the confines of personal identity" (488).

73. See Freund, "Tyranny of Interpretation," and Catherine Belsey, "Disrupting Sexual Difference: Meaning and Gender in the Comedies," in John Drakakis, ed., *Alternative Shakespeares* (London: Methuen, 1985), 166–90.

74. The most plausible psychological reading of Viola's sincere courtship can be found in Alexander Leggatt's fine chapter on the play in *Shakespeare's Comedy of Love* (London: Methuen, 1974), 221–54. Freund cleverly summarizes Viola's possible motives, which she then takes pains to deconstruct, in "Tyranny of Interpretation," 485.

75. For more on the homoerotics of the play, see Valerie Traub, *Desire and Anxiety: Circulations of Sexuality in Shakespearean Drama* (London: Routledge, 1992), 137ff.

76. John Hollander, *The Figure of Echo: A Mode of Allusion in Milton and After* (Berkeley: Univ. of California Press, 1981), 22.

77. Arthur Golding, *Shakespeare's Ovid: Being Arthur Golding's Translation of the Metamorphoses*, ed. W. H. D. Rouse (London: De La More Press, 1904), 3:477–78; hereafter cited in text (by book and line numbers) as Golding, *Metamorphoses*.

78. Anthony Brian Taylor, "Shakespeare and Golding: Viola's Interview with Olivia and Echo and Narcissus," *English Language Notes* 15, no. 2 (December 1977): 103–6.

Samuel Daniel's speaker in *Delia* (c. 1592) addresses Echo in a familiar way:

> Echo, daughter of the air,
> Babbling guest of rocks and hills,
> Knows the name of my fierce Fair,
> And sounds the accents of my ills:
> Each thing pities my despair,
> Whilst that she her lover kills.

Elizabethan Lyrics, ed. Norman Ault (New York: Wm. Sloane, 1949), 158. The ambiguous pronouns in the last line suggest that the Echo and Narcissus paradigm commonly involves a slippage of identities between the lover and the beloved.

79. One other suggestive, complicating parallel emerges at the end of *Twelfth Night*, when Viola instructs her brother: "Do not embrace me, till each circumstance / Of place, time, fortune, do cohere and jump / That I am Viola" (5.1.249–51). Along with the odd Christian implications of *Noli me tangere*, the lines may harken back to the description of Narcissus's "passing pride": "That to be toucht of man or Mayde he wholy did disdaine" (3.441–42).

80. Viola and Olivia are not the sole Ovidian descendants in *Twelfth Night*. In one of Orsino's first conceits in the play, he imagines himself as a love hunter, pursuing "the hart." Imagistically, he metamorphoses at once into Actaeon—

not seeking but sought, yet not sought by the beloved but rather his own urges: "my desires, like fell and cruel hounds, / E'er since pursue me" (1.1.22–23). Orsino's hunting image, drawn like the Echo and Narcissus story from *Metamorphosis*, book 3, provides an active, bodily complement to the passive incorporeality of narcissistic self-imperiling; Actaeon, Echo, and Narcissus all die radically defaced, without bodies. Actaeon's tragedy proleptically comprises the Echo and Narcissus tale, especially after his transformation into a stag:

> But when he saw his face
> And horned temples in the brooke, he would have cryde alas,
> But as for then no kinde of speach out of his lippes could passe.
> (Golding, *Metamorphoses*, 3.236–38)

In anticipating both Narcissus (beholding his unrecognizable image) and Echo (in a state of verbal insufficiency and frustration), the Actaeon story prepares Ovid's reader for the vision of failed, bodiless self-love. Perhaps remembering Actaeon's fate and subconsciously seeking romantic dismemberment, Orsino tells Cesario on his first embassy to "be clamorous and leap all civil bounds" (1.4.21).

81. It might be argued that Olivia's abasement is deliberately not malefactored; it thus *prevents* that fantasy of courtier dominance common in the court of Queen Elizabeth.

82. Caren Greenberg, "Reading Reading: Echo's Abduction of Language," in Sally McConnell-Ginet, Ruth Borker, and Nelly Furman, eds., *Women and Language in Literature and Society* (New York: Praeger, 1980), 305. Greenberg further explains that "when Narcissus rejects Echo's love, she repeats his words in such a way as to express her own love for him. Echo's repetition is, therefore, a reading. Echo has abducted the first person pronoun, and the negation of passion simultaneously becomes an expression of passion" (307).

83. Holt, *Duke of Anjou*, 120.

84. Read, *Mr. Secretary Walsingham*, 2:21 n. 1.

85. Even though Olivia suggests she "would not have him miscarry for the half of my dowry," her comment betrays Malvolio's purely material worth to her. This is the same dehumanization that the steward movingly describes in his imprisonment: "They have here propertied me" (4.2.94). In his brutal comeuppance, he becomes *mere* material, "matter for a May morning": matter for cruel jest on the one hand, for Olivia's marriage activities on the other.

86. Salingar, "The Design of *Twelfth Night*," *Shakespeare Quarterly* 9 (1957): 119.

87. Read, *Mr. Secretary Walsingham*, 2:25–26.

88. For "Sebastian" as a name with homosexual overtones in the Renaissance, and for a further meditation on the significance of his nominal relation with Antonio, see Cynthia Lewis, " 'Wise Men, Folly Fall'n': Characters Named 'Antonio' in English Renaissance Drama," *Renaissance Drama* 20 (1989): 197–236.

89. Neale, *Queen Elizabeth I*, 316.

90. More on Antonio's luckless career can be found in Read, *Mr. Secretary Walsingham*: "At the beginning of the year 1581 Don Antonio, with a price of

twenty thousand ducats on his head, was practically a fugitive. His whereabouts were not even certainly known; his cause appeared to be absolutely desperate" (2:51). I have also consulted the entry on "Antonio, Prior of Crato" in the *Encyclopedia Britannica*, 11th ed. (New York, 1910). The names "Antonio" and "Sebastian" recur, with no apparent relevance to the Anjou match and no homoerotic (but plenty of political) implications, in *The Tempest*.

For further suggestions that the central referentiality of *Twelfth Night* hovers around the year 1580, see the pages on the play in Eva Lee Turner Clark, *Hidden Allusions in Shakespeare's Plays*, 3d ed. (Port Washington: Kennikat Press, 1974), 364–92. Clark briefly mentions Sebastian and Antonio ("important names to [Elizabeth's] court circle in 1580" [380–81]) and reminds us that the Brownists, to whom Sir Andrew objects, were "by the end of 1580 . . . grown to sufficient numbers to be of official concern" (389, 390), but they had lost real power as an historical force by 1583. I owe this reference to Shannon Prosser.

Index

Composition: Com-Com
Text: 10/13 Sabon
Display: Sabon
Printing and binding: Braun-Brumfield, Inc.

Living Your Colors

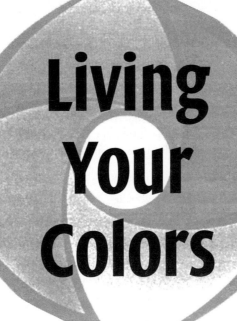

Living Your Colors

Practical Wisdom for Life, Love, Work, and Play

TOM MADDRON, M.S.

WARNER BOOKS

An AOL Time Warner Company

Warner Books, Inc., 1271 Avenue of the Americas, New York, NY 10020
Visit our Web site at www.twbookmark.com.

 An AOL Time Warner Company

Library of Congress Cataloging-in-Publication Data
Maddron, Tom.
    Living your colors : practical wisdom for life, love, work,
and play / Tom Maddron.
        p. cm.
    ISBN 0-446-67911-9
    1. Typology (Psychology) 2. Color—Psychological aspects. I. Title.

BF698.3 .M24 2002
155.2'64—dc21   2002025891

Book design by Fearn Cutler de Vicq

Printed in the United States of America

First Printing: December 2002

10 9 8 7 6 5 4 3 2 1

This book is dedicated to J. Krishnamurti whose writing, teaching, and conversation have opened so many hearts to the simple, loving observation of life and of human beings.

Acknowledgments

I would like to acknowledge the twenty-year partnership with Ed Forbes, LCSW, and Jeremy Howell, LCSW, which has resulted in the development of much material very helpful to human service professionals and to people in general. In addition, to my wife Margaret Maddron, M.Ed., I want to acknowledge our professional relationship that has greatly enriched all my efforts, and our marriage and friendship that have helped me to survive some very hard times with strength and joy. And to the thousands of Colors participants, thank you for making the Colors seminars a powerful opportunity for developing understanding of natural human differences.

Contents

CHAPTER 1

Assessing Your Colors

Welcome! This is a book about you . . . and about me. This is a book about personality styles. It is based on ancient traditional wisdom and also on modern research. The human patterns it reveals are natural, positive, and valuable. When you have assessed your own personality style and read about the styles of the important people in your life, you will have a new understanding and appreciation of the remarkable balance and harmony that is possible in human relationships. There are no wrong answers in your personal assessment. All the "Colors" are equally valuable and important. So enjoy! Celebrate the richness of human differences.

A "COLORS" QUIZ

Below you will find a questionnaire for determining your "Colors" profile. As you fill out the questionnaire, set aside what you've been told to be like and try to think of yourself as you are when you're most comfortable and natural.

Of course, we all have some of all these qualities, and they may come out more strongly at different times. For purposes of this quiz, however, try to look beyond specific situations, set aside what others think you "should" be like, look past the demands of your job, and forget for the moment about the requirements of your role in life. Just be yourself as you most naturally and comfortably are. *Please note:* Extra assessment sheets are provided at the back of the book.

Directions

In each of the 10 items,
- Put a **4** by the set of words that seems to describe you best.
- Put a **3** by the set of words that describes you second best.
- Put a **2** by the set of words that describes you third best.
- Put a **1** by the set of words that seems the least like you.

When you have completed the 10 items,
- Total the a's. Enter the a total beside "Gold" in the spaces provided at the bottom of the page.
- Total the b's. Enter the b total beside "Blue" in the spaces provided at the bottom of the page.
- Total the c's. Enter the c total beside "Green" in the spaces provided at the bottom of the page.
- Total the d's. Enter the d total beside "Orange" in the spaces provided at the bottom of the page.

Your highest totals indicate the Colors that you chose as being most like you in the quiz. Some people find that one or two Colors are really strong and the others very weak. Some people find that all four Colors are about equal in strength.

As you read on through the book, you may find changes in your sense of which Colors best describe you. You may feel that the relative weight of the Colors in your life is different than you thought or even than the quiz might suggest. Remember, you are always the best judge of what is right for you.

Living Your Colors

A Colors Quiz:

Rank the four sets of words in each item, **4, 3, 2, or 1** according to how well they describe you. (**4 is most like you.**)

1. a. ___3___ solid, steady, careful
   b. ___4___ feeling, sympathetic, kind
   c. ___2___ cool, clever, independent
   d. ___1___ lively, witty, energetic

2. a. ___3___ reasonable, moral, hardworking
   b. ___4___ sensitive, sincere, caring
   c. ___1___ logical, abstract, moral
   d. ___2___ skillful, playful, fun-loving

3. a. ___2___ dependable, faithful, devoted
   b. ___4___ close, personal, involved
   c. ___3___ curious, scientific, thoughtful
   d. ___1___ daring, energetic, brave

4. a. ___3___ reliable, organized, serious
   b. ___4___ peaceful, harmonious, warm
   c. ___1___ impatient, perfectionist, heady
   d. ___2___ here-and-now, impulsive, active

5. a. ___1___ consistent, structured, planned
   b. ___4___ meaningful, spiritual, inspired
   c. ___2___ analyzing, testing, model making
   d. ___3___ high impact, persuasive, generous

6. a. _4_ sane, faithful, supportive
   b. _2_ poetic, musical, artistic
   c. _1_ theoretical, studious, principled
   d. _3_ performing, playing, creating

7. a. _3_ commit, follow through, persist
   b. _4_ communicate, encourage, nurture
   c. _2_ inform, discuss, question
   d. _1_ energize, compete, engage

8. a. _2_ conserve, maintain, protect
   b. _4_ inspire, understand, appreciate
   c. _3_ design, invent, construct
   d. _1_ promote, excite, activate

9. a. _1_ value, honor, provide
   b. _4_ share, connect, express
   c. _3_ respect, stimulate, dialogue
   d. _2_ touch, pleasure, surprise

10. a. _1_ traditional, loyal, conservative
   b. _4_ belonging, involved, cooperative
   c. _2_ skeptical, nonconforming, fair
   d. _3_ free, independent, rebellious

Totals

a. Gold _23_ **b. Blue** _36_ **c. Green** _20_ **d. Orange** _19_

THE COLORS IN A NUTSHELL

	GOLD	BLUE	GREEN	ORANGE
Basic Need	Order	Authenticity	Rationality	Freedom
Strongest Values	Service Responsibility	Honesty Empathy	Objectivity Integrity	Action Individuality
Key Experience	Judgment	Emotion	Logic	Sensation
Learning Style	Concrete Organized Practical	Enthusiastic Cooperative Participatory	Independent Data-Based Analytical	Hands-On Skill-Based Physically Active
Greatest Joys	Accomplishment Service Recognition	Spiritual Insight Intimacy Love	Wisdom Discovery Innovation	Skill in Action Excitement Victory
Sexuality	Rewarding/Giving Private Fitting and Proper	Romantic Emotional Creative	Exploratory Inventive Thoughtful	Energetic Skillful Fun
Troubled By	Disorder Instability Lack of Responsibility	Disharmony Dishonesty Lack of Feeling	Illogic Injustice Sentimentality	Authority Regulations Pomposity
Encouraged By	Recognition of Contribution	Appreciation Emotional Support	Affirmation of Intelligence	Freedom Respect Applause
In Groups	Organization Commitment Follow-Through	Communication Inspiration Cooperation	Analysis Ingenuity Independence	Physical Skill Creative Energy Playfulness
On the Job	Stability Organization	Support Enthusiasm	Ingenuity Pragmatism	Energy Innovation
Personal Troubles	Overload Rigidity Bossiness	Moodiness Volatility Dreaminess	Indecisiveness Superiority Coldness	Carelessness Quick Temper Impulsiveness
Seeks in Relationships	Seriousness Responsibility Loyalty	Meaning Intimacy Affection	Autonomy Respect	Sensuality Excitement

CHAPTER 2

Introduction to Colors

THE POWER OF PICTURES AND STORIES

How we picture ourselves, how we tell the story of our lives, has a big effect on how we live. For example, if I ask you to list all your faults in one column and all your strengths in another, which will be easier? Which list will be longer? For some reason, most people's faults list is easier and longer. Maybe we fear being conceited. Maybe we are taught to be humble. The fact is, most of us are more aware of what's "wrong" with us than what is "right" with us. This book is about what is right with us.

There are many ways to be okay in this world. If there really were only one right way to be, very few of us would measure up to it, and we'd tend to be very judgmental about ourselves and others. We would argue and fight and exert pressure on one another to try to conform to that one right way. Fortunately, thank goodness, there are many right ways to be. The fundamental differences among us are natural. They complement one another and enrich our lives in many ways. When we tell our human story this way, so that human differences are natural and good, it relieves us of a lot of the need to be judgmental and frees us up to appreciate ourselves and each other in new ways.

This book is about this change in our pictures and stories about ourselves. It is about making small changes in our story now that will lead to big changes down the line. It is about an ancient idea, the idea of temperament. An idea taken from ancient Greece with surprising support from cultures the other side of the world, and from modern science.

This is not a book about "Truth." The four Colors, and the temperaments they represent, should be seen as a set of lenses for looking at the world. This is a very old set of lenses that has survived for thousands of years in more than one culture.

These lenses demonstrate certain natural differences among people. These natural differences can be appreciated and accepted. And as we all know only too well, these differences can also be argued about, rejected, and fought over.

The good news is that when we decide to appreciate and accept these natural differences, much of the trouble seems to go out of life. New understanding and new acceptance of others follow closely on the heels of a new attitude about the self—new pictures and stories. New pathways open up. Strengths are discovered. Limitations are accepted. Cooperation is improved. We move from conflict to an appreciation of our natural differences. This is the reason for this book. Little changes now. Big changes down the line.

THE HISTORY OF THE IDEA OF FOUR TEMPERAMENTS

The four Colors in this book are used to represent the four temperaments—which date back to the ancient Greeks in Europe. The early Greek philosophers of medicine identified four basic categories of human personality. They explained the categories in terms of a balance among the four bodily "fluids" that they believed were central to human health and behavior. When one of the personality types appeared, it was explained that a certain fluid was dominant.

As European science developed over the centuries, the idea of the four fluids was replaced by more sophisticated understanding of the body and of behavior. The idea of the four temperaments, however, survived. In the Yup'ik culture of western Alaska, one of the central religious symbols is called, in English, the Eye of Awareness. This symbol portrays the spirit acting through four basic elements that make us human. These elements are the body, the emotions, thinking, and culture or will.

The correlation between the old Greek ideas and the ancient Inuit culture is surprising and exciting. It suggests that temperament is something deeper than culture—something simply human.

In traveling and training across cultures, I have found this to be true. With the African American and Latino community of south-central Los Angeles, with the Yup'ik Eskimo community of western Alaska, with representatives of more than one hundred Native American tribes and villages from Alaska and the lower forty-eight states, with Asian Americans in the Central Valley of California, with exchange students from Southern African culture, and with European Americans of all ages and social classes, the Colors activity works just the same. A Yup'ik grandmother commented that doing Colors reminded her of listening in her childhood, many decades ago, to her own grandmother talking about "the different ways people choose to be."

The psychologist and philosopher, Carl Jung, made a major contribution to the idea of personality types when he published a book on the subject in 1921. Jung's work was taken up by Katherine Briggs and her daughter and son-in-law, Isabel Briggs and Peter Myers. This family effort resulted in the Myers-Briggs Personality Indicator, a popular and well-respected psychological test currently in use throughout the world.

In their book, *Please Understand Me*, psychologist David Keirsey and his co-author, Marilyn Bates, brought together the four temperaments of the Greeks with the sixteen personality types of the Myers-Briggs test. Whereas the Myers-Briggs Temperament Indicator is a highly defined, scientifically validated set of personality categories, *Colors* defines a flexible spectrum or profile, a rainbow of human qualities.

Over the centuries, these four elements of personality have interested people for the same reason that they interest us today. The four temperaments shed light on certain natural differences among people that make sense, differences that help us understand and relate to ourselves and the people around us.

Contemporary research, particularly some remarkable studies of identical twins, indicate that we are much less of a blank slate at birth than was once thought. The four temperaments are one way of describing some of our inborn personality differences— differences that don't seem to come from family or culture.

The Colors paint a picture of a human community made up of natural and complementary strengths, strengths that can work together to do wonderful things. The Colors also shed light on the endless conflicts, difficulties, and misunderstandings that are common to all cultures throughout history.

This book gives you comprehensive, accessible, and useful information about the temperaments. It is written in language much of which came directly from people just like you. I have carried out Colors seminars with more than eight thousand people, and their words echo through the practical wisdom of *Living Your Colors.*

The Colors provide a flexible profile, a rainbow of human qualities. Whether in romance, family, work, or friendship, the insights in this book are easy to understand and to remember. You will recognize yourself and the people around you on every page. In addition, *Living Your Colors* focuses on what is good, strong, and valuable about our personalities. This is no catalog of sins, but rather a celebration of the miracle of balance that gives the human community such flexibility and adaptability, that has contributed so much to our successes and our future possibilities.

THE FOUR COLORS

It is important to remember that the pure Colors do not exist. They are more like compass points in a map of human personality traits. Studying the four Colors builds a remarkable familiarity with the natural differences among people. Some of us are very close to one of the compass points. Some of us are near the center of the compass, with elements of all the directions.

Put simply, the influence of the four elements can be described as follows: Some of us lead with our hearts; some with our physical bodies and sensations; some, with our analytical thinking minds; and some, with our judgments and standards.

- **Gold.** Those of us who lead with judgment and standards show the characteristics of what we call the Gold personality style.

- **Blue.** Those of us who lead with our hearts show the characteristics of what we call the Blue personality style.
- **Orange.** Those of us who lead with our physical skills and sensations show the characteristics of what we call the Orange personality style.
- **Green.** Those of us who lead with our analytical thinking minds show the characteristics of what we call the Green personality style.

WHAT IF I SEEM TO HAVE SOME OF ALL THESE COLORS?

Naturally, each of us is a blend of all these characteristics. In fact, the word *temperament* comes from a Greek word meaning "mixture." Each of us is really a rainbow of Colors.

Sometimes we may be more Blue; our hearts may be more active and alive, and everything may seem personal and full of feeling.

Sometimes we may be more Orange—more physical, energetic, and impulsive.

Sometimes we may be more Green—more reserved, deliberate, and analytical.

Sometimes we may be more Gold—more organized, traditional, committed, and practical.

Still, it's important to notice that most of us have a strong, underlying style, a certain combination of the Colors, that stays with us . . . perhaps even throughout our lives.

This underlying style is really positive, fundamental, and long-lasting. We can let go of the constant effort to change it. We can accept our temperament and learn to live with it successfully, rationally, fully, and beautifully.

Just as important, we can let go of the effort to change the personalities of the other people in our world. We can learn to live with them as they are.

WHAT ABOUT RELATIONSHIPS?

Chapter 8 focuses on the six basic relationships among the four Colors. The Colors are a great help in understanding the complicated field of relationships in which we find ourselves. It's interesting to think about how these relationships work.

I start with a relationship with myself . . . I and myself . . . how I wish to be and how I am.

Then there is my relationship toward others . . . I and you, I and they . . . how I wish to be seen and accepted.

In addition, others have ways of relating to me . . . they see me a certain way, they act toward me a certain way . . . a world of people around me.

Lastly, I care about how others are relating to each other around me . . . fussing and feuding, loving and harmonious . . . I affect their relationships, and their relationships affect me.

It goes in circles. Let's say that my Blue side meets my Gold side. They work together, they argue and discuss, I make a decision. I talk to you about it, and my Blue/Gold decision runs smack into your Green/Orange point of view. You react to me in a certain way. Perhaps we disagree. So you go talk to John and Mary about it. John agrees with you. Mary agrees with me. You and John agree with each other, and you both argue with Mary. Mary sends me flowers, and John sends me a brick. I begin to doubt myself or to feel good about myself. Maybe I change my decision. Maybe I stick to it. And so the wheel turns.

WHY DO THE COLORS SEEM SO REAL AND ACCURATE?

When they first look at their Colors, people are often shocked to find very personal and private thoughts, feelings, and experiences described so accurately. After many years of working with Colors, however—after seeing so many people go through the seminar activity—I no longer find it a mystery why Colors works so well. It is a simple way of sorting out the world of human experience. It's based on the idea that there are four very basic elements that shape human experience and behavior, four basic psychological functions.

Once these elements are selected and identified, it becomes apparent that each person presents a different mixture, a different balance of the functions. Some people are very much influenced by one or two of the Colors. Others show a balance among three or four. These preferences lead to natural and understandable differences in how people see the world and how they behave in it.

HOW CAN I LEARN TO RECOGNIZE AND UNDERSTAND THE COLORS?

For most of us, the best method of learning is to read, observe, and talk over these differences with other people in our daily life. A good Colors training or seminar can give us the opportunity to see the Colors in action. But there's nothing like daily life as a laboratory to watch the Colors unfold.

There's nothing like seeing ourselves mirrored in our relationships with others who have a similar temperament. There's nothing like seeing the range of familiar differences that show up in family, friends, acquaintances, coworkers, fictional characters, movie actors, politicians, and all the great parade of human types that we see throughout our lives.

THE PAYOFF!

My years of study of these natural differences have brought about a great change in me. A very positive change. I wish the same for you. The best part is that I no longer feel that people are setting out to annoy me with their contrary ways. I no longer feel the need to get into disputes with others about ways of being. I now see myself and the personalities around me as the natural working out of these four basic human elements, and it all makes sense!

All in all, I now see the world as a magical blend of personal styles, strengths, and relationships. I love the Yup'ik idea that we are all spirit at the center and that our differences arise from the four natural elements. As I watch it all work out, I see that we can accomplish just about anything if we learn to accept our natural, inevitable, and valuable differences and get on with *Living Our Colors.*

COLORS REVEALED

Keep in mind that each of us can be seen as a blend of the four Colors, a rainbow or spectrum, a "mixture" in that ancient meaning of the word *temperament.* The pure Colors don't exist. Some of us, however, are very strongly one way or another. Very Gold. Very Blue. Very Orange. Very Green. Some of us are a balanced mixture of three or four of the Colors. Most of us fall somewhere in between.

In understanding people, it is always helpful to know their first two Colors, at least. A Gold/Orange person may act quite differently from a Gold/Green or a Gold/Blue person. The three will have similarities due to having the Gold in common, though, each of the three will be very different according to his or her Color.

In learning to think about Colors, it is helpful to separate out and heighten the differences among the four. In the next four chapters, we will look at the very Gold Golds, the very Blue Blues, the very Orange Oranges, and the very Green Greens. Later on we will look at the six basic pairs of Colors, both as they interact with each other, and as they work out together, blended in one person.

Read on! I know you'll be glad you did.

CHAPTER 3

GOLD

Protect and Serve

"Tradition, good order, and good work"

I am solid, traditional, hardworking, and productive. I use my skills and energy to help things work out and go well. I like things to run smoothly.

I respect the wisdom that has been handed down in customs and traditions. I need security in my work and in my relationships.

I know that love means loyalty and responsibility. It's very easy for things to get muddled up and to fall apart, so I take good care to keep it all together.

I make plans and lists and I follow through on them. I am on time and cooperative in groups. I try to get other people to get with the program, but I often end up carrying most of the load. People depend on me.

I try to measure up to high standards, and I feel guilty when I don't meet them. I'm pretty successful, and I do it the old-fashioned way: "I earn it!"

Gold. What the Greeks called the melancholic temperament. What the Yup'ik Eskimos describe as spirit acting through culture and duty.

Golds judge the world according to standards of excellence. These standards are carried over from past experiences. The past may be ten centuries ago or ten minutes ago, but it is the solid Gold's best and surest source of wisdom and best guide for action.

Standards may evolve and change to some degree, but for Golds the underlying values are eternal ... hard work, duty, responsibility, commitment, order. These are the things that give life meaning and make it livable.

Golds' standards and principles form a mental and emotional map. The map gives order to life and shapes how things are seen. When new things are discovered, they are examined in comparison to the best of the past, and corrections are made in an effort to help things measure up to the standard.

This correction of things toward the standard is one of Golds' most important contributions. Extreme Golds see criticism as a sacred duty, an obligation to serve quality. Rarely does anything seem perfect just as it is. Improvement is always possible, therefore it is always possible to make a contribution toward improvement.

For Golds, this process of correction and improvement is a positive thing, one of the most positive. Of course, the other Colors often complain and accuse Golds of being negative and overly critical. But for Golds, praise seems to be deserved only rarely. Worse yet, easy praise is actually a threat to quality and therefore to order and stability. It would be insincere and possibly even destructive to give praise just to make others feel better. Easy praise tarnishes the standard, and the standard is most important.

We have all heard that judgment is a two-edged sword, and it certainly cuts both ways for Golds. Having high standards for others is just part of having high standards for themselves. These high standards expose the Golds to much stress and guilt. Their own failures to measure up are much more painful to them than the failures of others, and a nagging sense of never being quite "up to snuff" is a common Gold complaint.

Golds experience life as basically unstable. It needs constant effort and attention to keep from deteriorating into chaos and confusion. The ground underfoot never seems to be quite solid. The shelter overhead is always threatening to leak. The picnic will bring ants. The parade will bring rain.

So Golds bring the bug spray and umbrellas. They prepare, provide, and give care. They never want to be on the receiving end. To be needy and dependent is a horror to Golds. Lists, priorities, plans, agreements, contracts, institutions, rituals, roles, and authority are ways Golds use to keep order, to stem the tide of chaos that always threatens to overwhelm. Left on its own, life goes downhill.

These basic concerns combined with high standards of order and quality lead to a pretty serious approach to life. Golds are noted for their seriousness, for their sense of duty and obligation, and for their sense of place.

Golds believe in institutions. They are not satisfied with patchwork and improvisation. The fundamentals must be sound. Punctuality is crucial. Concrete outcomes and accomplishments count. Dreams and plans have no substance until they are executed and the paperwork is complete. "The day's work counts!"

The social order is very fragile, and a proper network of obligations, duties, and roles provides the only possible security. Love and affection are too fleeting and untrustworthy to be relied upon. Energy and enthusiasm are passing things. Intellectual analysis often undermines order. It is loyalty, duty, authority, and reward and punishment that keep things from falling apart. Public opinion, status, and proper appearances are not incidental. They are essential.

This means work before play, and the play is likely to be well organized and productive, too. Exercise for health. Travel to broaden the mind. Not just skiing, but being on the ski patrol. Responsible play, a Red Cross backpack, and free ski-lift tickets, too! Sex in its proper place, well deserved, giving and receiving, a heaven-sent relief from the toils and tribulations of maintaining order and productivity, a sign of commitment and the natural order of love.

Of all the Colors, Golds have the hardest time ever going on vacation. If there's a phone nearby, they report that they might as well be at the office. If they can be reached, or even if they could call in, they are really not "away." And when they do manage to get really "away"—say, on a white-water rafting trip—thoughts of the mess that is building up at the office are never far from their minds. Golds know that the price of vacation will be the cleanup afterward.

This isn't just how Golds see the world. It's usually how it actually works. The other Colors count on Gold to carry the load, and the Golds oblige in order to get things done and to get them done "right." It's a circular process, and the other Colors are quite content as the burdens shift toward the Golds. Everyone knows that the Golds will carry the burdens if humanly possible. Everyone counts on that.

This means Golds are always at risk of being overloaded and even overwhelmed. Worst of all, they try not to show it. They try to tough it out like the Stoics of old. Always careful about appearances, Golds often tighten up their image as the pressure mounts. They may look their best just before they go over the edge. The cues may be subtle and indirect—weight loss or gain; paleness; dark circles under the eyes; illness.

In a troubled family or organization, the Gold will be trying to keep it all together. The child trying to parent the parents. The grandmother trying to keep a disintegrating family from self-destructing. The business partner in the shaky business, burning the midnight oil, struggling to keep the ship afloat.

We must protect and care for our Golds. They look strong, and they are reluctant to ask for help. We'd better help them anyway, without being asked, if we want them to survive to continue to make their contribution.

One way to help is to pay attention. Golds are supported and enlivened by public recognition. It needs to come spontaneously, and it must be earned. A word of recognition, a pat on the back . . . or much better yet, a plaque, a bonus, and a raise. Real, concrete recognition and a job well done—these are among the highest joys for Golds.

The flip side of this need for recognition is a common Gold experience of bitterness based on slights, lack of respect, and lack of recognition. The difficulty that the other Colors experience with Golds' authoritarian style often leads to criticism and resistance or simply to silence rather than respect and acknowledgment.

Money has a special place for Golds. They often report that earning money is better than finding money or winning money, that they have rarely if ever overdrawn a checking account, that they prefer to accumulate money rather than spend it, that money means more to them than merely the power to buy—it's a concrete symbol that they are doing all right as people, and that there is some degree of security for the future.

Across cultures, the Golds are the caretakers of the traditions, the ceremonies, the ways of the community. They show deep respect for their elders and for the proper authorities of the established order. They resist and reject revolutionary ideas and often are deeply suspicious of things that are new or the influences of other cultures.

Strong Golds can be quite fierce and even warlike in defense of their community. This can be true whether the community is an ancient religious heritage, a country, an ethnic group, or a family tradition.

Gold Dislikes

Golds see much in the world that does not measure up to their generally high ideals and their belief in traditional standards. Perfection is very rare. Flaws and imperfections stand out. Golds tend to see things as they should be, and the reality rarely measures up.

Golds understand that order is fragile and that chaos awaits around every turn. Their high need for security and stability leads to a deep concern about anything that threatens orderly living. When the ground is shaky underfoot, the Gold experiences very real anxiety. The anxiety leads to dislike of anything eccentric or revolutionary.

Golds are committed to hard work, productivity, success, and the smooth running of institutions and procedures. Punctuality and adherence to routine are high values. Anything that seems to threaten these values is met with intense dislike. Nonconformity, insubordination, disobedience, and irresponsibility head the list of threats to order. Confronted with these things, the Gold will complain and criticize.

Confusion is a Gold nemesis. One of the main contributors to confusion is a lack of clear leadership with clearly defined roles for the leader and the follower. Golds see definite hierarchy and legitimate authority as essential in avoiding confusion and getting the job done. They abhor a power vacuum, confused and uncertain leadership, or no leadership at all. Unclear expectations and fuzzy goals are simply impossible to deal with.

Golds tend to have many strong dislikes. They are often rather grumpy. They experience a lot of guilt and the burdens of responsibility, and may be annoyed by cheerfulness and playfulness in others. Slobs, procrastinators, and idlers are of no use to Golds.

CHAPTER 4

BLUE

Create Harmony

"True feelings and real relationships"

I lead with my heart and dream of a better world. I feel things deeply, both joy and pain. I love to discover beauty in people and in nature. I love to nurture and care for people and things and watch them grow. I'm very romantic.

Personal relationships are important to me. Honest sharing and real communication are some of the highest things in life. Being with other people can be hard, especially when they are selfish and uncaring.

I always try to make peace, but I would rather be alone than be with people who can't or won't get along. I am sometimes moody, and old feelings and experiences from the past stay with me a long time.

I always want to find the best in people. I value cooperation and goodwill. I am interested in spiritual things. I wish for "the peace that passeth understanding."

Blue. What the Greeks called the choleric temperament. What the Yup'ik describe as spirit seeing and acting through emotion.

Blues swim in a sea of feelings. They are usually quite good at this kind of swimming, accepting and flowing with emotions that would thoroughly upset the other Colors. Of all the Colors, however, extreme Blues most often report that they wish they were some other Color. They often wistfully admire the Oranges with their carefree grace and playfulness, the Golds for their orderliness, and the Greens for their cool heads. But Blues find themselves destined to live with the joys and sorrows of being the deeply feeling Color.

The heart is a sensitive and powerful instrument for Blues. It registers all the subtleties and nuances of relationships as well as all the ups and downs of the personal self. Joy and pain, pangs and twinges of eagerness or shyness, a constant music of emotional sensation accompany every aspect of daily life.

These emotions are as real as a toothache for Blues, deep physical sensations that cannot be ignored. The other Colors often misunderstand, believing that the Blues are "thinking" these emotions, "acting as if" these personal and relational things were important, "deciding" to be this way. Not so.

For Blue, a heartache is a bodily sensation, as real as a broken arm. Inspiration and enthusiasm flood the body with emotional energy. Fear is a consuming physical presence. Shame reddens the face and brings tears, and tears are never far away for Blues. Love and sympathy are all-consuming.

Parting is no sweet sorrow for Blues. Every good-bye is a loss, often filled with anxiety and sadness. The other Colors are sometimes confused by Blue's careful attention to the little partings and separations that are so frequent in daily life. A very Blue family might gather at the window to wave good-bye when some family member leaves for the grocery store! My own family, for example.

Rage is fierce for Blues, fiercer perhaps than for any other

Color. Often this rage comes from another particularly Blue characteristic, the hatred of injustice. Everything is personal to Blues, and persons are precious. All fragile things are precious. When a Blue sees a child being badly treated, an animal abused, nature trampled, social injustice, sorrow easily gives way to righteous anger. Though the fuse is long, it is a big bang.

Self-righteousness is a Blue specialty. Since they are particularly sensitive to the subtleties of personality, Blues know where other people are vulnerable. When the self-righteous rage does come out, Blues often go for the jugular of the person they are attacking. Blues are so averse to conflict that when they do go to war, they usually try to go for a single knockout punch in the first round. "The she-bear and her cubs." Beware the angry Blue.

The Blue's sensitivity makes a wonderful contribution to the community. Blues are enthusiastic, generous, and inspiring. They are process-oriented, and they want to bring out the best in others. Warm and sympathetic, they are good at promoting smoothly flowing relationships and at bringing out the full participation of all group members. They love to nurture things, groups, people, and watch them grow.

In intimate relationships, Blues are very romantic and attach great meaning to small gestures, gifts, sweet nothings, and tokens of affection. Sex expresses loving and caring. It is part of Blues' endless search for self-expression and self-realization and may be very creative. It usually reflects the kind of intimacy that takes place between two people. Blues may feel deeply betrayed if their sexual partner finds such intimacy with another person. They are prone to getting into relationships they can't seem to get out of—even when they want to—for fear of hurting the other person.

Blues feel conflict coming a mile away and try to finesse it before it happens. Usually very flexible, Blues will set aside their own interests and ideas in service to group harmony. They easily adopt a nonjudgmental attitude and are keenly aware of the points of view of others. All this flexibility and goodwill can come to a screeching halt, of course, when the Blue is out of sorts, self-righteous, and resentful.

Blues tend to be intuitive and good with words. Natural and effective communicators, they are skillful at getting their point across in a variety of ways. Their idealism combines with their natural enthusiasm, and they strive to influence others to a better life, often a spiritual life, a self-actualized life.

Blues account for a small percent of the total population. They are, however, naturally drawn to helping professions and other influential occupations. In education and social-service settings, Blues are often in the majority, along with the Golds.

Blues often believe that the Blue way of life is the healthy way of life. They see intimacy and emotion as the keys to health and happiness, and they urge these values on the people around them. Greens, Golds, and Oranges are sometimes made to feel that their ways are wrong, even that there's something wrong with them as people.

Blues' sensitivity can work against them. They sometimes see themselves as pathologically undefended: no armor, no facade, no mask. It is remarkable how often Blues speak of feeling "crushed." This is a special word for Blues. It means feeling inwardly devastated by personal failures, slights, misunderstandings, or mistreatment, real or imagined.

Encouragement and emotional support are crucial for Blues. Left on their own without any feedback from others, they usually assume the worst. Other people's silence is interpreted as negative, and Blues spiral down in their feelings.

Criticism is also hard for Blues to take. Since everything is personal, criticism is personal. Blues don't naturally separate themselves from their actions, so criticism of actions is criticism of self. None of the other Colors is so vulnerable about this issue. To Oranges, put-downs and competition are natural, even fun. To Golds, criticism of self and others is a sacred responsibility, the key to maintaining high standards. To Greens, skepticism and critical judgment mean intellectual rigor, and they thrive on the precision that results. For Blue, criticism just means failure.

This fragility of the self is a key to the Blue temperament. Not only are persons precious, they are fragile and unique. Hurt feelings are real hurts. The consequences last a long time. This fragility breeds anxiety. Blues do not heal quickly from emotional hurts. For Blues, all emotional experience lasts a long time, with feeling memories often carried from early childhood into the last stages of life with the full emotional load intact.

Loss, emotional trauma, and betrayal are not going to be gotten over easily for Blues. When the other Colors are ready to move on into the future or just into the here and now, the Blue is still in the throes of the past. To some degree, this must simply be accepted. Skillful grief work, artistic expression, careful communication, and good therapy may all have their place, but the fact is that, for Blue, feelings from the past will always be easily resuscitated and brought to life.

Fragility goes hand in hand with the constant Blue quest for meaning, for actualization and the highest possible realization of self. The quest for spiritual awareness, for transcendent understanding, for direct awareness of highest things is a common denominator for Blues.

To some extent, this quest is fostered by the intensity of suffering that Blues endure in the rough-and-tumble of daily life. The heart that feels great pain is capable of great joy. The suffering of Jesus, the Sufi's wine of love, the compassion and joy of the Chassidic Jewish tradition, the peace that passeth understanding, all the ecstatic religious paths have great appeal. For the Blue, the goals of religion are freedom, realization, and direct experience, rather than dogma, ethics, or morality.

Blues are often on a mission, driven by a utopian ideal or a meaningful experience. Though sometimes overly romantic and unrealistic, Blues often bring real vision to the community. With a global perspective, looking beyond facts and actions, Blues often bring a view of the whole and of great possibilities.

Blue Dislikes

Blues' dislikes grow out of their special concern for relationships, the intensity of their feelings, and their deep commitment to the sanctity of persons.

Unpleasant emotional experiences are a frequent occurrence for Blues, and they will go to great length to avoid them. Blues have long feeling memories. Emotional events are remembered, and the power of the feelings comes back along with the details of who, what, when, where, and why. Bad sex is as bad as it gets, leaving its traces for years to come. Their strong reactions include a kind of hysteria, as well as that remarkable Blue rage.

Very high on the list of dislikes for most Blues is hypocrisy or insincerity. Blues are outraged by people who put on the appearance of virtue, generosity, or kindliness while contradicting these appearances in their behavior.

Injustice and exploitation are deeply troubling to Blues. Being in the presence of unfairness or hurtful behavior is just about more than a Blue can stand.

A list of Blue dislikes would include: deception, insincerity, artificiality, competition, domination, impersonalness, disharmony, lack of feeling, dishonesty, emotional coldness, injustice, stress and conflict, judgmental people, rigid structure, lack of communication, isolation, detail work, being yelled at, cruelty of any kind, bossy negative people, heartlessness, and compulsiveness.

CHAPTER 5

ORANGE

Just Do It!

"Moving. Happening. Going. Doing."

I want to be free to act. I want to make things happen. I love to be good at lots of things. I love to compete with others and do my best. I love to win!

I don't understand how people can sit around all day and endlessly talk, talk, talk. Life is an adventure. Action and excitement are the spice of life. I want to move, and laugh, and achieve things. I want to be with people who want to do things.

I'm impulsive and spur-of-the-moment. Too much planning, too much seriousness, too much thinking—they all get in the way of living now! I want to be respected for my skill, my creativity, and my energy.

Live and learn, that's what I say. Learn by doing. Hands on. Then do something with it, for heaven's sake, or what's the point?

Now, what did you say was the next activity? Let's get going!

Orange. What the Greeks called the sanguine temperament. What the Yup'ik describe as spirit seeing and acting through the body.

When it's time to ride the rocket, Orange will be the first to volunteer. Others may provide the vision, the design, the detail work and organization, but Orange will fly the machine with skill and daring.

Action and sensation are the keys to the Orange experience, the life of the senses and the physical body. Orange seems to make up about a third of the population, equal in percentage to Gold, making Orange and Gold the two predominant Colors. This means that physical action is an influence equal to order and tradition in the human community.

From shaking the slats of the crib to rocking a chair over backward in a grade school classroom, riding a motorcycle on two-lane blacktop, starting an independent business, and building a house from the ground up without any blueprint, Orange must act!

This action is not a decision. It doesn't stem from an idea, a philosophy, or an emotion. It comes from the actual muscular and hormonal energy of the body. Thinking about it, explaining it, giving reasons for it—these come later. In the beginning is action.

This intense, physical demand for action leads to an absolute need for freedom. If forced to sit still and listen for long, the knee begins to bounce up and down, the pencil waggles in the fingers, the hands beat out a rhythm under the table, the mind wanders, sleepiness sets in, and various ideas begin to pop up about ways to generate some entertainment.

Some Oranges are quiet in their demeanor, physically still. But the inner experience is the same. Energy, impatience, restlessness, action for its own sake, the desire to *do* something!

Life without enjoyment simply makes no sense to Orange.

What is all this seriousness, routine, and drudgery for, anyway? Is there something wrong with delight, excitement, and play? Or sex? What about the development of skill entirely for its own sake, getting really good at something just because you can, acting for the sheer joy of it? And why should everything have a reason, a purpose, a meaning? Can't things just exist for their own sake? Okay, so we need to get in enough food for the winter. Let's at least whistle while we work!

Needless to say, Orange meets with some difficulty in dealing with the orderly Gold and Blue worlds of school and of various occupations, with their demands for conformity and physical restraint. Commitments and obligations often have the same stultifying effect.

Thus *freedom* becomes a key word for Orange. The experience of being bound, of being held still or tied down is too unpleasant. It is a real and powerful suffering, an explosive physical discomfort, and it must be avoided as much as possible.

When this demand for freedom turns into a battle with the other Colors, as it sometimes does, Orange can become really rebellious, oppositional, and defiant. Green's reasons, Blue's emotions, and Gold's duties are like words in a foreign language to an Orange who needs to move, and move now.

Extreme Oranges live in the here and now. Urges, whims, and impulses don't happen in a long field of past, present, and future. They occur now, and now is what there is. This gives these impulses great power and reduces the power of restraints.

Self-control, organization, limits, boundaries, plans—none of these things comes naturally for Oranges. They need external structure. They need someone to tap them on the shoulder and mention that, at their current speed, they won't make it around the next curve. This is Oranges' deepest dilemma. They may need help in dealing with the high level of organization required by modern school, work, and life in general. Yet while such help with external structure is needed, it may be very hard to accept.

But what a contribution Oranges make to the community . . . ! Energy, skill, charisma, grace, accomplishment, laughter, competition, spirit, play, camaraderie, creativity . . . all these and more enliven the group, generate action, and prevent stagnation.

Oranges thrive on crisis, handling it with skill, sometimes even generating it when they feel that things need to be shaken up. They are tool handlers, often mechanically inclined, with a high tolerance for discomfort and intense effort.

Oranges like to work and play in teams with a strong sense of team loyalty and camaraderie. They make work into play. They handle projects well when they are given specific goals, timelines, and outcomes but are left to get the work done on their own. They are strong negotiators. They are self-starters and long-distance runners—when the incentives are right and they are truly engaged.

Oranges develop alternative lifestyles, lifestyles that give free rein to the spontaneity, creativity, energy, and impulsiveness that is their natural style. In the arts, skilled crafts, performance, sports, sales and marketing, or entrepreneurship of all kinds, Oranges often create unique roles for themselves within or outside the system.

They are rarely interested in broad, liberal-arts intellectual pursuits, or in knowledge for its own sake. When they get to college, they often outperform everyone. They chose it, they know why they're there and what they want out of it. They are self-motivated and bring all their energy to bear on the outcome they want. Oranges want to learn by doing and achieve concrete results. Once again, immediacy takes the place of long-term goals and objectives, and the Orange heads out into the job market or into an alternative lifestyle that lets him or her be free.

It's important to note that there are many Orange women. Just as the Blue man may have difficulties due to macho cultural stereotypes, the Orange woman may struggle with female stereotypes of all kinds. Blue and Gold women often find that their temperaments lead them in directions more traditionally "female." Orange and Green women, with their tendencies toward physical adventure and intellectual coolness, often see themselves as marching to a different drummer when it comes to matters of gender.

But Oranges usually love to challenge limits anyway. Orange women are physically skillful, energetic, spontaneous, competitive, often humorous or even sarcastic, and it is a delight to see the many interesting roles and lifestyles that they develop for themselves.

For both male and female Oranges, sex is just about the most exciting and fun activity in life. They approach it with great good humor and with the characteristic freedom and creativity that marks everything they do. They do not see sex as tangled up with all kinds of sober relationship issues, but as a joy in its own right.

On the other side of the coin, Oranges often conceal their nature from others who do not understand, or who judge them negatively. One of the joys of a Colors activity is to watch people from each Color discover their strength and worth—*and* those of all the other Colors. The Oranges often show this the most of all as they come into their own with pride and self-respect.

Orange Dislikes

For Oranges, the world needs to be a free-play zone. All their strengths—spontaneity, energy, creativity, enthusiasm—depend on having room to move. When they are confined and constrained, their dislikes are intense. And given their action-oriented nature, Oranges are inclined to rebel against what frustrates them.

Overstrict and rigid authority usually leads the list of things most hated by Oranges. The strong hand holding them back simply makes no sense to them. To Oranges, control often seems to be arbitrary and unreasonable. It feels to them as if someone were simply trying to dominate them, to defeat them in a power struggle. Oranges do not like to be told what to do or not to do. They don't like pompous people, and they will not be condescended to.

When Oranges are seriously out of sorts they may become rude and aggressive, dismissive, and harsh in their communication.

Routines and boredom fall right in alongside rigid authority as a burr under the Orange's saddle. It is a physical agony for Orange to have to do the same rote task over and over again. Boredom is not just a state of mind for Orange. It is a physical discomfort of major proportions. The muscles fill up with thwarted energy, which finds its way into all kinds of restless activity and ultimately to an explosive release. Oranges become very good at finding ways to release this energy, turning work into play, making a competitive game of a task, or stirring up playfulness in their relationships.

While Oranges will practice endlessly a skill or behavior that interests them—a jump shot, a musical scale, the effective use of a tool, a game strategy, a sales gambit, a dance step—it is their interest, their creativity, and their active participation that drive them. The imposed routine of no immediate interest or reward drives them crazy.

Just as difficult as rote and routine is the challenge of having to be physically still. The classroom can be a trial. The lecture hall, a torture chamber. The desk, a prison. The library, a tomb.

Equally tough is the lack of a real challenge. The Orange thrives on challenge, on novelty, and on reaching for new heights of performance. An easy task is of no interest unless it pays well. A long string of easy tasks leads to boredom and the search for something new.

In general, Oranges don't like interruptions, rigid timelines, paperwork and bureaucracy, rigid people, slow people, slow drivers (!), standing in lines, too much talk, couch potatoes, negativity, lack of money, or lack of sex.

GREEN

Figure It Out

"Information, exploration, and analysis"

I love to solve problems and create new ideas. I need freedom to explore, to learn, to experiment, and to gather information and knowledge.

I need time to think and analyze before I make a decision. Getting at the truth isn't easy. It's hard to get hold of. The facts won't put up with any foolishness. There are lots of possible answers to any question. I am very curious, and I need my independence in order to understand.

I like to learn about the things that interest me, and I am interested in lots of things. I don't like to be told what to do or to think about. I don't like or trust authority unless it really proves itself. I don't like to do the same things over and over again. I like to create and move on, letting others handle the details.

I am more comfortable with ideas and things than I am with feelings and relationships. I want people to appreciate my special contribution to the world. I have strong feelings and I care about what other people feel, but I prefer not to talk about it too much.

Green. What the Greeks called the phlegmatic temperament. What the Yup'ik describe as spirit acting through thought.

In all the trainings that I have done, Greens have nearly always been in the minority. Whatever the actual proportion may be, Greens are unique and special, and often alone among the other Colors.

Greens lead with the power of the thinking mind, approaching all situations with skepticism, seeking new ideas, concepts, designs, and understandings, and relying first, last, and always on their own analysis.

If the Green reader has read this far in this book, it is quite certain that he or she has raised many objections, counterarguments, and skeptical analyses of what is being said. For many Greens, the whole idea of Colors will have seemed overly simplistic, unscientific, and confining.

If the Green reader's interest has been held, it may well be because this idea of Colors has an interesting background with its roots in the Greeks and its relation to Native culture. Or the idea of the types may have sparked an interest, promising a new mental model for analysis and understanding, a new power of comprehension. Greens like powerful models.

One thing is for sure. Whether attending a training or reading this book, Greens doubt everything. If something doesn't make sense to them, they will not just ignore it and go on as if nothing is wrong. They may speak out or raise a challenge. Or they may hold their peace and turn inward. They may close the book or get up and leave the meeting. Depending on their interests and what they want in the situation, they will make up their own minds and act accordingly.

Greens operate based on the evidence. Just the facts, ma'am. They aren't swayed by Blues' personal sentiments or enthusiasm. They mistrust elegant Gold appearances, glossy presentations, and traditional ideas. They will refuse to be caught up in Orange action for its own sake. For Green, it's always a matter of "Let's think this thing over."

Thus, personal integrity and independent analysis are basic keys to understanding extreme Greens. They don't have to have genius-level intelligence. They may have traveled some quite different, independent, nonconformist path in life.

Sometimes Greens' intelligence is overlooked by important people in their lives. On close inspection, it usually turns out that they have been underestimated due to their slow, patient, careful analysis, their refusal to rush to judgment, their unwillingness to give quick and easy answers, and their refusal to simply conform to the prevailing ideas of the people around them.

Greens are interested in applying knowledge: prediction and control, elegant design, problem solving, and dealing skillfully with complexity. They love to feel ingenious, to be experts in everything, to create solutions through their accumulated know-how. Their sexuality partakes of this same intense exploratory quality. Sex is full of curiosity for Greens. Once past the barriers of their overall reserved nature, sexuality is a broad landscape to be explored and enjoyed. It can be a game or a serious expression of deep meaning, but either way, it will be full of experimentation and an opportunity for a kind of vulnerability that many Greens don't find in other areas of life.

But they are even more deeply interested in knowledge and analysis for its own sake. They want to be known as truly complex individuals with great analytic ability. The exercise of intelligence itself, more than its practical application, has the most meaning. "I think, therefore I am," is a good theme for Greens.

Greens prefer to think a thing over rather than to decide about it or arrive at final conclusions. They enjoy looking at a problem afresh each time it is encountered. They like to set aside old approaches, look for a new perspective, a clever insight, an underlying principle, a novel approach, a different outcome.

One unique and recognizable thing about Greens is their hatred of repetition and redundancy. Sometimes it seems almost comical how averse a Green will be to repeating something, or to having to hear it a second time. Green wants it terse, compact, and to the point. "Do not imply that I am stupid by telling me something a second time." "What's the matter, weren't you listening? I already told you once."

Greens doubt their own past conclusions as much as they doubt the ideas of others. Very self-critical, Greens are not personally defensive about their ideas. They are eager for self-improvement and they simply follow knowledge and ideas wherever they lead, even if the ideas contradict what was thought yesterday or ten minutes ago. If someone shows them a real error in their thinking or a truly convincing new idea, the past is left behind easily.

This easy, honest intellectual movement breaks down, however, when Greens feel inferior, inadequate, or out of their depth. At these times, a brittle defensiveness may come into play. Greens are deathly afraid of appearing stupid and inadequate or of actually discovering for themselves that they don't know everything about everything. Fear of humiliation is powerful for Greens.

This constant, here-and-now cogitation sometimes gives the very Green a particularly recognizable appearance: a look of preoccupation sometimes bordering on bewilderment that goes along with a grasping about among a lot of ideas. This highly intellectual, analytical person often seems picky and perfectionist, a bit tense and irritable, especially as ideas are colliding and confusion threatens.

Very Green people can be recognized by their interests. The eccentric, absentminded professor of mathematical linguistics; the librarian specializing in North African topographical maps; the expert statistical theoretician relating the rise and fall of baseball batting averages over the last fifty years to the materials and construction of the ball; the adolescent who knows the inside of Dungeons and Dragons or the motherboard of the computer or the levels of Doom as well as most of us know our address and phone number; the six-year-old with the extensive collection of insect larvae organized by species . . . all are examples of the special worlds of information and knowledge that are created and inhabited by Greens.

The everyday social world can be a real nuisance for Greens. They don't enjoy small talk. They often find that others don't stay with them long enough to relate to their complex interests. The teacher doesn't wait for the answer to her question. She may not even understand her own question as well as the Green does. It is one of a Green's toughest challenges that teachers, parents, and the other Colors tend to drift away while the Green is working the way through a maze of interesting and thoughtful information. Greens are at risk of becoming isolated and eccentric.

In addition, when Greens are out of sorts, they are quite capable of becoming acid-tongued, insolent, and arrogant. When others complain about their attitude or criticize their ideas, they may respond with a sarcastic and condescending smile.

Greens love riddles, mental tricks and games, paradoxes, satire, clever repartee, and intricate intellectual exercises of all kinds, and they enjoy demonstrating their mental power to others. This sometimes makes others feel uncomfortable and on their guard.

Greens can also be rather ruthless when the logic demands it. They will do what's required without much attention to feelings or traditional ways. They often appear puzzled and more than a little irritated when Blues and Golds resist their logic with some nonsense about feelings or about preserving the old ways.

Like Blues, Greens are very inward people. Their feelings run very deep, and they take them very seriously. But for Greens, talking about feelings seems false and contrived. After all, words and feelings are two different things. Talk is not feeling. Greens often say that all the talk about feelings is artificial. It cheapens the feelings. On the other hand, since their feelings are so deep and often unexpressed, Greens are at risk of being seen as cold, distant, uninvolved, and uncaring, even when they care deeply.

Greens contribute a very valuable emotional coolness and deliberateness in situations and relationships. They are not much moved by the subtle emotional messages that people send out with body language and voice tones. If it's not explicit, it gets no attention. There may be an underlying refusal on the part of the Green to be manipulated by these little pressures and emotional subtleties. Greens often see these messages as sneaky, manipulative power games—emotional blackmail—and Greens are not fools to be pushed around in these ways.

On a really excellent, perfect day, a Green has the chance to keep a cool head in a crisis, to bring encyclopedic knowledge to bear on the situation, to weigh up the facts and the options, to design and construct a brilliant, realistic, and effective plan, to consult while others carry out the plan successfully (no tedious effort required of the Green), to save the day, and then humbly and modestly to receive due praise and appreciation from the others for his or her brilliance. For a Green, this is as good as it gets.

Green Dislikes

Greens depend on the integrity of their own autonomous thinking process and the free actions that grow out of it. Some of their deep dislikes tend to be organized around situations that violate rationality and integrity—events that throw their hard-won analyses into disarray.

Illogic and irrationality are among the deepest dislikes for Green. Greens often report that the people around them seem "stupid"—that is, that these people do not think things through until they arrive at logical conclusions that will guide their actions.

Greens gather information, analyze it, and base their actions on the analysis. It is hard for them to understand that others don't necessarily operate this way. The Gold going along by tradition and precedent; the Blue following the lead of feelings and relationships; the Orange acting and then figuring it out later . . . all of these other approaches seem to be illogical, confusing, and ultimately doomed to the deliberate, thoughtful Green.

Greens are not easy in social situations. Most social interaction seems to them to be useless, illogical, and chaotic. They hate prejudice, injustice, unfairness, irrationality, thoughtlessness, stupidity, and overemotionalism . . . in other words, gossip and small talk.

When they are thoroughly disgusted, they tend to drag their feet and become noncompliant. They engage in put-downs and show their scorn for the people and things that have upset them. They often withdraw into a sense of superiority. Their sarcasm is a wonder to behold, and they are masters of the silent treatment.

Redundancy, sloppy thinking, oversimplifying, and mechanical repetition of old ideas will drive a Green from the room. Authoritarian control, intimidation, rigidity, and know-it-alls (particularly those who disagree with them) are great bugaboos. Distractions, time pressure, rote tasks, and nonsense schedules will send a Green looking for another job.

CHAPTER 7

Troubles

Each of the Colors has its own special troubles. Carried to its extreme, each Color has some serious drawbacks and pitfalls. It's a good thing that all the Colors coexist, so that they can check and complement one another. Each Color is often good medicine for the extremes of the others. When there is love, respect, understanding, and communication, we can all help each other get through the worst of our muddles.

GOLD TROUBLES

Golds are usually pretty successful. Their organization, their commitment, and the value they place on accomplishment usually pay off. Still, there are some common difficulties that plague them.

In troubled families, Golds are often stretched to the limit trying to keep things together. It may be Grandma struggling to get the kids on the right track, trying to save marriages, and keep a roof over everybody's head. It may be a child trying to keep peace in the parents' marriage or parenting an irresponsible adult. Wherever the Gold is positioned in the troubled family, he or she will be working hard, and often exhausted and near the breaking point.

Overload and exhaustion are common pitfalls for Golds. "If no one else is doing it, I will have to," is a common Gold lament. Just as in a troubled family, Golds will struggle to keep a troubled organization afloat, and again the stress and strain will take their toll.

In addition to these difficulties, extreme Golds are subject to various behavior patterns that can be self-defeating and can alienate other people. Their commitment to organization and structure can turn into rigidity. They may become highly judgmental and negative toward others. They may become completely authoritarian and uncompromising. "My way or the highway" may become their motto.

The flip side of authoritarianism is blind following, and this is a common problem when Gold becomes too Gold. Authority is to be respected and obeyed, and this is true whether I am the sheep or the shepherd. Golds can fall into an unquestioning good-soldier mentality, following orders, forgetting to question, surrendering their own independent judgment, and giving all to the cause.

Golds are prone to anxiety and endless hand-wringing. Worry may never leave them. Holidays may be impossible. Worse yet, ambitious vacations may turn into harder work than work. They are also inclined to complaining and self-pity, which is often pretty well justified considering how hard they're working and how little gratitude they get.

Fatigue may become exhaustion. Hypochondria may set in, and real physical complaints may not be far behind. Both Golds and Blues tend to convert life stress into illness or psychosomatic problems. Their sex lives may suffer from accumulated resentments, becoming another of the burdens they carry instead of a release and relief.

Golds need Oranges around. Oranges are frequently irritating to Golds, but they do insist on play, on spontaneity, and on generally "lightening up!" This is a good counterbalance to Gold's tendency toward all work and no play. Golds need Blues as well. Blues offer inspiration and sympathy, and liven up the heart. And they need Greens to question, to be skeptical, to provide alternatives, and to balance Golds' reliance upon precedent and authority.

But above all, Golds need help getting the work done. It is undeniable that the other Colors *all* are happy to let the drudgery fall to the super-responsible Golds. If the Oranges, Blues, and Greens know what's good for them, they will give loving care to the Golds.

BLUE TROUBLES

The deepest troubles for Blues come from the power of their emotions, the depth of their personal sensitivity in relationships, their dreaminess, and sometimes from a kind of self-absorbed narcissism. At the extreme, they are prone to deep anxiety, serious depression, and emotional explosiveness.

Distress in social situations may become almost unbearable. Conflict, rejection, and criticism are very painful, and Blues lose confidence in themselves easily. When things are tough, Blues will often become withdrawn and sulky. Emotional blackmail and passive aggression often come easier for Blues than direct confrontation of issues.

For all their commitment to honesty and authenticity, Blues will lie. They tend to be masters of the little white lie that saves face or avoids emotional unpleasantness. They will lie to save face or cover up their own shortcomings as well. Failure as a person is so painful to Blues that denial and keeping up appearances may seem like the only way out.

Trouble in romantic relationships can be all-consuming. Blues always say that they would rather have a broken arm than a broken heart. When asked to explain, the answer is always the same. The broken arm will heal. The broken heart will hurt forever. Breaking off a bad relationship, like all forms of loss and separation, may be just too hard. Blues often find themselves locked into unhappy situations because it is so hard to say no or to say good-bye. Their sexuality is inextricably entwined with their overall emotional state and may become simply impossible when the life of the heart is out of kilter. On the other hand, illegitimate sexual acting out also may occur, rooted in the depths of loneliness, a sense of powerlessness, and/or self-isolation.

Blues are often dreamy and distracted, living out fantasies while the practical realities tumble down around them. They may have a hard time setting limits, meeting deadlines, getting motivated to carry out their responsibilities.

The demand for self-actualization and self-expression can lead Blues to serious frustrations and overexcitement. They are easily caught up in outlandish belief systems, and they may act out a messianic zeal for whatever happens to be their current enthusiasm. They are also prone to dilettantism, sampling many and various interests and activities, but mastering none.

When Blues are cornered, or when they finally feel justified in their anger, they may be quite emotionally explosive, confrontive, even violent.

Blues can profit greatly from the presence of the other Colors. Gold helps with a firm grasp on practical reality and the ability to bring stability and order. Orange helps with a light heart and emotional resiliency. Green brings calm rationality, pragmatism, and clear boundaries. All of these can be a great help to the over-wrought Blue.

ORANGE TROUBLES

Oranges often get a lot of heat in life. They are criticized, called immature, lazy (which they are *not*), hyperactive, careless, noisy, and so on. Concerned or hostile Golds are after them about risk and disorder. Unfriendly Blues are after them about insensitivity. Unhappy Greens treat them as thoughtless and superficial. Once mighty warriors, hunters, sailors, or respected farmers, mechanics, and artisans, Oranges have a much narrower field of play in the modern world.

Most Oranges rise above all this. They get enough love, enough respect, enough opportunity, enough room to move, and they get along just fine. In fact, they often excel. They may leave school early and never read a book, but they will always be skillful, and they will find ways for that skill to pay off for them.

Some Oranges are not so fortunate, and when Oranges are unhappy, resentful, and rebellious, they act out, they lie, they drop out of school, they run away. They may become rude and defiant in school, in the workplace, in the family, and on the street.

It may become a badge of honor to break laws and rules. Their own lack of respect for comfortable hypocrites and petty tyrants may seem to justify an outlaw lifestyle, or various activities right on the edge of legality or respectability. Lying, cheating, and stealing may become a way of life. Physical aggression may be part of it as well. Overly aggressive sexuality or violation of sexual taboos is not uncommon in stressed-out or unsocialized Oranges who are seeking release for some mighty intense physical demands.

Extreme Oranges are usually looking for the buzz. They tend to prefer stimulants, seeking to heighten their excitement, eliminate fear and anxiety, and reach maximum, ultra-maximum, super-ultra-maximum, radically, devastatingly ultra-super-ultra-maximum intensity, and all this just preparing to *really* go for it the next time around.

Oranges are adventurers and risk takers. Bungee jumping, sky-diving, hang gliding . . . pretty soon they are all passé and some new thrill must be found. "Been there, done that" is a common Orange complaint. "No fear!" is an Orange motto.

Oranges are hard to rein in once they have really slipped the leash. They must be approached largely on their own terms: directly, strongly, and often physically. They are not likely to be moved by Blue's appeals to sympathy, by Gold's lectures on order and responsibility, or by Green's arguments and analyses. In the end a change must appear to them to be in their own best interest, and it is on those terms that they must be approached.

Any or all of the offerings from the other Colors *will* be helpful if and when the Orange decides to make a change. But it is no good trying to turn an Orange into a Gold, a Blue, or a Green. Life will always be an adventure for Oranges, and they will keep it lively for the people around them as well.

GREEN TROUBLES

Greens' most serious troubles involve isolation and the power of emotions. Social interaction is never easy for Greens. In extreme situations, they can become seriously disconnected from others. They may have a difficult time finding their way back in.

Greens are well able to build their own world of information and imagination. In the most serious circumstances, they may simply go and live in their inner world. Children and youths may withdraw into comic books, Dungeons and Dragons, the whole world of virtual reality and video games. Adults may disappear into the Internet or into any number of other complex and isolated pathways.

Greens are prone to disgust and cynicism toward their fellow human beings. They may tend to write people off. They are also very vulnerable to feeling rejected, feeling odd, feeling like an outsider. In addition, they may have strong feelings of superiority toward a world that doesn't understand or respect their intelligence, and this superiority may lead them to snobbishness or to strange and eccentric behavior. The search for power can lead troubled Greens down some very unpleasant paths.

On the other hand, Greens are also vulnerable to feelings of inadequacy when they can't comprehend a situation, when they don't know enough, or when they simply don't have the capacity to measure up to their own standards. Feelings of humiliation are deadly to Greens, and they will go to any length to avoid them.

Greens are never easy with emotions. When feelings do well up and come to the surface, Greens sometimes feel overwhelmed and helpless. A flood of feeling can sometimes wash away the power of the intellect to manage things. Deep confusion often results, and it may seem like drowning or like losing all control.

Greens are often prone to indecisiveness in the face of the sheer volume of the information that they possess. Their perfectionism may be overwhelmed by the complexity of a situation.

Their performance anxiety may prevent action and decision. They may try to "baffle them with bull*!#." Or they may become paralyzed, noncompliant, uncooperative, and uncommunicative.

The most common serious difficulty faced by Greens is that others may come to think they are cold and uncaring. This can be a deep wound for a Green, who really cares very deeply. It's the expression that gets in the way. Talk is cheap to a Green. Worse yet, it seems to cheapen the real depth of authentic feelings. One of Greens' worst fears is that no one will ever know how much they really care.

Greens need the support and feedback of the other Colors. Blues can help them to cope with the sea of feelings. Golds can help to bring them back to the concrete world of duty, responsibility, time, and commitment. Oranges, as always, can help them to lighten up, to laugh, to get tough, and to get back on the horse and ride.

CHAPTER 8

Relationships

When Colors Meet Each Other

Richard was a handsome fireball of a salesman with an eye for
the uniqueness of a product and a preference for the special
quirk, the exotic material, the nifty detail that showed the arti-
san's genius. He was also an incorrigible flirt from the word *go*.
In addition, he was always on the lookout for the really big
deal—the deal that, after showing great promise, usually col-
lapsed in a pile of broken dreams. His life had seen a long series
of relationships, a couple of broken marriages, and a current marriage that looked like it was going on the rocks, too.

Jeanne, Richard's wife, was a quiet, attractive brunette with
special skills at organization and personal relations. She was a
working mother, a longtime office manager with a flawless work
record. She loved her home and her children and wished for a
quiet life. Her children were leaving the nest, and Jeanne was
faced with the question of whether she wanted to spend the rest
of her life with Richard. She was pretty tired of the strain.

Richard and Jeanne spent many hours deep in tiresome repetition of their age-old struggle to change each other. To Jeanne,
Richard was immature, insensitive, and irresponsible, and she felt

pain in her heart at what she saw as his lack of caring. Her reading of self-help books led her to hold him up to an image of "the perfect modern man" that was miles from who and what Richard was. To Richard, Jeanne was nagging, dependent, and just too darn sensitive about every little thing. He had been raised in a traditional male household where his father had ruled the roost and brooked no opposition from "the females."

The funny thing was, they really loved one another. In a strange way, it was exactly the things Jeanne criticized in Richard that she loved . . . his spontaneity, his wit, his fearlessness, not to mention his strong, attractive, energetic body. She even enjoyed it that other women found him attractive. The reverse was true for Richard. He loved the sense of peace that he felt when he was with Jeanne. He loved her grace, her delicacy, and her refinement. And above all, he loved her love for him!

One day, Richard's company brought in a Colors trainer to teach selling skills based on the natural differences among customers. The trainer also talked about how the different personalities made different kinds of salespeople. At one point, Richard found himself sitting in a group of people who had identified themselves as Orange. He recognized himself to some degree in every one of them. He enjoyed hearing the trainer describe him and his fellows as a normal, natural, and much-needed segment of the population instead of as a bunch of men and women who never grew up.

As the session went on, he found himself looking across the room at another group of people who had identified themselves as Blue. Suddenly he realized that he could hear Jeanne's voice in every word they spoke: in their wishes and hopes, in their dreams and fears, in their values and needs. He felt the old feeling of love and tenderness rise up inside, and decided then and there to share the Colors experience with Jeanne.

By the time Richard had arranged for Jeanne to join him at a Colors seminar, there were already major changes in their relationship. Richard's views had already begun to change, and he'd used the Colors materials to help Jeanne understand what he had been learning about. They had talked over the differences in their backgrounds, but above all, they had begun to realize that their basic differences were natural, that their personality differences were normal, and that there was nothing wrong with either of them! This realization made all the difference. The pattern of bickering was broken. Evenings of cold silence were replaced by romantic evenings of love and mutual exploration. The children leaving home was no longer a terror for Jeanne. She actually looked forward to the nights when the kids were "sleeping over" with friends, now that she enjoyed "sleeping over" with her husband again. Richard began to understand the way it hurt Jeanne when he was too openly flirtatious, and he found he could let some of that go.

When Richard and Jeanne came to the next seminar, it was plain for all to see that they were discovering each other all over again like a couple of newlyweds. Their marriage is still going strong to this day, more than ten years later.

It has been said that "life is relationship." So what happens when two people's Colors meet? When we study the Colors, we can learn a lot about how we are going to get along with others. Let's turn our attention to mapping out the Colors relationships, discovering where our tensions and conflicts will pop up and what the various Colors have in common with one another. Let's look together at how the relationship will actually work.

Can we know in advance which pairs will be happy and successful and which will not? Can we say which Color makes the right partner for each other Color? Unfortunately—or perhaps fortunately—it's not quite as easy as that. Though we might wish that there were some simple key to matching Colors successfully, there are no cut-and-dried answers. Even two people of the very same Color can get seriously crosswise with each other or bring out shared weaknesses in one another that can spiral into real problems.

As I have traveled around the country meeting thousands of people in Colors seminars, I have seen each of the six possible Colors pairs and the four same-Color couples represented by happy and successful marriages, healthy working relationships, solid and loving parent–child relationships, and so on. When I ask people how many are the same Color as their partners, almost no hands go up. When I ask how many are with someone of different Color than themselves, more than 90 percent of the hands go up ... every time. It is clear that the differences attract each other and that many factors besides temperament bring people together, though many couples share the same basic Color.

It appears to me that sex is a wild card in the coming together of the Colors in couples. I suspect that this helps nature create a rich and varied gene pool. The Colors intrigue each other. They also complement each other with offsetting strengths and values. The key is in getting along. In courtship, however, we don't always show our "true colors." We play up the things that the other person seems to like and play down the rest of our stuff. Once committed to one another in marriage, we gradually relax into our natural ways of being. This image management is natural and human. It has gone on from time out of mind. But how much better it would be to enter into long-term relationships with a realistic understanding of one another, based on the knowledge that all the Colors are good and necessary and that we will always have to adjust to our differences.

We can observe that some matches are more difficult than others, but we can only understand this when we look closely at the specific profiles of the people involved. Most obviously, if my highest Color is your lowest Color, we will nearly always have difficulties. If I am very Gold and have little Orange to speak of, while you are all Orange with little or no Gold, we are likely to rub each other the wrong way a lot. Love and acceptance will have their work cut out for them. You will be jumping in head-first while I am still reading the NO LIFEGUARD sign, day in and day out. I'll be planning for retirement while you're having your fun, wanting to spend the money now! At the same time, our other Colors, Green and Blue in this example, will play a role between us, sometimes helping, sometimes throwing in a monkey wrench.

There is no one kind of successful relationship. For some of us in some relationships, we do not need a great deal of intimacy and caring. We may only need to be businesslike and effective, or independent and mutually supportive. This is certainly true in most business and professional relationships. Mutual acceptance and support are important in these relationships for them to be successful in their purposes. Many quite successful marriages are based on independent lifestyles that come together for purposes of parenting, coordination of financial or business interests, family alliances, management of property, and so forth. Even sex may or may not be a part of the marriage contract. Gold and Green, particularly, may find themselves in very businesslike marriages or may intentionally seek them out. When we really understand natural human differences, we see that relationships can take a nearly infinite variety of forms.

Love is not a Color. In the Eye of Awareness, the Yup'ik symbol mentioned in the second chapter, the center of the circle is an open spiritual space, free of color. It is the energy that transcends all four Colors. When we have this loving energy—that is, when we have open affection, understanding, respect, and acceptance in our hearts—then the natural differences among our Colors will be a source of shared strength, of mutual challenge, of enrichment and variety in our lives. Here in our center, affection, understanding, respect, and acceptance are attitudes that we all can share, whatever our Color. Our friend, lover, spouse, workmate, parent, or child will bring richness to our lives, a richness that can outweigh the various frustrations that are inevitable when our differences are strong.

GOLD IN RELATIONSHIPS

So, my Gold friend, how are you doing with the important responsibilities and burdens you are carrying? Are you on your own? Are you surrounded by the other Colors or do you have some other fairly strong Golds around helping you carry things? Are you struggling to keep the ship afloat pretty much on your own, pursuing your goals and the good of the community? For you, relationships are usually about trying to get the other Colors to pitch in, to do some work—and about trying to get them to do it right! Sometimes it's better for you to just do the task yourself. You'll have to clean up the mess later anyway, if you delegate it.

The other Colors are glad you're there. They will usually admit how much they depend upon you. You are usually so good at working your fingers to the bone, and doing it without letting others know how much stress you're feeling, that they forget how much they need you. I think you would be wise to remind them in concrete terms, and do so fairly often. Take a sick day once in a while just on general principles. This will help others remember. If you build in some reminders for them before your resentment builds up too much, they might even pitch in and help. But when your hurt and resentment mount up and make you sulky and sour, the other Colors will run and hide—or else they will counterattack. Relationships will suffer.

You have very high standards of behavior, of belief, and of appearances. These standards are an important part of your contribution to the community of strengths represented by the Colors. You work hard to meet these standards, and you may expect that you can encourage others to do so as well. This turns out to be a doubtful proposition, however. The other Colors cannot simply conform to your standards any more than you could give them up. Look for their strengths and build standards for them that match what they can do. When they are doing the best at what comes naturally to them, they will be better able to meet your expectations, and they will also be making their best contribution to whatever it is that needs doing.

Gold and Gold

Let's suppose a new person comes into your life. You notice that the first thing they do is to look around and find out what it is that's important to you, what important burdens you are carrying. You notice that they respect your values and priorities. Once they understand what's really important to you, they set about helping in some practical way if they can. They don't offer reassuring hugs. They don't propose some sort of fun or restful escape. They don't offer a ten-page analysis of the situation and tell you what to do about it. They simply, carefully, and skillfully set about being helpful in getting the job done, and done right.

Is it a miracle? No, it's just another Gold who has taken a genuine interest in you. They will follow up on the helpfulness with spontaneous acts of generosity and thoughtful gifts. If it's courtship, it will be solid and enjoyable. If it's a new work relationship, it will be really helpful. In addition, the person will put on their best appearance for you or for your customers or colleagues. They'll be on time for things. If they are late, it won't be because they were goofing around. It will be because of other serious commitments that they are honoring, and this may be the first hint of where difficulties can arise between you.

So much will be right for you about this Gold person. At the same time, however, if they have other commitments—and chances are they will—you will find that they are sometimes caught between them, and you may not always come first in line for time and attention. Especially after the honeymoon is over. In a marriage, you can expect that their loyalty to their family of origin will be as strong as yours, and you know how strong that is.

Along the same lines, if you have differences of opinion about important values or social issues, work approaches on the job, religious differences, parenting, sexuality, or other behavioral differences at home, your partner will be just as stubborn as you are. Here comes "my way or the highway," which is especially strong with other Golds.

With a Gold spouse, you will share the strong-willed, traditional lifestyle and a firm and steady pace of living. Unless one of you craves a bit more spice, a more adventuresome sexuality, a bit more sentiment, or a bit more intellectual stimulation, Gold and Gold will get along well. The checkbook will always balance. The yard will be mowed. The family, both nuclear and extended, will be remembered and cared for. Surprises will be kept to a minimum.

Gold and Blue

Here's someone who will join you in keeping the peace. They will do it for very different reasons than yours. For them, emotional harmony is the highest goal in relationships. They avoid emotional pain wherever possible . . . both in themselves and in others. You, on the other hand, keep the peace as part of your duty to the success and stability of the family or work group. Between the two of you, the people around you will be taken care of.

You'll know the Blues by the tone of sympathy they bring to your conversations, especially when they find out how hard you are working, the stress you are under. The Blue will be more likely at first to give you a hug or put flowers on your desk than to pitch right in with the work itself. You will find them to be most concerned with the state of your heart—your emotional heart, that is. "How are you feeling?" "How do you feel about it?" "How does this feel?" are the questions most often asked by Blues. They live in their feelings, and they will look to your feelings as the key to your relationship. If you are happy with them, it won't matter to them that quarterly profits are down, that the well has run dry, or that there's nothing in the refrigerator for dinner.

You will find that the Blues are attracted to the same social settings as you. If you are working in a service industry, a social-service agency, or an elementary school, there you'll find Blues on every side, along with other Golds. Once again, they are there out of the needs of their hearts, while you are there out of a duty to the community. They will be focused on the interpersonal process and relationships. You will be getting the job done. In a marriage, they will be looking for expressions of feelings. They want to hear "I love you" several times a day, whereas you would be content with some help around the house, remembered birthdays and special occasions, and a good social impression as a solid couple. They will want sex to be full of romantic words and gestures of assurance that you really care, and in return they will be deeply generous and inventive in their lovemaking. For you, it must fit into a busy schedule, and nothing too out of the ordinary.

You will share a deep concern for the children, a deep sense of parental responsibility. For you, this will show itself in the practical care you give, the safe environment you provide, the expectations you insist upon. Love will be shown by all the things you do and give. For the Blue, much more will be expressed in words, emotional expressions, and gestures of affection. If you are facing a life-threatening surgery, you will want the children to know where their next meal is coming from. The Blue will want them to know they are loved. They will want to pass on a last word or two of wisdom, while you're making sure they know where the will is and who gets Grandfather's pocket watch.

You will find the Blue a bit hard to understand when it comes to what they call *authenticity* or some such word. You will be carrying on quite successfully in a certain course of action when suddenly the Blue will bail out or call a halt because it "doesn't fit," or "it's just not me!" When you dig a little deeper, you'll find that the success they're seeking isn't really much about money, security, or recognition, but about some sort of personal realization or development that's hard as heck to figure out. All you can do is love or tolerate it. It goes with the package. The good news is that the Blue will generally love and look out for the best in you, celebrate your happiness along with all your other lovely emotions, empathize with your sorrows and feelings of failure, and let you off your own hook when it comes to your high standards.

Gold and Orange

Look out! Here comes some excitement. There's an old Chinese curse that goes, "May you live in interesting times." For the Orange, this is no curse. It's what they hope for every day. I knew a strong Orange in high school who used to sit in math class looking out the window and wishing and hoping that the butte south of town would erupt just for the sheer fun of it (and so that school would let out!).

You can feel the energy when an Orange walks into the room. Except for the few quiet Oranges, their bodies are almost never still. They love fast-paced action and lots of stimulation. They can work with the radio on, study while pedaling an exercise bike or jogging on a treadmill. They are deeply independent in action, automatically resisting authority unless it squares with where they want to go anyway.

If you meet an Orange with a strong Gold second Color, they will show you how to be Gold with energy and enthusiasm, how to make work a game, to compete with yourself and others just to make it interesting. Your love life won't involve just quiet intimacies and thoughtful gifts; rather, the Orange will bring impulsive expressions of affection and fun and a vigorous sexuality. They may forget your anniversary, but every day will have the quality of a celebration.

When it comes to loyalty, they will be tempted when they are away from you to love the one they're with. Depending upon circumstances, and depending upon the strength of their other Colors, they may or may not succumb. I have known Golds who had open-marriage agreements with their spouses, but for most Golds, this loyalty issue will be one hard thing about pairing up with an Orange. Really, it's more about living up to commitments and agreements than about loyalty per se. Orange lives in the here and now, and words that were spoken weeks, months, or years ago seem pretty far away when the moment is full of new opportunities.

Oranges are very nonjudgmental. "Live and let live" is more natural to them than "my way or the highway." Still, they very much share your Gold concrete practicality. They love money and the things it can buy, though they want to spend it now while you might want to save it for the future. They love good appearances, though their ideas about fashion may be a bit more flamboyant than yours . . . maybe more than a bit. They like the fresh and new where you prefer the tried and true.

As a couple, you will have the energy and the organization to do whatever you put your minds to. There will probably be some head-butting along the way, but if the two of you understand these differences and see the value of your individual contributions, the sky's the limit for accomplishment.

Gold and Green

This is where things get serious. When Gold and Green are attracted to each other, it is usually around a very businesslike approach to life. Unless Orange is also strong in one or both, Green and Gold combine talents for serious purposes. Neither you nor the Green is much for devil-may-care, kick-off-your-shoes fun and games, unless you are in the right place at the right time, unless you have made sure that the situation is safe, the curtains are drawn, and business is buttoned down tight.

Once again, depending upon the mix of your other Colors, you and your Green partner are not inclined to indulge in romantic nonsense. You have deeper satisfactions. Real accomplishment. Quality in what you do, what you think, what you believe. Down-to-earth matters. Achievement. Freedom from foolishness, childishness, error. Perfection is a high goal. It involves commitment and ability. Between you, you and your Green partner may just have what it takes to reach it. But you both know that your performance can always be improved upon.

If you are attracted to a serious Green, the chances are that you are also attracted to the toughest, most difficult and exacting sort of work and activities. You may be in the professions with lives depending upon you. You may be practicing skills that require utmost dedication and constant work. Your Green partner will either join you in that work, contributing their powerful analytical intelligence, or they will be pursuing similar interests of their own. This may result in your leading parallel lives, respecting one another's endeavors, meeting outside of work for times of mutual appreciation, rest, and the joy that comes from someone understanding your accomplishments.

Difficulties will arise when the Green's endless analysis begins to impair your demand for action and productivity. For them, there simply can never be enough data, and the latest fact uncovered can turn an entire plan right on its head. Deadlines may seem meaningless as the Green follows the pace of the information instead of the pace of the project.

At home, the Green spouse may fail to take notice of the detail work involved in maintaining the household. Other interests occupy them, and these other interests may look to you like "just sitting around" as they spend their time reading, watching the latest documentary or film on TV, or pursuing quiet hobbies in the workshop, while you maintain the wardrobe and environment, or try to keep up appearances for the neighbors. Green pays little attention to appearances. It's the quality of the content that matters to them. Appearances seem superficial, and people who focus on appearances may seem shallow to the intellectual Green.

Green brings an inventiveness and exploratory quality to sex. Their interests may explore directions that are a bit too unusual for your tastes. Gold and Green is not usually the relationship that sparks fireworks and causes the earth to move. This is the relationship that designs and builds the stable platform from which the fireworks may be fired, and invents and markets the machinery to measure the movements of the earth.

BLUE IN RELATIONSHIPS

It must have been a Blue who said that "life is relationship." As a strong Blue, you may not live entirely for relationships, but whatever you live for, your active, emotional heart will be reacting to relationships pretty much all the time. You'll value justice and abhor injustice. You'll spend much time in sympathy and compassion for the downtrodden, worrying about mistreated children and animals, and wishing the best for underdogs everywhere. Relationships are deeply moving to Blues. They are the source of belonging and the field in which life takes place. They are also the source of most of the pain in your life.

As a Blue, you feel this special sensitivity in all your relationships. You want this sensitivity from others, but many others simply don't share it. You want to bring out the best in everyone you meet and you expect others to share this wish . . . but not everyone does. You take criticism personally, whereas many people thrive on being critical. For a strong Blue, sex is completely wrapped up with emotion, commitment, and romantic love. For many non-Blues, especially Greens and Oranges, sex is just sex—a good time, a release, or a well-deserved reward.

Blue and Blue

When you meet another Blue, there may be a special sharing that takes place. If you have been living with mostly Oranges, Golds, and Greens, it will be a relief to meet someone who shares your Blue feelings. You will find that you have much in common. If you meet as intimate friends or lovers, chances are you will share your dreams, your emotions, your rich fantasy life, and a mutually affirming sexuality. If you meet in a work setting, you will likely share opinions about the culture of your workplace, whether it's people-friendly and caring, or cold, efficient, and hard on employees. You will find that similar things make you angry and other things make both of you happy or sad.

It is a common experience when two Blues are in a relationship that you may reinforce the patterns you have in common, including your difficulties. You may find yourselves spiraling down into a shared depression or gloominess as you discover your agreements about hard and negative things in life. Of course, you may also share and support each other's joys. For better or worse, you will both be likely to give special attention to feelings and emotions. Feelings last a long time for Blues, therefore your past experiences, positive or negative, will have important effects over time.

If you marry a Blue, this mutual reinforcement of feelings will have a major impact on the quality of your marriage. If you are considering marriage, it will be important to pay attention to which way this shared feeling process commonly takes you. Courtship is a time of putting your best foot forward, and Blues are extremely good at adjusting to the wants of others, but you can always find subtle hints of the underlying patterns that may become major elements of your relationship over time.

Blue and Gold

As a Blue, when you meet a Gold, your emotional sensitivity must allow for their emphasis on order and productivity. In a lover, you will be looking for the typical elements of intimacy: gentle touches, quiet moments, deep sharing, loyalty, creativity, and the expression of feelings. These will be the things you try to communicate to the Gold. Golds are often happy to meet Blues in this way. They enjoy sharing these things, especially when the sharing contributes to a successful relationship. That's what Golds want: a successful, solid, orderly, productive relationship.

Golds want to be appreciated for their hard work and their

good qualities, and as a Blue, you are more than willing to give them the recognition for which they are longing. As the relationship settles down for the long term, your Gold partner will live more and more fully in their hardworking, practical style. Some of the delightful moments of intimate sharing and subtle tenderness will tend to fall away as the Gold settles into deeply held values about hard work, productivity, maintaining good appearances, and fulfilling social responsibility.

Your style of following inspiration, of "leading with your heart," and your tendency toward dreaminess will bump into the Gold's practicality and reliance on the past, on precedent and procedure. If you are trying to build a house together, you will bring many innovative ideas, even eccentric ones, while the Gold will be deeply concerned with maintaining an acceptable image in the community.

Your sense of forgiveness and sympathy will clash with the Gold's more conservative morality and tendency to judge people according to traditional standards. Your intimate expressions of love, affection, and appreciation will meet the Gold's style of showing love by giving gifts and doing things for others. They may look for gifts and practical help as evidence of your affection for them while you are sending them great waves of love and affection through your own language and gestures—which they may not understand or appreciate. You may come to feel that their reliance on things and their practicality are really not very romantic; you may even come to doubt an authentic love for you simply because it's expressed in a different way than you're accustomed to.

Unless Gold is a pretty strong influence in you as well, you will have a hard time dealing with their critical nature, their commitment to standards and results, and their impatience with sentimentality. For all these differences, however, you and Gold have much in common. You both value good work and cooperation in the community, helpfulness and order in relationships. If you are working together in a service occupation, you will often find yourselves natural allies—though once again the Gold will be more focused on a well-running organization while you are dedicated to well-served clients. As a couple, you will find yourselves sharing community activities and a genuine concern for the welfare of others.

Obviously, conflict will arise when the Gold's emphasis on duty, roles, appearances, and productivity come up against your emphasis on persons, feelings, emotional harmony, and creativity. When you fight with each other, you will tend to accuse the Gold of being rigid and unfeeling. The Gold will counter that you are overly emotional, romantic, dreamy, naive, and wishy-washy. You will make up when you remember and appreciate your common ground. Service and good relationships often bridge the natural differences between you. Together, you carry tremendous responsibility in the community.

Blue and Orange

When you meet an Orange, there may be an immediate dislike, or there may be a strong attraction. To you as a Blue, the Orange will appear to have a freedom and a sense of fun and creativity that you might dearly love to possess yourself. You may envy this freedom or you may resent it. Either way, as you become closer to one another, there is likely to be a strong reaction between you. Blue and Orange are the nonlinear, right-brain Colors. This means emotion and sensation. Orderly analysis and strict structures do not come naturally to either Color. Feelings run high—but for the Orange, feelings are physical and they are of the moment, here and now. Feelings are simpler for them than they are for you, and they don't last so long. Tomorrow is a new day. Yesterday's argument is past and gone. Whereas for you, yesterday is a live issue. As is last week and ten years ago. The Blue heart has a long memory.

Blues often fall in love with Oranges for their physical grace and emotional freedom. But with Orange, a sting can be waiting. Orange moves easily from relationship to relationship. Good-byes are not difficult. Hellos are natural and comfortable. For you, as we have seen, every good-bye is like a little death, and even something as simple as not being noticed by someone can feel like being cut off and thrown away.

This is the price of Blue loving Orange. Orange will not naturally take care of the Blue's deep sensitivity in relationships. They will forget anniversaries and birthdays. They will be deeply involved in a game or an activity and completely miss your cues that you need their attention, their reassurance, their affection. There is no malice or lack of affection in this, though the Blue tends to see it that way. It is simply that Orange is doing what they are doing at any given moment. Their basic message to all of us is, "Lighten up. Do something. Get back on the horse. You're tougher than you think you are."

It's wonderful when Blue learns the lessons that Oranges are teaching. They can help you find the freedom they enjoy. Their creativity fits in well with yours. It enriches yours and takes it in directions you haven't even thought of, or have been afraid to attempt. They can help you lift your spirits when you're "blue," and Blues are frequently "blue." Oranges are not intimidated by authority or tyrannized by rules and bureaucracy. They can show you how to "just do it" and not always wait around for the approval of some authority figure. They live by the motto "I'd rather be told 'Stop!' than be told 'No!'"—so they boldly and blithely go off in creative directions that, as a Blue, you wouldn't dare.

Orange tends to prefer general camaraderie to quiet intimacy. For the Orange, sex is playful, often even athletic. Those quiet moments with long lingering glances and whispered intimacies are not a necessary part of their sexuality. They live in the body primarily, and sex is about sensation for them. You may find the Orange to be impatient with your need for a certain atmosphere before sex can be enjoyable. As a Blue, you will find that when you are upset about something, especially something in your relationship, sex just isn't the thing for you. In all honesty, Blues are not above withholding sex when they are angry or upset. This is part of Blues' survival strategy in life, which often involves passive-aggressive strategies that make up for their lack of pure, straightforward aggression. For your Orange partner, on the other hand, sex may be just the thing to take their mind off whatever is troubling them . . . or troubling you!

You'll find that for Orange, life is a game, and winning is the best thing of all. They love risk and the excitement of new sensations. Depending upon their second Color, you may find them quite unable to join you in your sensitive concerns for others and for the world. They are strongly independent and take care of their own first. They tend to be impatient with your willingness to sacrifice, because it goes against their deeply held appreciation for individual responsibility and autonomy. They will make an exception, however, when your self-sacrifice works to their bene-fit. Why look a gift horse in the mouth, eh?

Unless you have some strong Orange in you, you will have a hard time with their impulsiveness, their sensation-seeking, and their inattention to sentiment. As we have seen, Oranges make up a bit more than one-third of the population according to the liter-ature. Only a fraction of these are extremely Orange. As with all potential partners, friends, or associates, the power of the other Colors will soften the impact of their primary Color. Take these things into account when deciding how far you wish to bring Orange into your life. Your creativity and your reliance on things other than cold reason and logic to guide you give you much in common. Your ability to experience real joy and excitement together can offset much that pushes you and Orange apart.

Blue and Green

Green shares with you the inward life. You look inward for guidance from your feelings. Green looks inward to their reason and understanding. Like you, Green is sensitive to input from the outside world, but their sensitivity often leads them to isolate and protect themselves, whereas you may set out to interact with the world and try to make it safe and right. Both of you share an abil-ity to find value in solitary activities and various kinds of medita-tion.

Greens have a great deal to teach you. They are able to make boundaries in life, whereas for you, life is all one big event, and it usually seems to be all mixed together. Work and home, commu-nity and family, religion and daily life ... everything flows together for you. Green can make compartments, putting work in its place, home in its place, community in its place, and so on. They know how to hold their tongues in situations where you may well blurt out your feelings inappropriately. They know how to say no in situations where you can't seem to keep from saying yes.

You may fall in love with their rationality, their ability to explain, to discover reasons and the logic of situations. Above all, you may admire, even envy, their autonomy. Green is as independent as Orange, if not more so, since Orange seeks out camaraderie. Greens think for themselves, and they are usually not afraid to disagree with others. They tend to put the facts ahead of relationships and are not willing to compromise the data just to keep someone happy or friendly toward them. For you, of course, the hostility of others is painful.

Tension between you and the Green will begin to arise when their logic and their love of problem solving run into your feelings and sensitivities. You will share a sadness, and they'll offer a solution. They will expect the solution to resolve the sadness and will become impatient with you if you would rather stay with the sadness. You will communicate an enthusiasm, and they will toss off a bit of logic or a few facts that completely pop your bubble. You will approach them for an intimate moment and they will turn away into an interest or preoccupation of their own. You will interpret silence as negative. They will see it as neutral or, better yet, a relief. You will look for words of appreciation or of love and affection, and they will be silent, letting their actions speak.

For you, sharing a feeling with someone makes it more real. For the Green, talking about deep feelings may seem to cheapen the feelings, to make them trivial. Greens have a quiet and deliberate emotional style, often seeming quite cool, even cold. Greens' sexuality often has an almost intellectual quality about it, far from the luxurious intimacy and romanticism that you enjoy so much. Greens like sex for its own sake, and for its inventive possibilities. Still, they definitely have some deep feelings. They care. They want to belong. They want to be appreciated. They just don't want to chat about it. Small talk doesn't interest them, and deep sharing is very difficult. This makes for some long silences when you're wanting to talk about everything under the sun.

You will probably be much more social overall than your Green friend, lover, or colleague. When you are seeking out human contact for its own sake, Green is finding ways to avoid having to deal with it. You will need to develop some independent relationships in order to take care of yourself in a marriage to a Green. They will have many independent interests of their own, but socializing probably won't be one of them. Greens can become very controlling and possessive when they are insecure; you may need to assert your social needs while at the same time reassuring them of your loyalty.

Unless you have some pretty strong Green in yourself, you will have a hard time with their tough skeptical nature, their impatience with your dreamy enthusiasms, their coolness and unwillingness to share feelings, and their stubborn independence. On the other hand, you share the inner world in its entirety between you. Blue and Green together can lead lives of deep meaning and spiritual search. While Gold and Orange provide the energy and structure of life, you and your Green partner will deepen the experience.

ORANGE IN RELATIONSHIPS

I'll keep this moving right along, my Orange friend. I know you've got things to do, places to go, people to see. Ah yes, but what people? That's the relationship question. Who are the good work partners, the best lovers? Who is enjoyable in small doses and who is a candidate for the long-term relationship? Are you even thinking about the long term? Are you looking for a life mate or a playmate? Do you want someone who will hit the deck at full speed, or who will at least make zero to sixty in eight seconds or less? Or are you looking for someone who can slow you down a bit, help with the details, keep an eye on the clock, remind you about the bank closing, the taxes coming due? Or maybe you're ready for some romance. Hearts and flowers. Sweet nothings in your ear. Maybe even make a baby or two. Or perhaps it's time in your life to study something, to really learn, to get at the meat of some subject that will take you where you want to go. Who do you want to go with you?

If you're like most Oranges, you're going to value a sense of humor. That means someone who doesn't take themselves or anyone else too seriously. A lot of good Orange humor comes out of a distaste for conceit, for people who are puffed up, who are too high on themselves. These are the folks you may enjoy bringing down a peg, and doing it in a way that shows them that you know something, too. This is probably not a firm basis for a long-term relationship, though it may be good for a few laughs in the short run. At work you may have no choice. You may have to put up with the boss or move on. But in a friend or a lover, you can choose.

To go along with that humor, you probably would appreciate a generally upbeat and active disposition. Not too much gloom and doom. As little whining as possible. Not too much sitting around and introspecting. An unexamined life may not be worth living, but an unlived life isn't worth examining, either. On the other hand, it might be nice to find someone who does enough thinking and reading and so on to carry on a decent conversation. A little wit, for sure. Dull people need not apply.

You might want to get with somebody who specializes in some of the things you aren't attracted to. Balancing the checkbook, for example, and of course contributing something to the bank account. Cleaning house. Keeping the wardrobe in good shape. You like to look sharp, and you like decent surroundings. It's all that upkeep that gets you down. Some people actually don't mind doing it as much as you do. You might be able to strike a deal where you take care of some things you enjoy and they take care of some things you don't. Deal making comes naturally to you, doesn't it? Right along with making life a game and enjoying a good win–win?

Of course, a little style wouldn't hurt, a little flair, a bit of creativity in outlook and presentation. It doesn't have to be Miss America or Mr. Olympia if the style and attitude are there. Casual. Cool. Active. Helpful. Nonjudgmental. Nothing to it. You must meet half a dozen people like that every time you go to the grocery store. *Not!*

You're probably going to want a socially active life. Most Oranges are quite gregarious. You love to chat and play and generally be around other human beings in friendly, low-stakes camaraderie or high-energy competition. For many of you, this group activity bridges easily into having several different romantic partners; from ongoing flirtation and bawdy humor right on into bed. Not so easy for most of the other Colors. Between fear of the consequences, fear of the body, fear of triangles, and just plain fear, the other Colors may actually hold that sexual energy of yours against you. If you're getting into something permanent, you'd better get clear about this issue. Your casual enjoyment may have a way of blowing up in your face down the road.

Getting into work groups and teams, you are a natural cheerleader and a goer/doer from the get-go. The work team needs your humor and excitement, but count on it, they also want more compulsiveness than you're comfortable providing. The clock, the calendar, the policies and procedures manual, the memo, that strong Gold in the next office or acting as crew chief . . . these can all be your friends. Stay on top of them and your relationships will prosper. Try to dodge them or stall them and it rarely works for long. Instead, become a speed reader. Learn touch typing. Make it a competition. Use your quick skills to beat the game on its own terms; ten minutes a day at your speed will put you well ahead of the pack. Then you'll be crew chief. You can do the micromanaging and be a nuisance to everyone else about deadlines and quality benchmarks. Or else work your way into self-employment and hire a Gold to keep the books and manage your schedule.

Orange and Orange

Now, this should be pure fun, right? Somebody just like you. Or are they? First of all, what's their second Color? An Orange/Green can cut you up with sarcasm and a devastating wit. An Orange/Gold has climbed the management ladder with drive, ambition, and an orderly approach and may just leave you in the dust. An Orange/Blue really cares about other people's feelings and may shake a finger at you about how long it's been since you called Mom. So first of all ... there's Orange and then there's Orange.

Now, maybe they really are just like you. Impatient, fun-loving, living in the here and now. If you've both been loved and cared for and have a healthy respect for yourselves and each other, the sky's the limit. It can be a really great time. Sex will be over the top! Of course, they can't keep track of their bank balance any better than you can. They love to live beyond their means as much as you do. They have the boss or the teacher down on their necks just like you do. They love a clean house but don't love to follow the routine that keeps it that way.

When two Oranges interact, there will often be a pattern of winding up or winding down. Maybe I wind down when you wind down and wind up when you wind up. Maybe the more I wind up, the more you wind down. Maybe the more you wind up, the more I wind down. For example, maybe when my voice gets louder, you tend to get quieter. Or maybe when you get louder, I get louder.

Two Oranges who both wind up can wind up pretty tight. When I get louder and you get louder, too, it can result in some pretty noisy conversation! Or take irritability and quick temper. I snap at you and you snap back and pretty soon, these emotions can wind up into quite a storm. The good news is that for Orange, when the spat is over, it's over. It can be like the sun coming out after a thunderstorm—almost instantaneous relief and the ability to just go on as if nothing ever happened. This is endlessly astonishing to Blues, for whom emotions have long tails.

Orange and Gold

Here is one of the most ancient and common arguments of all: spontaneity versus order, freedom versus rules, entertainment versus earnestness. It is also one of the most ancient of complementarities, a lovely batch of balancing strengths. Orange and Gold are the two concrete, action- and results-oriented Colors. You won't find that Gold partner or colleague spending much time navel-gazing or going in for endless hair-splitting. Action is the order of the day for both of you. Your Gold buddy will bring the map and the flashlight, and you will bring the excitement and the love of risk and adventure. Between you, you just might have what it takes to get the mountain climbed, the jungle mapped, the source of the Nile tracked down.

Of course, all the way up the Nile you'll argue with each other. The Gold will tell you that you are childish and immature. You will counter that they're rigid and uncreative. In return, you will be told to settle down and face facts, to which you will reply that life is too short to settle and that you were the one who had the guts to take on this adventure in the first place. If your Gold partner gets a little pompous and conceited, you will find yourself spontaneously coming up with practical-joke strategies. They will provide the nose in the air, you will provide the banana peel under their shoe. They'll inflate the balloon, you'll provide the pin.

On the other hand, your Gold will sure be good looking, making the best of their assets, showing real care for their appearance. The image won't be flashy, but it will have class. They'll have nice things. Once again, class. They'll be successful, too. They will have done what it takes to be sure that they are. While you have played the angles, exploited your natural talents to the max, and taken every shortcut you could find to get where you are as quickly and painlessly as possible, the Gold will have planned, studied, practiced, met the standards one by one, and earned the paper, the title, or the position. They'll have earned a lot of the things you would love to have.

You and the Gold will share a deep impatience with slow-moving, dreamy, intellectual, and romantic types. Fortunately for you, you and your Gold counterparts make up a substantial majority of the human race at any given time, while the dreamers and analyzers are left in the minority. The good Lord in infinite evolutionary wisdom selects action and energy, Orange and Gold, as primary over the more passive, responsive temperaments, the Blues and the Greens. Still, your Gold partner will probably act more cautiously than you would in most situations. Sex will be more appropriate and constrained. It may well be a Gold driving that poky car ahead of you, the one that just cost you your chance to make it through the intersection on yellow instead of having to take it on red so that you now have to visit with this nice police-man.

Orange and Blue

Whether in work, in friendship, or as a couple, your own active passions will have more appeal than the spectator activities of art appreciation, sports watching, or reading the words of others. Obviously, there are many exceptions to these observations. But what's important in the Orange–Blue relationship will always be some form of spontaneous creativity, an openness to the new, a lack of standard judgments in favor of a gut-level appreciation of anything open, energetic, freewheeling, fresh, passionate, perceptive, whole.

Practicality and concrete order go out the window in favor of the first impression, the quick association, the laugh or the tear; for things done for the fun of it, for the challenge of it, for the excitement of it. The body and its sensations loom large in the Orange–Blue world. The heart and its "rays and pangs" is like a furnace generating power, heat, and emotion at the center of the organism. Physical movement comes out of the musculature and the heart. It is ecstatic and creative just for its own sake. Everything exists for its own sake.

Time is rhythmic and circular for Orange and Blue. The past is judged alongside the present on an equal footing. It has no special authority just because it has stood the test of time. For the Orange, the standards of the past are to be competed with, improved upon . . . always the personal best is out there to be reached for.

The really good news for the Orange about Blue is that Blue really loves passionately. Your Blue partner will appreciate things about you that you don't even know about yourself. They will admire, even envy your freedom, the way you seem to live without pain while they are feeling their own pain and everybody else's. *Passion* is a key word in this relationship. In a work setting, the Blue will want to find ways to feature your skill, talent, and creativity. They may fight with you to get you to be more sensitive to others' feelings, but they are not likely to join forces with the Golds who may want to put a muzzle on you.

In a marriage, Blue loves to love you. As long as there is some romance, some gentleness and intimacy, sex will be good . . . creative and adventuresome. When your Blue partner's out of sorts, however—feeling used or unappreciated, or unhappy about completely unrelated things—sex is not only unpleasant, it's practically impossible. Far from being an enjoyable escape from emotional unpleasantness, sex must come from a positive emotional background or Blue won't play. If they stuff their feelings and go ahead just to please you, the bad energy will accumulate.

When Blues have had enough, they blow big time. "Long fuse, big bang": That's Blue. When they blow, I call it the Samson syndrome. I imagine the Blue standing between two support pillars that hold up the entire temple, their long hair flowing, their rage at injustice cranked up to ten, and suddenly they pull the whole world down around the ears of the gathered multitude. That's the fed-up Blue. And they are especially good at it, since they have an instinct for the jugular. During the buildup phase, they have been protecting your vulnerable points. Now, at rage time, they head straight for them. In addition, Blue feelings don't go away immediately the way your Orange ones do. It's a long time, if ever, before the Blue gets over it—whatever it is.

Orange and Green

Now, here comes somebody who goes places you may never have really explored, like the reference room at the library. You'd be surprised at what they are looking for in there. You probably think they're searching for facts and information about some fourteenth-century monastic order or the essential principle of the solenoid, and they may be doing just that. If you look a little closer, though, you'll discover that what they are really digging out of those musty old tomes is power. In the Green world, whether it's the university, the Mensa study group, the engine repair shop, the vegetable garden, or the stock market, knowledge is power. As an Orange, chances are you share with the Green a love of power. You gather it in order to win in open combat. They gather it to have and to hold and to measure out in careful, strategic doses.

You may well enter into a strategic alliance to fight against having power exerted over you. You won't be told what to do. Green won't be told what to think. Between you, authority figures will have a rough time. You both probably enjoy exercising power, each in your own way. Green likes to keep a low profile with power, and being the boss may require more "bossiness" than the Green enjoys exerting. You, on the other hand, pretty much thrive on the exercise.

You will be more of a team player than the Green, who tends to prefer a more solitary and independent relationship to the group. They enjoy making their input from a little distance and often leave it to others to carry out their insights. The Green becomes a long-distance runner. The Orange likes a nice line of scrimmage.

You will be generally more impetuous than your Green friend or partner. They will prefer to think things through in advance, to anticipate the bumps in the road, to apply just the right leverage at just the right places to get the job done with a minimum of effort and hassle and, above all, a minimum risk of failure or humiliation. Humiliation is what it means to lose, to fail, to make a goof. Looking stupid is just about the ultimate horror to most Greens. They are generally relentless in their analytical criticism of the performance of others, and equally so of their own. Their own failures and humiliations are just about the only places where Greens will turn away from the facts, hiding their errors or putting the best face on them when they can.

Often the Orange spouse will tell me that it's common for their Green partner to "suddenly" decide that they want to move forward on an idea that was proposed to them six months ago. Of course, the Orange had almost forgotten about the darn idea in waiting for a response. Green wheels grind slowly, but they grind exceedingly fine.

Sexually, both of you will have considered open marriage unless your Blue or Gold influences have prevented it. I recommend that you handle this issue aboveboard with one another rather than doing it on the sly. Greens are vulnerable to feeling that they have been made fools of, and you are vulnerable to feeling tricked by the Green's excellent strategies. Better to put it on the table and have some clear agreements. When the agreements are in place and working, the sex will be inventive. The Green will probably take you places you have never thought of before while you provide the rocket fuel that keeps the fire burning.

As work colleagues, you will each have your eye on the prize in your own way. Once again, putting this on the table will prevent misunderstandings and bloodletting. Find the win–wins between you. If there are to be win–lose transactions, let the outside competition take the losses rather than either of the two of you. Competition can be fun, though, as you well know. Greens can enjoy it, too, especially if it gives them a chance to demonstrate their smarts. Nice open competition with well-defined playing fields and some clear rules can generate a lot of energy in service to the goals of the team. Covert, high-stakes competition for perks within the organization (like promotions) can leave blood on the tracks. Don't deny the combative aspect of your natures. Really, there's no use in trying—they're there for both of you. Get them out in the open and put them in service to your outfit.

This can work in a marriage, too. Banter. Clever repartee. Open competition. Play fighting. Real fighting. Fair fighting. The thrill of victory, the agony of defeat. Many marriages continue from "I do" unto death with this constant spirit of battle as the glue that holds the couple together. Blues and Golds have a hard time understanding it, but it's none of their business anyway. Now, if you are an Orange/Blue and your partner is a Green/Gold, the spirit of the battle can easily turn sour since it may really be a battle between your second Colors, Blue and Gold. They don't know how to fight for the fun of it. They actually think that winning and losing may have eternal consequences. Fortunately for the true Orange–Green relationship, time is fleeting. Nothing lasts long. Round Seven. When you hear the bell, come out fighting. And don't forget to check out the gorgeous girl carrying the round-number card. Ah, Orange.

GREEN IN RELATIONSHIPS

Greens, I would like to invite you to turn your cool, appraising eye on relationships. Though I know that you tend to be very sufficient unto yourself, even the Greenest of us seeks companionship: perhaps wishing to raise children, perhaps hoping to find someone to share diverse or specialized interests, someone to share a physical relationship, and—above all, perhaps—someone to appreciate the intelligence and insight that you possess in abundance. Naturally, in addition, there are the inevitable and unavoidable relationships involved in work and professional activities.

Most Greens report that they have felt pressure in their lives to be more social, to be part of the group, the work team, or the family. Your need for independence in thinking and analyzing contributes to an impression of cool distance. Your needs for space, solitude, and time for processing add to people's misunderstanding. Your high demand for personal integrity has probably made it difficult for you to conform to the terms of belonging of the groups with which you've been involved. The subtlety and complexity of your thoughts get thrown into disarray when you try to fit in with irrationality, rigidity, or excess emotion. The gears don't mesh.

Greens have told me how wonderful it is to find someone who is really interested in their thoughts, really appreciative of their special knowledge and understandings, someone who really admires their wit and intelligence. "Whew!" they say; "what a relief not to be completely alone." Of course, in the next breath they express their gratitude for the space and solitude they still have. Or else they share their frustration with the loss of these precious commodities if they've had to give them up to make a relationship work.

Above all, they report what a joy it is to be appreciated for their unique contributions to the unfolding of the group, whether it is the academic discipline, the work group, the family, or the marriage. Greens often have deep fear of being perceived as uncaring and isolated. Your caution about communicating your deepest thoughts and feelings, your dedication to the integrity of your values and style, may have given the impression that you don't care to belong. At the same time, your ability to analyze and solve serious problems confronting the group demonstrates your contribution and the real value of your participation. Your commitment of time, effort, money, and thought to your spouse demonstrates your love. You make a contribution on your own terms. Your sexuality is not necessarily tied together with deep intimacy and personal affection. You show love in your own way. You always have. If only these things were recognized, the three little words wouldn't be necessary.

All of these challenges may be unfamiliar to you if you've been raised with people who have valued you as you are. In that fortunate case, you will know your own worth. You will approach relationships with a confidence born of that knowledge. The majority of your Green brethren will envy you your good luck as they deal with relationships filled with misunderstanding. If you know or work with other Greens, you will see all sorts of variations on these themes.

Green and Green

Ah, here comes someone with a mind! Great. Let's learn together. When Greens get together, there will either be an appreciative and understanding silence, or there will be a very interesting conversation.

If they have interests in common, there will be much to talk about in that field. If each person's premises and conclusions agree with those of the other, the conversation will move harmoniously and enjoyably through the information. There may be some competition about who knows best, but with common premises it should work itself out nicely. If the premises and conclusions are different, there will be a lively dispute, perhaps even a battle. Depending upon how much Orange the Green people share, this battle can be fun and exciting—or it can become bitter and divisive. You will have to be convinced before you will change your conclusions, and so will your partner or colleague. Or you may have to agree to disagree. This process can range from matters of child-rearing to marital behavior or serious professional disputation. Your tolerant attitude will usually come to your aid in dealing with differences, but the differences will not simply go away on their own.

In all your relationships, much depends upon your sense of safety with regard to the chance of looking foolish. As I've said before, humiliation is usually about the worst possible relationship experience for Greens. Discovering that you have been dead wrong, publicly, about something important; blundering into a position of illogic; being laughed at for your errors—these are deeply painful moments for most Greens. Other Greens are very good at discovering and pointing out such goofs, and they may not be particularly gentle about doing so. Thus differences about facts or principles can take on a very high-stakes energy for you in your relationships with other Greens.

On the other hand, no one can understand what these situations are like as well as another Green, and if you meet in an attitude of love and respect, your lives can be deeply enriched. It means a lot to have shared the "Green experience" growing up . . . the solitude, the intellectual interests, the social awkwardness, the sexual curiosity, the pressure to conform . . . it can be a wonderful thing to meet someone who understands. As with all Colors, the influence of your second Color will make a profound difference in these matters. Once you resolve these Green–Green issues, you will be left to enjoy or to struggle with the differences and commonalities that arise from your second Colors.

Green and Blue

When you cross paths with a Blue, you may find them to be rather mysterious . . . illogical, emotional, intuitive, tangled up in half a dozen confused relationships, enmeshed with their families, boundaryless, interested in all sorts of nonrational philosophies and experiences . . . just what the heck is going on with them?

It may be good news or bad news that they seem to be very interested in you! They care what you think and seem to have affection for you even before they know you very well. Instead of arguing with you when you have a difference, at least at first they try to understand. They may even express agreement, changing their position to make it harmonious with yours. You may not trust this kind of flexibility until you "get it" that what they care about is not the intellectual content so much as harmony in the relationship. For Blue, peace is often more important than intellectual integrity. They are willing to be wrong if it serves to smooth relations. Your life, on the other hand, is probably filled with situations in which you have chosen to be right instead of superficially happy.

Even more puzzling and sometimes annoying is the Blue's emotionalism. They seem to switch in a matter of moments from despair to joy and back again. Then they may become depressed for days over nothing. Or else they may become irrationally delighted or enthusiastic for weeks about some simple fact or event in the world, or—worse yet—become irrationally enthusiastic over something very suspicious or even obviously wrong.

Emotions often overrule facts, and the Blue may seem to be practically incapable of getting the facts straight. Sometimes you just can't reason with them. Sex is one and the same as emotion and communication to the Blue. There's no setting aside the emotional issues for a moment of physical enjoyment. There's no simple "setting the facts in order" so that intimacy can occur. Blues just don't divide life up into different areas. It's all one big homogeneous whole. When things are not in order, there is no sexuality.

Still and all, their intuitions often prove true. When they say, "I feel that thus and so may happen . . ." it fairly often does. They read other people well and know what it takes to please or displease others. They are socially pretty much at ease, meeting people where they are, shifting social Colors like a chameleon. Their kisses and hugs are heartfelt. Their love is genuine and it feels good to receive it . . . up to a point. They see your deep concerns and share them with easy passion. They even have words for all those subtle or even powerful emotions that sometimes seem to flood you beyond your control. They can actually help when the emotions boil over in you, as they occasionally do.

In work, Blues benefit from your quick intellect, and especially your ability to set boundaries. They really appreciate your help in sorting out the world, which to them is just one big mass of relationships. They also appreciate it when you express some vulnerability and uncertainty. They don't enjoy rubbing your face in it the way some others do, but seek out the best in you and try to help you get through the situation with as little pain as possible.

Then all of a sudden, they blow up in a white-hot anger like you've never seen before. They go for the knock out in the tirade that follows. They may accuse you of all those things you've heard before—of being uncaring and cold, of not sharing your feelings or not having any, and so on. They have been setting aside their own interests in service to you and feel that you haven't appreciated it, or in some other way they are feeling that a deep injustice is taking place. As a spouse, they may feel that you are not available to the children. As a coworker, they may feel that you are not sensitive to the needs of others. The surprising thing is the force of their rage. It's as strong as their love and passion. This is the biggest challenge of being with Blues.

Green and Gold

At last, here is a detail person. The Gold is someone who will cross the t's and dot the i's while you take care of the sophisticated data manipulation, solve the complex problems, and come up with the big ideas. The Gold can follow directions explicitly, even when they don't understand the underlying logic of the plan. They take work seriously and want it done right. They are never dreamy or emotionally volatile, and they don't play around on the job.

They value the impression they make on you and others. They put things in their proper places and find a time and a place for everything. They are a great help in keeping you in touch with the practical realities of daily life and the expectations of others as you pursue your inward agendas.

The Gold brings you a reality check, keeps a tidy house, keeps your calendar current and your important papers in some kind of order. They respect your work space and will tidy it if you wish, but they will also respect your boundaries as long as you don't impose your mess on them, which is more than they can stand. Here is someone who can finally keep order around you. If they are Gold/Blue, they will guide you through the complexities of the irrational world of emotions. If they are Gold/Green, they will join you in your seriousness and your commitment to productivity. If they are Gold/Orange, they will be a driving force moving you forward in an organized and energetic way.

Your Gold partner or coworker will be focused on concrete realities. They are not introspective; nor are they especially analytical. If anything, they will accuse you of thinking too much instead of acting, going off on tangents instead of carrying out practical tasks. They will appreciate your skill at problem solving more than the complex reasoning behind it. When it comes to expressions of love or appreciation, they will enjoy unwrapping presents and opening birthday cards. Like you, they value concrete expressions of love more than emotional words and sentiments. At work, they will appreciate public recognition and rewards more than any other Color. At home, they will value traditional holiday celebrations, family traditions, and a rewarding sexuality. If you value your relationship with a Gold, remember your anniversary! For solid, serious commitment, good order, and a meaningful place in the community, Gold will be your best bet.

Green and Orange

Hurrah for a fellow rebel! When it comes to poking holes in pompous, puffed-up authority figures, the Orange is for you. Some Oranges carry out their independent lifestyle quietly with occasional bursts of energy and excitement. Most of them wear their energy on their sleeve every day. Together, Green and Orange are a danger to everything conceited and tyrannical.

On the other hand, if you value your position, power, and authority, you may want to avoid the maverick Orange. At work, they will likely resist your attempts at micromanagement, preferring to receive clear objectives and timelines and to be left to their own devices in getting the job done—which they will do. Fortunately, this is most often Green's preferred style of management anyway, and when Oranges are on your side, they can't be beat for energetic action.

At home, their lives are lived for the joy of novelty, sensation, laughter, and impulsiveness. Your Orange spouse may not be too cautious about stepping on your toes or pointing out those embarrassing errors that we talked about above. If life is a game, then catching a smart person like you in an error is a definite win, even when they love you dearly. Still, they appreciate new things, and that includes new ideas, at least as long as they lead to action and the talk doesn't go on too long. Their enjoyment of sex usually includes a delight in novelty and adventure that you will probably find amusing and enjoyable. You'll rarely find an Orange sticking up for traditional ideas and values when new ones are being discovered or tested. Like you, the Orange is not caught up in the past, but looks at each day and each situation afresh.

You will share a love for clever and successful dealings in business, deal making, and professional matters. Oranges enter into these activities with the enthusiasm of an athlete and with a highly competitive zeal. You come to them with a serious, analytical shrewdness, but also with a great desire to win. The Orange will be more impulsive than you are, more willing to take risks for the thrill of it, but they want to win and there is a natural alliance between their competitive skill and your clever intelligence.

Orange is very social—not in the intimate and sensitive way Blues are, but with a gregarious, energetic, physical enthusiasm that can be very infectious. They may like team play while you may prefer more solitary sports or the rich intellectual tradition of baseball, for example. Orange loves an open competitive challenge, while you prefer to work at your own pace and reveal the power you have achieved in your own way and your own time, if you ever reveal it at all. You both love power in your different ways, and this can lead you to compete with each other for it unless you choose to join forces.

In your arguments, you will accuse the Orange of having a "ready, fire, aim!" mentality, of thoughtlessness and inconsistency. The Orange will counter that you think too much and are too serious for your own or their good. Both of you are more motivated by personal drives than by community interest. Your common tendency toward self-centeredness may make sharing and cooperation difficult at times, but the fact that you have it in common definitely helps. Chances are you will develop somewhat independent lives over time if you become partners. But however you choose to live, together you are the salt of the earth. Each of you brings a special savor that keeps the world from ever becoming dull and stuck in its ways.

Notice that there are six pairs of different Colors. There are ten pairs if you count the four same-Color combinations: Blue and

Blue, Green and Green, et cetera. There are twenty-four different orders that the four Colors can take in a Colors profile. In addition, if you look closely at the quiz, you'll notice that each Color's influence can be weak or strong as represented by the numerical score. Put all these differences together and the Color numbers have many thousands of different combinations of strengths. Ten pairs, twenty-four different profiles, thousands of patterns of relative strength . . . Colors does not reduce us to four simple types; far from it! Like the four cardinal points of the compass, there are infinite directions in between. But knowing North, East, South, and West is mighty helpful in finding our way.

CHAPTER 9

When the Colors Blend

Look at your first *two* Colors. There are six possible pairs. The effects of the second and even the third and fourth Colors can be very important. They give unique texture to every individual profile. It is very interesting to look at some of these subtleties, but it's also possible to get lost in a hurry if we try to go too deep. So let's take a look at the six pairs, which I have dubbed Sunburst, Mystic, Diamond, Firecracker, Torchbearer, and Homebuilder.

WHEN BLUE AND ORANGE BLEND—"SUNBURST"

Sunburst loves the bright, active, passionate life. You'll find him or her to be right-brained all the way, full of physical energy and lots of strong feelings that come bubbling out at all the right times—and also the wrong ones. Work is a very personal adventure, but highly engaged with other people. Love is emotional and creative, full of fantasy, fiery feelings, and experimentation. Sunburst demands the freedom to explore in a world of love and passion, while paying close attention to precious personal emotions, values, and possibilities. Physical energy is strong. The heart is lively. Moving, going, and doing combine with sensitivity.

Love is a passion. But so is everything else. Idealism is a big part of the passion. So is sexuality in a love affair or a marriage. Enthusiasm follows enthusiasm, with occasional bouts of exhausted depression. Negative feelings can be as strong as positive ones. Passionate anger can follow passionate affection. The anger can be a flash and gone, or sometimes it can be a lifelong preoccupation. Creativity is a very high value, and freedom an even higher one. Disorder and confusion may reign in practical matters. These are not Sunburst's concerns. Structure will need to come from outside, from other people or from social situations. The Blue/Orange Sunburst brings the energy; somebody else had better have the organizational chart.

Inner conflicts tend to occur between Sunbursts' powerful impulses to action and their concern for other people. Sometimes they simply must follow an impulse, even if it will cause pain to someone. Blue guilt will follow. Sometimes they suppress the impulse in service to someone else, and then find themselves feeling resentful and controlled. High energy and strong feelings are a double-edged sword for the Sunburst.

WHEN BLUE AND GREEN BLEND—"MYSTIC"

Here we go into a world of deep inner experience. The Mystic lives in a world in which deep thought interacts with profound feelings. Sacred texts, wise sayings, philosophical understandings—all are part of daily life. Dreams are important. They are thought over, talked over, perhaps interpreted according to some method or practice. Material things are seen in the light of their deeper meanings. Precious objects may be kept nearby, and may be assigned special value and power. The meanings of those objects are either deeply personal or seen as sacred to the collective. Matters of personal identity and spiritual influence are given close attention.

Lovemaking is a mystery, a spiritual journey, a way to be in contact with sacred energies or objects. Emotions are personal, to be shared with care and gentle respect. Gift giving takes on a deeply personal, often spiritual significance. Organized religious structures may be avoided or downplayed. The Mystic makes an independent spiritual journey. Certain places are filled with meaning. Visiting them and caring for them often has a ritual quality. Other cultures and ancient ways hold fascination.

The Mystic is very sensitive to shocks, both physical and emotional. The surface calm overlies reactive passions that run deep and strong below, and a delicate balance must be maintained. Small shocks can seem powerful jolts to the Mystic sensitivity. These are not people cut out for the rough-and-tumble of the marketplace. In all likelihood, they will strive to make for themselves a quiet space where inner exploration can go on with serene intensity.

Here, problems can occur around inwardness and passivity. It may be hard to act. Indecision and fear of others' reactions combine to suppress spontaneity. In addition, the sentimental Blue feelings argue with the Green rationality—and once again, action is postponed. There will be a tendency toward withdrawal as a preferred life strategy. This may or may not work out for the best.

WHEN GREEN AND GOLD BLEND—"DIAMOND"

Diamonds know the value of things and love quality. Pride and humiliation are the two ends of their measuring stick. Beauty, order, refined skill, special knowledge, careful appearances, and recognition—these are the hallmarks of success. Diamonds value physical attractiveness, careful hygiene, quality gifts given and received, good clothes, a well-cared-for home . . . class all the way. Responsibility, duty, and service are highly valued, and power is sought carefully and quietly. Diamonds appreciate being able to lead from behind. They wish to maintain a low profile while exercising an effective guiding hand.

Diamonds have a calm and deliberate demeanor. They express little emotion. Gushy sentiments seem shallow and gauche to them. They do not wish to be fawned over and have a hard time giving praise. But well-deserved recognition is not sentimental, and Diamonds wish to be recognized for the true value of their actions and way of life. In work, they feel that their rewards are justly earned, and they recognize the same worth in others. In love, duty and mutual respect are very important—but agreements carefully arrived at may allow for open marriage or other forms of independence. Family loyalty, diligent work, honorable service, a no-nonsense commitment to a community or a relationship . . . these are the real evidence of love to Diamonds. Love means doing and giving, not fine phrases or emotionalism. Careful analysis, correct and thoughtful action, tough but clear business dealings, respectful giving are the shining facets of the Diamond.

The conflict between the demand for action and the wish for "a little more information first" can keep the Diamond in a quandary. Impulses of social responsibility and goal-orientation are strong in the Gold side, while a desire for seclusion and autonomy arises from the Green. Sometimes a pattern of self-doubt results from this combination. There is also a tendency toward elitism stemming from the high standards and careful style of the Diamond. This can sometimes lead to resentment or even rebellion among associates.

WHEN ORANGE AND GREEN BLEND—"FIRECRACKER"

Hide your conceits; here come the devastating wits, the great stand-up comics, the masters of satire and irony. For a seminar leader, Firecrackers are the dreaded "trainer killers." They are independent, excitable, and have a very low tolerance for stuffed shirts. They love to poke fun at people who put on airs, people who are condescending to others. Firecrackers are not sentimental, and they're not impressed. The Orange side brings physical energy and social aggressiveness. The Green side brings sharp insights and clever language. Both Colors bring the demand for independence. All traditional ways are in danger!

Firecrackers think for themselves. They can be quite cantankerous and eccentric at times. They love clever ideas and ingenious things. Forever skeptical of others, they often fall in love with their own ingenious ideas. Firecrackers are not moved by a lot of talk about feelings and emotions. Their lovemaking is vigorous and creative, even eccentric. Both Green and Orange contribute to the pattern of deep feelings not talked about, even with closest friends and spouses. Romance is foreign to them. Anything mushy or touchy-feely is like fingernails scraping on a blackboard to Firecrackers.

In work, they will be masters of their specialty. In love, they will be autonomous and independent. You will rarely put anything over on them—though they may . . . on you.

When they reinforce each other, Orange and Green temperaments bring out a very sharp-tongued and sometimes tactless social style. Inwardly, the physical impulses and sensation-seeking of the Orange argue with the cool logic of the Green. Firecrackers often find themselves cleverly talking their way out of trouble once they've gotten there by following impulses.

WHEN ORANGE AND GOLD BLEND—"TORCHBEARER"

"In the beginning was the deed" would be a good motto for Torchbearers. They're full of drive, energy, and social responsibility. They carry the load and whistle while they work. They love tough tasks and laughter. They love accomplishment more than anything. They like to do things—fun things, productive things, team things. And they like to run things, they like to be in charge, and they usually run things very well. Just about every Torchbearer whom I've met has been a manager of some sort. Goals, purposes, timelines, schedules top their lists. And they do make lists, at least in their minds. A spirit of competition adds to the fun, along with a focus on concrete realities. Torchbearers are all action. Meditation is not on the agenda. They have a little difficulty relating to sensitive philosophy and mad emotionalism.

Torchbearer lovemaking is vigorous but it must fit into the schedule. It may or may not be a priority. While Torchbearers are very practical and energetic, they may not be highly emotional. Still, they value family and relationships highly. Gregarious and socially responsible, they sell the most tickets to the upcoming benefit concert, and they probably booked the orchestra and the hall and handled the publicity as well. Any organization is lucky to have them. If you're not looking for too much sentiment, a Torchbearer will make a loyal and fun life partner.

Speed seems to be the essence of the Gold/Orange Torchbearer. This combination can result in a highly aggressive personality, for better or for worse. Once again, we see the argument between the Orange impulses and, in this case, the orderly, goal-directed motives of the Gold. The Torchbearers I have known have reported the strongest internal conflicts of any of the combinations. Given the high energy and action orientation of both Colors, this shouldn't come as a surprise.

WHEN BLUE AND GOLD BLEND—"HOMEBUILDER"

Homebuilders are serious, down to earth, and tenderhearted. They love to care for places, people, children, animals, gardens, communities . . . in short, the world. Love is both emotional and responsible for Homebuilders. Lovemaking is a warm, affectionate, and natural act with deep roots in the home, in the meaningful relationship, and in the making of children. Commitment runs deep. It is expected in return . . . not a selfish possessive commitment, but a commitment to the things that matter and to practical efforts on behalf of those things.

Homebuilders are grounded in a deep feeling for the practical and meaningful things of the world, of nature, of home, and of the human community. Work is a part of this grounded commitment. Romantic love and deep personal loyalty are the foundation of sexuality for Homebuilder. Many hold to the view that sex is really for procreation—and even when it isn't, it should be treated with that same reverence. They could be called "Schoolteachers," since elementary schools, kindergartens, and preschools are staffed in large part by this combination of Blue and Gold. But beyond the schools, wherever service is the order of the day, there you will find Homebuilders in great numbers. They are playful and serious in their natural and proper seasons. I look for Homebuilders—solid, endlessly helpful—wherever I go. I know that they will help and guide me through whatever situation I find myself in.

The inner life of Homebuilders is a conversation between various sensitivities and sympathies on the one hand, and practical realities on the other. Both impulses tend to work for the good of those around them, which makes this combination so helpful in the community. Still, it's not always easy to resolve the tension between duty and compassion. A quiet sadness often results. Homebuilders often tell me that they wish they could change Colors. Personally, I'm very glad they're around.

The Workplace

Leadership means managing people—one of the most difficult of all tasks. It means coordinating the actions of others in service to a common goal. It means establishing that goal and developing the consent of others to be governed by that goal. Each Color has its own way of carrying the burdens of leadership. Each has particular talents that lend themselves to good leadership, and each needs the support and, to some extent, the skills of the other Colors in order to be successful.

Working style, on the other hand, refers to the way people respond to the demands of work and the pressures of supervision. Each Color has its own motivations for performing and producing effectively. Each Color has its own satisfactions with regard to work, and what motivates one Color may be completely meaningless or even problematic to another.

Let's take a look at the various Colors' leadership and working styles.

GOLD LEADERSHIP STYLE

Golds are often in leadership positions, but they do not seek the limelight for its own sake. They are rarely moved by the desire for public visibility and fame. Golds lead because someone has to, because the work is important and must be done right, because they are personally committed and responsible, and because they value the status, the recognition, and the rewards. They accept positions of authority as the natural and inevitable result of their effort and dedication.

Hard work is the key to Golds' leadership style. They work hard themselves, and they expect others to do the same. Golds "do it the old-fashioned way: They earn it." It may be fun to find a dollar lying by the road, but it is deeply satisfying to earn one.

Golds have a sixth sense for what really needs to be done. In a business, in a family, in the community, Golds have an eye on the foundations, the necessities, the infrastructure, the moral and legal framework, and the bottom line. If something isn't getting done, they will do it or see that it gets done. They are usually decisive and sure of their ground.

Their standards are high. The ideals are clear and well defined. It takes a great deal of hard work to live up to them. In actual practice, though, those standards are hardly ever fully met. This means that Golds almost always see things falling short of their ideal. This is true even when things are going quite well. This sense of falling short drives them to expect more of themselves and of the people around them.

Golds are dedicated to the institutions they serve. This dedication applies to the family, the school, the business or corporation, the military organization, the nation, the ideology, the tradition, the religion, the way of life.

Gold leaders are always painfully aware of the potential for slip-ups, confusion, chaos, and failure. Delegation is a gamble.

"If something can go wrong, it will," is a Gold motto. This leads them to strive at all times for stability and good order, for well-defined procedures that must be carefully followed, and for tough accountability and real consequences. It is always a temptation for Golds to micromanage, since the farther from them the work is done, the less likely it is that the work will meet the standard.

Tradition is a primary value for Golds. The ways of the past are proven ways. Even if they may not be the most efficient and up-to-date, traditional ways have stood the test of time. Clever ideas and a fascination with the new for its own sake are frivolous. Once again, frivolous things threaten the foundations of order.

Organization is essential. Well-defined missions set the course. Plans implement it. Roles with defined responsibilities bring order out of the chaos of individual ideas, talents, and energy. Procedures coordinate the roles. Job descriptions and task analysis connect people to what must be done. Only in this way do day-to-day, moment-to-moment activities have their place in the grand scheme of things. Order out of chaos.

There must be accountability throughout the organization and conformity to the norms and policies. This means hierarchy, levels of responsibility, levels of authority. Managers must manage. Standards must be set and enforced. Subordinates must measure up. Golds are not shy about letting go someone who is not contributing. Sentiment has its place, but not at the expense of the organization. There is a sternness about a strong Gold. Expectations are high, and they are serious. This seriousness cuts both ways, and Golds feel the sting of their own failures most of all.

In negotiations, Golds strike a hard bargain. Contracts are at the core of working relationships. Tough bargaining means clear, enforceable contracts with the best possible terms. Golds know value. They believe in fairness, but they seek and respect competitive advantage as well. They are not sentimental about business relationships, though they do place a high value on loyalty and trust, on win–win solutions and cooperation wherever possible. Negotiation tends to be firm but fair.

Thoroughness, good use of time and energy, efficiency, punctuality—all are high values for Golds. Golds hate to be late. They are irritated when others are late. They make lists. Sometimes they make lists of lists. They often report that the next day is carefully planned before they go to sleep at night, the next week is pretty well thought out, and both fit into the plan for the month and the year.

Golds have a special relationship with money. To them, money is valuable in and of itself, and they love to see it accumulate. Spending is enjoyable when done with care and attention to value, but seeing the bank account grow, the net worth increase, the jars of jams and jellies row upon row in the larder . . . this is real satisfaction, safety, relief.

The outward and visible signs of success mean much to Golds. Money serves as one measure of that success, and Golds expect their pay to be commensurate with their efforts and their position. They don't like to see money lying idle. It should be working and earning just like people.

Every bit as important as money, however, is public recognition. Honors, testimonials, certificates of appreciation, promotions based on merit, Citizen of the Year—these can mean more than money for the Gold. So often it seems that no one knows how hard they really have worked, how much they have contributed. Spontaneous recognition of their achievement brings tears of gratitude and profound joy.

GOLD WORKING STYLE

Golds take work very seriously. They often report that a job well done is their highest joy. They want to contribute, to be successful and productive, and they respond well to recognition, rewards, and incentives.

Golds fill the ranks of management at every level. They make good administrators and respond well to shouldering important responsibilities. Public administration is a popular field with Golds, and they represent their institutions with dedication.

In the professions, Golds are orderly and productive. In medicine, they gravitate toward clearly defined specialties and often find their way to medical administration. In law, they lean toward the corporate and financial side, administrative law, prosecutorial positions, and the bench. Law enforcement is another popular occupation for Golds.

Auditing, accounting, home economics, and fiscal responsibilities are a natural fit for orderly Golds. They are attracted to the military, where they make decisive leaders and responsible soldiers.

Along with the Blues, Golds swell the ranks of public education and institutional health and social services. They make solid, responsible teachers and education administrators. In hospitals and clinics, they are nurses, technicians, orderlies, and clerical staff. They make fine librarians, curators, and archivists. They also provide support services throughout both public and private institutions, handling clerical and custodial jobs efficiently.

Their teaching style emphasizes community, tradition, and values. They establish clear expectations, and their discipline is firm and fair. The expectations come from traditional standards . . . the three r's and plenty of drill and practice.

In an office or factory, Golds prefer useful tasks, and they handle detail well. They mistrust abstractions, preferring to deal with the concrete. They like clear structure, firm expectations and timelines, and well-defined responsibilities, a clear notion of right and wrong. They need to know that they are on track, and they look to people in authority to tell them. They are punctual, arriving on time and leaving on time.

Golds make good salespeople. They present a good appearance, and they have the ability to order and organize the work of selling so that contacts are made and followed up, details are handled, time is well utilized and closing is solid. Selling requires hard work, persistence, and organization, and Golds often take to it well.

Golds also do well in merchandising. Their strong sense of value and their easy way with order and bookkeeping make them good buyers and managers throughout the retail and wholesale worlds. Golds love quality things, and they love a good appearance. Hairdressing, cosmetology, and retail apparel sales are favorite fields for them.

Golds make good employees. If they have a clear idea of what is expected of them and if the rewards are sufficient for their needs, they will be hardworking and productive.

BLUE LEADERSHIP STYLE

For Blues, the central driving force in leadership style is commitment to the people involved and to a strong sense of community. Blue leaders want to nurture people, to see the best come out in each member of the group. They are oriented to individual strengths, to relationships, and to participation.

Indeed, participation is a key value. Blues are reluctant to exercise arbitrary authority. Instead, they seek consensus based on communication and involvement. They are willing to be patient. They will sacrifice a certain amount of well-regulated efficiency in favor of maintaining harmony in relationships. The whole idea of team or community is very important to Blues.

These personal and community values lead Blues toward a democratic management style. They value input and pay serious attention to the points of view of employees or coworkers, whom they tend to think of as fellow participants in a joint venture. Blues give abundantly of appreciation and support. They want to be loved, and they want to manage with love.

Blues like flexible and creative solutions that arise from the people involved. They favor flexible procedures and put a high value on day-to-day learning and adaptation.

It is usually uncomfortable for a Blue to adopt an attitude of authority. Laying down the law can be very difficult. Blues are fundamentally egalitarian in their outlook, and the idea of one person lording it over another pushes a hot button of indignation or shame.

Tough negotiations can be a real challenge for Blues. Their desire for consensus and win–win solutions can undermine their ability to strike a hard bargain. Their aversion to people's dissatisfaction and conflict can make closing a deal a real nightmare for them.

Closing a sale or a deal is usually a bumpy process under the best of circumstances. Often, no one is completely satisfied. Empathetic Blues go to the utmost to keep everyone happy. They may well feel buyer's remorse in advance for all sides. On the other hand, this careful, empathetic approach and the consuming desire to please can lead to great teamwork, to very solid and satisfactory outcomes, and to considerable customer loyalty.

Having to fire someone, to let someone go, is nearly always traumatic for the Blue manager. It is one of those "little deaths" that Blues try to avoid at all costs. As leaders or managers, Blues will usually bend over backward to avoid having to do so. It is a common experience for Blue managers to lie awake nights, losing sleep over the incompetence or disruptiveness of an employee, while postponing the inevitable confrontation.

That powerful Blue anger, that righteous wrath that can wither flowers, will sometimes come out in crisis situations. There may be a long period of avoiding conflict and confrontation. But at some point, there will be enough wrongs or a last straw, and a real outburst is due. When the outburst comes, it can be frighteningly powerful and may lead to long-term regrets and recriminations.

In addition, when Blues lose confidence in themselves, when they feel ashamed and defeated, or when they feel that they have done harm, their depression can be deep and infectious. A kind of paralysis can set in, and it will last until the cloud lifts, usually through making amends, receiving emotional support, finding a sense of forgiveness, and arriving at a new inspiration. It is tough for Blues to move on from disaster. Loss of trust in others is very hard to repair.

In addition to all these people-centered aspects, there is a special visionary quality to the Blue leadership style. Blues are holistic thinkers. They see a big picture and they are inspired by what they see. They often have the ability to inspire others with the vision.

Such vision and emotion result in an enthusiasm that can be an infectious motivator. Suddenly, going to the moon sounds like a really beautiful idea, or gathering the family for a wonderful get-together in a new setting, or moving the company into fascinating, uncharted seas.

Blues are usually good communicators. They convey not only the idea, but also the feeling behind the idea. They are catalysts, and can rally the troops to new heights of endeavor, holding out an exciting vision for all to see, expressing deep faith in the abilities of the people around them.

Strong Blues are deeply intuitive. They look inside and get readings on things that the other Colors often miss. When a Blue says, "I've got a feeling about this," it's usually a good idea to listen carefully. Their hunches sometimes border on ESP, if not actually going over the line into that strange domain.

Blues want to educate, to lead people toward meaningful things. They are drawn to the arts and to the spiritual dimension of life. They will move companies toward community involvement, toward doing well by doing good, investing for the long term in customer loyalty and social participation, caring for the environment even at some cost to the bottom line.

Cooperation, inspiration, personal growth, community development, investment for the good of all . . . these are watchwords for the Blue leader.

BLUE WORKING STYLE

As employees or group members, Blues wish for an open social atmosphere. They naturally form relationships with coworkers, customers, and employers, and they need the freedom and permission to care for these relationships. When the demands of the work, strict supervision, or organizational culture prohibit such relationships, Blues will suffer.

They value honesty, but not brutal honesty. To Blues, honesty equates to fair dealing and a lack of manipulation. Blues will tell little white lies, and even some pretty big ones, to avoid inflicting emotional pain, or to protect themselves from pain. Still, they are very sensitive to and suspicious of confidence games and motivational strategies. Blues give their best when they feel that they are trusted and can trust in return.

Emotional support is a key factor for Blues. They will give it, and they need to receive it. When Blues are left without feedback, they assume the worst about themselves. This leads them to spiral down into anxiety, self-doubt, and depression. Good, clean information about performance delivered in a caring and supportive manner does the trick.

Blues often value another person's affection more than his or her praise or admiration. "I'm glad you're here. I sure enjoy working with you. You're a real asset to the team"—all are high praise to a Blue.

Blues thrive in a positive, creative, service-oriented environment. They are troubled by intense competition. Conflict is painful. Heavy production orientation and mechanization may block relationships. Manipulative selling strategies and sharp business practices offend them and make them anxious. Blues fear meeting dissatisfied customers in the future and facing the shame of not having served them well.

They make good doctors, nurses, medical technicians, and hospital workers based on their excellent bedside manner. This is based more on their love of people than on easy technical mastery. The emotional suffering of patients can be hard for Blues. Harder still can be the apparent callousness of some medical professionals about a patient's pain.

Blues' love of people in general attracts them to the helping professions. They do well as clergy and in service positions related to church or charitable organizations. They do well in the service sector generally. They make great receptionists and public relations people. They present their best face to the community and represent the business or institution in a positive manner. In the office, they look to the needs of the staff as well as the customer.

Along with Golds, Blues tend to dominate the education, counseling, and social-service professions. As teachers, they are attracted to the early grades by their love of children. They put participation at the top of the priority list and work to develop student self-esteem, bringing out the best in each student's unique makeup. Discipline is usually personal, flexible, and inclusive, and they rely for motivation on inspiration and appreciation more than duty and consequences.

Blues are often artistic or musical with good speaking and writing skills. They are attracted to the arts and humanities and make good media people, creative marketers, actors, and entertainers. The opportunity to express feelings in creative ways is a real joy to Blues. The magic and mystery of the arts spread over into the realm of the spiritual, which is usually a Blue's highest aspiration.

ORANGE LEADERSHIP STYLE

Orange leaders are focused on action. When they are bright and talented, when they have the resources, when they have the bit in their teeth, the sky's the limit. Action is at the center. Institutional structures and procedures are never an end in themselves. Everything else exists to make action possible. Everything that blocks or frustrates action must be set aside.

Deeply bound up with action is skill. Skill in action. "Show me the problem, give me the tools, and get out of the way!" "Call in the guys who know what they're doing, and turn them loose on the job!" "Get me the best!" Time present. Here and now. Let's get to work.

The tools must be in hand. The right tool for the job. If the right tool isn't handy, we'll invent it. Troubleshooting is our middle name. Getting the bugs out. Improvising. Making it work.

Oranges are blessed with an entrepreneurial spirit. They love to work for themselves, to be their own boss, set their own pace, and work to the best of their ability. In middle management they respond well to project assignments when they are given the latitude to get the job done in their own way.

Oranges lead by example, setting a standard of performance for others to follow. Coaching is a good metaphor for the Orange style. They learn by doing. They don't enjoy learning from manuals or from verbal instructions, and they teach as they learn, more by showing than by telling. Cheerleading, enthusiasm, and encouragement combine with strong expectations, pushing the coworker, the student, or the employee to perform.

Orange leaders can be quite brusque and authoritarian in their management style. They are impatient with opposition, and they expect their directions to be followed. They are usually going full throttle themselves, and slowness or resistance in others feels like a very bumpy road. Orange leaders often physically touch people, moving bodies around with a matter-of-fact and playful strength. "Stand here. Grab hold here. Lift and release. If they push hard, you push harder!"

This intrusive style is frequently tempered by an infectious sense of humor, a feeling of genuine physical camaraderie, and a natural ability to move on from difficult situations without much ado. Oranges are capable of holding grudges and of acting on them. Still, their general here-and-now orientation keeps them moving forward in a positive way most of the time.

Oranges are realists. Their goals are concrete, actual, material. Action is physical. There must be movement. Less talk, more do! Get the job done and move on to the next one. The abstract is of little interest to them. Opportunities. Results. Product. Dollars. Winning.

Did someone say winning? Oranges compete! Competition means everything, and competition is to win. Oranges often report that winning is better than sex, and they usually like sex a lot. The Orange leader is competing all the time, competing with past performance, with business or sports competitors, with others within the organization, with heroes and significant figures from the past, with deeply held personal goals.

Orange leaders use competition as a motivator. They enjoy

managing via competition, challenging employees and coworkers to outdo one another, and leaping right into the fray themselves. Oranges like to see their coworkers physically active and competitive off the job as well. They expect it.

This competitive, entrepreneurial spirit makes for master negotiators, deal makers, and deal closers. Oranges' good verbal skills combine with tactical cleverness and a deep understanding and enjoyment of the game. Someone else can watch out for the incidentals. Orange negotiators are thinking many moves ahead, and they have their eye on the prize.

Above all, Orange leaders welcome change. The old ways can be improved upon. The new is an adventure, a challenge, the very stuff of life. Oranges are flexible and confident. Fear is the enemy, a waste of time. Utter devastation and complete failure are just events along the way. People are tough. They're not made of porcelain and crystal. They fall down. They break. They mend. They get up. They go on. "How else have we ever gotten anywhere that was worth a damn, anyway?" says the Orange.

ORANGE WORKING STYLE

Oranges love to work. They are sometimes thought of as too carefree and playful to be good workers. As young people, they are often turned off to traditional kinds of work when it's boring and when bosses are too authoritarian. It's easy to thwart and block their potential with too much structure and suppression. When Oranges are doing what they love to do, they are the hardest workers of all the Colors.

As in their leadership style, the key factors for Orange are energy and skill and the freedom to use them. It is very common for an Orange to work at something from dawn until late at night. The clock has no meaning. Punishment and reward are forgotten. All that matters is the challenge of the task at hand. Productivity is sky-high when work is play.

Oranges turn tasks into creative play. They love to develop their skills and performance to the highest possible level. The quiet Orange craftsperson may linger endlessly over creative detail work. The highly physical and mobile Orange construction worker may strive to outdo the previous day's performance. They love economy, precision, and grace in movement, finding the most efficient and elegant way to get the job done.

Movement, variety, and immediacy bring out the best in Oranges. They thrive on crisis situations and love to think on their feet. Physical problem solving is a natural strength. Sensory and concrete, they are grounded in the realities of tools and materials.

At their most skilled, they make excellent surgeons and craftspeople of the highest order. They are attracted to engineering and technical fields where they may work with materials either on the most massive scale or on the most intricate and delicate.

Oranges are tool users. Show an Orange a backhoe, a bulldozer, a police car, an ambulance, or an airplane, and he or she will want to climb aboard, turn it on, and go. Give them a soldering iron, a metal lathe, a scroll saw, or a scalpel and they will want to put it to use immediately.

Oranges love to build things. I know an eighty-year-old Orange man who decided one day that he needed a twenty-four-foot-square, two-room cottage on a corner of his property. After eyeballing the site, the man excavated it with pick and shovel, built the forms, poured the foundation, framed the walls and roof, finished the exterior and interior in fine style, and was ready to move in in a couple of weeks, all without a single plan on paper!

Farming, ranching, forestry, fishing, hunting, guiding— Oranges naturally love the outdoors. They love the independence, self-reliance, and endurance that go along with working outside.

Oranges like people, and they work with people in a spirit of teamwork, competition, and camaraderie. Teaching, coaching, and youth work are often a good fit. Oranges love children. They frequently have a natural, unforced rapport and an easy authority with young people.

As teachers, the Oranges rely on an up-tempo style with lots of hands-on activity and group camaraderie. They tend to keep the structure pretty fluid, with lots of room for taking advantage of the unexpected. Learning is concrete, visible, and relevant. Discipline is usually built around a sense of team building, challenge, enthusiasm, and personal responsibility without strong traditional value judgments. The Orange teacher is sometimes prone to power struggles.

In business, selling is a strong point. Though Orange salespeople may need help around the detail work, they have an instinct for the bottom line. Their enthusiasm and love of the chase give them energy galore, and they capitalize on every opportunity to move the customer toward the close.

Law enforcement and public safety work appeals to the Orange sense of adventure. Technical specialties like nursing, dental hygiene and assisting, or respiratory therapy give Oranges the opportunity to be moving and doing with skill.

Oranges are not natural followers, and they thrive on the

opportunity to build all the skills necessary for an independent life. Their entrepreneurial tendencies can take them in any direction in which skill and self-reliance pay off. A few examples that I know of include an independent chef with his own small, quality catering business; a pushcart vendor in an open-air market; and the owner of a toy factory deep in the woods. For Oranges, the possibilities are endless.

Oranges also make great entertainers in all fields. Wherever they work, they bring fun, humor, witty conversation, and energy. A workplace without the Orange influence can be a pretty dull place.

GREEN LEADERSHIP STYLE

Greens bring intellect, ingenuity, pragmatism, and design to the leadership role. Working smart is what matters to Green . . . seeing the whole picture, understanding the details that make it up, relating the details to the whole, creating pathways and activities that move things forward, applying technology, solving problems, and adjusting goals in a realistic way.

The Green leader tries to take account of the whole complex field of factors and influences in a situation. This means thorough assessment, sufficient information, careful reasoning based on the information, planned action, attention to feedback, and adaptation to new information. Greens don't shoot first and ask questions later. They don't defend the old in the face of the new. They aren't moved by sentiment and enthusiasm. They want to follow the facts wherever they lead.

The big picture is apparent to Greens. The analytical Green mind synthesizes, drawing on a broad field. All the detailed care and deliberation must relate to the whole. Greens work conceptually, relating information to constructs and paradigms that make sense to them. These underlying ideas are often rooted in theories and philosophies that cross disciplines and go well beyond the task at hand.

Greens can explain what they are doing. They can explain what their organizations are doing. They can explain their expectations and instructions to their subordinates and coworkers. Often their understanding and explanations go well beyond the ability of others to understand. This can be a problem for the Green leader.

Greens have an uncanny ability to sort out complex situations and design systems to manage them. It is a real delight to watch this Green mind at work, weighing and measuring, categorizing and systematizing, anticipating and planning, creating tools and processes that meet many contingencies and challenges.

The big-picture view is the strategic view. Greens make strategy, and they make it for the long term. In addition to attending to the dynamics within their organization, family, or group, Greens take account of the larger movements around their organization and position things accordingly.

The Green leader uses schematic diagrams, illustrates concepts and processes, makes maps, develops grids and diagrams, and lays out pathways. Greens tend to be systemic thinkers, working from the whole to the part and back again. This analytical process is second nature to Greens. It's fun for them, the most fun there is.

Whenever relevant, science and technology are familiar necessities to Greens. They are proud of their skill and knowledge in complex technical fields, and they enjoy being the specialist in a field of laypeople. They keep themselves up to date on the latest developments and enjoy applying them in ingenious ways.

Certain things are to be avoided at all costs, most particularly any form of stupidity. Greens detest stupidity. Stupid things include redundancy, confusion, emotionalism, hidebound traditionalism, irrationality, and impulsiveness.

Redundancy is a particular bugaboo for Greens. It is practically impossible for Greens to repeat themselves. They just can't get the words out. "It's already been said, for heaven's sake. Weren't you listening? You already said that. Do you think I didn't understand?" Green readers will notice that this has been said in a previous chapter.

Green leaders expect people to pay attention, to be genuinely interested, and to get it the first time. Repetition is an insult to everyone's intelligence, and that's a very great sin. This expectation that people will pay attention and understand is a key to the Green's leadership style. Greens give the information and move on. Failure to act on the information is the listener's responsibility.

Individual autonomy and responsibility are also strong values for Green. They are very reluctant to exercise power over others. Stating the facts of the case should be sufficiently compelling. Intelligent minds should work together around the data and the plan. As independent individuals, we either cooperate or we go be independent somewhere else. Greens are not sentimental about these things. Firing someone seems almost overdramatic. A parting of ways should be obvious from the facts of the situation.

Greens love to teach. They want to contribute to growth and

competence in others and to enrich the volume of knowledge in an organization. They frequently lead by instructing, teaching principles and techniques that others are to apply. They like to bring in outside experts, good reading materials, interactive learning tools and training. Learning is a catalyst to Green, stimulating creative problem solving and ingenuity. Research is essential to organizational functioning.

The niceties of social interaction tend to escape Green leaders. They are not much interested in subtleties of feeling and relationship. In fact, they don't pay much attention to them. Their leadership style is rather dry, focused on the vision and on analysis of tasks and information. They are not overly given to praise and give little thought to emotional support. The facts speak for themselves. Good work is good work. Everyone knows it. Why all the fuss?

GREEN WORKING STYLE

Greens like to know why they're doing what they're doing. The rationale is everything. They need the freedom to arrive at their own conclusions, and to act on them. Greens think for themselves.

In the workplace or profession, Greens are motivated by curiosity. Their minds tend to probe deeply into things, pursuing underlying structure, process, and significance. They do their best work in this way. Given free rein, Greens develop understanding, and they can make a major contribution to any setting.

They love data and information of all kinds. They read. They compute. They analyze. They understand specs. They strategize.

They design. Then they move on. Routine follow-through is not their strong suit.

Greens love the abstract and the intellectual, in technology, in the arts and humanities, in scientific research, in systems design, in management, in education, in comic books, in video games, in science fiction. Greens learn and teach. They write and do research.

Their focus is on the information. They are skeptical and analytical. They don't settle for easy answers and they mistrust glibness, tradition, and sentiment. Greens pride themselves on not being gullible. They often possess a dry and trenchant wit and sometimes a scathing tongue. They do not suffer fools gladly, and they refuse to be fools themselves.

In the law, they love the intricacies of argument, the fine detail of precedent, ingenious case making, stratagems, telling facts, and the demonstration of compelling and powerful intelligence. In science and medicine, they are attracted to the cutting edge of research and theory, the subtleties of evidence, rigorous and relentless analysis, absolute expertise, the finely honed specialty.

Computers are a playland for Greens, requiring all their analytical skills, all their intelligence and ingenuity. Data analysis, engineering, and systems design often leave the other Colors behind, but here Greens can come into their own.

Greens are not highly social and gregarious by nature. They do best in fields that give them a little distance in relationships. Photography and journalism are two common examples.

In any work setting, Green workers need this sense of space. They are independent by nature, and they don't like to promote themselves. They do, however, want to be recognized and utilized for their intelligence, their competence, and their pragmatic vision. They find their way into management based on their expertise in the field, rather than on their natural people skills.

As teachers, they are brought to education by whatever subject area they are teaching; by the content more than by the students. They tend to be attracted to the higher grades where content is more sophisticated. They expect their students to be there out of interest in the information and to be self-motivated. For this reason, their disciplinary style tends to be very laissez-faire with strong reliance on natural consequences and learning through experience.

In the open market, Greens can sell very well in technical fields where information and expertise sell the product, but they are shy about cold calling and the other extrovert people skills that come into play in general sales. They are ingenious at creating marketing strategies, but would rather get the other Colors to make the calls.

This is a key factor in managing the Green worker to best advantage. They do best at the analytical, creative level—research, data management, analysis, design, teaching—and routine follow-through is often best left to others.

Green workers are unique, and usually very much in the minority. They can be quite touchy, withdrawn, even eccentric. But their special gifts are essential in any dynamic organization. They often need special care if their gifts are to flower.

The next page lists some suggestions about the particular fields of work that are often enjoyed by the different personality styles.

SAMPLE OCCUPATIONAL PREFERENCES BY COLOR

Gold

Administrators	Military
Managers	Nurses
Factory or site supervisors	Health technicians
Clerical supervisors	Medical secretaries
Surgeons	Editors
Lawyers	Teachers
Dentists	Librarians
Social-service workers	Clergy
Police, detectives	Home economists
Auditors, accountants	Hairdressers
Retail and commission sales	Cosmetologists

Blue

Clergy	Marriage and family counselors
Educators	Rehabilitation workers
Physicians	Child-care workers
Nurses	Service-sector business
Media specialists	Writers
Teachers	Artists
Education consultants	Editors
Librarians	Musicians
Psychiatrists	Entertainers
Psychologists	
Social workers	

Orange

Engineers	Heavy-equipment
Electrical technicians	operators
Mechanics	Emergency technicians
Teachers	Managers, administrators
Coaches	Entrepreneurs
Farmers	Commission sales
Dental assistants	Auditors
Dental hygienists	Child-care workers
Storekeepers	Receptionists
Nurses	Religious workers
Bookkeepers, accountants	Musicians
Marketing personnel	Performing artists
Police, detectives	Artisans

Green

Lawyers	Librarians
Researchers	Writers
Physical scientists	Artists
Social scientists	Entertainers
Doctors, surgeons,	Photographers
medical technicians	Marketing personnel
Computer programmers	Sales (technical)
Systems analysts	Journalists
Chemical engineers	Managers, administrators
High school teachers	Mortgage brokers
University teachers	Accountants

CHAPTER 11

Children

THE GOLD CHILD

Gold children need security based on an orderly life and on high standards of quality and effort. Concrete, practical realities are of the highest significance to them. The ground under their feet must feel secure. The lawn needs to be mowed. The roof mustn't leak. The baby needs changing. Meals should be on time.

From an early age, Gold children will try to correct anything that threatens the order around them. Parents can expect their Gold children to parent *them* if need be; to correct their language, to resist their impulsiveness or impracticality, to count their money, to judge their competence, their house, their cars, their success. There is often a comic seriousness to the righteous attitudes of the Gold child.

Security and order mean predictability to Gold children. Accustomed and proven ways are best. Novelty and new ideas are not to be trusted. New situations are very challenging, and they are met with ordering strategies from the past. Knowing what's worked before, who's in charge, and what the rules are brings safety.

Gold children appreciate routine, and they like to organize

things. They are very good at meeting the demands of everyday life in an orderly way. When routines are disrupted, they become confused and anxious. There may be clutter, but rarely is there mess. If there is mess, it is *their* mess and they know how it works. Certain things need to be done at certain times in certain ways, day by day.

Roles and defined relationships are important to Gold children. This is Uncle John. Uncle John does certain things and doesn't do others. Grandpa is Grandpa. Grandma is Grandma. Father is a certain way. Mother another. Older siblings have their roles. Younger siblings theirs. The cop on the beat has his or her job. Just as the firefighter, the teacher, the minister, and the doctor do. And I have my role, too. These things are fundamental. They are not to be tampered with.

Rules go right along with roles. There are certain ways to act and not to act. These rules come from proper authority. They are handed down from the past. Justice should be swift and sure when the rules are violated. Consequences should be fair, appropriate, and immediate. Injustice or chaotic justice is deeply upsetting and confusing. Somehow, order must be restored.

This emphasis on roles and rules goes along with a need and respect for authority. Gold children are obedient to legitimate authority, and they see most authority as legitimate. They have a strong sense of right and wrong based on the "shoulds" and "oughts" that come from tradition. They see nothing wrong with the stern and proper exercise of power in the name of order. In their turn, they expect their own authority—whether it comes from their birth order, their family role, or their social position—to be respected and obeyed.

Territory and ownership are strong values for Gold children. It is my toy box, in my room, in our house, in our town, in our state, in our country. Boundaries must be set and respected. Property is sacred. Ownership is a right. Stewardship is a responsibility.

Along with rules, roles, authority, territory, and ownership go appropriate rewards and deserved status. Gold children pay careful attention to who has earned what, and they expect just rewards for their efforts. They are strongly motivated by honors and recognition. They work hard and carry much responsibility, and it is only right that they should receive their due praise and be paid well.

Appearances are always important to Gold children. Quality work and an orderly workshop are essential. When company comes, appearances are to be preserved. If there must be mess, it should be tucked away to be cleaned up later. Roles and responsibilities in the family and community require that we present ourselves decently. Neatness of dress and appearance mean a great deal. How we are seen by others is a fundamental concern. Serious developmental education such as education about sex need to be handled in a calm manner that stresses natural order and safety.

Gold children pay attention to time. They are punctual and dependable and they get the job done. Work before play is an obvious necessity. In school, they expect an orderly and traditional classroom, practical and profitable, with concrete learning, fair rewards and punishments, and public recognition for a job well done. They contribute to the family and community. They do their duty. They preserve tradition and look out for the continuity of the past.

Gold children are no more angels than any other Color. They can be very stubborn and willful, especially in relationship to an emotional Blue, a playful Orange, or an abstract Green. In general, however, they tend to make less trouble than other children. This can be a burden for them, and sometimes the potential joy and adventure of childhood get lost in the search for security and accomplishment.

THE BLUE CHILD

Blue children are emotionally sensitive and reactive. Feelings are always near the surface. From the earliest times, Blue children cry and laugh easily. Unhappiness and discomfort are intense. Happiness and merriment are infectious. Life is an emotional roller coaster. Sleep may be restless and full of dreams. The Blue child responds to attention and can be very rewarding to the parent, deeply engaged and responsive from the beginning. The happy Blue child is helpful and supportive of others, a contributing member of the family.

When Blue children feel emotionally safe, they are very social, gregarious, and responsive to the people around them. They like to have lots of friends, and they look for intimacy in the family. They often act as a sort of emotional barometer of what's going on among the people around them.

This interpersonal sensitivity is keyed to the rises and falls of persons in the rough-and-tumble of daily life. Persons are precious to Blues. The social successes and failures, gains and losses, triumphs and humiliations of people have life-and-death importance for the Blue child. Unfairness and injustice are very significant. Social failure and rejection are crushing. Blue children root for the underdog.

This social sensitivity reaches below the surface of things.

When people around them are wearing masks, smoothing over their conflicts and difficulties, being sneaky and mean under a respectable facade, the intuitive Blue child senses these undercurrents and reacts to them. While the child may not be permitted to react openly, he or she will show distress in moodiness, sullenness, illness, misbehavior, and sometimes open rebellion. A good question to ask a child showing these behaviors is, "Is this a mad thing or a sad thing you're feeling?" It will usually be one or the other.

Attachment is a key to Blue children: attachment to objects, to people, to pets, to special places, to books or ideas. Loss is an especially important theme in their lives. Blue children mourn deeply, and they mourn a long time. This mourning may be about things that seem trivial to the other Colors—a toy, a doll, an article of clothing, a special activity with a special person. Major losses can be really debilitating for them.

Blue children are often highly imaginative, even dreamy. They love to pretend. Their inner life is usually full of imagery, and the images are full of emotional significance. They are often spontaneously artistic or musical, and their creations can have real insight and power from an early age. Their imagination can take them to the heights of joy and inspiration and to the depths of fear and despair. Dreams and nightmares are powerful. Blue children invest an almost magical significance in certain key symbols. They learn well from symbolic play—dolls, sandbox play, art, charades, music—Blue children will reveal their inner world in their play.

Blue children often need help with structure and motivation. Their dreaminess, imaginative fearfulness, and emotionality sometimes undermine their ability to act, to do rote learning, or to carry out repetitive tasks that need to be done. They don't respond easily to rigid structures. They move more naturally and easily with flexible routines. But they do not seek chaos, either. Emotional safety is the key, for themselves and for the people around them. If structure keeps people safe and happy, it is welcome. If it is punitive, arbitrary, and unjust, it is rejected.

As with all their emotions, anger is strong for Blue children. It can be quite startling when the sensitive, artistic, and nurturing Blue child suddenly lets loose with righteous wrath, indignation, or injured rage. This anger easily becomes sullen and brooding if it doesn't clear. It is part of the price of leading with the heart, making strong attachments, and valuing personal justice so highly.

Blue children need emotional nourishment and support. As with Blue adults, they feel hurt by criticism and assume the worst from silence. In the classroom, they do well when they are inspired, intrigued, allowed to dream and create in an open, interactive environment. While they need external help with boundaries, limits, and deadlines, they thrive on loving touch and encouraging words. While they want to express themselves and their creative imagination, Blue children will choose belonging and harmonious relationships over success.

Competition is not motivating to Blue children. It threatens the smooth emotional flow that they seek. Victory at too great a cost to someone else is uncomfortable to Blues.

Duty in the abstract doesn't carry much weight with them, either. It is the personal aspect of duty, the emotional responsibility to another, that will motivate them.

Serious developmental learning usually takes place through what is modeled by others. Blue children are particularly attuned to what is communicated between the lines. No matter what is being said, it's what people actually do and—above all—what people actually feel that Blue children respond to. If they see warm, loving touch and contact between parents and other adults, it's the most wonderful feeling in the world to them, and the best possible sex education and relationship education generally. All their lives, it will be the relationships among the people around them that give them their sense of safety or threat.

Blue children are not selfless and endlessly in service to others. They can be quite selfish. Often they avoid hurting others because that hurt may come back around on them in the future. Blues are not just altruistic. Their pain is powerful, and it is primarily their own pain they fear. But they feel pain when others feel pain, and that is a very powerful influence and restraint upon their behavior.

THE ORANGE CHILD

Orange children are physically active. They love challenges and they take risks, girls and boys equally. They need boundaries for safety, but within the boundaries they need room to move. Striking this balance between boundary making and freedom is the challenge in caring for Orange children.

Structure and routine are a real challenge for them. They are not naturally inclined toward order and boundaries. Safety is not of the highest concern. They love danger and have a high tolerance for pain. They are proud of their endurance and their toughness. A parent's worry and concern simply feel like fussiness and interference.

In fact, worry and concern are not a good approach to keeping Orange children safe. They need a more direct authority, even a physical authority, and it needs to be conveyed in a spirit of strength, respect, and camaraderie.

The Orange child responds well to a straight-from-the-shoulder, in-your-face kind of supervision. The caregiver's message needs to be, "You are strong. I love how strong you are. I am strong, too. We are both strong, and for your own safety I'm in charge of you!" Underlying this authority, there needs to be a real affection and respect for the Orange child's energy, skill, and creativity. To respond well, the child needs to respect the authority and to feel respected in return.

If a parent tries to plead with the Orange child, or to wheedle him or her into cooperating, the child loses respect and the authority is undermined. If the parent is a pushover, it will be more of the same. If the parent tries to simply dominate, however, exercising arbitrary authority based on the parental role, the Orange child is likely to rebel. What works is a relationship of strength between equals, where one is more equal than the other for purposes of safety and learning. We hope that one will be the parent.

It is important not to confuse the physical energy and activity of the Orange child with hyperactivity or to give it some other negative label. Orange children live in the body and in sensations. Given firm, respectful care in a safe and challenging environment, active Orange children live joyful, energetic, and productive lives.

Not all Orange children are loud and physically rambunctious. Some are rather quiet and physically still, until they meet a challenge. Then their physical power comes out. And during their quiet times, their Orange humor, competitiveness, and love of freedom are all there, under the surface, awaiting their opportunity to emerge.

Subtleties of emotion, the demands of duty and order, and fine intellectual pursuits are simply not very interesting to Orange children. They live in the same concrete, physical world that Golds prefer. But rather than trying to keep order in this world, Orange children want to have an impact on it. They want to play in it, to be skillful in it, to exercise power over it. Not to talk.

Simple do's and don'ts with natural consequences work best. Orange children will not adapt their behavior based on moral theories or appeals to altruism, but rather on consequences and self-interest. These are things we do and these are things we don't do and here are the consequences either way. Language about right and wrong tends to fall on deaf ears. This can be hard on the Blue and Gold parents whose values tend to be rooted in deeply held beliefs.

Orange children are highly skillful. They learn by doing, by direct physical involvement with things. This is the key to successful education for Orange children. Their senses are keen, and their reactions are quick. They tend to be well muscled and well coordinated. They usually love the outdoors and all physical challenges. Elementary school has been called the "big sit" by Oranges who crave movement. They will accept the "big sit" as long as they can count on recess, lunchtime play, and some hands-on pedagogy. Hard physical effort doesn't faze them as long as it's fun or challenging. Unless they are being forced into some boring physical task, they just want to get better at whatever they do.

Orange children are highly motivated by competition. They love team play and they love to win. They assume that everyone in the game is strong and capable, so they don't lose much sleep over the losers. They hate to lose, but they don't even lose much sleep over their own losses. The Orange child just gets back up and goes at it again.

Orange children love to perform. They enjoy the limelight and want to show others what they can do. They're not much into spectator sports. They want to be on the field, in the thick of things. They know they can do it, and they want the opportunity to prove it.

They have trouble with passive activities like listening and reading. Still, if they have a meaningful goal, they will do whatever it takes to develop the skill and knowledge to achieve it. This is why Orange students really come into their own in the higher grades and in college, where they can follow their interests and choose their goals.

If they are allowed to apply what they learn in action, and if they don't have to wait too long to get that chance, Orange children can endure much. Rote practice and discipline are all right as long as they serve an active purpose. Orange children love change and novelty, but they will put up with repetition if it builds skills and helps get them where they want to go.

In the modern, urban world, Orange children often have a tough time. Our schools, communities, and workplaces are not usually designed for their energetic style. The other Colors have often lost touch with the primordial importance of Orange. Out on the prairies, in the woods, on the sea, in cultures and communities that need tough physical skills, the Orange child is a star on the way to being a really important adult.

THE GREEN CHILD

Green children are born thoughtful. Naturally, not much actual thinking is going for the first few months, but a watchful, inward quality becomes apparent from the beginning. The analytical mind that will emerge has its roots in the quiet, self-contained infant.

Green independence shows itself early. Green children are processing . . . looking, listening, thinking things over, trying to make sense of things. This requires space, time, autonomy. The parent who is expecting immediate intimacy and lots of interaction will be puzzled and sometimes concerned by the Green child.

Green children want to come to a new situation on their own terms with the freedom to move in and out, check things out, compare things with other things, make some tentative judgments, test the judgments, adapt and adjust. They mistrust all quick responses.

The inner workings of the Green child's mind are not easy and fluid. The analytical mind takes things apart, chooses and selects, sees things in chunks, looks for pattern among different elements. This is not the quick approximation and correction of the Orange, the emotional intuitive flow of the Blue, or the orderly application of precedent of the Gold. The Green process takes time, and like any fine instrument, its mechanism is delicate.

This complex inner world is easily thrown off by distractions and confrontations. Green children avoid intrusions. They want to focus. They want to follow their interests where they lead. This is the natural unfolding of their information gathering and analysis. They are capable of being completely absorbed in some investigation for hours, days, even years.

Green children are very inward. Like Blues, they live very much within themselves. Strong emotion is in there, but it can be one of the major intrusions that interfere with the smooth workings of the analytical mind. Green children project a calm and deliberate emotional style most of the time. They tend to be upset by emotions, however, when they arise. Blue children swim in this sea of feelings and keep their heads above water, most of the time. The equally inward Green is subject to being overwhelmed by these feelings. Strong emotions often have a life of their own. They may not be rational, and they can be very difficult to control. Speech chokes up. Tears well up. Confusion sets in. No place to hide. Humiliation. A disaster.

This is further complicated by Green children's need to maintain the integrity of their analysis. This integrity is built into the analytical process. Why should a person analyze if the analysis isn't allowed to determine action? Why think carefully for yourself only to be pushed around by some flood of irrational emotions, whether they are your own or someone else's?

The same basic principle of thinking for themselves leads Green children to question authority and routine at all times. Why? Why? Why? And the explanation had better make some sense. This can be very challenging to a parent who is acting from feeling, from impulse, from tradition, or just trying to get through the day. Green children ask tough questions. Parent and educator might have to learn something in order to answer.

Green children usually seem older than their years. They show that wise, thoughtful demeanor before they can walk. When they start talking, well, it can be a bit unsettling. Not all Green children are geniuses, but they are all thoughtful. They often begin achieving mentally at an early age. They may follow many pathways and interests, and some of them seem strange to the other Colors, like a fascination with bugs or with the inside workings of living things.

Green children don't mind being alone; in fact, they often seek it out. Socializing for its own sake has little interest for them, though they love to talk about whatever does interest them. They are delighted when someone understands and cares—better yet, when someone *knows* something.

They want to be loved and respected like any other child, and like any child, that love needs to be on their own terms. Give them the facts of sexual development as they show curiosity and readiness to find out. Stay with the facts and maybe just a brief statement about what the facts may mean. Long, redundant lectures on any subject are torture to Greens of all ages. Listen for questions both out loud and between the lines. A smothering, emotional approach will close them down and drive them into themselves.

Intellectual challenges are fun for Green children. Rough physical camaraderie may be simply too disorienting, unless the Orange is right there behind the Green. Holidays are okay, but family duties and traditions may feel stultifying.

Both at home and in the classroom, the best approach to Green children includes a lot of watching and listening. Be there, but keep a respectful distance. Challenge them, encourage social contact, but don't interfere too much. Set limits and expect things of them, but don't micromanage. Above all, be willing to learn along with the child in a spirit of calm adventure and safe exploration. Green children need to know that the parent or teacher is there with them and for them, that they belong, that the world is safe so that they can pursue their independent interests.

The next page provides an outline of child needs, strengths, and challenges that should be helpful to parents and teachers, and to anyone who loves children. The following chapter explores the parenting styles of the four Colors.

THE GOLD CHILD

Needs	Strengths	Challenges
Safety	Creating safe space	Risky activities
Security	Organizing	Unpredictability
Stability	Putting things in order	Instability
Organization	Defining appropriate structure	Chaos
Belonging	Fitting into group	Isolation
Participation	Contributing to group/family	Lack of guidance and clear values
Predictability	Serving group order/productivity	Irrational consequences of actions
Continuity	Sustaining group identity and ways	Lack of connection over time
Tradition	Maintaining tradition	Novelty, newness for its own sake
Clear expectations	Meeting expectations	Irrational expectations
Others to be responsible	Setting expectations	Others fail to meet expectations
Rules	Making and supporting rules	Anarchy
Boundaries	Finding and supporting boundaries	Constant change and fluidity
Authority	Supporting/carrying out authority	No one in charge
Roles	Carrying out roles	No defined roles
Responsibilities	Carrying responsibility	No defined responsibility
Work	Working hard	No meaningful work
Appreciation	Thriving on recognition	No sensible recognition
Clear status definition	Supporting clear status definition	Unclear status hierarchy
Permission to relax	Perseverance	Constant pressure to perform

THE BLUE CHILD

Needs	Strengths	Challenges
Encouragement	Giving encouragement/ support	Others' inattention
Support	Able to receive nurture	No structure, arbitrary structure
Nurture	Takes feedback seriously	Others' indifference
Feedback	Gives understanding	Caustic, critical environment
Understanding	Makes self understood	Strong conformity demands
Self-expression	Identifies with group	Balancing expression/ group role
Belonging	Participation	Isolation, alienation
Involvement	Bringing others in	To be seen and not heard
Inclusion	Friendliness	Loss
Friends	Generosity	Aloneness
Honesty	Sensitivity to hidden feelings	Emotionally charged secrets
Harmonious relationships	Imagination	Conflict with others
Others to get along	Peacemaking	Conflict among others
Sensitivity	Intimacy	Stoicism
Pretend play, art, music	Creativity	High expectation of compliance
Flexible structure	Self-management	Routine, impersonal standards
Freedom to be alone	Positive solitude	Enforced participation in conflict
Gentle touch	Loving touch	Rough touch, no touch
Reality checks	Dreaminess	Lack of boundaries, defined roles

THE ORANGE CHILD

Needs	Strengths	Challenges
Independence	Active initiation	Compliance, following
Self-reliance	Autonomy	Blending in
Freedom within limits	Self-motivation	Taking direction
Flexible structure	Thinking on their feet	Accepting structure
Action	Energy	Expectation of quiet/ stillness
Adventure	Risk taking	Being safe
Challenge	Love of the new	Being appropriate
Fun and excitement	Enjoyment	Taking things seriously
Change and variety	Adaptability, flexibility	Managing routine
Attention	Not shy	Attention seeking
Stimulation	Can handle much stimulation at once	Boredom
Hands-on learning	Natural physical understanding	Following the directions
Physical involvement	"Body smart"	Introspection, analysis
Competition	Plenty of drive	Self-sacrifice
Performance	Expressive, daring	Playing anonymous roles
Modeling of skills	Imitation, learning by doing	Taking verbal instruction
Skill practice	Focus (when interested)	Focus (when not interested)
Doing, not watching	Active participation	Quiet observation
Camaraderie	Gregarious	Solitude, working alone
Firm, strong touch	Physicality	Intimate touch
Respectful boundaries	Responds to respect	All arbitrary boundaries

THE GREEN CHILD

Needs	Strengths	Challenges
Rationality	Clear reason	Dealing with the irrational
Time	Perseverance (when interested)	Perseverance (when not interested)
Patience	Takes own sweet time	Hurrying, being hurried
Space	Handles solitude well	Crowding
Autonomy	Thinks for self	Being told
Constant learning opportunities	Love of learning	Rote, repetitive activities
To explore	Loves new experience/ information	Redundancy
Investigation	Loves to inquire	Being fed canned information
Questioning	Needs to see reasons	Accepting things on faith
Explanations	Needs to see cause/ effect	Settling for surface appearances
Challenge	Loves intellectual challenge	Routine
Many interests	Wide-ranging mind	Lack of information resources
Rational authority	Personal integrity	Arbitrary authority
Solitude, social distance	Good at being alone	Enforced social demands
Independence	Self-reliance	Team play
Social encouragement	Learns social skills (if necessary)	Small talk, emotional intimacy
Help with decisions	Complex analysis	Arbitrary deadlines, criteria

CHAPTER 12

Parents

GOLD PARENTS

Commitment and dedication are at the heart of the Gold parenting style. Golds place the highest value on doing important work in life. They often see family and child-rearing as the most important of all work.

For Golds, family values and traditions are the foundation of family life, often of life itself. They expect good order based on proper roles and responsibilities. The traditions are to be respected. Routines and rituals are to be followed with respect. It is this good order that gives safety, predictability, and stability to life.

Great effort and attention are spent in making sure that things are running smoothly and securely. Careful attention is given to details and appearances. Chores are to be done on schedule. Responsibilities are taken seriously. Work and school come first. Privileges are earned, not just taken for granted. Work before play.

As in all areas of life, Gold parents insist on high standards in all things. There are right ways and wrong ways of living and of doing things. Values are central. Life must be held up to the standard. Where it is found wanting, it must be corrected. Constructive criticism is essential.

The Gold parent strives to be a good role model, to lead by example, to be above reproach. This is a tough challenge, and Golds rarely feel that they have measured up. Their answer to this is to redouble their efforts, not to lower the standard. This quality strongly influences their parenting.

For Golds, life is effort. Things that are easy and fun are mistrusted. Feelings and emotions are too unreliable. Clever thinking and analysis can be deceptive. Work is essential. Without work, we have chaos and failure.

Children are expected to carry out their responsibilities and strive for high standards. Parenting must be held to a standard as well. Gold parents must pay attention to all the details. They must make and enforce rules and hold up high expectations. They expect honesty and hard work.

Their parenting style is authoritarian. They are the parents. They are responsible, and they are accountable for the results. It is their job to manage things, to supervise the child for success. A child's failure is the parent's failure, and success comes from doing the right thing.

Organization, planning, routine, punctuality, neatness, a good appearance, respect for tradition, and hard work lead to success. Rewards are appropriate, but they must be earned. Self-worth is a more understandable idea than self-esteem. Self-worth is earned. It doesn't come free.

Discipline is essential, and it is good for the child. It is tied to the values and standards that the Gold parent holds dear. Consequences must be available for misbehavior. Punishment is corrective. It builds character and prepares the child for the rigors of life. Above all, it upholds the standard.

Obedience is required and expected. Gold parents see obedience as belonging to the natural role of the child, just as authority belongs to the role of the parent. Gold parents were usually obedient children. They see this authority of the generations as essential to orderly life. Respect for elders and for those in authority is a key to the stability of the community.

Change must be anticipated and planned for. The child must prepare for each step of the life path. Goals and directions must be established, and action must be directed toward the goals. The parents' duty is to keep the child on track and focused. Children must be involved in appropriate community activities and cultural traditions. Career goals must be set. Social participation and responsibility must be instilled.

Gold parents are often deeply concerned about their dreamy, sensitive Blue children, their impulsive, competitive Orange children, and their independent and skeptical Green children. The right way to live seems so obvious to the Gold. Duty and responsibility, hard work and well-earned rewards make such good sense to them.

Gold parents can be very helpful to their children of other Colors. They can provide a secure base, an orderly foundation upon which the Blue, Orange, or Green children can build their own unique lives.

BLUE PARENTS

For the Blue parent, everything starts with a deep emotional connection with the child. The moment of birth is sacred. Throughout life, contact, communication, and empathy with the child are among the highest values. The responsiveness of the child is very important, and Blue parents take it to heart.

Blues love intensely, and they need to be loved in return. They often hope and expect that their relationship with the child will be the most intimate in their lives. This can lead to pain when the child shows independence, gets angry, rebels, or simply turns away to follow his or her own interests.

We don't get to choose the Colors of our children. The other Colors are not as focused on emotional intimacy as is the Blue parent. Over time, parenting is likely to be an emotional roller coaster for the Blue parent, just like the rest of the Blue life.

Close families based on emotional connection and affection are the Blue ideal. Blues are devoted to family. They invest great energy in the family, often sacrificing their own needs and interests in the process. They expect the same of their spouses and children. To the Blue, family closeness is only natural. Everyone should feel it spontaneously.

Holidays, birthdays, hellos, good-byes, births, deaths, and all the other significant family events are very important to the Blue parent. If someone is really not interested or is going through the motions out of duty, it's deeply troubling to Blue parents. Rejection, coolness, and distance are always troubling for Blues, and these things can really show up around family rituals and important family events.

The family is the most intense arena in life for Blues. Their deep sensitivity makes them particularly vulnerable to the open and hidden conflicts of family life. Marital conflict, trouble between father's family and mother's family, issues with mothers-

and fathers-in-law, sibling rivalry—these are all particularly troubling for Blues.

When things are going well, Blue parents are affectionate, nurturing, emotionally supportive, and enthusiastic. Persons are precious to Blues, and raising children is the cultivation of precious persons. They want to bring out the best in everyone around them. They support the development of true potential in their children, and they value the children's self-expression.

They want to contribute to their child's development, to be important in the child's life and growth. They want to be a positive influence, building self-esteem, nurturing potential, providing emotional safety.

Blue parents rely on the emotional relationship to guide behavior. They try to use as little discipline as possible, preferring to nurture and to guide rather than to structure and provide consequences. They hope and expect that the child will behave well out of love for the parent, high self-esteem, and loyalty to the family.

Conflict is, as always, to be avoided at all costs. Discipline is democratic and personal. Flexibility is valued highly, and whole situations are taken into account. Rigid rules and structures are avoided in favor of serious talks and expressions of concern. This may lead to inconsistency and emotional subjectivity in discipline, and the deep Blue anger and righteous wrath may overflow from time to time.

Sometimes Blue parents use their own pain as a lever to try to influence the child. They may try to act more as a friend and confidant than as an authority figure. Sometimes the child is invited from a very early age to share the emotional trials and tribulations of the Blue parent, and this can be a great burden for the child.

Blues care deeply about their children. They invest great energy and dedication in the work of being a parent. They value differences and support uniqueness, special talents, and special personal qualities. They provide a rich, nurturing environment in which their children can grow and develop.

ORANGE PARENTS

For Orange parents, life is a challenge and an adventure. It is there to be enjoyed. Family life is not about meticulous details, musty traditions, sentimentality, or intellectual discourse. It is about challenge, camaraderie, and fun.

Children should be raised to be strong, independent, self-reliant, and resilient. They don't need to be fawned over, organized, or analyzed. They need to play, to do their own thing. Children don't need constant attention from their parents, and Orange parents must have their own freedom if they are to be healthy and happy.

The Orange home is a relaxed and casual environment. It may be very spare, almost unimportant—a place to eat and sleep, a base of operations for action and adventure in the wider world. It may be a work of art with all kinds of unique and original furnishings and architecture. Or it may be a complex playground full of workshops, awash in the clutter of hobbies and games, a gymnasium, or grand central station for the entire neighborhood.

Orange parents communicate this sense of openness and action to their children. They must live this way themselves, and they wish to carry their children right along with them. They are optimistic, flexible, and here-and-now-oriented. They love to laugh, and they avoid dark, heavy intellectual or emotional experiences.

Boredom is the enemy. Routine and ritual have no appeal. Family gatherings are not about duty and sentiment. They are about fun. Change and action are the order of the day. Oranges love change, novelty, variety. Each day is a new opportunity to try new things.

The Orange emotional life is about involvement and camaraderie. Oranges are usually quite social, and the Orange family is usually a hub of activity. Big families are common, with lots of visiting back and forth. Parenting is a shared project. Everyone is involved. Aunts and uncles, grandparents, family friends, all are invited to care for the children.

Competition is part of everything. Orange parents love to challenge their children, to play hard and build strength and power. Winning is important in play and in life, but in a funny way it's less important to Oranges than to the other Colors. It doesn't have the personal quality that it has for Blues. It doesn't mean order versus chaos as it may for Golds. It doesn't suggest disorienting failure the way it may for Greens.

Work is done in spurts of tremendous energy. It is not approached as an ongoing daily routine, to be kept up with moment by moment. Get a Dumpster and clean the house in a day. Make it a game. Get everyone in the neighborhood involved. Invite the family. Door prizes!

As stated before, Oranges love skill, and they will work hard in a focused way to develop it. But it must be useful skill. Orange parents love to teach skills, and they show by doing all the time with their children. Skill in action is the highest value for the Orange. They want their children to be as good as they can be at whatever interests them.

Orange parents aren't committed to any particular way of parenting, preferring to deal with things as they come along. They are not consistent disciplinarians, but they do expect to be obeyed. They tend to rely on their personal power and direct, immediate solutions, rather than on routines, emotional connectedness, or reasoning. They would rather not have to discipline at all, and rarely plan how they will do it.

When the need to discipline pops up in a situation, Orange parents respond in terms of the immediate circumstances. They are not troubled by routine misbehavior. They like pluckiness and mischief, and they respect children's willfulness as strength. It is only when the children are really at serious risk, or when they are disrupting the parent's life, that discipline becomes an issue.

Oranges are often quick to anger, and just as quick to forgive and forget. They tend to be somewhat manipulative themselves, and they see through children's manipulations fairly easily. It's hard to con an Orange. They try to keep things light and humorous, laughing off troubles as much as possible, and they separate easily when their children are ready to be on their own.

Orange parents give their children an energetic and creative home environment full of fun and action. The Blue child may find it somewhat emotionally stressful. The Gold child may try to parent the Orange parent and stabilize things in the family. The Green child may pull back and watch. But all the children will get the message. Life is short. Do something!

GREEN PARENTS

Green parents are thoughtful, parenting with reason and rationality. They often read books and apply parenting methods that make sense to them. They want to know what the experts have to say, but they will think the problem through for themselves before deciding how to act.

Green parents are very interested in the growth and development of the child, particularly his or her intellectual and educational development. Life is about learning and understanding. It is about curiosity, interests, exploration, experiment, and information.

Motivation comes from within for Greens. They expect their children to have interests that will guide their lives. They talk things over and draw out the children's interests, feeding them and nurturing them with opportunities to learn.

They love to question and to challenge the child's understanding, opening up new pathways and new ideas. Intellectual discussion is play, and they love to see children move toward their full creative potential. They love intellectual games, puns and plays on words, complex puzzles, and *Jeopardy!*

Green parents give a high value to competency, to rigorous understanding and careful application of principles. They expect their children to think about consequences before they act—to use their heads. Thoughtlessness and stupidity are the great sins. "God put a wonderful brain in your head. It isn't there just to hold up your hair and keep your ears apart. Your highest duty is to use it."

Greens are skeptical and independent by nature. They do not accept authority easily themselves, and they do not impose it easily on their children either. Greens prefer reason and logic to rules and consequences. They give reasons for their decisions. They prefer to give information that will guide their children's decisions, to influence rather than enforce.

Green parents try to be logical, objective, and fair. They listen to the facts of the case. Weigh the possible outcomes and consequences. They are not in a hurry. They want to talk things over and be sure before going ahead. They are not moved by impulses, emotionalism, or tradition. They want the facts, and they question the facts, too.

Greens refuse to quarrel. Discussion is a high art. It is to be carried out in a reasonable and respectful way. They have no patience, however, for obvious stupidity. They don't "suffer fools gladly," as the old saying goes. They can be quite acid-tongued and sarcastic about foolishness. When someone has acted stupidly and the consequences are happening, well, that's just how it works, doesn't it? Learn from it.

As parents, Greens can be prone to lecturing. The Blue, Gold, or Orange child may become somewhat deaf to the Green logic. Green parents are often at a loss about what to do with a highly emotional Blue child, a stubborn Gold child, or a willful Orange one. When reason fails, the Green parent may simply withdraw. Strong, authoritarian interventions may be just too unsettling.

Autonomy is a very high value to Greens. People shouldn't have to be pushed, ordered about, or bossed. Intellectual freedom, freedom of speech, choice, and thought are essential. The Green parent may feel that it is best for children to just learn from consequences rather than to be forced against their will.

Green parents rely on clear communication of important information. Confusion is seen as the main source of trouble. If the facts are clear, action can be clear. Learning can take place. A rational critique of someone's thinking or behavior is an expression of caring. Repetition should not be necessary. Once a thing has been pointed out, then that should be enough.

As stated before, emotions run deep for Greens, but they are very uneasy about communicating them. They deeply mistrust what they see as easy emotionalism. Constant expressions of love, appreciation, pride, and praise in a family seem false and intrusive to Greens. They expect people to infer their caring and appreciation from their investment and commitment. This emotional stoicism drives Blues nuts.

Green parents expose their children to the deep questions about life. They bring to their families the life of the mind. They are democratic, rational, and open-minded, and they bring out the natural curiosity and creativity of their children.

PARENT STRENGTHS AND CHALLENGES

Gold Parent Strengths	Gold Parent Challenges
Responsible	Being flexible
Dedicated	Accepting differences
Stable	Sharing authority
Family-oriented	Dealing with uncertainty
Hardworking	Responding to change
Helpful	Dealing with rebellion
Good role model	Dealing with irresponsibility
Authoritative	Supporting creativity
Strong values	Handling emotional sensitivity
Clear expectations	Dealing with noise and confusion
Values rules	Handling lack of appreciation
Establishes routines	Handling disrespect
Traditional	Playing and being spontaneous
Organized	
Practical	
Objective	

Blue Parent Strengths	Blue Parent Challenges
Nurturing	Exercising authority
Devoted	Setting limits and boundaries
Emotionally sensitive	Dealing with conflict
Values closeness	Dealing with loss
Values persons	Saying good-bye
Good communication	Handling rejection
Supports potential	Being disliked or criticized
Encourages self-expression	Being consistent
Harmonious in relationships	Being objective
Builds family cohesion	Putting needs before wants
Flexible	Putting business before feelings
Democratic	
Disciplines through caring	
Warm	
Enthusiastic	
Spiritual	
Noncompetitive	

Orange Parent Strengths	Orange Parent Challenges
Optimistic	Being consistent
Flexible	Exercising authority
Direct	Planning and organizing
Accepting	Handling time and schedules
Loves change	Attending to duties
Adventurous	Putting work before play
Relaxed	Encouraging neatness
Casual	Being emotionally sensitive
Nonjudgmental	Being serious
Friendly	Being intellectual
Engaged	Being patient

Emotionally strong

Handling quick anger

Here and now

Hands on

Playful *and* hardworking

Expects obedience

Green Parent Strengths	**Green Parent Challenges**
Logical	Exercising authority
Objective	Enforcing limits and boundaries
Emotionally calm	Making firm decisions
Uses guidance and influence	Avoiding too much lecturing
Uses information	Avoiding sarcasm and withdrawal
Uses parenting methods	Dealing with illogic
Gives reasons	Dealing with rebellion
Thinks things through	Communicating feelings
Pays attention to cause/effect	Handling others' emotions
Uses independent judgment	Noise and distraction
Values growth	Confusion and conflict
Encourages development	Handling details, time pressure
Proud of accomplishments	Social participation
Intellectually stimulating	
Sets high intellectual standards	
Uses natural consequences	

TEACHING AND LEARNING STYLES

Gold Teaching Style	**Gold Student Learning Needs**
Strong work ethic	Order and structure
Clear routine	Clear expectations and directions
Lots of structure	Goals and action sequences
Repetition and practice	Specific content

Well-organized activities

Traditional learning content

Emphasis on community traditions

Emphasis on appearances
  and propriety

Detailed, tried-and-true lesson plans

Demand for student accountability

Use of text, precedents, references

Strict and firm discipline

Repetition and practice

Learning from the foundation up

Freedom from mess and confusion

Responsibility and authority

Visible recognition and rewards

Consistent discipline

Justice based on rules and authority

Blue Teaching Style

High participation

Personal encouragement

Emotional safety

Affection

Physical contact

Emphasis on the positive

Individualized learning

Variety

Creativity

Inspiration and aspiration

Cooperation over competition

Expects motivation through
  self-actualization

Discipline through understanding

Emphasis on fairness

Blue Student Learning Needs

Emotional safety

Harmonious relationships

Personal encouragement
  and recognition

Openness and interaction

Group learning in a safe
  atmosphere

Minimum conflict

Inspiration, exploration, creativity

Personal expression

External challenge/structure

Conceptual/global learning

Personal fairness

Discipline based on
  understanding/inclusion

Orange Teaching Style

Spontaneous

Free-flowing structure

Relevant

Orange Student Learning Needs

Competition

Immediacy

Application of learning

Here and now	Skills over knowledge
Applied	Action over talking/listening
Concrete	Movement over sitting
Immediate	Learning by doing
Hands-on	Discovery
Action	Variety of experience
Variety	Camaraderie
Novelty	Firm, respectful, consistent
Challenge	discipline
Upbeat competition	External structure
Humor and fun	
Situational discipline	
Control through personal power	

Green Teaching Style	Green Student Learning Needs
Lecture/dialogue	Understanding of cause and
Explanation	effect; "Why, why, why?"
Theory	Exposure to concepts/ideas
Critical analysis	Time for thought
Exploration	Freedom to doubt/question
Independent thinking	Teacher patience
Skepticism	Time to answer questions
Expects motivation based	Independent learning challenges
on interest	Relevance
Values student autonomy	Recognition of capabilities
Emphasizes personal responsibility	Minimum repetition/redundancy
Disciplines through	Reality checks and timelines
guidance/suggestion	Minimum forced intimacy or
Uses natural consequences	participation
Reluctant to enforce structure	Rational discipline
	Natural consequences

CHAPTER 13

Moving Forward with the Colors

Understanding the natural differences between and among people will be useful to you in different ways depending upon your Color mixture. As we have seen throughout the book, the motivations and rewards that are meaningful to each Color differ in predictable ways.

Those of us with considerable Blue in our temperament will tend to see the wholeness and balance of the differences as beautiful and deeply meaningful. We will resist any tendency to pigeonhole our fellow creatures. At the same time, we will rejoice in the detailed exploration and rich appreciation of human differences that Colors makes possible. For Blues, it is a joy to discover these new ways to find and highlight the value of persons, and to contribute to the blossoming in health and delight of "children and other living things," as the saying goes. We will also find new ways to appreciate the other Colors whose priorities and ways of life may have seemed so mysterious and even harsh to the Blue heart. In addition, Colors gives us permission and puts a much-needed blessing upon our sensitivity and emotionality. Especially for the Blue men among us, it is of great value to let go of the stiff upper lip and swim freely in the sea of emotion.

For those of us who are deeply rooted in Gold, the value of the

Colors will have a more practical aspect. Golds will probably still be irritated by Blue sentimentality, Green studiousness and vacillation, and Orange rambunctiousness. Still, by virtue of understanding the inevitability of these qualities, Golds will be able to focus on finding keys to cooperation that work for the good of the tradition, the family, the community, or the project.

One metaphor that Golds often find helpful is to see the temperaments of other people as being akin to the weather. Indeed, this weather metaphor can be helpful to all the Colors. We can all waste enormous time and energy complaining about the weather, but how much more efficient it is simply to dress appropriately for whatever weather comes our way. Very important for us as Golds, then, is the growing understanding of ourselves that Colors brings, the permission it offers for us to be who we are with our emphasis on serious matters, our focus on good order, work, and traditional values, and the high standards that we impose upon ourselves and others.

When we are deeply Green by nature, we are usually very skeptical of any attempt to categorize us. Of all the Colors, we tend to be the most aware of our own uniqueness, and it has great value to us. We look forward at the end of our days to looking back over a life lived in our own authentic way. At first, Colors may seem to threaten that authenticity. In the end, however, we see that Colors blesses our differences and our Green authenticity. In addition, as Colors reveals itself to us as Greens, we begin to realize its power as a tool in analyzing others. Through this pathway, we often find its value in helping us understand and accept ourselves.

Colors can be a bridge for us as Greens in finding our way into the inner life of others. Most of us have rarely sought deep intimacy, though we may be interested in understanding others. Our inner world is precious to us, and it is not to be cheapened by a lot of glib chitchat and emotional sharing. Still, we do need to know and understand others in order to pursue our ends and make our contribution to the community, and it is here that Colors can help by shedding light upon the inner world of others. In addition, Colors helps others understand and accept us as we are. It lets the other Colors know how deeply we do feel and how much we do care, but without the embarrassing and unpleasant process of self-disclosure.

For those of us who are filled with that wonderful energy called Orange, Colors gives us the permission that we have needed all our lives. "Sit down, hush up, slow down, grow up, don't be so immature, think before you act!" Unless we are very lucky Oranges, we have felt entirely too much of this thumb of oppression pushing down on us. Okay, so we need to take some of this advice, fine! Every Color needs to have its extremes checked and corrected to some degree, doesn't it? That's at least partly what relationships are all about—finding good balance.

In these and in many other ways, Colors has its special payoffs for each of us. Its special blend of payoffs will be finely tuned to our own balance of personal qualities. It's amazing how much you will be able to tell about the people you meet as you listen and watch their Colors unfold. Their politics, their pleasures and preferences, their ways of relating—all become rather transparent.

This is, of course, part of the fun and the positive value of Colors, but it also raises a challenge. My suggestion to everyone I talk to about this is to go easy, to be gentle, and above all, to work on letting go of your prejudices against your lowest Colors. I think this is the best advice of all. If you can love your lowest Color when you find it in yourself and others, I assure you, you will gain the maximum value from your understanding of Colors . . . and you will do the least harm.

LESSONS LEARNED: NEWFOUND RESPECT

The Colors will always be with and around you. If Golds drive you nuts, try learning to have sympathy and concern for their heavy burdens. Try to understand the ways they don't live up to their own expectations. Notice the pain that this brings them, even when they're expecting others to do what they themselves can't. Learn to value their contribution to all the efforts they are engaged in. Then you will be able to get along in a friendly and effective way with Golds. You will be able to see what their deep concerns and responsibilities are and lend a hand. This will endear you to Golds more than any other thing. Help them with whatever really concerns them. That's the key to getting along with Gold.

If the Blues make you crazy with their emotionalism and end-less talk about relationships, try to appreciate the sensitivity they bring to the process of the community, the way they soften the edges and humanize the expectations. Help them feel emotion-ally safe and valuable as people. Then they will give heart and soul to whatever projects or activities you may be engaged in. Appreciate their vulnerability. Above all, however, show a little vulnerability yourself. This is the real key with Blues. Allow some of your own softness and uncertainty to show through, and you'll bring out trust and support from them. As they often say to me: "When you show your vulnerability, it brings out the best in me."

On the other hand, if all they see is your armor, they will resist you and defend themselves, expecting pain.

If Oranges are just too rambunctious and playful for your taste, try sitting back and observing their energy for a while. Notice where it is focused. Learn to appreciate how they direct and channel all that voltage. Learn from them to find some of that power in yourself. This last part can be a tough challenge for each of the other Colors, but Oranges really respond to the Orange in others. Good strong physical presentation, high-fives, team energy, and—above all—mutual respect will win Oranges' acceptance and affection. It will bring out their respect for you and motivate them to give their very best participation. It is one of the key messages of the whole Colors experience that Orange is not immaturity waiting to grow up! Orange is a valid adult style, a natural quality that is predominant in as much as a third of the population as a whole. Oranges don't need another lecture on character development. They need to be respected, and they need strong, direct, respectful communication.

If Green is your lowest Color, and if the cool, detached, intellectual style of Greens is hard for you to take, the key to dealing with it is to learn to learn. Learn to love to learn! Even if it's just during those times when you are with Green folks, become a fellow student with them. Learn from them. Learn with them. Share something you have learned (but be sure to let them share what they know about the subject as well). This is the ground upon which they can meet you. In learning, they feel a degree of social safety. This is the ground upon which they will feel most able to open up. Once you get some rapport established through shared learning, then you may be able to shift the ground a bit to your feelings, your responsibilities, or your playfulness. Until Greens feel sure that their intelligence and information will be respected, they won't feel safe with the strengths of the other Colors. When you think about it, this is the key for all of us. Until we know that our own strength is valued, we won't want to show our weakness.

Ultimately, with an understanding of Colors come new responsibilities. We know people's strengths by knowing their temperament, but we may also learn something of their weaknesses and vulnerabilities. How we use this understanding is an ethical challenge to which each of us must respond.

As a final note, I like to remember that the Yup'ik Eskimo symbol places the four different Color elements around the edge of the hoop—but the middle of the hoop, the very center of things, is left open for the spirit, for the soul, for the clarity of life itself, in which there is no Color. In this way of thinking, spirit is neither heart nor body nor intellect nor duty. Spirit is what underlies and enfolds them all, and watched from the perspective of that center, our understanding of the lesser qualities of our personalities can shed much light on our lives and behavior.

It seems to me that the four Colors, seasoned and illuminated by the spirit, provide a rich, broad, and meaningful map of human life. And in the end, it seems that *Living Our Colors* means really, fully living our lives.

Appendix: Extra Quiz Sheets

A Colors Quiz:

Rank the four sets of words in each item **4, 3, 2, or 1** according to how well they describe you. **(4 is most like you.)**

1. a. _____ solid, steady, careful
    b. _____ feeling, sympathetic, kind
    c. _____ cool, clever, independent
    d. _____ lively, witty, energetic

2. a. _____ reasonable, moral, hard-working
    b. _____ sensitive, sincere, caring
    c. _____ logical, abstract, moral
    d. _____ skillful, playful, fun-loving

3. a. _____ dependable, faithful, devoted
    b. _____ close, personal, involved
    c. _____ curious, scientific, thoughtful
    d. _____ daring, energetic, brave

4. a. _____ reliable, organized, serious
    b. _____ peaceful, harmonious, warm
    c. _____ impatient, perfectionist, heady
    d. _____ here-and-now, impulsive, active

5. a. _____ consistent, structured, planned
    b. _____ meaningful, spiritual, inspired
    c. _____ analyzing, testing, model-making
    d. _____ high-impact, persuasive, generous

6. a. _____ sane, faithful, supportive

   b. _____ poetic, musical, artistic

   c. _____ theoretical, studious, principled

   d. _____ performing, playing, creating

7. a. _____ commit, follow-through, persist

   b. _____ communicate, encourage, nurture

   c. _____ inform, discuss, question

   d. _____ energize, compete, engage

8. a. _____ conserve, maintain, protect

   b. _____ inspire, understand, appreciate

   c. _____ design, invent, construct

   d. _____ promote, excite, activate

9. a. _____ value, honor, provide

   b. _____ share, connect, express

   c. _____ respect, stimulate, dialogue

   d. _____ touch, pleasure, surprise

10. a. _____ traditional, loyal, conservative

   b. _____ belonging, involved, cooperative

   c. _____ skeptical, non-conforming, fair

   d. _____ free, independent, rebellious

Totals

a. Gold _____ b. Blue _____ c. Green _____ d. Orange _____

A Colors Quiz:

Rank the four sets of words in each item **4, 3, 2, or 1** according to how well they describe you. (**4 is most like you.**)

1. a. _____ solid, steady, careful
b. _____ feeling, sympathetic, kind
c. _____ cool, clever, independent
d. _____ lively, witty, energetic

2. a. _____ reasonable, moral, hard-working
b. _____ sensitive, sincere, caring
c. _____ logical, abstract, moral
d. _____ skillful, playful, fun-loving

3. a. _____ dependable, faithful, devoted
b. _____ close, personal, involved
c. _____ curious, scientific, thoughtful
d. _____ daring, energetic, brave

4. a. _____ reliable, organized, serious
b. _____ peaceful, harmonious, warm
c. _____ impatient, perfectionist, heady
d. _____ here-and-now, impulsive, active

5. a. _____ consistent, structured, planned
b. _____ meaningful, spiritual, inspired
c. _____ analyzing, testing, model-making
d. _____ high-impact, persuasive, generous

6. a. _____ sane, faithful, supportive

b. _____ poetic, musical, artistic

c. _____ theoretical, studious, principled

d. _____ performing, playing, creating

7. a. _____ commit, follow-through, persist

b. _____ communicate, encourage, nurture

c. _____ inform, discuss, question

d. _____ energize, compete, engage

8. a. _____ conserve, maintain, protect

b. _____ inspire, understand, appreciate

c. _____ design, invent, construct

d. _____ promote, excite, activate

9. a. _____ value, honor, provide

b. _____ share, connect, express

c. _____ respect, stimulate, dialogue

d. _____ touch, pleasure, surprise

10. a. _____ traditional, loyal, conservative

b. _____ belonging, involved, cooperative

c. _____ skeptical, non-conforming, fair

d. _____ free, independent, rebellious

Totals

a. Gold _____ **b. Blue** _____ **c. Green** _____ **d. Orange** _____

TOM MADDRON, a graduate from the University of Oregon with a Master of Science in Counseling Psychology, has made his living first as a marriage, child, and family therapist, and then traveling and training human relations skills in business, education, and social services. Known as the "Colors Guy," he has explored the personality styles of thousands of persons of all walks of life. He lives with his wife, Peggy, a teacher, in the coastal town of North Bend, Oregon.